AI-based 3D Point Cloud Coding

Wei Gao

AI-based 3D Point Cloud Coding

Methods, Standards, and Applications

Springer

Wei Gao
School of Electronic and Computer Engineering
Peking University
Shenzhen, China

ISBN 978-981-95-0659-0 ISBN 978-981-95-0660-6 (eBook)
https://doi.org/10.1007/978-981-95-0660-6

This Springer imprint is published by the registered company Springer Nature Singapore Pte Ltd.
The registered company address is: 152 Beach Road, #21-01/04 Gateway East, Singapore 189721, Singapore

Preface

Recent years have witnessed the wide applications of 3D vision in many burgeoning technologies, such as autonomous driving, interactive games, virtual and augmented reality, intelligent robots, unmanned aerial vehicles, etc. As an efficient 3D visual data representation format, point clouds can depict 3D objects and 3D scenes with high precision geometry coordinates and the corresponding attributes. The recent advancements of artificial intelligence (AI) have significantly promoted 3D point cloud processing and understanding technologies for human and machine perception improvements. The increasing adoptions of 3D point cloud technologies generate a burden in data storage and transmission, and therefore the compression problem has attracted much attention from academia and industry to conduct research and propel the standardization efforts. The success of deep learning usage into image and video coding evidenced the potential of the same approach for 3D point cloud coding. The AI-based 3D point cloud coding can outperform traditional approaches, and become the mainstream direction to renovate the point cloud compression paradigm.

This book discusses different technological aspects of AI-based 3D point cloud coding with 12 well-organized chapters. It presents fundamental theories, efficient methods, technical standards, and application issues of AI-based 3D point cloud coding. The major concerns of these chapters can be described as follows.

Chapter 1 serves as an introduction, providing the background knowledge on the importance of point cloud data coding and its applications. Chapter 2 delves into the fundamentals of deep learning-based point cloud coding, establishing a foundation for understanding the subsequent chapters. These chapters lay the preliminary knowledge for readers.

Chapter 3 focuses on quality assessment and perception models for point clouds, which are crucial for understanding how point cloud data is evaluated and perceived, and are essential for developing coding algorithms that improve perceptual quality.

Chapters 4, 5, and 6 constitute the core part of the book, covering various technical aspects of deep learning-based point cloud coding. Chapter 4 addresses the geometry coding of static point clouds, while Chap. 5 discusses the attribute coding of static point clouds. Chapter 6 extends the discussion to dynamic point clouds, including the challenges and critical techniques for point cloud coding. These chapters provide detailed explorations for effectively applying deep learning models to compress point cloud data.

Chapters 7, 8, 9, and 10 present more advanced topics. Chapter 7 discusses human and machine perception oriented 3D point cloud coding, emphasizing the importance of coding techniques that consider human visual experience and machine perception utility. Chapter 8 deals with the compression artifacts removal problem, which is a critical aspect of point cloud coding to elevate signal quality. Chapter 9 explores the current status of AI-based 3D point cloud coding standards, providing insights into industry practices. Chapter 10 extends the discussion to several practical issues, such as lightweight implementations of point cloud networks, point cloud streaming and communication systems, and point cloud rendering and display.

Finally, Chap. 11 provides an overview of open source projects related to AI-based 3D point cloud coding, offering practical resources for readers interested in hands-on experience. As the last chapter, Chap. 12 concludes this book with future research directions and challenges in the field of AI-based point cloud coding.

The book is designed for readers who are interested in the intersection of 3D visual data compression, 3D visual information processing, and deep learning applications. From this book, readers will gain a comprehensive understanding of the current status and future potentials of the fast-growing technologies in AI-based 3D point cloud coding. In addition, for readers who are interested in the advanced technologies of image and video coding in the current AI era, please refer to our composed sister book titled *AI-based Image and Video Coding: Methods, Standards, and Applications* published by Springer Nature.

Shenzhen, China Wei Gao

Acknowledgments During the past years, many colleagues, collaborators, and graduate students have joined the research for 3D point cloud coding methods, standards, and applications. The accomplishment of this book cannot come true without their efforts, help, and support.

The technical chapters and some of the research works presented in this book were developed in collaboration with our students and colleagues at Peking University. Particularly, we would like to thank Kangli Wang, Chenhao Zhang, Yuqi Ye, Zhuozhen Yu, Haoruo Liu, Shihao Li, Kaiyu Zheng, Wang Liu, Shunzhou Wang, Jingxuan Su, Zhaojian Yao, Huiming Zheng, Liang Xie, Wenxu Gao, Xingming Mu, and Changhao Peng. Moreover, these postdocs and graduate students, and some other graduate students also helped edit this book, and spent much time in proofreading and figure drawing, including Qianxi Yi, Wei Cheng, Chengwei Wang, Zijian Zhang, Shangkun Sun, Junhong Lin, Xiaoyu Liang, and so on.

We also would like to thank many colleagues and friends for working together to promote the 3D point cloud coding research and its corresponding standardization efforts, including those from the School of Electronic and Computer Engineering at Peking University, the Audio Video Coding Standard (AVS) Workgroup of China, the IEEE Computer Society Data Compression Standards Committee (DCSC), as well as many other universities, research institutions, and high-tech companies. Many colleagues and friends have collaborated closely to develop advanced 3D point cloud technologies and applications, and consistently provided their substantial dedication and support.

We are very grateful to the Springer Nature team for helping us to create this book.

Competing Interests The author has no competing interests to declare that are relevant to the content of this manuscript.

Contents

Acronyms

ACR	Absolute Category Rating
AE	Autoencoder
AQ-IRN	Adaptive Quantization Enhanced Inception-Residual Network
AR	Augmented Reality
ASIC	Application-Specific Integrated Circuit
AVS-PCC	Audio Video Coding Standard—Point Cloud Compression
AWI	Adaptively Weighted Interpolation
BCE	Binary Cross-Entropy
BPOV	Bits Per Output Value
BPP	Bits Per Pixel
CNN	Convolutional Neural Network
DASH	Dynamic Adaptive Streaming over HTTP
DCT	Discrete Cosine Transform
DL	Deep Learning
DNN	Deep Neural Network
DPCC	Dynamic Point Cloud Coding
DSCQS	Double-Stimulus Continuous Quality-Scale
DSIS	Double-Stimulus Impairment Scale
EM	Entropy Model
FFT	Fast Fourier Transform
FLANN	Fast Library for Approximate Nearest Neighbors
FPGAs	Field-Programmable Gate Arrays
FR	Full Reference
GCN	Graph Convolutional Network
GNN	Graph Neural Networks
G-PCC	Geometry-based Point Cloud Compression
HISPOC	High-Performance 3D Point Cloud Accelerator
HSV	Human Visual System
IoU	Intersection over Union
ISO	International Standardization Organization
JND	Just Noticeable Distortion

JPEG	Joint Photographic Experts Group
JSCC	Joint Source-Channel Coding
KABM	KNN-Attention Block-Matching
KD-tree	K-Dimensional Tree
KNN	K-Nearest Neighbors
LiDAR	Light Detection and Ranging
LLMs	Large Language Models
LoD	Level of Details
LoRA	Low-Rank Adaptation
MMF	Multi-scale Motion Fusion
MPEG	Moving Picture Experts Group
MSR	Multiscale Sparse Representation
MV	Machine Vision
NCR	Numerical Category Rating
NGS	Neural Graph Sampling
NOV	Negatively Occupied Voxel
ViT	Vision Transformer
VR	Virtual Reality
V-PCC	Video-based Point Cloud Compression
PCAC	Point Cloud Attribute Coding
PCC	Point Cloud Coding
PCGC	Point Cloud Geometry Coding
PCL	Point Cloud Library
PCQA	Point Cloud Quality Assessment
POV	Positively Occupied Voxels
RAHT	Region-Adaptive Hierarchical Transform
RANSAC	Random Sample Consensus
RD	Rate-Distortion
RD-Curve	Rate-Distortion Curve
RoI	Region of Interest
SOPA	Sparse Occupancy Probability Approximation
SOTA	State-of-the-Art
SS	Single-Stimulus

Chapter 1
Introduction to 3D Point Cloud Coding

Abstract This chapter introduces the fundamentals of 3D point cloud coding, covering key aspects including 3D visual data formats, widely used point cloud datasets, traditional non-learning-based compression standards, and emerging AI-driven approaches. First, various 3D visual data formats are analyzed, highlighting the advantages of point clouds in explicitly representing 3D geometry structures and associated attributes. Afterward, representative point cloud datasets and their applications are reviewed. The discussion then addresses the necessity of 3D point cloud coding, examining key challenges and the growing shift toward AI-based methods that demonstrate superior efficiency and reconstruction quality. Additionally, quality assessment methodologies are examined, including both subjective evaluations and objective metrics. By establishing this foundation, the chapter provides essential context for understanding the problem of point cloud coding and the transformative potential of AI in this domain.

Keywords 3D visual information representation · Point cloud datasets · Point cloud coding · AI-based coding · Point cloud quality assessment

1.1 3D Visual Data Representation

This section will briefly introduce several common 3D visual data formats, including point cloud, voxel grid, and mesh, which can support different kinds of 3D visual information processing tasks.

1.1.1 Point Cloud

Point cloud data can be primarily acquired through Light Detection and Ranging (LiDAR) scanners or depth cameras. This type of data consist of unstructured, unordered 3D points that capture the spatial distribution and surface properties of objects. For instance, when scanning a building, each point corresponds to a real-

W. Gao, *AI-based 3D Point Cloud Coding*,
https://doi.org/10.1007/978-981-95-0660-6_1

world surface feature, such as windows, stairs, or walls, and carries attributes like color, intensity, and incident direction. In addition to LiDAR, point clouds can be generated using RGB-D cameras, which simultaneously capture color images and depth maps. By leveraging camera parameters, these frames are converted into 3D point representations [1–16]. Generally speaking, point cloud data have the following characteristics.

- **Disorder.** The pixels in the 2D image have fixed positions, but when the positions of the point cloud are read in different orders, there are many possibilities.
- **Unstructured.** Neural networks structure 2D image data into a matrix form, but point cloud data are unstructured and are very difficult to directly input into the network.
- **Density inconsistency.** Real scenes contain objects of different categories, so the corresponding point cloud data spatial attributes are also different. When the density of acquired data changes, how the model handles it has also become a research issue.
- **Incomplete information.** Due to problems such as occlusion, complete attribute descriptions cannot be obtained, and low-resolution sampling contains relatively one-sided information.

The original point cloud data retain the richest and most detailed information, with the least loss of input information among all methods. However, in this case, the amount of data that needs to be processed is large and the processing speed is slow. The current mainstream point cloud data file formats are as follows.

- **PTS.** Laser scan data format.
- **PTX.** ASCII-based interchange format for point cloud data.
- **XYZ.** Based on Cartesian coordinates.
- **LAS/LAZ.** The most common format for exchanging point clouds.

These files typically contain information such as the 3D coordinates, reflection intensity, and color of point clouds, using common PTS files. A PTS file is a plain text format designed to store LiDAR-scanned point cloud information. The first line indicates the total point count, followed by multiple rows containing seven data fields per point. These fields consist of 3D spatial coordinates (X, Y, Z), an intensity measurement, and RGB color values. The color parameters range from 0 to 255 (8-bit unsigned), while the intensity value quantifies surface reflectivity, with 0 denoting minimal reflection and 255 indicating maximal reflectance. To optimize storage and processing, voxelization and octree structures are commonly employed for compressing and organizing such point cloud data.

Voxel Voxel is the smallest unit of digital data segmentation in 3D space, similar to the smallest unit pixel of a 2D image. It can be simply deemed as a 3D pixel, which is a kind of quantitative and fixed-size point cloud data. 3D convolutional neural networks can be directly applied to this representation. The size of voxels and the number of points that each voxel can accommodate require parameter settings, which inevitably leads to information loss since voxel grids have fixed resolutions.

Typical voxel-based methods include VoxelNet [17], Voxel-FPN [18], RPCGC [19], etc. Voxel data are mainly stored in BINVOX files.

Octree In 1982, Donald Meagher introduced the application of octrees in 3D computer graphics [20], proposing a method to construct an octree from a point cloud. The octree framework organizes 3D geometry entities into voxels, ensuring uniform temporal and spatial complexity. By recursively partitioning space, 3D objects are decomposed into a hierarchical graph with root nodes. Within this structure, voxels sharing identical attributes merge into a leaf node. Otherwise, they undergo further subdivision into eight smaller cubes. The leaf nodes correspond to the finest resolution—for instance, a resolution of 0.01 m yields cubic leaves with 1cm edge lengths. The storage structure of an octree can be used for the recursive search of elements. Generally speaking, the nodes of the generated octree can be divided into the following three categories.

- **Grey node.** The corresponding cube is partly occupied by the searching elements.
- **White node.** The corresponding cube has no searching elements.
- **Black node.** The corresponding cube is fully occupied by the searching elements.

1.1.2 Mesh

Mesh is a data structure used in computer graphics to model various irregular objects. Therefore, continuous things in reality can only be simulated using discrete structures in the computer. The surfaces in physical environments are fundamentally composed of innumerable microscopic polygonal segments. When these segments are interconnected, they create what is referred to in computer graphics as a mesh structure. Although meshes can theoretically incorporate diverse polygonal shapes—ranging from quadrilaterals to more complex polygons—triangular elements have become the de facto standard. This predominance arises from a key geometric principle, i.e., all planar polygons can be systematically triangulated. Consequently, triangular meshes have emerged as the most prevalent method for modeling object surfaces.

Generally speaking, a mesh contains the geometry and attribute information of an object. The geometry information mainly includes the follows.

- 3D coordinates of vertices.
- Index of vertices that make up the face.

The attribute information mainly includes the following.

- Parameters for mapping 2D planar regions to mesh surfaces.
- Attribute maps.
- Attributes associated with each vertex (color, reflectivity, normals, transparency, etc.).

A tetrahedron has four vertices, four faces, and four normal vectors of faces. The mesh data structure can be written to a file for use by other programs. There are various file formats for storing mesh data, among which the most common are OBJ files and VRML files.

- **OFF.** Object File Format. OFF files only store information about the points, faces, and edges of the object.
- **PLY.** Polygon File Format also known as the Stanford Triangle Format. In addition to geometry information, PLY files can store attribute information such as color, surface normals, texture coordinates, and transparency.
- **OBJ.** The OBJ format is a geometry definition standard originally created by Wavefront Technologies for its Advanced Visualizer animation suite. Now an open format, it has been widely adopted by various 3D graphics software developers. Typically, an OBJ file stores vertex positions, texture coordinates (UV mapping), surface normals, and polygonal faces—the latter represented as sequences of vertices and texture vertices.
- **VRML.** The Virtual Reality Modeling Language (VRML) is a standardized file format designed for creating 3D interactive vector graphics, primarily for use on the World Wide Web. Using a text-based structure, it enables the definition of 3D polygons by specifying vertices, edges, and surface properties such as color, UV-mapped textures, reflectivity, and opacity.
- **X3D.** The Extensible 3D (X3D) is a royalty-free ISO/IEC standard designed for the declarative representation of 3D computer graphics. It supports various graphics file formats, along with programming-language APIs and runtime specifications, enabling the delivery and integration of interactive, network-ready 3D content. The latest version, X3D 4.0, has been approved by the Web3D Consortium and is currently undergoing final ISO/IEC review as an updated International Standard.

In addition, meshes can be divided into static meshes and dynamic meshes in terms of timing. Static meshes can be divided into surface meshes and volume meshes, and currently, the majority of compression methods are focused on surface meshes.

1.2 Typical Datasets of 3D Point Clouds

Point cloud datasets serve as valuable experimental resources and validation foundations for the study of point cloud coding technology. Conducting compression experiments on point cloud datasets with varying scales and complexities enables researchers to assess the performance of diverse point cloud coding algorithms, identify potential issues, and refine these algorithms. Additionally, these datasets can be utilized to train and evaluate AI-based compression algorithms, thereby enhancing both compression efficiency and reconstruction quality. The datasets mentioned are detailed in Table 1.1.

Table 1.1 General information of point cloud datasets. Source: Author

Dataset	Year	Institution
ShapeNet	2015	Stanford University, USA
ModelNet	2015	Princeton University, USA
S3DIS	2016	Stanford University, USA
MVUB	2016	Microsoft Inc., USA
8iVFB	2016	8i Labs Inc., USA
Owlii	2017	Owlii Inc., China
ScanNet	2017	Stanford University, USA
SemanticKitti	2019	University of Bonn, Germany
nuScenes	2020	nuTonomy, USA
Ford	2020	Ford AV LLC, Dearborn, USA
PCSOD	2022	Peking University, China

In the realm of artificial intelligence and point cloud coding, the advent of 3D datasets heralds a new era of possibilities. These datasets, repositories of spatial and temporal richness, serve as the linchpin for the development, training, and evaluation of algorithms tasked with compressing and enhancing 3D visual content. This section sheds light on the foundational aspects of 3D datasets, unveiling their significance in the intricate tapestry of AI-driven point cloud coding.

3D point cloud datasets come in various forms, each tailored to specific applications and domains. Two primary categories emerge, each representing a distinct facet of the 3D world, including Graphics-based 3D Datasets and Scene-based 3D Datasets.

1.2.1 Graphics-Based 3D Datasets

The mesh, as previously mentioned, is composed of numerous triangular facets. However, it should be noted that a point cloud can be generated by sampling the mesh. Therefore, this section presents both the mesh and point cloud datasets, which are collectively referred to as Graphics-based 3D Datasets. This part will introduce ShapeNet, MVUB, 8iVFB, Owlii, ModelNet, S3DIS, and PCSOD. It should be noted that the datasets are obtained by either Computer-Aided Design (CAD) models or camera acquiring.

ShapeNet In the rich tapestry of 3D datasets, ShapeNet stands as a foundational marvel, offering a diverse and comprehensive collection of 3D models that has become an instrumental dataset in the realm of 3D learning-based methods. With thousands of objects collected in the real world shown in Fig. 1.1, it becomes one of the broadest and richest 3D datasets. Nowadays, ShapeNet has indexed more than 3 million models, 220,000 of which are grouped into 3,135 categories (WordNet synsets).

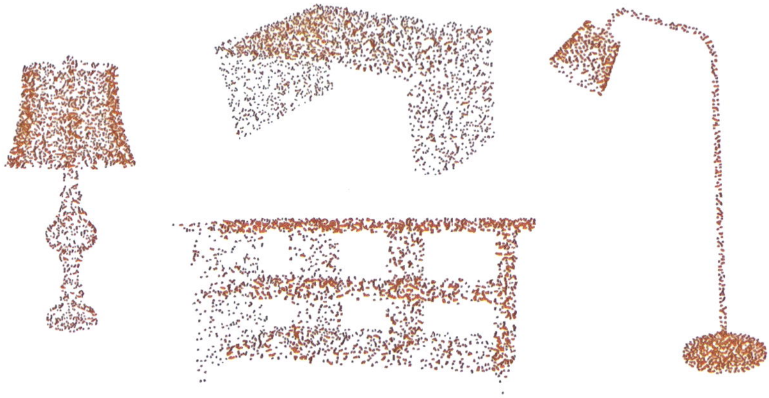

Fig. 1.1 Examples in ShapeNet dataset. Public-domain open-access image [21]

MVUB Microsoft Voxelized Upper Bodies (MVUB) contains five subjects, known as Andrew, David, Phil, Ricardo, and Sarah, which are captured by RGB-D cameras. As one of the famous point cloud datasets, it provides two spatial resolution versions: 512×512×512 voxels and 1024×1024×1024 voxels, respectively. These two versions are also known as depths 9 and 10. Besides, it is also a dynamic dataset with 30 fps and 7–10 seconds length. Moreover, it contains attributes, with RGB information in occupied voxels. The examples of the MVUB dataset can be seen in Fig. 1.2.

8iVFB 8i Labs provides a Voxelized Full Bodies dataset (8iVFB). The 8iVFB stands as a high-standard landmark in point cloud and mesh datasets, as demonstrated in Fig. 1.3. It is excellent in creation, captured by 42 RGB cameras, which makes itself an attribute dataset. The dataset has four sequences: Longdress, Loot, Redandblack, and Soldier, and each of them shares with one spatial resolution: 1024×1024×1024. Alike MVUB, it is a dynamic dataset at 30 fps, and each sequence is over 10 seconds.

Fig. 1.2 Examples in MVUB dataset. The displayed point cloud data are made available under the CC BY License as part of a JPEG Open Access (OA) publication (Copyright ©1988–2024, www.jpeg.org) [22]

Fig. 1.3 Examples in 8iVFB dataset. The displayed point cloud data are made available under the CC BY License as part of an MPEG Open-Access (OA) publication. (Copyright ©1988–2024, www.mpeg.org) [25]

Owlii Provided by Owlii Inc., Owlii is a set of dynamic human textured mesh file sequences, as shown in Fig. 1.4. Owlii contains four sequences with $1024 \times 1024 \times 1024$ spatial resolution, namely Basketball_player, Dancer, Exercise, Model. The dynamic dataset is at 30 fps, with a duration of 20s. The RGB attribute information is preserved.

ModelNet ModelNet [23] is a large-scale dataset extensively utilized for 3D shape recognition and understanding, developed and released by the Computer Science and Artificial Intelligence Laboratory at MIT. This dataset encompasses a diverse array of 3D models across various categories, sourced from multiple repositories including Google 3D Warehouse, Trimble 3D Warehouse, as well as custom-generated models. The included models represent common object categories such as tables, chairs, beds, sofas, bookshelves, monitors, among others—totaling 40 distinct categories, as shown in Fig. 1.5. ModelNet is available in two versions: ModelNet10 and ModelNet40. ModelNet10 comprises approximately 3,991 3D models per category while ModelNet40 contains around 9,843 models per category. These models are stored in OFF format and include vertex and facet information with consistent size and orientation [24].

S3DIS The Stanford 3D Indoor Segmentation (S3DIS) dataset [27], a benchmark for point cloud semantic segmentation, is derived from the Stanford 2D-3D Semantic dataset. Comprising 271 rooms across six indoor environments, S3DIS contains 13 annotated categories such as walls, tables, bookshelves, and ceilings.

Fig. 1.4 Examples in Owlii dataset. The displayed point cloud data are made available under the CC BY License as part of an MPEG Open-Access (OA) publication (Copyright ©1988–2024, www.mpeg.org) [26]

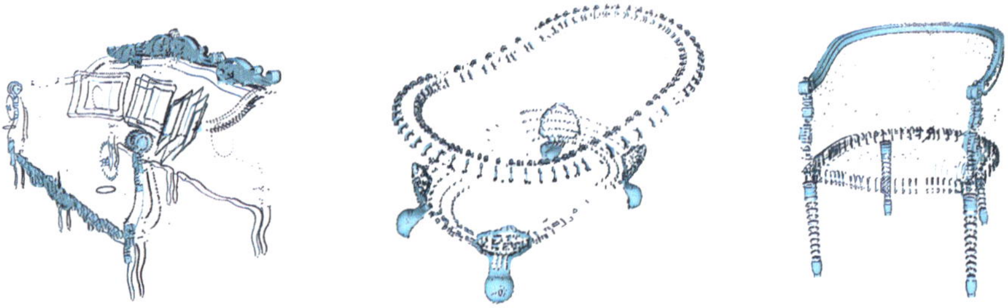

Fig. 1.5 Examples in ModelNet dataset. Public-domain open-access image [23]

As illustrated in Fig. 1.6, each point in the cloud is assigned a semantic label and carries both geometry (3D coordinates x, y, z) and attribute data (RGB values and normals). During preprocessing, the point cloud is typically divided into 1 m×1 m blocks, with 4,096 points randomly sampled from each block for model training.

PCSOD PCSOD is the first dataset designed for point cloud salient object detection (SOD) [28], comprising 2,872 object samples. These samples encompass everyday 3D objects from both indoor and outdoor environments, categorized into 12 superclasses (e.g., furniture, public utilities, artifacts, and buildings) and further refined into 138 subclasses (such as "table," "bridge," "doll," and "playground"), as

Fig. 1.6 Instances of S3DIS dataset. Public-domain open-access image [27]

Fig. 1.7 Categories of PCSOD dataset. Public-domain open-access image [28]

illustrated in Fig. 1.7. The dataset features hierarchical annotations, where each view includes category labels, segmentation maps, and bounding boxes (see Fig. 1.8). For practical use, PCSOD can be split randomly into a training set (2,000 samples) and a test set (remaining samples), approximating a 7:3 ratio [29].

1.2.2 *Scene-Based 3D Datasets*

The previous part introduces Graphics-based 3D Datasets, which mainly focus on one specific object or human in the real world. Besides, Scene-based datasets emerge as dynamic sources of spatial depth, capturing the screen with precision. These datasets, mainly rooted in LiDAR technology, play a pivotal role in applications like autonomous vehicles, robotics, and environmental mapping.

SemanticKitti The SemanticKITTI dataset stands out as a foundational benchmark, uniquely combining precise spatial point clouds with rich semantic annotations. Every point in SemanticKitti with its own annotation constructs a real-world understanding of the task of semantic segmentation. Figure 1.9 gives several frames of the dataset with annotations. Because of the indeed need for compression in real-

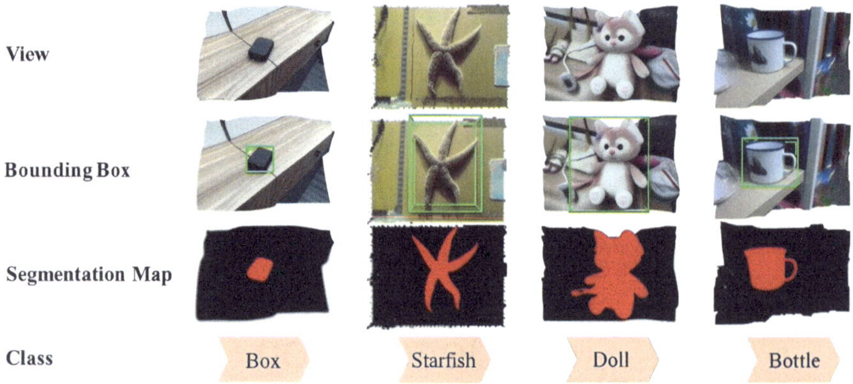

Fig. 1.8 Samples in the PCSOD dataset labeled with hierarchical annotations, such as superclass/subclass, bounding boxes, and segmentation maps. Public-domain open-access image [28]

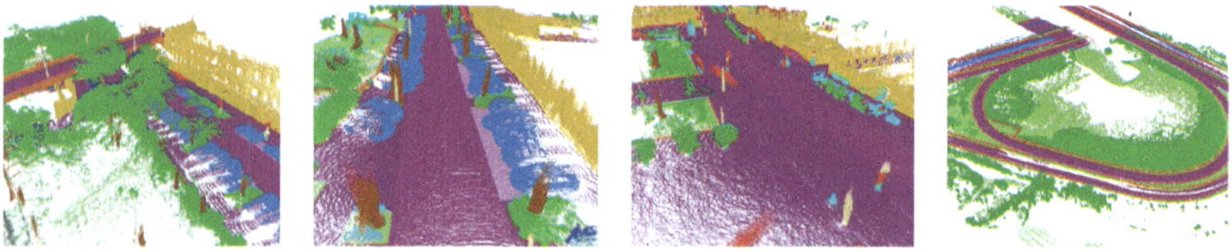

Fig. 1.9 Examples in SemanticKitti dataset. Public-domain open-access image [30]

world scenarios and the clarity for depicting the 3D world, the dataset is served as both a training set and a test set in learning-based point cloud coding.

Ford Ford dataset is used in the MPEG point cloud coding standard, which contains three sequences with more than 4,500 frames in total. Figure 1.10 gives several frames of the dataset. Ford dataset is so challenging that it provides seasonal variation in weather, lighting, construction, and traffic conditions. It is applied as a test dataset frequently.

ScanNet ScanNet lies a comprehensive exploration of indoor environments, captured with precision and realism through depth sensors and RGB cameras, as

Fig. 1.10 Examples in Ford dataset. Public-domain open-access image [31]

Fig. 1.11 Examples in ScanNet dataset. Public-domain open-access image [32]

shown in Fig. 1.11. The dataset contains 1,513 objects with at most 21 classes of annotations, which will be provided for semantic segmentation and instance segmentation. The dataset also provides 2D and 3D versions for a single frame.

1.3 Non-Learning-Based Point Cloud Coding Standards

1.3.1 The Need of Point Cloud Compression

Compression involves decreasing the size of data files while maintaining quality or minimizing quality loss. In contemporary digital environments, media compression is crucial for tackling the growing challenges related to data storage, transmission, and processing. A typical 1,500-frame LiDAR point cloud sequence, such as "Ford_01," is approximately 6GB in size. Compared to images and videos, point clouds have significantly larger data volumes, which presents greater challenges for storage and transmission [33–39]. Uncompressed point cloud data occupy a substantial amount of storage space, which not only increases storage costs but may also result in inefficient use of storage resources. By employing point cloud compression technology, the data volume can be significantly reduced, thereby minimizing storage requirements and optimizing the utilization of storage resources. Compressed point cloud data can be transmitted more rapidly, reducing network bandwidth usage and enhancing transmission efficiency. This is especially critical in application scenarios requiring real-time transmission of point cloud data, such as autonomous driving and telemedicine. Moreover, the accuracy, compression ratio, and real-time performance requirements for point cloud data vary across different application scenarios. Investigating point cloud coding techniques enables the selection of suitable algorithms and parameters tailored to specific application needs, thereby optimizing compression performance.

1.3.2 MPEG Geometry-Based Point Cloud Compression (G-PCC) Standard

In the domain of volumetric video representation, the Moving Picture Experts Group (MPEG)—the preeminent international consortium for visual coding standards—has established Geometry-based Point Cloud Compression (G-PCC) as a comprehensive solution [40–44]. This advanced standard provides flexible compression options, including: (1) lossless preservation of point cloud data, (2) lossy compression with configurable quality levels, while maintaining the integrity of both 3D geometry structures and their corresponding surface attributes [34, 37, 38, 45, 46]. G-PCC employs two primary methods for compressing point cloud geometry, i.e., octree-based coding and predictive geometry coding [47].

Octree-Based Geometry Coding Octree-based coding serves as a core method in G-PCC for point cloud geometry compression. This approach organizes 3D space into a hierarchical tree structure, where nodes represent spatial cubes, and leaf nodes denote voxels potentially containing point data. Initially, the entire point cloud is enclosed within a bounding volume, which undergoes recursive partitioning into eight smaller sub-cubes (octants). The subdivision process iterates until achieving the target resolution or until voxels meet specified occupancy conditions. Finally, the presence or absence of points within each voxel is efficiently compressed using entropy coding, enabling compact storage of geometry data.

Predictive Geometry Coding Predictive geometry coding is another technique used in G-PCC to further improve compression efficiency. This method leverages the spatial correlation between points in a point cloud to predict the location of points in surrounding voxels. By predicting the geometry, the amount of information that needs to be transmitted can be reduced. Predictive coding can use various strategies, such as angular coding, to predict the direction and distance from a known point to a new point, thus reducing the bits required to encode the new point's position. This method is particularly useful when points are sparsely distributed, as it can effectively capture the geometry structure with fewer bits. Both octree-based and predictive geometry coding methods are designed to work together within the G-PCC framework to achieve high compression ratios while maintaining the quality of the decompressed point cloud data. These techniques are crucial for applications such as 3D modeling, virtual reality, and autonomous driving, where efficient transmission and storage of 3D data are essential. In terms of attribute compression, two key methods within the G-PCC framework are transform-based attribute coding and predictive attribute coding.

Transform-Based Attribute Coding Transform-based attribute coding in G-PCC utilizes the Region-Adaptive Hierarchical Transform (RAHT) to exploit the correlation between attribute values. This method involves segmenting the point cloud into regions and applying a hierarchical transform to decorrelate the attributes, thus reducing redundancy and enabling efficient compression. The RAHT is particularly effective for attributes that exhibit smooth variations and can significantly improve compression efficiency.

Predictive-Based Attribute Coding Predictive attribute coding in G-PCC leverages the spatial correlation of attribute values between neighboring points in the point cloud. By predicting the attributes of a point based on its neighbors, the codec can reduce the amount of information that needs to be transmitted, thereby achieving compression. This approach is especially useful for point clouds with attributes that have strong spatial correlations, such as color or intensity values that change gradually across the point cloud.

These attribute coding methods are designed to work in conjunction with G-PCC's geometry compression techniques to achieve an overall high compression ratio while maintaining the quality of the decompressed point cloud data. The combination of geometry and attribute compression methods in G-PCC makes it a comprehensive solution for point cloud coding, suitable for a wide range of applications, including 3D modeling, virtual reality, and autonomous vehicle mapping.

1.3.3 MPEG Video-Based Point Cloud Compression (V-PCC) Standard

The main idea of the Video-based Point Cloud Compression (V-PCC) standard [48] is to not directly encode the point cloud in 3D space, but to project the 3D point cloud data into 2D planes, and then use the mature video coding technologies to fulfill the point cloud coding task [1, 2].

The rapid development of 3D sensing technologies—including LiDAR, depth cameras, and photogrammetry—has established point clouds as a key format for representing 3D data. These datasets play a critical role in fields such as autonomous vehicles, virtual and augmented reality (VR/AR), 3D mapping, and immersive media. Nevertheless, raw point clouds are extremely large, frequently containing millions or billions of points along with attributes like color, reflectance, and surface normals. This creates substantial storage and bandwidth demands, driving the need for effective compression techniques. To tackle this challenge, the Moving Picture Experts Group (MPEG) introduced the Video-based Point Cloud Compression (V-PCC) standard, optimized for dynamic point clouds, such as those capturing moving objects or evolving scenes. V-PCC works alongside the Geometry-based Point Cloud Compression (G-PCC) standard, which focuses on static point clouds, providing a complete framework for 3D data compression.

The significance of V-PCC lies in its ability to enable efficient storage and streaming of 3D content. By achieving compression ratios of 10 to 100 times without perceptible quality loss, V-PCC drastically reduces bandwidth requirements. This makes it particularly valuable for real-time applications like VR/AR, telepresence, and live 3D broadcasting. As part of the MPEG-I standard (ISO/IEC 23090-5), V-PCC ensures interoperability across various devices and platforms, fostering widespread industry adoption. Today, it is already being utilized in autonomous vehicles for LiDAR data compression, metaverse applications, and 3D teleconferencing, highlighting its versatility and impact. From a technical perspective, V-PCC leverages well-established video compression techniques, such as HEVC/H.265, by projecting 3D point clouds into 2D video frames. The process begins with preprocessing and segmentation, where the point cloud is decomposed into patches—local surface regions that approximate planar surfaces. An occupancy map, acting as a binary mask, is then generated to indicate which pixels in the 2D frame correspond to actual 3D points. Next, geometry and texture projection are performed, mapping 3D patches onto 2D planes using orthographic or perspective projection. This step produces two types of video streams: a geometry video, which encodes 3D coordinates (x, y, z) as depth maps, and an attribute video, which encodes color (RGB), reflectance, or other attributes. These videos are subsequently compressed using standard video codecs like HEVC/H.265 or VVC/H.266, employing motion estimation and inter-frame prediction to exploit temporal coherence between consecutive frames for higher compression efficiency [48].

During reconstruction, the decoder decompresses the 2D videos and reprojects them back into 3D space using the occupancy map and auxiliary data, such as patch metadata. V-PCC also incorporates advanced features like layered coding, which prioritizes critical regions (e.g., foreground objects) for adaptive streaming, and supports both lossy and lossless compression modes to balance quality and compression ratio. Additionally, its scalability allows for progressive decoding, making it adaptable to varying network conditions. Despite its advantages, V-PCC faces several challenges. The computational complexity of real-time encoding remains high, particularly for high-resolution point clouds. Dynamic occlusions, where newly revealed areas in moving scenes must be handled, add another layer of difficulty. Looking ahead, future developments may integrate AI-based compression techniques, such as neural network predictors, to further enhance efficiency. In conclusion, MPEG V-PCC serves as a critical bridge between 3D data acquisition and practical deployment, offering an efficient compression solution for immersive technologies. As the demand for 3D content continues to grow in fields like the metaverse, autonomous systems, and next-generation media, V-PCC is poised to play an increasingly pivotal role in shaping the future of digital experiences [48].

1.3.4 AVS Point Cloud Compression (PCC) Standard

The year 2019 witnessed a significant advancement in point cloud coding technology when China Audio Video Coding Standard (AVS) Working Group released the AVS Point Cloud Compression (PCC) standard [49] in March. As a specialized compression framework, it addresses the critical need for efficient representation of LiDAR-generated 3D point data, offering comprehensive solutions for environments ranging from completely static settings to complex scenes with multiple moving objects.

The AVS PCC standard establishes a comprehensive framework that defines an advanced encoding methodology and detailed decoding protocols both specifically designed to accommodate both lossless and moderately lossy compression of geometry data. Beyond this core functionality, the specification also facilitates the streamlined encoding of high-precision, large-volume point cloud datasets. By optimizing data compression efficiency, the standard significantly improves the storage capacity and transmission performance of point cloud information, thereby enabling its widespread adoption in diverse fields. These include but are not limited to geospatial mapping, smart city development, and the advancement of self-driving vehicle technologies. AVS PCC includes two types of geometry coding techniques, i.e., octree and predictive tree, and three types of attribute coding techniques, i.e., the prediction, the prediction and transform, and the multilayer transform.

Octree for Geometry Coding The octree-based geometry compression process divides space using an octree structure. Each voxel's occupancy, which indicates whether points are present, is represented by an occupancy code. This occupancy code is subsequently entropy-encoded using context models that consider neighboring patterns. AVS PCC effectively utilizes the unique characteristics of point cloud spatial distribution, implementing different context models for datasets with varying densities to achieve efficient compression of geometry information. The design of the context model is the main difference between AVS PCC and GPCC in octree coding [50].

Predictive Tree for Geometry Coding The predictive tree is a structure that creates parent–child relationships among points. Unlike the octree, where each voxel represents a fixed spatial area, the predictive tree is more suited for sparse point clouds or areas with low density [50]. Compared to the predictive tree in MPEG, the predictive tree structure in AVS PCC is simpler and does not include any specialized mode. Due to the uneven distribution of points, relying on the overall density of the point cloud to determine the geometry coding method for the whole frame of point clouds may not be effective. Instead, the predictive tree is incorporated into a macro-block framework in AVS PCC, allowing for the selection of geometry coding methods based on the density of individual macro-blocks.

Prediction for Attribute Coding AVS adopts the Hilbert order as the baseline sequence for attribute prediction. It maintains a reference set with a predefined maximum capacity, storing both the coordinates and attributes of previously encoded points [50]. During the encoding process, AVS PCC dynamically selects reference points from this set by leveraging geometry data. The final attribute prediction is derived by analyzing the spatial and attribute correlations among the selected references.

Prediction and Transform for Attribute Coding The prediction and transform method for attribute coding is a single-layer transform, which reduces redundancy in attributes by creating a linear framework for transformation between groups of points. Initially, it segments the ordered points into groups of varying sizes. Next, it employs cross-group prediction to enhance relationships among the groups. Subsequently, the method applies the Discrete Cosine Transform (DCT) to further eliminate redundancy [50]. Additionally, the transform coefficients from different groups are sorted in an alternating manner to boost the efficiency of entropy coding. This structured approach ensures a more compact representation of the data.

Multilayer Transform for Attribute Coding The multilayer transform utilizes a bottom-up framework to minimize redundancy in attributes by transforming them in pairs. This approach allows for the simultaneous incorporation of all attributes, making full use of global correlations, but does not enable point-by-point processing. It employs a hierarchical Haar transform to organize the attributes into clusters, subsequently applying the basic Haar wavelet transform in pairs to effectively rearrange the data. If RAHT in MPEG is considered as a transformation based on octree, the multilayer transform can be considered as a binary tree transformation applied to 1D data after converting the 3D point cloud into one dimension.

1.4 AI-Based Compression Requirement for Point Clouds

The integration of artificial intelligence into point cloud coding has opened up new possibilities for handling 3D spatial data. By employing deep neural networks and advanced machine learning algorithms, this cutting-edge approach significantly enhances traditional compression methods [19, 51–58]. Given the ever-growing utilization of point cloud data in diverse application scenarios and continuous breakthroughs in AI technology, such intelligent compression solutions, as discussed in [59], are poised to play an increasingly important role in both academic research and industrial implementations.

Although traditional methods have provided a stable solution for point cloud coding, their compression ratio is still insufficient, hindering the widespread application of point clouds in areas similar to video. Deep learning–based approaches leverage neural networks to extract features of point cloud data, thereby demonstrating significantly better performance in compression ratio compared to traditional methods while preserving high reconstruction quality, making them a focal point of research.

Current AI-driven point cloud coding techniques can be broadly categorized into three main methodologies. (1) Point-based methods: Unlike voxelization, these approaches operate directly on raw point clouds, leveraging deep learning models to extract and compress geometry features without intermediate representations. For instance, Yan et al. [60] proposed an end-to-end network for efficient feature learning from unstructured points. (2) Voxel-based methods: These methods convert point cloud data into a volumetric voxel representation, which is then compressed through deep learning frameworks. Prior studies, such as Wang et al. [55, 61], have demonstrated the effectiveness of this strategy in handling sparse 3D data. (3) Octree-based methods: This paradigm utilizes hierarchical octree partitioning to recursively subdivide 3D space into octants, enabling multi-resolution detail representation. The compression is achieved by neural networks that exploit contextual dependencies across octree levels.

Looking ahead, AI-based point cloud coding is both a challenging and a promising technique. The MPEG and AVS working groups are actively investigating standardization efforts for AI-based point cloud coding. Through ongoing research and optimization, it is anticipated that deep learning point cloud coding technology will play an increasingly significant role across various domains in the future. Moreover, AI-based compression also provides more potentials for optimizing coding performances for machine perception tasks [28, 62–67].

1.5 Point Cloud Coding Performance Evaluation

During the implementation of point cloud coding algorithms, the introduction of geometry and attribute distortions remains an unavoidable phenomenon. Consequently, comprehensive performance evaluation of compressed point clouds necessitates a dual-focus approach incorporating: (1) human perceptual assessment through subjective quality evaluation methodologies and (2) quantitative analysis employing mathematically-defined objective quality metrics [68–75].

1.5.1 Subject Quality Assessment

Compared with objective quality assessment (QA), subjective QA can obtain a more accurate measurement of a specific medium content [1]. Based on practical experiments, subjective QA contains five steps, i.e., selecting content, introducing distortion, designing the rendering scheme and viewing protocol, displaying and scoring the point clouds, and processing the opinion scores. After selecting specific content for subjects of QA experiments and introducing distortion (usually by quantization), subjects will be presented with the experimental scheme and protocol, ensuring experiment subjects to fairly and correctly treat every sample. In the step of displaying and scoring, there are many recommended standards to obtain a fair result of opinion score. Lastly, the mean opinion score will be generated after collecting and processing.

1.5.2 Objective Metrics for Compressed Quality

Unlike traditional image quality assessment, the evaluation of point cloud quality requires consideration of both texture and geometry distortions [1], as both factors significantly impact perceptual fidelity. In recent years, significant research efforts have been devoted to advancing quality assessment methodologies in point cloud coding, leading to the development of various objective metrics. Among these, point-based error measurements such as Point-to-Point (P2P) and Point-to-Plane (P2Plane) distances are widely used to quantify geometry inaccuracies. For signal fidelity evaluation, Peak Signal-to-Noise Ratio (PSNR) remains a fundamental benchmark, while compression efficiency is typically analyzed through Rate-Distortion Curves (RD-Curves) and their derived metrics including Bjontegaard Delta Rate (BD-Rate) and Bjontegaard Delta PSNR (BD-PSNR). Additionally, perceptual quality models like the Point Cloud Quality Metric (PCQM) [76] have emerged to better align with human visual perception, providing a more comprehensive assessment framework for compressed point clouds.

Point-to-Point Error As a fundamental geometry assessment metric, the point-to-point (po2po) error [1] computes the spatial displacement between homologous points in two point clouds—the original reference and its distorted version. This approach characterizes reconstruction quality through aggregating individual measurement errors across the entire set of point correspondences.

$$po2po(A, B) = \frac{1}{N_A} \sum_{\forall a_i \in A}^{N_A} \|E(a_i, b_i)\|_2^2, \tag{1.1}$$

where A and B are two point clouds need comparison, and b_i is the nearest neighbor of a_i in B. $E(\cdot, \cdot)$ is denoted as the calculation of the Euclidean distance between two points. Point-to-point error effectively identifies subtle geometry distortions due to its straightforward calculation and broad applicability. However, this approach overlooks the reality that points in a point cloud often represent a structure's curved surfaces. Consequently, it may not accurately reflect human visual perception, leading to discrepancies between the objective quality assessment and subjective evaluations.

Point-to-Plane Error In 3D point cloud quality assessment, the point-to-plane (po2pl) error [1] criterion serves as a geometry fidelity measure. Its core mechanism involves two computational stages: first, identifying spatially correlated points between reference and distorted clouds; second, quantifying perceptual distortion through a composite metric that combines Euclidean distance with normal vector angular differences. The mathematical representation of this error metric takes the following form:

$$po2pl(A, B) = \frac{1}{N_A}\sum_{i=1}^{N_A}(\overrightarrow{v}(a_i, b_i) \cdot \overrightarrow{N}(a_i))^2, \tag{1.2}$$

where $\overrightarrow{N}(a_i)$ is the unit normal vector of a_i, and $\overrightarrow{v}(a_i, b_i)$ denotes the vector from a_i to b_i, and b_i is the nearest neighbor of a_i in B. However, the point-to-plane error is sensitive to distortions caused by translation or scaling. Additionally, the point-to-plane error calculation relies on the presence of a normal vector at each point in both the reference and distorted point clouds.

PSNR Peak Signal-to-Noise Ratio (PSNR) [1] is a commonly employed metric for assessing the quality of compressed media by evaluating its fidelity to the original, uncompressed version. This metric computes the logarithmic ratio between the peak signal power and the noise power introduced during compression, with results expressed in decibels (dB). A higher PSNR value indicates better preservation of the original content's quality. Mathematically, it is defined as:

$$\text{PSNR} = 10\log_{10}\left(\frac{p^2}{\text{MSE}}\right), \tag{1.3}$$

where MSE is defined previously (point-to-point error and point-to-plane error), and p represents the peak error. The point-to-point error is also referred to as D1-MSE, while the point-to-plane error is referred to as D2-MSE. Consequently, the PSNR corresponding to the point-to-point error is termed D1-PSNR, and the PSNR corresponding to the point-to-plane error is termed D2-PSNR.

Rate-Distortion Curve (RD-Curve) For compression algorithms, a higher bit rate generally implies better image quality and less distortion. However, it also demands more storage space and increases the burden on network transmission. Therefore, identifying the optimal balance between rate and distortion to achieve the best compression performance is crucial. This approach is known as rate-distortion optimization. In practical applications, the RD-Curve [1] is utilized to evaluate the performance of various compression codecs. It provides insights into the trade-off between the quality of the compressed image or video and the resources required for compression and decompression, such as computational power and bandwidth.

BD-Rate BD-Rate [1] quantifies the average performance gap between two rate-distortion (RD) curves. Its computation involves comparing the normalized area integrals of the two curves: the integral of the lower curve is subtracted from that of the upper curve, with both values scaled by their respective integration intervals. In practical terms, BD-rate reflects the additional bitrate required by the optimized algorithm to maintain equivalent video quality compared to the original method.

A negative BD-Rate value signifies enhanced coding efficiency, demonstrating the superiority of the improved algorithm.

BD-PSNR BD-PSNR [1] represents the improvement in objective quality of the optimized algorithm compared to the original algorithm at the same bit rate. The unit of BD-PSNR is dB. Optimizing BD-PSNR for the regular representation enhances the coding performance of the algorithm. A larger BD-PSNR indicates better performance of the proposed algorithm, resulting in a higher PSNR at the same code rate.

PCQM Point Cloud Quality Metric (PCQM) [76] represents an innovative approach in full-reference PCQA, uniquely integrating geometry and color features. It achieves this by merging geometry-based attributes derived from curvature analysis with color-based attributes, which are ascertained through comparisons of lightness, chroma, and hue. Specifically, the method employs three geometry-focused features developed through curvature calculations using quadric surface fitting, along with five color-focused features. Given a point $p \in R$, where R is the reference point cloud, PCQM involves calculating quadric surface fitting based on a set of nearest neighbors $p_i^D \in D$ of p by minimizing:

$$\sum_i \|z_i - Q(x_i, y_i)\|^2, \tag{1.4}$$

where the neighbor p_i^D of p has coordinates (x_i, y_i, z_i), and Q is the quadric surface denoted as $Q(x, y) = ax^2 + by^2 + cxy + dx + ey + f$. Then the curvature ρ can be directly computed from the coefficients of the fitted quadric surfaces by

$$\rho = \frac{(1 + d^2)a + (1 + e^2)b - 4abc}{(1 + e^2 + d^2)^{\frac{3}{2}}}. \tag{1.5}$$

PCQM considers three geometry features based on curvature, which are curvature comparison, curvature contrast, and curvature structure. The color-based features considered are lightness comparison, lightness contrast, lightness structure, chroma comparison, and hue comparison. However, although PCQM takes into account the fusion of geometry and color features, the design of this fusion is relatively simple. At the same time, the method is sensitive to the selection of neighborhood size, and the calculation of curvature is time-consuming.

1.6 Organization of the Book

This book provides a comprehensive overview of the emerging research field of AI-based point cloud coding, leveraging the power of deep learning to process and compress 3D data efficiently. The structure of this book is designed to guide readers from the basics of point cloud coding to advanced topics and future research directions. It can be divided into four major modules:

Introduction and Fundamentals Chapter 1 serves as an introduction, providing the background knowledge on the importance of point cloud data coding and its applications. Chapter 2 delves into the fundamentals of deep learning–based point cloud coding, establishing a foundation for understanding the subsequent chapters. These chapters lay the preliminary knowledge for readers.

Quality Assessment and Perception Models Chapter 1 serves as an introduction, providing the background knowledge on the importance of point cloud data coding and its applications. Chapter 2 delves into the fundamentals of deep learning–based point cloud coding, establishing a foundation for understanding the subsequent chapters. These chapters lay the preliminary knowledge for readers.

Deep Learning–Based Coding Methods Chapters 4, 5, and 6 constitute the core part of the book, covering various technical aspects of deep learning–based point cloud coding. Chapter 4 addresses the geometry coding of static point clouds, while Chap. 5 discusses the attribute coding of static point clouds. Chapter 6 extends the discussion to dynamic point clouds, including the challenges and critical techniques for point cloud coding. These chapters provide detailed explorations for effectively applying deep learning models to compress point cloud data.

Advanced Topics Chapters 7, 8, 9, and 10 present more advanced topics. Chapter 7 discusses human and machine perception-oriented 3D point cloud coding, emphasizing the importance of coding techniques that consider human visual experience and machine perception utility. Chapter 8 deals with the compression artifacts removal problem, which is a critical aspect of point cloud coding to elevate signal quality. Chapter 9 explores the current status of AI-based 3D point cloud coding standards, providing insights into industry practices. Chapter 10 extends the discussion to several practical issues, such as lightweight implementations of point cloud networks, point cloud streaming and communication systems, and point cloud rendering and display.

Open-Source Projects and Future Directions Finally, Chap. 11 provides an overview of open-source projects related to AI-based 3D point cloud coding, offering practical resources for readers interested in hands-on experience. As the last chapter, Chap. 12 concludes this book with future research directions and challenges in the field of AI-based point cloud coding.

The book is designed for readers who are interested in the intersection of 3D visual data compression, 3D visual information processing, and deep learning applications. From this book, readers will gain a comprehensive understanding of the current status and future potentials of the fast-growing technologies in the field of AI-based 3D point cloud coding.

1.7 Summary

This chapter provides a comprehensive overview of the related issues about 3D point cloud coding. Beginning with a comparative analysis of different 3D visual information representation formats, it highlights the advantages of point clouds in explicitly representing 3D geometry structures and associated attributes. Popular point cloud datasets are then enumerated, underscoring their critical role in deep learning, where high-quality data significantly influences model performance. The discussion proceeds to examine the challenges of point cloud coding, explaining why it remains an active research area and emphasizing the growing prominence of learning-based approaches. Key evaluation methodologies and metrics for point cloud coding are subsequently presented. Finally, the organization structure of the book is outlined. For readers who are interested in the related technologies of AI-based image and video coding, please refer to [77].

Exercises

1. What are the differences between point clouds and images in terms of information representation?
2. If no compression is performed, and the bit width of a frame is 10 bits, how large is the geometry information of a point cloud containing 100,0000 points?
3. If no compression is performed, the geometry bit width is 10 bits, and the attribute information is 8-bit color information. How large is the point cloud containing 250 frames with an average of 1,000,000 points per frame?
4. In practical situations, the number of faces in most mesh files is twice that of points. Assuming that an OBJ file only stores the coordinates of points and the vertex index of triangular faces, with the coordinates stored in the form of double-precision floating-point numbers and the index stored in the form of 32-bit integers. What is the proportion of storage space occupied by vertices and faces?
5. Why is mesh representation important in 3D visual data formats?
6. What role can the coding standards like MPEG G-PCC, MPEG V-PCC, and AVS PCC play in the compression of 3D point cloud data?
7. How might subjective quality assessment differ from objective metrics for quality assessment in the context of 3D point cloud coding performance evaluation?
8. What are the advantages and disadvantages of point clouds (based on voxel or octree) and meshes for 3D scenes and objects?
9. Please explain the difference between octree-based geometry coding and predictive geometry coding in MPEG G-PCC. Why are both methods used together in point cloud coding?

10. Please describe two methods used for attribute compression in MPEG G-PCC and explain their advantages.

References

1. G. Li, G. Wei, W. Gao, *Point Cloud Compression: Technologies and Standardization* (Springer, Berlin, 2024)
2. W. Gao, G. Li, *Deep Learning for 3D Point Clouds* (Springer, Berlin, 2024)
3. S. Sun, X. Liang, B. Qu, W. Gao, Content-rich aigc video quality assessment via intricate text alignment and motion-aware consistency. arXiv preprint arXiv:2502.04076 (2025)
4. S. Sun, B. Qu, X. Liang, S. Fan, W. Gao, Ie-bench: advancing the measurement of text-driven image editing for human perception alignment. arXiv preprint arXiv:2501.09927 (2025)
5. Y. Ye, W. Gao, LLM-PCGC: large language model-based point cloud geometry compression. arXiv preprint arXiv:2408.08682 (2024)
6. Q. Xu, L. Meng, G. Zhang, W. Gao, G. Li, Coding-free multiscale latent variables for lossless point cloud attribute compression, in *2025 IEEE International Conference on Multimedia and Expo (ICME)* (2025)
7. L. Meng, Q. Xu, S. Liu, W. Gao, G. Li, Towards specialized and generalizable geometry restoration of compressed point clouds, in *2025 IEEE International Conference on Multimedia and Expo (ICME)* (2025)
8. W. Liu, W. Gao, X. Mu, Fast inter-frame motion prediction for compressed dynamic point cloud attribute enhancement, in *Proceedings of the AAAI Conference on Artificial Intelligence*, vol. 38(4) (2024), pp. 3720–3728
9. Z. Yang, W. Gao, X. Lu, Danet: Density-adaptive network for geometry-based point cloud compression artifacts removal, in *2023 IEEE International Conference on Visual Communications and Image Processing (VCIP)* (IEEE, New York, 2023), pp. 1–5
10. X. Fan, G. Li, D. Li, Y. Ren, W. Gao, T.H. Li, Deep geometry post-processing for decompressed point clouds, in *2022 IEEE International Conference on Multimedia and Expo (ICME)* (IEEE, New York, 2022), pp. 1–6
11. X. Zhang, G. Liao, W. Gao, G. Li, Tdrnet: transformer-based dual-branch restoration network for geometry based point cloud compression artifacts, in *2022 IEEE International Conference on Multimedia and Expo (ICME)* (IEEE, New York, 2022), pp. 1–6
12. Z. Li, G. Li, T.H. Li, S. Liu, W. Gao, Semantic point cloud upsampling. IEEE Trans. Multimedia **25**, 3432–3442 (2022)
13. R. Zhang, W. Gao, G. Li, T.H. Li, Qinet: decision surface learning and adversarial enhancement for quasi-immune completion of diverse corrupted point clouds. IEEE Trans. Geosci. Remote Sens. **60**, 1–14 (2022)
14. R. Bao, Y. Ren, G. Li, W. Gao, S. Liu, Flow-based point cloud completion network with adversarial refinement, in *ICASSP 2022–2022 IEEE International Conference on Acoustics, Speech and Signal Processing (ICASSP)* (IEEE, New York, 2022), pp. 2559–2563
15. J. Chen, G. Li, R. Zhang, T.H. Li, W. Gao, Pointivae: invertible variational autoencoder framework for 3d point cloud generation, in *2022 IEEE International Conference on Image Processing (ICIP)* (IEEE, New York, 2022), pp. 3216–3220
16. R. Zhang, J. Chen, W. Gao, G. Li, T.H. Li, Pointot: interpretable geometry-inspired point cloud generative model via optimal transport. IEEE Trans. Circuits Syst. Video Technol. **32**(10), 6792–6806 (2022)
17. Y. Zhou, O. Tuzel, Voxelnet: end-to-end learning for point cloud based 3d object detection, in *Proceedings of the IEEE Conference on Computer Vision and Pattern Recognition* (2018), pp. 4490–4499

18. H. Kuang, B. Wang, J. An, M. Zhang, Z. Zhang, Voxel-fpn: multi-scale voxel feature aggregation for 3d object detection from lidar point clouds. Sensors **20**(3), 704 (2020)
19. L. Xie, W. Gao, H. Zheng, G. Li, Roi-guided point cloud geometry compression towards human and machine vision, in *Proceedings of the 32nd ACM International Conference on Multimedia* (2024), pp. 3741–3750
20. D. Meagher, Geometric modeling using octree encoding. Comput. Graphics Image Process. **19**(2), 129–147 (1982)
21. A.X. Chang, T. Funkhouser, L. Guibas, P. Hanrahan, Q. Huang, Z. Li, S. Savarese, M. Savva, S. Song, H. Su, et al., Shapenet: an information-rich 3d model repository. arXiv preprint arXiv:1512.03012 (2015)
22. C. Loop, Q. Cai, S.O. Escolano, P.A. Chou, Microsoft Voxelized Upper Bodies (MVUB). Microsoft Corporation, Tech. Rep., 2005, available from the JPEG Pleno Database. http://plenodb.jpeg.org/pc/microsoft/
23. Z. Wu, S. Song, A. Khosla, F. Yu, L. Zhang, X. Tang, J. Xiao, 3D ShapeNets: A deep representation for volumetric shapes, in *Proceedings of the IEEE Conference on Computer Vision and Pattern Recognition* (2015), pp. 1912–1920
24. L. Xie, W. Gao, H. Zheng, G. Li, Roi-guided point cloud geometry compression towards human and machine vision. arXiv preprint arXiv:2504.14240 (2025)
25. E. d'Eon, B. Harrison, T. Myers, P.A. Chou, 8i Voxelized Full Bodies—A Voxelized Point Cloud Dataset. ISO/IEC JTC1/SC29/WG11, Macau, Tech. Rep. m41658 (2017). http://plenodb.jpeg.org/pc/8ilabs/
26. Y. Xu, Y. Lu, Z. Wen, Owlii Dynamic Human Mesh Sequence Dataset. ISO/IEC JTC1/SC29/WG11, Macau, Tech. Rep. m41658 (2017). https://mpeg-pcc.org/index.php/pcc-content-database/owlii-dynamic-human-textured-mesh-sequence-dataset/
27. I. Armeni, O. Sener, A.R. Zamir, H. Jiang, I. Brilakis, M. Fischer, S. Savarese, 3D semantic parsing of large-scale indoor spaces, in *Proceedings of the IEEE Conference on Computer Vision and Pattern Recognition* (2016), pp. 1534–1543
28. S. Fan, W. Gao, G. Li, Salient object detection for point clouds. arXiv preprint arXiv:2207.11889 (2022)
29. W. Gao, G. Li, Deep-learning-based point cloud enhancement I, in *Deep Learning for 3D Point Clouds* (Springer, Berlin, 2024), pp. 71–97
30. J. Behley, M. Garbade, A. Milioto, J. Quenzel, S. Behnke, C. Stachniss, J. Gall, Semantickitti: A dataset for semantic scene understanding of lidar sequences. arXiv preprint arXiv:1904.01416 (2019)
31. F.M. Company, Ford av dataset: autonomous vehicle data set (2024), accessed on 2024-09-20. https://blog.gitcode.com/6de81fbe00eed5b4c8f451d1b00a558e.html
32. A. Dai, A.X. Chang, M. Savva, M. Halber, T. Funkhouser, M. Nießner, Scannet: richly-annotated 3d reconstructions of indoor scenes, in *Proceedings of the Computer Vision and Pattern Recognition (CVPR)* (IEEE, New York, 2017)
33. T. Qin, G. Li, W. Gao, S. Liu, Multi-grained point cloud geometry compression via dual-model prediction with extended octree. ACM Trans. Multimed. Comput. Commun. Appl. **20**(9), 1–30 (2024)
34. W. Gao, H. Yuan, G. Li, Z. Li, H. Yuan, Low complexity coding unit decision for video-based point cloud compression. IEEE Trans. Image Process. **33**, 149–162 (2023)
35. Y. Shao, W. Gao, S. Liu, G. Li, Advanced patch-based affine motion estimation for dynamic point cloud geometry compression. Sensors **24**(10), 3142 (2024)
36. Y. Shao, F. Song, W. Gao, S. Liu, G. Li, Texture-guided graph transform optimization for point cloud attribute compression. Appl. Sci. **14**(10), 4094 (2024)
37. Y. Shao, X. Yang, W. Gao, S. Liu, G. Li, 3d point cloud attribute compression using diffusion-based texture-aware intra prediction. IEEE Trans. Circuits Syst. Video Technol. **34**(10), 9633–9646 (2024)
38. J. Zhang, Y. Chen, G. Liu, W. Gao, G. Li, Efficient point cloud attribute compression framework using attribute-guided graph fourier transform, in *ICASSP 2024–2024 IEEE International Conference on Acoustics, Speech and Signal Processing (ICASSP)* (IEEE, New York, 2024), pp. 8426–8430

39. Y. Shao, G. Li, Q. Zhang, W. Gao, S. Liu, Nonrigid registration-based progressive motion compensation for point cloud geometry compression. IEEE Trans. Geosci. Remote Sens. **61**, 1–14 (2023)
40. H. Yuan, W. Gao, J. Wang, Dynamic computational resource allocation for fast inter frame coding in video conferencing applications, in *2021 IEEE International Conference on Multimedia and Expo (ICME)* (IEEE, New York, 2021), pp. 1–6
41. W. Gao, Q. Jiang, R. Wang, S. Ma, G. Li, S. Kwong, Consistent quality oriented rate control in hevc via balancing intra and inter frame coding. IEEE Trans. Industr. Inform. **18**(3), 1594–1604 (2021)
42. H. Yuan, W. Gao, A new coding unit partitioning mode for screen content video coding, in *Proceedings of the 2021 5th International Conference on Digital Signal Processing* (2021), pp. 66–72
43. Y. Guo, W. Gao, S. Ma, G. Li, Accelerating transform algorithm implementation for efficient intra coding of 8k UHD videos. ACM Trans. Multimed. Comput. Commun. Appl. (TOMM) **18**(4), 1–20 (2022)
44. Z. Cai, W. Gao, Efficient fast algorithm and parallel hardware architecture for intra prediction of AVS3, in *2021 IEEE International Symposium on Circuits and Systems (ISCAS)* (IEEE, New York, 2021), pp. 1–5
45. F. Song, G. Li, W. Gao, T.H. Li, Rate-distortion optimized graph for point cloud attribute coding. IEEE Signal Process Lett. **29**, 922–926 (2022)
46. F. Song, G. Li, X. Yang, W. Gao, T.H. Li, Fine-grained correlation representation for graph-based point cloud attribute compression, in *2022 IEEE International Conference on Multimedia and Expo (ICME)* (IEEE, New York, 2022), pp. 1–6
47. G. Li, W. Gao, W. Gao, MPEG geometry-based point cloud compression (g-PCC) standard, in *Point Cloud Compression: Technologies and Standardization* (Springer, Berlin, 2024), pp. 135–165
48. G. Li, W. Gao, W. Gao, MPEG video-based point cloud compression (v-PCC) standard, in *Point Cloud Compression: Technologies and Standardization* (Springer, Berlin, 2024), pp. 199–218
49. G. Li, W. Gao, W. Gao, AVS point cloud compression standard, in *Point Cloud Compression: Technologies and Standardization* (Springer, Berlin, 2024), pp. 167–197
50. W. Gao, W. Gao, X. Mu, C. Peng, G. Li, Overview and comparison of AVS point cloud compression standard. APSIPA Trans. Signal Inf. Process. **14**(2), 1–33 (2025)
51. Y. Zhang, W. Gao, G. Li, Openpointcloud-v2: A deep learning based open-source algorithm library of point cloud processing, in *Proceedings of the 1st International Workshop on Advances in Point Cloud Compression, Processing and Analysis* (2022), pp. 51–55
52. L. Xie, W. Gao, Learningpcc: a pytorch library for learning-based point cloud compression, in *Proceedings of the 32nd ACM International Conference on Multimedia* (2024), pp. 11234–11238
53. C. Fu, G. Li, R. Song, W. Gao, S. Liu, Octattention: octree-based large-scale contexts model for point cloud compression, in *Proceedings of the AAAI Conference on Artificial Intelligence*, vol. 36(1) (2022), pp. 625–633
54. C. Zhang, W. Gao, Adadpcc: adaptive rate control and rate-distortion-complexity optimization for dynamic point cloud compression, in *Proceedings of the AAAI Conference on Artificial Intelligence* (2025)
55. K. Wang, W. Gao, Unipcgc: towards practical point cloud geometry compression via an efficient unified approach, in *Proceedings of the AAAI Conference on Artificial Intelligence* (2025)
56. K. Zheng, W. Gao, H. Zheng, Octree-based learned point cloud geometry compression: a lossy perspective, in *2025 Data Compression Conference (DCC)* (IEEE, New York, 2025)
57. Z. Qi, H. Liu, W. Gao, Variable-rate point cloud compression with channel-wise entropy modeling, in *2025 Data Compression Conference (DCC)* (IEEE, New York, 2025)

58. H. Zheng, W. Gao, Z. Yu, T. Zhao, G. Li, Viewpcgc: view-guided learned point cloud geometry compression, in *Proceedings of the 32nd ACM International Conference on Multimedia* (2024), pp. 7152–7161
59. G. Li, W. Gao, W. Gao, MPEG ai-based 3d graphics coding standard, in *Point Cloud Compression: Technologies and Standardization* (Springer, Berlin, 2024), pp. 219–241
60. W. Yan, Y. Shao, S. Liu, T.H. Li, Z. Li, G. Li, Deep autoencoder-based lossy geometry compression for point clouds. arXiv preprint arXiv:1905.03691 (2019)
61. J. Wang, D. Ding, Z. Li, X. Feng, C. Cao, Z. Ma, Sparse tensor-based multiscale representation for point cloud geometry compression. IEEE Trans. Pattern Anal. Mach. Intell. **45**(7), 9055–9071 (2022)
62. S. Luo, W. Gao, A general framework for rotation invariant point cloud analysis, in *ICASSP 2024–2024 IEEE International Conference on Acoustics, Speech and Signal Processing (ICASSP)* (IEEE, New York, 2024), pp. 3665–3669
63. D. Yang, W. Gao, Pointchd: a point cloud benchmark for congenital heart disease classification and segmentation. IEEE J. Biomed. Health Inform. **29**(4), 2683–2694 (2025)
64. Z. Pan, N. Zhang, W. Gao, S. Liu, G. Li, Less is more: label recommendation for weakly supervised point cloud semantic segmentation, in *Proceedings of the AAAI Conference on Artificial Intelligence*, vol. 38(5) (2024), pp. 4397–4405
65. Z. Pan, G. Liu, W. Gao, T.H. Li, Epcontrast: effective point-level contrastive learning for large-scale point cloud understanding, in *2024 IEEE International Conference on Multimedia and Expo (ICME)* (IEEE, New York, 2024), pp. 1–6
66. N. Zhang, Z. Pan, T.H. Li, W. Gao, G. Li, Improving graph representation for point cloud segmentation via attentive filtering, in *Proceedings of the IEEE/CVF Conference on Computer Vision and Pattern Recognition* (2023), pp. 1244–1254
67. Z. Pan, W. Gao, G. Li, Distribution guidance network for weakly supervised point cloud semantic segmentation, in *Advances in Neural Information Processing Systems* (2024)
68. L. Xie, X. Mu, G. Li, W. Gao, et al. PKU-DPCC: a new dataset for dynamic point cloud compression. APSIPA Trans. Signal Inf. Process. **13**(6), 1–23 (2024)
69. H. Yuan, W. Gao, W. Gao, Opensep: an open source subjective experiment platform, in *Proceedings of the 32nd ACM International Conference on Multimedia* (2024), pp. 11248–11251
70. Z. Guo, W. Gao, H. Wang, J. Wang, S. Fan, No-reference deep quality assessment of compressed light field images, in *2021 IEEE International Conference on Multimedia and Expo (ICME)* (IEEE, New York, 2021), pp. 1–6
71. S. Fan, W. Gao, Screen-based 3d subjective experiment software, in *Proceedings of the 31st ACM International Conference on Multimedia* (2023), pp. 9672–9675
72. J. Wang, W. Gao, G. Li, Zoom to perceive better: no-reference point cloud quality assessment via exploring effective multiscale feature. IEEE Trans. Circuits Syst. Video Technol. **4**(7), 6334–6346 (2024)
73. J. Wang, W. Gao, G. Li, Applying collaborative adversarial learning to blind point cloud quality measurement. IEEE Trans. Instrum. Meas. **72**, 1–15 (2023)
74. H. Li, W. Gao, Information exploration of projected views for point cloud quality measurement. IEEE Trans. Instrum. Meas. **74**, 1–14 (2025)
75. S. Fan, W. Gao, Z. Chen, G. Li, G. Liu, Q. Wang, Stochasticity-aware no-reference point cloud quality assessment, in *International Joint Conference on Artificial Intelligence* (2025)
76. G. Meynet, Y. Nehmé, J. Digne, G. Lavoué, PCQM: a full-reference quality metric for colored 3d point clouds, in *2020 Twelfth International Conference on Quality of Multimedia Experience (QoMEX)* (IEEE, New York, 2020), pp. 1–6
77. W. Gao, *AI-based Image and Video Coding: Methods, Standards, and Applications* (Springer, Berlin, 2025)

Chapter 2
Fundamentals of Deep Learning–Based 3D Point Cloud Coding

Abstract With the rapid advancement of 3D sensing technologies, point cloud data have emerged as a fundamental representation of 3D information. Unlike structured images, point clouds consist of irregular, unstructured spatial points that accurately capture object geometry while presenting unique challenges for efficient compression. We first examine essential deep learning (DL) architectures and their advantages in processing point cloud data, including Convolution Neural Networks and Sparse Convolutions. The discussion then analyzes various point cloud representation formats and their respective trade-offs in coding efficiency. Furthermore, we present typical DL frameworks for point cloud processing and systematically outline the general pipeline for DL-based 3D point cloud coding. Critical components including quantization techniques and entropy modeling are thoroughly investigated. The chapter ultimately establishes a cohesive theoretical framework for advancing point cloud coding research through deep learning methodologies.

Keywords Convolutional neural network · Sparse convolutional network · Point cloud data representation · Point cloud network · Point cloud coding · Entropy model

2.1 Introduction

This chapter delves into the theoretical foundations of deep learning–based point cloud coding. First, it introduces the fundamentals of deep learning, including Convolution Neural Networks (CNNs) and Sparse Convolutions, which possess unique advantages in processing point cloud data. Next, it discusses various representation formats of point cloud data, including points, voxels, and octrees, analyzing their application scenarios and pros and cons in point cloud coding. It presents typical network architectures of deep learning for point clouds. Afterward, it introduces the general framework of deep learning–based 3D point cloud coding

W. Gao, *AI-based 3D Point Cloud Coding*,
https://doi.org/10.1007/978-981-95-0660-6_2

and introduces the basic entropy model. Finally, it summarizes the content of this chapter by recapitulating key points.

2.2 Basics of Deep Neural Networks

In the contemporary landscape of artificial intelligence (AI) development, deep learning has emerged as the cornerstone driving technological advancement. CNNs, and Sparse Convolutional Networks models serve as basic blocks of deep learning, each fulfilling pivotal roles in this progression. CNNs, leveraging their robust feature extraction capabilities, have established the foundation for image processing. Sparse Convolutional Networks, conversely, specialize in the efficient processing of sparse data structures. Their architecture has demonstrated particular efficacy in handling 3D data, making significant contributions to domains such as 3D object recognition, point cloud processing, and medical image analysis.

2.2.1 Convolutional Neural Networks

Since CNNs' initial proposal by LeCun et al. in the 1980s, CNNs have gained widespread popularity due to their exceptional performance in image processing tasks. Particularly, the success of AlexNet rapidly established CNNs as a core technology in computer vision [1]. The convolution operation is the cornerstone of CNNs, extracting local features by applying filters (or convolution kernels) to input data. Mathematically, a 2D convolution operation can be expressed as:

$$S(i, j) = (I * K)(i, j) = \sum_{m} \sum_{n} I(i + m, j + n) K(m, n), \tag{2.1}$$

where I represents the input matrix, K is the convolutional kernel, and S is the output feature map. CNNs capture local spatial features, which is the source of their powerful feature extraction capability.

In conclusion, CNNs, as a cornerstone of deep learning, provide valuable insights for point cloud data processing based on their success in 2D image processing. Despite the challenges in handling point cloud data, continuous research has led to the emergence of CNN variants and improved methods, driving advancements in the field of 3D vision.

2.2.2 Sparse Convolutional Networks

Sparse Convolution is a specialized convolutional technique designed for sparse data structures, particularly suited for processing sparse data. This type of data, typically generated by sensors like LiDAR, are characterized by uneven distribution and substantial empty regions in 3D space. Traditional convolutional neural networks are inefficient in processing such data, as they waste computational resources on numerous empty regions. The advent of sparse convolution offers an effective solution to this problem.

Submanifold Sparse Convolutional Networks are a significant framework for implementing sparse convolution, demonstrating powerful feature extraction capabilities in 3D data processing [2]. The core concept of sparse convolution is to perform convolutional operations only on non-zero elements of the input data, thereby significantly reducing computational overhead. Its mathematical definition can be expressed as:

$$S(i, j, k) = \sum_{(m,n,l)\in\mathcal{N}(i,j,k)} I(m, n, l)K(i - m, j - n, k - l), \tag{2.2}$$

where $\mathcal{N}(i, j, k)$ represents the neighborhood of the position (i, j, k) in the input data I, such that there is an overlap with the convolution kernel K and at least one non-zero element in K. I is the input sparse tensor, K is the sparse convolution kernel, and S is the output feature map. This method improves computational efficiency and memory utilization by representing input data as sparse matrices and computing only non-zero elements.

Sparse convolution has shown exceptional performance in 3D fields. Network architectures like SparseConvNet can achieve real-time object detection and semantic segmentation when processing large-scale sparse point cloud data. These applications not only showcase the robust capability of sparse convolution in handling sparse data but also demonstrate its broad potential in practical applications [3].

Despite its superior performance in computational efficiency and memory utilization, sparse convolution faces certain challenges. First of all, the representation and manipulation of sparse data often require specialized data structures and algorithmic support, potentially increasing implementation complexity. Additionally, sparse convolution may encounter issues with insufficient feature extraction when dealing with extremely sparse data. As deep learning applications in 3D data processing continue to expand, sparse convolution technology is evolving. Moreover, the application of sparse convolution in other fields, such as bioinformatics and network traffic analysis, shows promising prospects.

In conclusion, sparse convolution provides an efficient solution for processing sparse data. Its successful application in the field of 3D vision offers valuable insights for sparse data processing in other domains.

2.3 3D Point Cloud Data Organization

2.3.1 Point Representation

Point cloud data representation is a fundamental issue in 3D computer vision and computer graphics [4–16]. Direct point representation has its advantages and disadvantages. The advantages include simplicity and intuitiveness, preservation of original information, and applicability to objects of various shapes and topological structures. Points are the most basic geometric elements in 3D space, capable of representing complex 3D structures without additional conversion or interpolation. However, this representation method also has some drawbacks. First, there is a lack of explicit connection relationships between points, making certain geometric and topological analyses difficult. Second, point representation is relatively sensitive to noise, where errors in a single point can significantly affect the results. Lastly, the irregularity of point clouds increases processing difficulties.

2.3.2 Voxel Representation

In the field of 3D data representation, following point cloud representation, voxel representation has emerged as another widely applied method. Voxel refers to the smallest unit in a regular grid division of 3D space. The process of voxelization essentially involves discretizing continuous 3D space into a regular 3D grid, where each voxel represents a cubic region in space, typically containing occupancy status or other attribute information. The implementation of voxelization generally follows these steps, i.e., (1) determine the resolution and boundaries of the voxel grid; (2) for each input 3D point, calculate its corresponding voxel index; (3) aggregate the point information into the corresponding voxel.

Compared to point cloud representation, voxel representation offers significant advantages. First, voxel data present a regular 3D grid structure, facilitating data storage and access. Second, the regular structure of voxels naturally lends itself to 3D convolution operations, enabling direct application of deep learning models to voxel data, as demonstrated in the research by Maturana and Scherer [17]. Furthermore, voxel representation preserves spatial occupancy information of objects, including voids and internal structures, which is crucial for certain application scenarios. Lastly, by adjusting voxel size, representations at different resolutions can be achieved, facilitating multi-scale analysis.

However, voxel representation also faces a severe data explosion problem. For a voxel grid of $n \times n \times n$, even at medium resolution (e.g., 256^3), over 16 million voxels need to be stored, imposing enormous pressure on storage and computation. One approach is to use hash tables to store non-empty voxels, significantly reducing memory usage. The VoxelHashing method proposed by Niessner et al. is a typical example, using spatial hash functions to map voxels to a hash table, storing only voxels containing actual data [18]. Another approach leverages the sparsity of 3D data, storing and processing only non-empty voxels. For instance, the Octree structure is a commonly used sparse voxel representation method that recursively divides space, refining only in areas containing data, thus greatly reducing storage requirements [19].

Additionally, some studies attempt to use deep learning models to learn more compact voxel representations. Wang et al. [20] proposed the O-CNN method, combining Octree structure with convolutional neural networks to achieve efficient 3D shape analysis and generation. This method not only addresses the data explosion problem but also maintains the advantages of voxel representation, providing new insights for 3D data processing.

In conclusion, voxel representation offers a structured and regularized approach to 3D data processing, particularly suitable for deep learning applications. Although facing challenges of data explosion, these issues are being gradually resolved through various optimization techniques such as hash tables, sparse voxel grids, and deep learning–based methods. As research progresses, we anticipate seeing more efficient voxel representation methods, further advancing 3D vision and computer graphics. Voxel representation complements point cloud representation, providing rich tools and methods for 3D data processing, enabling us to better understand and utilize information from the 3D world.

2.3.3 Tree Representation

Tree structures play a crucial role in representing and processing 3D data, with KD-trees, binary trees, and octrees being the most commonly used tree structures.

Octrees are tree structures that recursively divide 3D space into eight sub-cubes [19]. Each node in an octree is either a leaf node or has eight child nodes. Octree construction begins with a cube encompassing point cloud. If the number of points in the current cube exceeds a threshold, it is divided into eight sub-cubes, and this process is recursively executed on each non-empty sub-cube. Octrees have important applications in point cloud data compression, enabling efficient lossy compression by organizing point cloud data into an octree structure [21].

Given a point cloud containing N points and an octree with a maximum depth of D, the space complexity of the octree is $O(N)$. In practical applications, the depth of the octree is usually limited to a small range, so the space complexity can be approximated as $O(N)$. The query complexity of an octree is related to the depth of the tree, averaging $O(\log N)$ in typical cases.

The precision of octree representation [21] is directly related to its maximum depth D. Assuming that the initial cube has an edge length of L, the edge length of the smallest voxel is:

$$L_{\min} = L/2^D. \tag{2.3}$$

The precision ϵ can be expressed as:

$$\epsilon = L_{\min}/\sqrt{3} = L/(2^D \cdot \sqrt{3}). \tag{2.4}$$

This formula shows that as depth D increases, precision improves exponentially. However, higher precision also means greater storage overhead and longer processing times. Therefore, in practical applications, a balance between precision and efficiency must be struck [22].

A typical application of octrees in point cloud coding is data reduction through voxelization [23]. The compression ratio can be expressed as:

$$\text{Compression Ratio} = \frac{\text{Original Point Count}}{\text{Leaf Node Count}}. \tag{2.5}$$

Experiments have shown that octrees can achieve compression rates of up to 33–50% while maintaining a certain level of precision [23]. In conclusion, tree structures provide powerful tools for efficiently processing large-scale 3D data. KD-trees excel in nearest neighbor searches, BSP trees have unique advantages in space partitioning and visibility determination, while octrees show great potential in point cloud coding and multi-resolution representation.

2.4 Typical Networks for 3D Point Cloud Processing

Point cloud data play an increasingly important role in fields such as robotics, unmanned aerial vehicles, and autonomous driving [24–32]. The importance of point cloud deep learning is primarily reflected in its ability to learn effective features directly from raw point cloud data, avoiding the limitations of manually designed features in traditional methods [33]. Through deep learning models, we can provide powerful tools for 3D scene understanding [34].

2.4.1 PointNet and PointNet++

To address the above challenges, researchers have proposed various innovative network structures. Among them, PointNet [35] and PointNet++ [36] are the most representative foundational networks. To extract features from point clouds, PointNet uses point-wise Multilayer Perceptrons (MLPs) and global max pooling operations.

PointNet contributions are: (1) It introduced spatial transformer networks through T-Net, enhancing robustness to point cloud rotations and other transformations; (2) it designed an effective global feature extraction method. However, PointNet also has limitations, mainly in its difficulty in capturing local structural information. To overcome this shortcoming, PointNet++ [36] introduced hierarchical sampling and grouping strategies, capturing multi-scale local features by recursively applying PointNet. Its core operation can be represented as:

$$F_l = \max_{i=1,\dots,N_l} \{h_l(F_{l-1}, x_i)\}, \tag{2.6}$$

where F_l represents the features of the l-th layer, h_l is an MLP, and x_i is the local neighborhood information of the sampled points.

2.4.2 Graph Convolutional Networks and Point Convolutional Networks

It is important to effectively capture local structural information in point clouds [37]. This leads to the emergence of two significant network types, including Graph Convolutional Networks (GCNs) and Point Convolutional Networks (PCNs). While these two categories of networks employ different approaches, they both aim to address the issues of unorderedness and irregularity in point cloud data, thereby achieving more effective feature extraction.

The core idea of GCNs is to view point clouds as graph structures and utilize relationships between points for feature learning. A typical representative of this approach is the Dynamic Graph CNN (DGCNN) [38]. DGCNN introduces the EdgeConv operation, which dynamically computes node adjacency relationships. The mathematical expression for EdgeConv is as follows:

$$\text{EdgeConv}(x_i) = \max_{j:(i,j)\in\mathcal{E}} h_\Theta(x_i, x_j - x_i), \tag{2.7}$$

where x_i represents the features of the center point, x_j represents the features of neighboring points, h_Θ is a learnable nonlinear function, and $\mathcal{E}$ denotes the edge set. This approach adapts to changes in geometric relationships between points, thus achieving more effective feature extraction.

On the other hand, PCNs attempt to apply traditional convolution operations directly to point cloud data. PointCNN [39] and KPConv [40] are representative works in this category. PointCNN introduces the X-transformation, which can be represented as:

$$\mathcal{X} = \text{MLP}(\text{Concat}(P - p, F)), \tag{2.8}$$

where P is the local point set, p is the center point, and F represents the corresponding features. This method enables the network to learn a canonical ordering of points, effectively handling the unorderedness of point clouds.

KPConv [40] proposes a kernel-based point cloud convolution operation, which can be expressed as:

$$(F * g)(x) = \sum_{x_i\in\mathcal{N}_x} g(x_i - x)F_i, \tag{2.9}$$

where g is the convolution kernel function, $\mathcal{N}_x$ is the neighborhood of point x, and F_i is the feature of point x_i. This allows KPConv to capture fine geometric details while maintaining computational efficiency. PointCNN attained an average IoU of 86.1% in the ShapeNet part segmentation task [39], while KPConv reached an average IoU of 67.1% in the S3DIS semantic segmentation task [40].

GCNs and PCNs each have their advantages. GCNs excel at capturing relationships between points and global structures, making them particularly suitable for processing point cloud data with evident topological structures. For example, in tasks such as human pose estimation or molecular structure analysis, GCNs may perform better. PCNs, on the other hand, focus more on extracting local geometric features, potentially offering advantages in tasks requiring fine local details, such as high-precision object segmentation.

In summary, GCNs and PCNs represent two important directions in point cloud feature extraction. Their emergence has significantly advanced point cloud processing technology, providing powerful tools for various practical applications.

2.4.3 Point Transformer

To handle large-scale point cloud data, Point Transformer [41] adopts a hierarchical structure. At each layer, the model first selects a set of key points using the FPS algorithm and then applies self-attention operations to these key points. Point Transformer has demonstrated excellent performance on multiple benchmark datasets. Point Transformer opens up new research directions for point cloud processing. Combining it with other advanced technologies, such as graph neural networks or sparse convolutions, may yield even more powerful point cloud processing models. Furthermore, applying Point Transformer to broader domains also presents promising research opportunities. Point Transformer not only provides a new paradigm for point cloud feature extraction but also offers fresh insights into addressing long-standing challenges in point cloud processing. As research progresses, we can anticipate Point Transformer and its derivative methods playing increasingly important roles in various practical applications.

2.5 General Deep Learning Frameworks for 3D Point Cloud Coding

Image and video coding methods have evolved from traditional hybrid structure-based methods [42–49] to deep learning-based methods [50–57], and the rate distortion performances have been significantly improved. Similarly, deep learning has significantly advanced the field of 3D point cloud coding by providing efficient and effective methods for compressing, reconstructing, and analyzing complex spatial data [11, 58–64]. These frameworks leverage neural networks' ability to learn hierarchical representations, enabling the extraction and preservation of intricate geometric and semantic features from point clouds. The primary approaches in this domain can be categorized into Point-based, Voxel-based, and Octree-based coding frameworks, each employing distinct strategies. Enhancement algorithms can further improve the compressed quality [64–71], which are also indispensable for the whole visual media processing system. Furthermore, AI-based point cloud coding methods can be much more easily optimized with the machine perception purpose [6, 24, 29, 31, 72–75].

2.5.1 Point-Based Framework

Point-based coding frameworks operate directly on raw point cloud data, treating each point as an independent entity characterized by its spatial coordinates and potentially additional attributes like color or intensity. Yan et al. [76] utilize an autoencoder architecture for lossy geometry compression. The encoder network compresses the point cloud into a compact latent representation. The decoder network reconstructs the point cloud from the compressed latent, aiming to preserve the essential geometric structures while reducing the data size. This approach effectively captures both local and global geometric features, achieving a balance between compression efficiency and reconstruction fidelity.

2.5.2 Voxel-Based Framework

Voxel-based frameworks convert point clouds into a regular voxel grid, facilitating CNNs for feature extraction and compression [77–80]. Wang et al. [81] leverage sparse tensors, the framework efficiently handles the sparsity inherent in point cloud data, reducing computational and memory overheads. The multi-scale representation allows the model to capture geometric details at various resolutions, enhancing both compression ratios and reconstruction quality [82–86]. These approaches [10, 81] enable scalable processing of large-scale point clouds, making it suitable for applications requiring high-resolution 3D data representations.

2.5.3 Octree-Based Framework

Octree-based frameworks utilize hierarchical tree structures to represent 3D point clouds, recursively subdividing space into octants to capture varying levels of detail [87–94]. Fu et al. [63] introduced *OctAttention*, an octree-based model that incorporates attention mechanisms for large-scale context modeling in point cloud coding. This framework enhances traditional octree representations by enabling the network to focus on relevant spatial regions, thereby improving compression performance without compromising reconstruction accuracy. The hierarchical nature of octrees allows for the adaptive allocation of computational resources, efficiently encoding regions with higher complexity or density.

2.6 Entropy Model in 3D Point Cloud Coding Networks

Similar to the hand-crafted entropy model, the learned entropy model also estimates distributions based on contextual information [87, 95–100]. An informative context is critical to improving the accuracy. According to the adopted data structure, the context can be roughly divided into voxel-based contexts and octree-based contexts. Different deep network structures are designed to model the dependency between points in the neighborhood and estimate distributions based on corresponding context structures.

2.6.1 Voxel-Based Context

In the voxel-based context, the point cloud is voxelized and multi-scale voxel occupancies are coded by an entropy encoder. In [101], the voxels are ordered with:

$$v_i = \begin{cases} 1, & \text{if } i\text{th voxel is occupied,} \\ 0, & \text{otherwise.} \end{cases} \tag{2.10}$$

The voxel-based context estimates distributions for each voxel v_i. This context is composed of various adjacent coded voxels centered on the currently coded voxel v_i. The reference voxel is characterized by its occupancy status, where 1 denotes occupied and 0 denotes empty, as represented in Eq. (2.10). The voxel-based context typically includes auto-regression, i.e., previously decoded voxels are introduced as contexts to predict the following voxels. Since voxels are coded in a strict 3D scan order, only the decoded voxels can be included in the context to keep the causality. Therefore, a mask is required to exclude undecoded contexts from the cubic voxelized context. This causes severe efficiency penalties since the voxels are limited to be coded in serial. For example, it takes thousands of seconds to decode a single point cloud, which is unbearable to practical applications. One of the solutions is to perform auto-regression at the level of groups. In other words, voxels are organized as groups, and the available contexts are only coded groups instead of all coded voxels, and the coding process is speeded up. Introducing multi-scale references from coarse voxel representations is also an effective strategy since these references have been coded.

Since the point cloud is generally sparse and hence most voxels are non-occupied, the efficiency of the 3D convolution can be improved by sparse convolution backbones such as the Minkowski Engine. The overall architecture of these voxel-based networks generally follows a ResNet structure, which is a stack of residual blocks with 3D convolution layers.

2.6.2 Octree-Based Context

Octree-based methods estimate the probability of the occupancy of octree nodes and then use the arithmetic encoder to code occupancy symbols losslessly. For ancestor-dependent context, each octree node is predicted according to low-resolution octree representations, which is like an upsampling prediction. This context structure is effective for sparse point clouds, because most voxels in the voxelized context are unoccupied in sparse scenarios, which provides little meaningful information. However, geometric structures of the original point cloud are implicit in the tree structure. Therefore, explicit localized geometric features expressed in voxel structure can be complemented to further enhance the compression performance. For example, voxelized context centered on the parent node is a reasonable context structure to achieve this. Furthermore, features from previously decoded sibling nodes can also be introduced in an auto-regressive way.

Features of nodes in the context include their bounding box coordinates, octant index, level index, and occupancy symbol. The tree-based entropy model generally adopts an MLP to predict distributions based on its ancestors. Meanwhile, 3D convolution is introduced to extract features from the fine-grained voxelized context, if available. Learned tree-structured entropy model is generally computationally efficient. Since ancestor nodes are completely known while coding the current level, all nodes within the current level can be coded in parallel. The inference of a typical learned tree-structured entropy model only takes tens of milliseconds on an octree with 16 levels. The overall coding latency is comparable to the hand-crafted methods such as G-PCC, i.e., around a few seconds.

2.7 Summary

This chapter explores foundational elements of deep learning relevant to point cloud processing, including CNNs, sparse convolutions, and Transformers. Various point cloud data representations are discussed, including raw points, voxels, and trees. Afterward, this chapter explores basic neural network architectures. Lastly, it discusses key concepts in point cloud coding, focusing on general framework and entropy coding techniques. In conclusion, this chapter provides a thorough examination of the intersection between deep learning and point cloud coding. For readers who are interested in the related technologies of AI-based image and video coding, please refer to [102].

Exercises

1. What is 2D convolution operation?
2. What is Rectified Linear Unit (ReLU) operation?
3. What is self-attention?
4. What is multihead self-attention?
5. What are representations for point cloud?
6. What a point can be represented?
7. Why can a voxel be used to represent a point cloud?
8. What kinds of trees can be used to represent point clouds?
9. What is the compression ratio?
10. Which networks are designed for point cloud deep learning?

References

1. A. Krizhevsky, I. Sutskever, G.E. Hinton, Imagenet classification with deep convolutional neural networks. Adv. Neural Inf. Proces. Syst. **25**, 1–9 (2012)
2. B. Graham, M. Engelcke, L. Van Der Maaten, 3d semantic segmentation with submanifold sparse convolutional networks, in *Proceedings of the IEEE Conference on Computer Vision and Pattern Recognition* (2018), pp. 9224–9232
3. C. Choy, J. Gwak, S. Savarese, 4d spatio-temporal convnets: Minkowski convolutional neural networks, in *Proceedings of the IEEE/CVF Conference on Computer Vision and Pattern Recognition* (2019), pp. 3075–3084
4. G. Li, G. Wei, W. Gao, *Point Cloud Compression: Technologies and Standardization* (Springer, Berlin, 2024)
5. Y. Ye, W. Gao, LLM-PCGC: large language model-based point cloud geometry compression. arXiv preprint arXiv:2408.08682 (2024)
6. S. Fan, W. Gao, Z. Chen, G. Li, G. Liu, Q. Wang, Stochasticity-aware no-reference point cloud quality assessment, in *International Joint Conference on Artificial Intelligence (IJCAI)* (2025)
7. Z. Yao, W. Gao, G. Li, T. Zhao, Collaborating constrained and unconstrained encodings for cross-modal salient object detection. IEEE Trans. Emerging Top. Comput. Intell. **9**(6), 3895–3909 (2025)
8. L. Xin, Z. Zhang, Z. Pan, J. Wei, D. Gao, W. Gao, Dreampbr: text-driven high-resolution SVBRDF generation with multimodal guidance, in *2025 IEEE International Conference on Multimedia and Expo (ICME)* (2025)
9. K. Wang, S. Li, Q. Yi, W. Gao, A novel benchmark and dataset for efficient 3d gaussian splatting with gaussian point cloud compression. arXiv preprint arXiv:2505.18197 (2025)
10. K. Wang, W. Gao, Unipcgc: towards practical point cloud geometry compression via an efficient unified approach, in *Proceedings of the AAAI Conference on Artificial Intelligence* (2025)
11. Z. Yu, W. Gao, When dynamic neural network meets point cloud compression: computation-aware variable rate and checkerboard context, in *2024 Data Compression Conference (DCC)* (IEEE, New York, 2024), pp. 600–600
12. S. Fan, W. Gao, Screen-based 3d subjective experiment software, in *Proceedings of the 31st ACM International Conference on Multimedia* (2023), pp. 9672–9675
13. J. Wang, W. Gao, G. Li, Zoom to perceive better: no-reference point cloud quality assessment via exploring effective multiscale feature. IEEE Trans. Circuits Syst. Video Technol. **34**(7), 6334–6346 (2024)

14. J. Wang, W. Gao, G. Li, Applying collaborative adversarial learning to blind point cloud quality measurement. IEEE Trans. Instrum. Meas. **72**, 1–15 (2023).
15. H. Li, W. Gao, Information exploration of projected views for point cloud quality measurement. IEEE Trans. Instrum. Meas. **74**, 1–14 (2025)
16. S. Fan, W. Gao, Z. Chen, G. Li, G. Liu, Q. Wang, Stochasticity-aware no-reference point cloud quality assessment, in *International Joint Conference on Artificial Intelligence* (2025)
17. D. Maturana, S. Scherer, Voxnet: A 3d convolutional neural network for real-time object recognition, in *Proceedings of theIEEE/RSJ International Conference on Intelligent Robots and Systems (IROS)* (IEEE, New York, 2015), pp. 922–928
18. M. Nießner, M. Zollhöfer, S. Izadi, M. Stamminger, Real-time 3d reconstruction at scale using voxel hashing. ACM Trans. Graph. (ToG) **32**(6), 1–11 (2013)
19. D. Meagher, Geometric modeling using octree encoding. Comput. Graphics Image Process. **19**(2), 129–147 (1982)
20. P.-S. Wang, Y. Liu, Y.-X. Guo, C.-Y. Sun, X. Tong, O-CNN: Octree-based convolutional neural networks for 3d shape analysis. ACM Trans. Graph. (TOG) **36**(4), 1–11 (2017)
21. R. Schnabel, R. Klein, Octree-based point-cloud compression. PBG@ SIGGRAPH **3**, 111–121 (2006)
22. A. Hornung, K.M. Wurm, M. Bennewitz, C. Stachniss, W. Burgard, Octomap: an efficient probabilistic 3d mapping framework based on octrees. Auton. Robot. **34**, 189–206 (2013)
23. Y. Huang, J. Peng, C.-C.J. Kuo, M. Gopi, A generic scheme for progressive point cloud coding. IEEE Trans. Vis. Comput. Graph. **14**(2), 440–453 (2008)
24. S. Fan, W. Gao, G. Li, Salient object detection for point clouds, in *European Conference on Computer Vision* (Springer, Berlin, 2022), pp. 1–19
25. S. Luo, W. Gao, A general framework for rotation invariant point cloud analysis, in *ICASSP 2024-2024 IEEE International Conference on Acoustics, Speech and Signal Processing (ICASSP)* (IEEE, New York, 2024), pp. 3665–3669
26. W. Gao, S. Kwong, Y. Zhou, Y. Jia, J. Zhang, W. Wu, Multiscale phase congruency analysis for image edge visual saliency detection, in *2016 International Conference on Machine Learning and Cybernetics (ICMLC)*, vol. 1 (IEEE, New York, 2016), pp. 75–80
27. W. Gao, S. Kwong, Y. Zhou, X. Wang, Phase congruency analysis of down-sampled and blurring images for foreground extraction, in *2015 International Conference on Wavelet Analysis and Pattern Recognition (ICWAPR)* (IEEE, New York, 2015), pp. 152–157
28. X. Lu, W. Gao, Attentivenet: detecting small objects for lidar point clouds by attending to important points, in *2023 IEEE International Conference on Visual Communications and Image Processing (VCIP)* (IEEE, New York, 2023), pp. 1–5
29. Z. Pan, N. Zhang, W. Gao, S. Liu, G. Li, Less is more: label recommendation for weakly supervised point cloud semantic segmentation, in *Proceedings of the AAAI Conference on Artificial Intelligence*, vol. 38(5) (2024), pp. 4397–4405
30. Z. Pan, G. Liu, W. Gao, T.H. Li, Epcontrast: effective point-level contrastive learning for large-scale point cloud understanding, in *2024 IEEE International Conference on Multimedia and Expo (ICME)* (IEEE, New York, 2024), pp. 1–6
31. N. Zhang, Z. Pan, T.H. Li, W. Gao, G. Li, Improving graph representation for point cloud segmentation via attentive filtering, in *Proceedings of the IEEE/CVF Conference on Computer Vision and Pattern Recognition* (2023), pp. 1244–1254
32. Z. Pan, W. Gao, G. Li, Distribution guidance network for weakly supervised point cloud semantic segmentation, in *Advances in Neural Information Processing Systems* (2024)
33. W. Gao, G. Li, *Deep Learning for 3D Point Clouds* (Springer, New York, 2024)
34. L. Liu, W. Ouyang, X. Wang, P. Fieguth, J. Chen, X. Liu, M. Pietikäinen, Deep learning for generic object detection: a survey. Proc. Int. J. Comput. Vision **128**, 261–318 (2020)
35. C.R. Qi, H. Su, K. Mo, L.J. Guibas, Pointnet: deep learning on point sets for 3d classification and segmentation, in *Proceedings of the IEEE Conference on Computer Vision and Pattern Recognition* (2017), pp. 652–660

36. C.R. Qi, L. Yi, H. Su, L.J. Guibas, Pointnet++: deep hierarchical feature learning on point sets in a metric space, in *Advances in Neural Information Processing Systems* (2017), pp. 5099–5108
37. L. Xie, W. Gao, H. Zheng, G. Li, Roi-guided point cloud geometry compression towards human and machine vision. arXiv preprint arXiv:2504.14240 (2025)
38. Y. Wang, Y. Sun, Z. Liu, S.E. Sarma, M.M. Bronstein, J.M. Solomon, Dynamic graph CNN for learning on point clouds. ACM Trans. Graph. (TOG) **38**(5), 1–12 (2019)
39. Y. Li, R. Bu, M. Sun, W. Wu, X. Di, B. Chen, Pointcnn: convolution on x-transformed points, in *Advances in Neural Information Processing Systems* (2018), pp. 820–830
40. H. Thomas, C.R. Qi, J.-E. Deschaud, B. Marcotegui, F. Goulette, L.J. Guibas, Kpconv: flexible and deformable convolution for point clouds, in *Proceedings of the IEEE/CVF International Conference on Computer Vision* (2019), pp. 6411–6420
41. H. Zhao, L. Jiang, J. Jia, P.H. Torr, V. Koltun, Point transformer, in *Proceedings of the IEEE/CVF International Conference on Computer Vision* (2021), pp. 16259–16268
42. Z. Yang, W. Gao, G. Li, Y. Yan, Sur-driven video coding rate control for jointly optimizing perceptual quality and buffer control. IEEE Trans. Image Process. **32**, 5451–5464 (2023)
43. F. Shen, Z. Cai, W. Gao, An efficient rate control algorithm for intra frame coding in avs3, in *2021 IEEE International Conference on Systems, Man, and Cybernetics (SMC)* (IEEE, New York, 2021), pp. 3164–3169
44. H. Yuan, W. Gao, J. Wang, Dynamic computational resource allocation for fast inter frame coding in video conferencing applications, in *2021 IEEE International Conference on Multimedia and Expo (ICME)* (IEEE, New York, 2021), pp. 1–6
45. W. Gao, Q. Jiang, R. Wang, S. Ma, G. Li, S. Kwong, Consistent quality oriented rate control in HEVC via balancing intra and inter frame coding. IEEE Trans. Industr. Inform. **18**(3), 1594–1604 (2021)
46. H. Yuan, W. Gao, A new coding unit partitioning mode for screen content video coding, in *Proceedings of the 2021 5th International Conference on Digital Signal Processing* (2021), pp. 66–72
47. W. Gao, On the performance evaluation of state-of-the-art rate control algorithms for practical video coding and transmission systems, in *Proceedings of the 2020 4th International Conference on Video and Image Processing* (2020), pp. 179–185
48. W. Gao, H. Yuan, G. Liao, Z. Guo, J. Chen, Pp8k: a new dataset for 8k UHD video compression and processing. IEEE MultiMedia **30**(3), 100–109 (2023)
49. W. Liu, W. Gao, G. Li, S. Ma, T. Zhao, H. Yuan, Enlarged motion-aware and frequency-aware network for compressed video artifact reduction. IEEE Trans. Circuits Syst. Video Technol. **34**(10), 10339–10352 (2024)
50. W. Gao, L. Tao, L. Zhou, D. Yang, X. Zhang, Z. Guo, Low-rate image compression with super-resolution learning, in *Proceedings of the IEEE/CVF Conference on Computer Vision and Pattern Recognition Workshops* (2020), pp. 154–155
51. W. Gao, S. Sun, H. Zheng, Y. Wu, H. Ye, Y. Zhang, Opendmc: an open-source library and performance evaluation for deep-learning-based multi-frame compression, in *Proceedings of the 31st ACM International Conference on Multimedia* (2023), pp. 9685–9688
52. W. Gao, H. Zheng, C. Zhang, K. Zheng, Z. Yu, Y. Li, H. Ye, Y. Zhang, Opendic: an open-source library and performance evaluation for deep-learning-based image compression, in *Proceedings of the 32nd ACM International Conference on Multimedia* (2024), pp. 11202–11205
53. Y. Wu, L. Xie, S. Sun, W. Gao, Y. Yan, Adaptive intra period size for deep learning-based screen content video coding, in *2024 IEEE International Conference on Multimedia and Expo Workshops (ICMEW)* (IEEE, New York, 2024), pp. 1–6
54. H. Zheng, W. Gao, End-to-end RGB-d image compression via exploiting channel-modality redundancy, in *Proceedings of the AAAI Conference on Artificial Intelligence*, vol. 38(7) (2024), pp. 7562–7570

55. L. Tao, W. Gao, G. Li, C. Zhang, Adanic: towards practical neural image compression via dynamic transform routing, in *Proceedings of the IEEE/CVF International Conference on Computer Vision* (2023), pp. 16879–16888
56. Y. Wu, W. Gao, End-to-end lossless compression of high precision depth maps guided by pseudo-residual, in *2022 Data Compression Conference (DCC)* (IEEE, New York, 2022), pp. 489–489
57. Y. Wu, Z. Qi, H. Zheng, L. Tao, W. Gao, Deep image compression with latent optimization and piece-wise quantization approximation, in *Proceedings of the IEEE/CVF Conference on Computer Vision and Pattern Recognition* (2021), pp. 1926–1930
58. L. Xie, W. Gao, H. Zheng, G. Li, SPCGC: scalable point cloud geometry compression for machine vision, in *2024 IEEE International Conference on Robotics and Automation (ICRA)* (IEEE, New York, 2024), pp. 17272–17278
59. L. Xie, W. Gao, H. Zheng, H. Ye, Semantic-aware visual decomposition for point cloud geometry compression, in *2024 Data Compression Conference (DCC)* (IEEE, New York, 2024), pp. 595–595
60. Z. Qi, W. Gao, Variable-rate point cloud geometry compression based on feature adjustment and interpolation, in *2024 Data Compression Conference (DCC)* (IEEE, New York, 2024), pp. 63–72
61. L. Xie, W. Gao, H. Zheng, End-to-end point cloud geometry compression and analysis with sparse tensor, in *Proceedings of the 1st International Workshop on Advances in Point Cloud Compression, Processing and Analysis* (2022), pp. 27–32
62. L. Xie, W. Gao, S. Fan, Z. Yao, PDNET: parallel dual-branch network for point cloud geometry compression and analysis, in *2024 Data Compression Conference (DCC)* (IEEE, New York, 2024), pp. 596–596
63. C. Fu, G. Li, R. Song, W. Gao, S. Liu, Octattention: Octree-based large-scale contexts model for point cloud compression, in *Proceedings of the AAAI Conference on Artificial Intelligence*, vol. 36(1) (2022), pp. 625–633
64. X. Zhang, G. Liao, W. Gao, G. Li, Tdrnet: transformer-based dual-branch restoration network for geometry based point cloud compression artifacts, in *2022 IEEE International Conference on Multimedia and Expo (ICME)* (IEEE, New York, 2022), pp. 1–6
65. W. Liu, W. Gao, X. Mu, Fast inter-frame motion prediction for compressed dynamic point cloud attribute enhancement, in *Proceedings of the AAAI Conference on Artificial Intelligence*, vol. 38(4) (2024), pp. 3720–3728
66. Z. Yang, W. Gao, X. Lu, Danet: density-adaptive network for geometry-based point cloud compression artifacts removal, in *2023 IEEE International Conference on Visual Communications and Image Processing (VCIP)* (IEEE, New York, 2023), pp. 1–5
67. X. Fan, G. Li, D. Li, Y. Ren, W. Gao, T.H. Li, Deep geometry post-processing for decompressed point clouds, in *2022 IEEE International Conference on Multimedia and Expo (ICME)* (IEEE, New York, 2022), pp. 1–6
68. W. Liu, W. Gao, Omni-scene perception-oriented point cloud geometry enhancement for coordinate quantization, in *Proceedings of the IEEE/CVF International Conference on Computer Vision* (2025)
69. R. Zhang, J. Chen, W. Gao, G. Li, T.H. Li, Pointot: interpretable geometry-inspired point cloud generative model via optimal transport. IEEE Trans. Circuits Syst. Video Technol. **32**(10), 6792–6806 (2022)
70. Z. Li, G. Li, T. Li, S. Liu, W. Gao, Information-growth attention network for image super-resolution, in *Proceedings of the 29th ACM International Conference on Multimedia* (2021), pp. 544–552
71. L. Zhou, W. Gao, G. Li, H. Yuan, T. Zhao, G. Yue, Disentangled feature distillation for light field super-resolution with degradations, in *2023 IEEE International Conference on Multimedia and Expo Workshops (ICMEW)* (IEEE, New York, 2023), pp. 116–121
72. Y. Guo, W. Gao, G. Li, Interpretable task-inspired adaptive filter pruning for neural networks under multiple constraints. Int. J. Comput. Vis., **132**, 2060–2076 (2024)

73. W. Gao, Y. Guo, S. Ma, G. Li, S. Kwong, Efficient neural network compression inspired by compressive sensing. IEEE Trans. Neural Networks Learn. Syst. **35**(2), 1965–1979 (2022)
74. Y. Guo, W. Gao, Semantic-driven automatic filter pruning for neural networks, in *2022 IEEE International Conference on Multimedia and Expo (ICME)* (IEEE, New York, 2022), pp. 1–6
75. L. Tao, W. Gao, Efficient channel pruning based on architecture alignment and probability model bypassing, in *2021 IEEE International Conference on Systems, Man, and Cybernetics (SMC)* (IEEE, New York, 2021), pp. 3232–3237
76. W. Yan, Y. Shao, S. Liu, T.H. Li, Z. Li, G. Li, Deep autoencoder-based lossy geometry compression for point clouds. arXiv preprint arXiv:1905.03691 (2019)
77. W. Gao, G. Li, H. Yuan, R. Hamzaoui, Z. Li, S. Liu, Apccpa'22: 1st international workshop on advances in point cloud compression, processing and analysis, in *Proceedings of the 30th ACM International Conference on Multimedia* (2022), pp. 7392–7393
78. W. Gao, G. Li, Point cloud compression, enhancement and applications: from 3d perception to large models, in *Proceedings of the 32nd ACM International Conference on Multimedia* (2024), pp. 11292–11293
79. L. Xie, W. Gao, Learningpcc: a pytorch library for learning-based point cloud compression, in *Proceedings of the 32nd ACM International Conference on Multimedia* (2024), pp. 11234–11238
80. L. Xie, W. Gao, Pchmvision: an open-source library of point cloud compression for human and machine vision, in *Proceedings of the 32nd ACM International Conference on Multimedia* (2024), pp. 11239–11243
81. J. Wang, D. Ding, Z. Li, X. Feng, C. Cao, Z. Ma, Sparse tensor-based multiscale representation for point cloud geometry compression. IEEE Trans. Pattern Anal. Mach. Intell. **45**(7), 9055–9071 (2022)
82. L. Xie, X. Mu, G. Li, W. Gao, et al., PKU-DPCC: a new dataset for dynamic point cloud compression. APSIPA Trans. Signal Inf. Process. **13**(6), 1–23 (2024)
83. S. Sun, X. Liang, S. Fan, W. Gao, W. Gao, Ve-bench: subjective-aligned benchmark suite for text-driven video editing quality assessment, in *Proceedings of the AAAI Conference on Artificial Intelligence* (2025)
84. B. Qu, X. Liang, S. Sun, W. Gao, Exploring AIGC video quality: a focus on visual harmony, video-text consistency and domain distribution gap, in *Proceedings of the IEEE/CVF Conference on Computer Vision and Pattern Recognition Workshops* (2024)
85. B. Qu, H. Li, W. Gao, Bringing textual prompt to AI-generated image quality assessment, in *2024 IEEE International Conference on Multimedia and Expo (ICME)* (IEEE, New York, 2024)
86. Z. Guo, W. Gao, H. Wang, J. Wang, S. Fan, No-reference deep quality assessment of compressed light field images, in *2021 IEEE International Conference on Multimedia and Expo (ICME)* (IEEE, New York, 2021), pp. 1–6
87. Y. Shao, X. Yang, W. Gao, S. Liu, G. Li, 3d point cloud attribute compression using diffusion-based texture-aware intra prediction. IEEE Trans. Circuits Syst. Video Technol. **34**(10), 9633–9646 (2024)
88. J. Zhang, Y. Chen, G. Liu, W. Gao, G. Li, Efficient point cloud attribute compression framework using attribute-guided graph fourier transform, in *ICASSP 2024-2024 IEEE International Conference on Acoustics, Speech and Signal Processing (ICASSP)* (IEEE, New York, 2024), pp. 8426–8430
89. W. Gao, H. Yuan, G. Li, Z. Li, H. Yuan, Low complexity coding unit decision for video-based point cloud compression. IEEE Trans. Image Process. **33**, 149–162 (2023)
90. Y. Shao, G. Li, Q. Zhang, W. Gao, S. Liu, Nonrigid registration-based progressive motion compensation for point cloud geometry compression. IEEE Trans. Geosci. Remote Sens. **61**, 1–14 (2023)
91. F. Song, G. Li, X. Yang, W. Gao, S. Liu, Block-adaptive point cloud attribute coding with region-aware optimized transform. IEEE Trans. Circuits Syst. Video Technol. **33**(8), 4294–4308 (2023)

92. Y. An, Y. Shao, G. Li, W. Gao, S. Liu, A fast motion estimation method with hamming distance for lidar point cloud compression, in *2022 IEEE International Conference on Visual Communications and Image Processing (VCIP)* (IEEE, New York, 2022), pp. 1–5
93. H. Yuan, W. Gao, G. Li, Z. Li, Rate-distortion-guided learning approach with cross-projection information for V-PCC fast CU decision, in *Proceedings of the 30th ACM International Conference on Multimedia* (2022), pp. 3085–3093
94. F. Song, G. Li, W. Gao, T.H. Li, Rate-distortion optimized graph for point cloud attribute coding. IEEE Signal Process Lett. **29**, 922–926 (2022)
95. T. Qin, G. Li, W. Gao, S. Liu, Multi-grained point cloud geometry compression via dual-model prediction with extended octree. ACM Trans. Multimed. Comput. Commun. Appl. **20**(9), 1–30 (2024)
96. Y. Shao, W. Gao, S. Liu, G. Li, Advanced patch-based affine motion estimation for dynamic point cloud geometry compression. Sensors **24**(10), 3142 (2024)
97. Y. Shao, F. Song, W. Gao, S. Liu, G. Li, Texture-guided graph transform optimization for point cloud attribute compression. Appl. Sci. **14**(10), 4094 (2024)
98. X. Mu, W. Gao, H. Yuan, S. Wang, G. Li, Adaptive LPU decision for dynamic point cloud compression. IEEE Signal Process Lett. **31**, 2370–2374 (2024)
99. C. Peng, W. Gao, Laplacian matrix learning for point cloud attribute compression with ternary search-based adaptive block partition, in *Proceedings of the 32nd ACM International Conference on Multimedia* (2024), pp. 10412–10420
100. T. Guo, H. Yuan, T. Wang, W. Gao, Graph filter-based fast motion matching for inter frame coding of MPEG G-PCC, in *2022 IEEE International Conference on Image Processing (ICIP)* (IEEE, New York, 2022), pp. 1151–1155
101. J. Wang, D. Ding, Z. Li, Z. Ma, Multiscale point cloud geometry compression, in *Proceedings of the Data Compression Conference (DCC)* (IEEE, New York, 2021), pp. 73–82
102. W. Gao, *AI-based Image and Video Coding: Methods, Standards, and Applications* (Springer, Berlin, 2025)

Chapter 3
3D Point Cloud Quality Assessment and Perception Models

Abstract This chapter focuses on quality assessment and perception models for point clouds. It begins with subjective quality assessment, addressing the selection of point cloud content, the introduction of distortion, rendering schemes, and viewing protocols, along with methods for displaying and scoring point clouds. This foundational discussion paves the way for understanding visual attention mechanisms and attention modeling. Subsequently, this chapter examines Just-Noticeable-Distortion (JND) specific to point clouds and relevant datasets, highlighting practical applications in point cloud processing and quality assessment. Finally, it introduces the concept of visual attention modeling, encompassing saliency detection and salient object detection, to elucidate how the human visual system extracts critical information from complex scenes. Overall, this chapter provides significant insights into the research and development of quality assessment and perception models for point cloud technologies.

Keywords Quality assessment · Point clouds · Perception models · Point could distortions · Point cloud rendering · Viewing protocol · Opinion score · Visual attention · Saliency detection · Salient object detection · Just-Noticeable-Distortion (JND)

3.1 Introduction

In recent years, the increasing use of 3D point clouds has revolutionized fields such as autonomous driving, augmented reality, and robotics [1–11], by enabling the accurate representation of complex 3D environments. Despite their advantages, ensuring the perceptual quality of point clouds remains a significant challenge [12–20]. Given the nonuniform and unstructured nature of point cloud data, assessing their quality is more intricate than traditional 2D media like images and videos. The human visual system (HVS) plays a crucial role in evaluating the perceived quality of these data, making both subjective and objective quality assessments essential in understanding how distortions affect user experience.

W. Gao, *AI-based 3D Point Cloud Coding*,
https://doi.org/10.1007/978-981-95-0660-6_3

The concept of Just-Noticeable-Distortion (JND) is also explored, which provides insights into the threshold at which degradations in point cloud data become perceptible to the human observer. Identifying these thresholds is pivotal for balancing compression efficiency and quality maintenance. Furthermore, the availability of appropriate JND datasets is essential for benchmark algorithms aimed at distortion detection.

In addition, visual attention models inspired by saliency detection mechanisms have emerged as a valuable tool in point cloud processing [21–33]. Such models aim to predict the most visually significant regions, which allows the prioritization of these areas during encoding and processing. This report examines the concepts of visual attention, saliency detection, and salient object detection in the context of 3D point clouds to provide a comprehensive understanding of how human-like perception models can enhance quality assessment techniques.

This chapter offers a detailed overview of both theoretical and practical approaches to the perceptual quality evaluation of 3D point clouds. It concludes with potential directions for future research and practical exercises to encourage deeper exploration of the discussed topics.

3.2 Quality Assessment of 3D Point Clouds

3.2.1 Subjective Quality Assessment

Compared with objective quality assessment, more accurate point cloud quality scores can be obtained by subjective quality, which can be used to design and evaluate the objective models [34–36]. This subsection primarily describes the main process and methods of existing subjective experimental research.

Subjective quality assessment is based on practical experiments. It can be separated into five steps: selecting point cloud content, introducing distortion, designing the rendering scheme and viewing protocol, displaying and scoring the point clouds, and processing the opinion scores. The selection of point cloud data for the experiment needs to be carried out in accordance with the experimental requirements, considering the geometry and attribute information, especially the latter, which includes colors, normal vectors, transparency, and other relevant attributes.

In terms of point cloud distortion, the distortion types commonly introduced are Gaussian noise, down-sampling, compression, and octree-pruning. By adjusting the parameters, the distortion of the point cloud could be controlled, thereby constraining the point cloud quality at various levels. Analyzing the relationship between the parameters and quality scores enables the examination of how different distortions impact quality. When rendering and visualizing the point cloud, the experimenter should consider the way of displacing points and the level of interactivity. Specifically, tester can independently choose how to observe the content.

In the displaying and scoring step, the experimenters should think about the type of visualization devices and the subjective scoring methods. Lastly, the mean opinion score is generated after being preprocessed to guarantee its validity. In the following subsections, we will illustrate related approaches corresponding to the five steps.

Selection of Point Cloud Content There are some factors that need to be considered when selecting original point clouds, including the density of point clouds, the normal vectors, the geometry structure of point clouds, and color features, among others. Besides, the type of content presented, such as human and inanimate point clouds, is another factor that should be taken into account.

Introducing Distortion The impact of distortions on the quality of point clouds is a primary focus of subjective experimental research. Intuitively, different kinds of distortion influence the point cloud quality in different fashions, and varying levels of distortion lead to different visual perceptions of the point clouds. Therefore, it is necessary to understand the types of distortion commonly used and how to adjust the level of distortion. Several distortion types and ways to adjust are described below.

Noise is one of the basic distortions usually introduced in order to simulate the real damage. A deviation arises between the attribute value of the distorted point and that of the original point after adding noise to one attribute of points. One of the most commonly used types is Gaussian noise, which refers to a type of noise that follows a Gaussian distribution. The probability distribution of all the deviation values should follow Gaussian distribution $\mathcal{N}(\mu, \sigma^2)$. The level of noise and the bias introduced into the point cloud attribute can be adjusted by modifying the mean μ and the variance σ^2.

The octree is a tree data structure [37]. Each internal node has eight children, corresponding to the octet partition structure of the 3D space. Thus, octree is mostly used to describe 3D data. By adjusting the depth of the octree, the number of points contained in each leaf node can be controlled. A deeper octree results in fewer points per leaf node and higher quality in the processed point cloud. Therefore, modifying the depth of the octree allows for the adjustment of the perceptual quality of point clouds.

Point cloud compression is often used to reduce the cost of storage and transmission [38, 39]. The commonly adopted compression methods are two point cloud compression standards defined by the Moving Picture Experts Group (MPEG): Video-based Point Cloud Compression (V-PCC) [40] and Geometry-based Point Cloud Compression (G-PCC) [41]. The distortion level of V-PCC can be controlled by quantization parameters, while the distortion level of G-PCC can be controlled by voxel size and block size. The detailed way to modify the performance of these compression tools will not be introduced here [42–49].

Down-sampling is an operation that reduces the number of points in a point cloud while preserving the 3D structure information of the point cloud. The different down-sampling methods sample the points in different ways, which leads to diverse visual feelings. Commonly used down-sampling methods are voxel down-sampling, uniform down-sampling, geometry down-sampling, and random down-sampling.

Adopting different down-sampling methods and adjusting the sampling ratio can modify the visual effect of distorted point clouds.

Rendering Scheme and Viewing Protocol Exploring the visual effects of different rendering schemes and visualization protocols is also one task of subjective assessment, which determines how point clouds are displayed to the tester.

Point cloud rendering approaches can be divided into two main categories, i.e., 3D-based approaches and projection-based approaches. The 3D-based approach can be further divided into the point-based approach, cube-based approach, and mesh reconstruction-based approach. Point-based and cube-based approaches mostly render point clouds by modifying the size and shape of the point and cube, while the mesh reconstruction-based approach adopts a point cloud surface reconstruction algorithm to render the point cloud as mesh [50]. The most regularly used surface reconstruction algorithm is Poisson reconstruction [51]. The projection-based approach projects the point cloud into images from different viewpoints. Vertical projection is the most commonly used projection method, which projects the points or voxels vertically to coordinate axis planes.

The viewing protocol involves the way that the assessor observes the content of the point cloud, which is mainly divided into passive approaches and interactive approaches. In the passive approach, the tester cannot control the point cloud but just watches the content designed by the experimenter, which is usually videos surrounding point clouds or projected images of point clouds. However, in the interactive approach, the assessor can adjust the parameters to observe point clouds, including viewing angle, point size, and render type.

Display and Score the Distorted Point Cloud In this design session, the experimenter should consider where to display point clouds, such as flat-panel displays and head-mounted devices. Meanwhile, specifying the subjective score method is an important part. Different methods correspond to different real scenarios. After gaining the rated quality scores, it is necessary to ensure the validity of these scores. Fan et al. proposed a screen-based 3D subjective experiment software designed for evaluating the perceived quality of 3D graphics with virtual reality [35, 52] in Fig. 3.1. Referring to ITU BT500-15, the commonly used subjective scoring methods can be divided into Single-Stimulus (SS) methods and Double-Stimulus (DS) methods. And the single-stimulus methods include Absolute Category Rating (ACR) and Numerical Category Rating (NCR). Meanwhile, the double-stimulus methods include the Double-Stimulus Impairment Scale (DSIS) and the Double-Stimulus Continuous Quality-Scale (DSCQS).

The SS methods do not provide a reference point cloud for scoring, which aligns more with the user's consumption habits of 3D content. In the ACR approach, testers are asked to assign image quality to a set of categories that are defined in semantic terms. In the NCR approach, observers should make judgments in categories on a linear scale. Since the categories are not limited by adjectives, the scale can be applied to a wide range of values. The DS methods provide unimpaired point clouds and distorted point clouds. In the DSIS method, each assessor is presented with an unimpaired point cloud and with the same distorted point clouds following. Then,

Fig. 3.1 Displaying the point cloud with virtual reality. Public-domain open-access image [35]

the tester should vote for the latter while keeping the former in mind. In the DSCQS method, the assessor is provided with a pair of point clouds: one is an unimpaired point cloud, and the other is the same one distorted. Following that, the assessor is asked to score the two point clouds.

Due to the differences in personal aesthetics and professional background of the experimental assessors, the obtained opinion scores need to be processed to remove any outliers among them. The most commonly used method to detect outliers is statistical analysis, which removes the opinion scores lie in $[MOS-2\sigma, MOS+2\sigma]$ (σ is the standard deviation of the opinion scores).

3.2.2 Objective Quality Assessment

This section provides an overview of full reference (FR), reduced reference (RR), and no reference (NR) methods. FR point cloud quality assessment (PCQA) methods, which require full access to the original point cloud. RR PCQA methods, which require only partial access, contrast with NR methods that operate independently of the original data. Classic FR metrics like point-to-point (p2po) [53], point-to-plane (p2pl) [54], point-to-mesh (p2m) [55], and plane-to-plane (pl2pl) [56] rely on geometric differences to assess quality. These techniques compute distances, such as the Euclidean distance between corresponding points, or error projections on normal vectors to measure deviations. The p2po metric specifically quantifies geometry distortion by calculating point-to-point distances. More complex metrics, including PSNR [57], Hausdorff [58], and Mahalanobis distances [59], supplement this analysis by providing additional context on point cloud errors.

While FR PCQA metrics offer clarity in geometric evaluations, they often fail to capture perceptual nuances, especially with texture-related distortions. Recognizing this, Meyer et al. [60] introduced a new metric—TQMCM—which integrates texture distortion with geometric error, extending traditional 2D methods to the 3D domain. Concurrently, other efforts by researchers such as Diniz et al. [61, 62] and Chetouani et al. [63] have focused on improving the perceptual accuracy of texture analysis using statistical models and neural networks.

The computational demands of PCQA, especially in scenarios where point clouds are transformed into images, have driven researchers toward image-based evaluation techniques. These methods leverage well-established image quality assessment (IQA) metrics like SSIM and VIF to assess the projected data. However, the FR and RR PCQA methods continue to face limitations in practical applications due to the need for reference data. RR PCQA, while alleviating some of these constraints, remains under-explored compared to its FR counterpart, despite the introduction of novel RR metrics focused on geometry and texture features.

Chettouani et al. [64] developed a method that leverages geometry properties such as distance, curvature, and grayscale features extracted from specific patches of point clouds, feeding these attributes into a convolutional neural network (CNN) for quality evaluation. Similarly, Tao et al. [65] introduced the PM-BVQA model, which converts 3D point clouds into 2D quality awarded features. The model integrates these features at multiple scales using a CNN-based joint feature extraction framework to improve quality assessment. Liu et al. [66] proposed PQA-Net, which performs joint features and fusion, combining it with a quality neural network. However, such deep learning–based approaches require significant amounts of training data. In response, Yang et al. [67] designed IT-PCQA, an innovative framework that leverages domain adaptation to transfer quality assessment capabilities from natural image domains to point cloud images. Liu et al. [68] also introduced a large-scale PCQA dataset[1] (LS-PCQA), alongside a novel NR PCQA model (ResSCNN). This method utilizes sparse CNNs to minimize computational costs when evaluating point cloud quality. To further optimize the evaluation process, Zhang et al. [69] developed MM-PCQA, a multi-modal fusion framework that deals with point clouds with sub-models and applies attention between point cloud and projected image data to enhance feature extraction. Additional research has focused on more specialized models, such as the 3D-NSS framework by Zhang et al. [70], which integrates natural scene statistics, entropy, and geometry features like curvature and planarity for regression-based quality prediction. Meanwhile, Wang et al. [71] introduced a dual-branch network that progressively learns quality metrics from multi-modal input data. Mu et al. [72] advanced this idea by employing a multi-view aggregation transformer (MVAT) to extract both contextual and geometry content from multiple projected images.

Recent developments reflect a growing interest in NR PCQA, driven by its flexibility across different scenarios and the promise of deep learning in improving

[1] https://github.com/lyp22/ResSCNN.

Table 3.1 Objective point cloud quality assessment methods. Source: Author

Method	Type	Advantages	Disadvantages
Classic FR metrics	FR	Calculates geometric differences, like distances, and error projections.	Ignores perceptual nuances, especially with texture-related distortions.
RR PCQA	RR	Focuses on geometry and texture features.	Faces limitation of the reference data
PQA-Net [66]	NR	Utilizes joint feature extraction and fusion for distortion classification.	Requires significant amounts of training data for deep learning network.
IT-PCQA [67]	NR	Transfers quality assessment capabilities from natural image domains to point cloud images.	Sensitivity to different types of distortions varies, dependent on training data.
MM-PCQA [69]	NR	Segments original point clouds and applies cross-modal attention between the point cloud and projected image.	Requires high demand on computational resources.
3D-NSS [70]	NR	Leverages natural scene statistics, entropy, and geometry features.	Requires a large amount of training data, and the training process and computational complexity are high.
Dual-branch network PCQA [71]	NR	Captures multi-modal features based on a dual-branch network.	Requires multiple projected images and original point cloud.

feature extraction. However, limitations remain, particularly concerning the impact of viewpoint changes and the lack of emphasis on multi-scale features. To address these gaps, new approaches incorporate information from diverse perspectives, accounting for variations in viewpoint and integrating both multi-scale and multi-modal data. These efforts represent significant progress in optimizing NR PCQA for real-world applications, promoting more efficient and perceptually relevant quality assessments. All methods are concluded in Table 3.1.

3.3 Just-Noticeable-Distortion of 3D Point Clouds

3.3.1 Concept of Just-Noticeable-Distortion

Just-Noticeable-Distortion (JND) refers to the minimum level of distortion that the human visual system (HVS) can detect, and it is a critical concept in the fields of visual perception and data processing. Leveraging the perceptual characteristics of the HVS, JND specifies the threshold at which distortion becomes noticeable to an observer under specific conditions (e.g., brightness, frequency, color, content, or scene). Its primary goal is to quantify the perceptual redundancy of the HVS, enabling the introduction of distortion without substantially compromising subjective quality. This facilitates the optimization of various applications, such as data compression, rendering, transmission, and noise processing [73].

JND originates from psychophysics and adheres to principles such as Weber's law, which states that the perceptual threshold is proportional to the intensity of background stimuli. For instance, on a bright background, HVS requires a larger change in brightness to perceive differences. JND studies determine the distortion threshold through subjective experiments, where observers compare original content with distorted version to assess whether the distortion is detectable. These thresholds vary depending on content characteristics; for example, distortions in smooth regions are more noticeable than those in complex textures. Additionally, HVS exhibits differential sensitivity across color channels, being most sensitive to changes in green and least sensitive to changes in blue.

In the domain of 3D point clouds, the concept of JND extends to both geometry information (point position) and attribute information (such as color). The analysis of point cloud JND must account for the perceptual characteristics of spatial structure and color distribution. Typically, its frequency components are examined using methods like Graph Fourier Transform (GFT), akin to frequency-domain modeling in image processing. Applications of JND encompass point cloud compression (reducing data volume while preserving quality), quality assessment (evaluating whether distortion is tolerable), and noise generation (simulating perceptible perturbations). The JND dataset obtained from subjective experiments serves as a foundation for developing perception-driven algorithms, thereby advancing efficient and realistic 3D data processing technologies. However, the absence of a point cloud JND dataset constrains its further application. Subsequently, we concisely elaborate on the implications and guiding significance of the law of JND in images and videos for constructing point cloud JND datasets and methodologies.

3.3.2 Enlightenment of Image and Video JND for Point Cloud JND

The principles of JND in images and videos offer crucial insights for constructing point cloud JND datasets and advancing related methodologies. Subjective experimental design serves as the cornerstone of image JND datasets. Point cloud JND should adopt these approaches to design standardized experiments, regulate display conditions, and gather sufficient observer data. The dataset must encompass various types of distortion (geometry distortion, attribute distortion) and include smooth, complex, natural, and artificial point cloud contents. For dynamic point cloud JND, the spatiotemporal model of video can be referenced to analyze the impact of inter-frame motion on distortion perception.

The research on image JND demonstrates that various masking effects are critical factors in JND modeling. The HVS exhibits higher sensitivity to distortion in low-frequency regions, such as smooth backgrounds, and lower sensitivity to high-frequency details, such as complex textures. Frequency components are typically analyzed using Discrete Cosine Transform (DCT) or wavelet transform. Video JND further incorporates the time domain, where distortions in fast-moving areas are relatively harder to detect. These principles imply that point cloud JND should integrate the frequency characteristics of geometry and attributes, leveraging GFT to decompose point cloud signals. A stricter threshold should be applied in low-frequency regions, while the spatiotemporal characteristics of dynamic point clouds should also be explored. Moreover, the JND difference between smooth and textured areas in images indicates that point cloud JND must account for local geometry complexity. For instance, distortions on flat surfaces are more perceptible, whereas complex curved surfaces can tolerate greater distortion.

3.4 Visual Attention Modeling of 3D Point Clouds

Visual attention plays a crucial role in the process of acquiring information from the outside world in humans and animals. Attention modeling is proposed to mimic this biological mechanism and has been widely used as a pre-processing procedure in many vision tasks, such as image compression and image quality assessment. For instance, in the image quality assessment field, we can allow the attractive regions of an image to have larger weights for the final quality score. In this section, we first briefly explain the visual attention mechanism and then introduce its two related research fields in computer vision, i.e., saliency detection and salient object detection, based on two representative works [21, 74] from these fields.

3.4.1 Concept of Visual Attention

Point cloud data contain rich spatial information and provide an immersive visual experience. Meanwhile, this also causes an explosion in the amount of data, which brings challenges to the practical transmission and processing of point clouds. However, for the 3D world, human eyes can easily process these massive amounts of information perceived from the outside world. The secret of the powerful data processing ability of the human eye is a special attention mechanism; that is, the human eye can quickly focus on the region of interest in a scene and obtain some coarse-grained perception of the scene. Then the coarse-grained perception is gradually refined under the repeated stimulation of external signals. This attention mechanism ensures that humans capture the most interesting information within their limited capacities. Visual attention modeling is proposed to mimic this biological attention mechanism by designing effective algorithms. In terms of the output types, attention modeling can be further categorized into saliency detection and salient object detection. Saliency detection aims to predict the heat maps that indicate the eye fixation of humans. Salient Object Detection (SOD) is dedicated

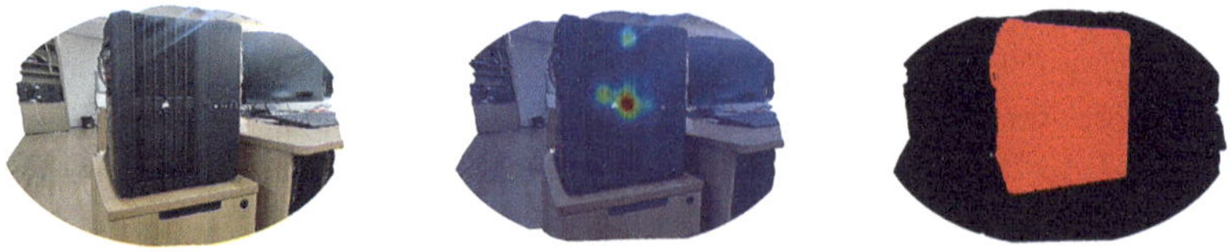

Fig. 3.2 The output comparison of saliency detection and salient object detection. The former produces the fixation map, while the latter predicts the segmentation map. Public-domain open-access image [21]

to identifying and fully segmenting the most visually attractive objects within a scene. The output comparison of these two attention modeling tasks is depicted in Fig. 3.2. Itti et al. [75] were the first to study attention modeling for 2D images. Following them, many excellent works [76, 77] were proposed, especially with the development of deep learning, and have been applied in many vision tasks as the pre-processing procedure.

Although compared with 2D images, point cloud data urgently need to introduce the biological attention mechanism to remove information redundancy, most of the existing attention modeling works are proposed for images, and only a few works [78–80] focus on 3D point clouds. Moreover, most attention modeling works for point clouds [74, 81–83] devote to saliency detection, while rare works involve object-level attention modeling. Attention modeling for point clouds has many challenges as the annotation of point clouds is often time-consuming and laborious, and tailored data processing methods need to be developed for point cloud feature extraction. In this section, we will select two representative works [21, 74] for introducing point cloud-based saliency detection and SOD, respectively.

3.4.2 Saliency Detection

Ding et al. [74] introduced a pioneering method for saliency detection in point clouds aimed at calculating the distribution of human attention for a specific point cloud sample. Their approach emulates key aspects of the human visual system, specifically local distinctness and global rarity, to assess visual saliency and determine attention distribution within point clouds. Local distinctness refers to the contrast between a point and its immediate environment, whereas global rarity reflects the frequency of occurrence of point cloud regions. The authors then craft an adaptive optimization framework to integrate various saliency cues. This framework, surpassing simple additive or linear combinations of saliency cues, achieves more effective saliency detection outcomes. Further details of this method will be discussed in the following sections.

Computation of Local Distinctness To characterize the local geometry features, a Fast Point Feature Histogram (FPFH) descriptor is adopted for describing the features of each point [84]. Specifically, let P represent a point cloud sample, where $p \in P$ is a point in P. The authors select k-neighboring points of each p_i in the sphere with radius r to define a Darboux uvn frame ($u = n_i$, $v = (p_j - p_i) \times u$, $\omega = u \times v$):

$$\alpha = v \cdot n_j, \tag{3.1}$$

$$\phi = (u \cdot (p_j - p_i)) / \left\| p_j - p_i \right\|, \tag{3.2}$$

$$\theta = arctan(\omega \cdot n_j, u \cdot n_j), \tag{3.3}$$

where p_j is a neighboring point of p_i. In this approach, the simplified point feature histogram (SPFH) can be calculated. For each point p_i, the final FPFH can be defined as:

$$FPFH(p_i) = SPFH(p_i) + \frac{1}{k} \sum_{j=1}^{k} \frac{SPFH(p_i)}{\left\| p_j - p_i \right\|}, \tag{3.4}$$

where $\left\| \cdot \right\|$ indicates the L_2 distance between two points. Due to the nonuniformity of point clouds, measuring the dissimilarity among points by the Euclidean distance cannot meet the relevant goals well. The authors [74] resort to the Chi-Square distance $\chi^2(\cdot)$ to measure the dissimilarity between the geometry features of two points p_i and p_j:

$$\chi^2(p_i, p_j) = \sum_{n=1}^{N} \frac{(FPFH_n(p_i) - FPFH_n(p_j))^2}{FPFH_n(p_i) + FPFH_n(p_j)}, \tag{3.5}$$

where N denotes the number of bins in the FPFH descriptor. The local distinctness of a point p_i can be calculated by combining its dissimilarities with all the surrounding points:

$$D(p_i) = 1 - exp(-\frac{1}{R} \sum_{j=1}^{R} \frac{\chi^2(p_i, p_j)}{1 + \left\| p_j - p_i \right\|}), \tag{3.6}$$

where $D(\cdot)$ indicates the local distinctness score of a given point p_i, and R represents the number of considered neighboring points. Since point clouds have a nonuniform point distribution, R is proportional to the density of points. In the experiments, too many points in a point cloud sample have considerable local distinctness scores. To suppress non-distinct and prevent detecting too many key points, a piecewise function as the suppression function is introduced [74]:

$$f(p_i) = \begin{cases} D(p_i), & D(p_i) \geqq h \\ D(p_i) \cdot D(p_i), & otherwise, \end{cases} \tag{3.7}$$

where h denotes the threshold determining the range of local distinctness score to be amplified or suppressed. $F(p_i)$ is the final local distinctness value. Inspired by the works [85] for image saliency detection, the authors utilize an adaptive threshold that allows the top 20% points with large local distinctness scores to be amplified.

Global Rarity The global rarity of point clouds is defined as point clusters, which can benefit the interference reduction of noisy points. A voxel cloud connectivity algorithm is utilized to partition the point cloud into compact clusters. The geometry features of each cluster are represented by the mean FPFH descriptions of all points in this cluster:

$$FPFH(c_i) = \frac{1}{C_i} \sum_{i=1}^{C} FPFH(p_i), \ p_i \in c_i, \tag{3.8}$$

where C_i denotes the number of points in the point cluster c_i. The initial global rarity score can be formulated as:

$$G(c_i) = 1 - exp\left(-\frac{1}{N} \sum_{j=1}^{N} \frac{\chi^2(c_i, c_j)}{1 + \|c_i - c_j\|}\right), \tag{3.9}$$

where $G(c_i)$ and N denote the initial global rarity score of the point cluster c_i and the number of clusters in the point cloud sample. $\|c_i - c_j\|$ indicates the L_2 distance between the point cluster centers of c_i and c_j. Since the initial global rarity score provides only a coarse estimation and does not precisely reflect the rarity within point clusters, a random walk algorithm is introduced to compute point-level global rarity, incorporating the local geometry properties of individual points. In practice, centroid points from selected clusters are classified as salient or non-salient using initial global rarity thresholds. When the rarity score exceeds t_1 or drops below t_2, the point nearest to the cluster center is assigned as a salient or non-salient seed, while all other points are considered unseeded. The authors set t_1 and t_2 to $\frac{1}{2}(G_{max} + \bar{G})$ and $\bar{G}$, where G_{max} and $\bar{G}$ are the maximum and average values of initial global rarity scores across all point clusters. With the seed points established, the random walk process measures how each unseeded point p_i is connected to its k-nearest seeded neighbors p_j.

$$w_{ij} = exp\left(-\frac{\|FPFH(p_i) - FPFH(p_j)\|}{\sigma_1^2}\right), \tag{3.10}$$

where $\sigma_1 = 3.7$ is constant. Once the weight matrix is constructed, the Laplacian matrix L is subsequently computed as follows [86].

Following the approach in [86], the probability vector P^s is optimized by minimizing the Dirichlet energy. Additionally, a fitting constraint is incorporated to ensure that the solution remains close to the initial global rarity score:

$$Dir[P^s] = \frac{1}{2}(P^s)^T L(P^s) + \frac{\eta}{2}(P^s - Y)^T (P^s - Y), \tag{3.11}$$

where η serves as a tuning parameter, and Y denotes the point-wise indication vector, which retains the initial global rarity scores. Equation (3.11) can be further simplified by setting the derivative of $Dir[P^s]$ with respect to the probability vector P_u^s (associated with unseeded points) to zero:

$$p_u^s = (L_u + \eta I)^{-1} \left(-B^T p_{seeds}^s + \eta Y_u^s \right). \tag{3.12}$$

Optimization Framework Upon calculating the values for local distinctness and global rarity, they merge these two saliency cues by optimizing the saliency values across all points [87]. The loss function can be defined as:

$$\ell = \sum_{k=1}^{2} \sum_{i=1}^{N} \left(\frac{s_i^2}{Z_k(p_i)} + Z_k(p_i)(1 - s_i)^2 \right) + \sum_{j \in R} W_{ij}(s_i - s_j)^2, \tag{3.13}$$

where $Z \in \{F, G\}$ with $Z_1(p_i)$ and $Z_2(p_i)$ indicating $F(p_i)$ and $G(p_i)$, respectively. N and R stand for the total point number and neighboring point number of p_i, respectively. The weight $W_i j$ means the influence of the neighboring point p_j on p_i, which can be formulated as:

$$W_{ij} = exp \left(-\frac{\|p_i - p_j\|}{\sigma_2^2} \right). \tag{3.14}$$

$\sigma_2 = 0.02$ is a constant. To assess the performance of the proposed framework, the authors carry out thorough experimental evaluations, which indicate that it consistently outperforms competing methods in generating salient point cloud representations [83, 87].

3.4.3 *Salient Object Detection*

Fan et al. [21] was the first to systematically study Salient Object Detection (SOD) for point clouds. Previously, point cloud SOD has been rarely studied due to the numerous intractable problems. The first problem to be solved is how to define the salient objects in point cloud scenes. Compared with 2D images, point clouds provide an immersive watching experience. In contrast to static image perception, human attention varies with viewpoint changes. The authors note that these changes in attention distribution can lead to saliency conflicts, where an object paradoxically falls into both salient and non-salient categories when viewed from different angles within the same point cloud sample. Given the saliency inconsistencies present in point clouds, it is essential to rigorously reinterpret the notion of saliency from images to 3D data. Despite the transformative impact of deep learning techniques [38, 39] on vision tasks, the absence of a well-established dataset for point cloud saliency object detection remains a major limitation, hindering further exploration in this field. Last but not least, since point clouds store 3D information as irregular and unordered points, existing well-designed algorithms for image-based SOD are not applicable for detecting salient objects in point clouds. While models exist for point cloud segmentation tasks, they fail to address the specific needs of SOD, leading to suboptimal performance on this task.

To enhance the understanding of salient objects in point clouds, the authors define point cloud SOD as identifying salient objects from any 3D perspective. The aggregation of segmentation maps from various viewpoints provides a full description of salient objects in the scene. To facilitate research, the authors introduce *PCSOD*, the first comprehensive dataset for point cloud SOD.[2] The dataset includes 2,872 annotated 3D views and can be used for various vision tasks beyond SOD.

Based on the proposed dataset, this work also contributes a baseline model for point cloud SOD, namely PointSal. The proposed model is an encoder–decoder architecture and primarily comprises a PointNet++ [88] encoder, a Feature Aggregation Block (FAB), a Point Perception Block (PPB), and a Saliency Perception Block (SPB). The network design is inspired by practices in the image processing field, where high-level features can become progressively diluted when transmitted through top-down fusion. Specifically, let $V = \{v_1, v_2, ..., v_N\}$ stand for a view with N points. Each point $v \in \mathbb{R}^{d_{in}}$ is represented by its spatial XYZ coordinates and corresponding point features such as RGB colors. The goal of point cloud SOD is to calculate the probability $p_i \in P$ of each point v_i being salient. To extract the hierarchical representations of input points, a PointNet++ encoder is first applied to extract multi-level features $\{F_l\}_{l=1}^4$. Each level of features contains a quarter of the number of features in the previous layer, and the feature dimension is doubled (the dimension of features in the first level is frozen to 64). To decode multi-level features into the final prediction, a novel decoder that incorporates three effective modules is introduced.

Given multi-level features from the encoder, the FAB is adopted to fuse them into compact representations F_c, in which high-level features are first up-sampled and then fused with low-level features. The up-sampling and fusion operations are common trilinear interpolation and concatenation, respectively. To make up the diluted high-level features, the PPB is developed to obtain global semantics and enhance the multi-scale representations of features. The global semantics F_s are

[2] https://git.openi.org.cn/OpenPointCloud/PCSOD#user-content-benchmark.

abstracted from the highest-level features F_4 via one PPM, while the multi-scale features F_m are extracted from the compact representations F_c by another PPM with varying configurations. The authors use the global semantics to improve the containing of high-level information in multi-scale features, which helps reduce the interference of non-salient backgrounds. To achieve this goal, the SPM is designed to integrate multi-scale features F_m and global semantics F_s and produce the final result P.

To enhance the high-level features, the PPB is proposed to capture global semantics and strengthen multi-scale feature representations. Global semantics F_s are extracted from the highest-level features F_4 using a PPM, while multi-scale features F_m are derived from compact representations F_c through another PPM with different configurations. The global semantics are then used to improve the integration of high-level information in the multi-scale features, reducing interference from non-salient backgrounds. This is achieved through the SPM, which combines the multi-scale features F_m and global semantics F_s to generate the final result P.

Extensive experiments indicate that the proposed baseline with tailored designs for SOD has visible superiority over other counterparts. The predictions from different methods on views of two typical scenes. As can be seen, the predictions from their proposed baseline have higher quality and are closer to the ground truths. The results of the comparison between point cloud quality assessment models are presented in Table 3.2.

Table 3.2 A comparative study of various point cloud quality assessment models. Source: Author

Basis	Methods	Modality	Color	Type
Global Geometric Distortion	point2point	point	colorless	Full-reference
	point2plane	point, normal	colorless	
	plane2plane	point, normal	colorless	
HVS Perception	Wu et al. [89]	point, image	color	
	GraphSIM	point, graph	color	
	MS-GraphSIM	point, graph	color	
	PCQM	point	color	
	PointSSIM	point	color	
Projection	Yang et al. [90]	image, depth	color	
Data-driven	ResSCNN	point	color	No reference
	PQA-Net	image	color	
	IT-PCQA	image	color	
	BM-PVQA	image	color	
	MM-PCQA	image, point	color	
	pmBQA	image, depth, texture, normal	color	

3.5 Summary

This chapter gives an introduction to quality assessment and perception models of point clouds. It discusses the methodologies of subjective evaluation and objective quality assessment modeling for point clouds. Following that, it provides the analysis of Just-Noticeable-Distortion (JND) that has the potentials to further optimize point cloud coding process by masking the unperceivable distortion. Finally, the visual attention modeling for point clouds can accurately predict where are mostly interested and can also guide the point cloud coding. For readers who are interested in the related technologies of AI-based image and video coding, please refer to [91].

Exercises

1. What is the aim of point cloud quality assessment?
2. How are distortions introduced in point cloud quality assessment studies?
3. What is the significance of rendering schemes in point cloud quality assessment?
4. How is the scoring of point cloud quality conducted in subjective assessments?
5. What is the concept of saliency detection?
6. What role do attention models play in point cloud quality assessment?
7. What is the concept of Just-Noticeable-Distortion?
8. What are the application areas of Just-Noticeable-Distortion?
9. How is multi-level Just-Noticeable-Distortion defined? Provide an example for illustration.
10. What is the reason for the scarcity of Just-Noticeable-Distortion datasets?

References

1. G. Liao, W. Gao, Q. Jiang, R. Wang, G. Li, Mmnet: multi-stage and multi-scale fusion network for rgb-d salient object detection, in *Proceedings of the 28th ACM International Conference on Multimedia* (2020), pp. 2436–2444
2. W. Gao, S. Kwong, Y. Zhou, Y. Jia, J. Zhang, W. Wu, Multiscale phase congruency analysis for image edge visual saliency detection, in *Proceedings of the International Conference on Machine Learning and Cybernetics (ICMLC)*, vol. 1 (IEEE, New York, 2016), pp. 75–80
3. W. Gao, Y. Guo, S. Ma, G. Li, S. Kwong, Efficient neural network compression inspired by compressive sensing. IEEE Trans. Neural Networks Learn. Syst. **35**(2), 1965–1979 (2022)
4. X. Zang, W. Gao, G. Li, H. Fang, C. Ban, Z. He, H. Sun, A baseline investigation: transformer-based cross-view baseline for text-based person search, in *Proceedings of the 31st ACM International Conference on Multimedia* (2023), pp. 7737–7746
5. G. Liao, W. Gao, G. Li, J. Wang, S. Kwong, Cross-collaborative fusion-encoder network for robust RGB-thermal salient object detection. IEEE Trans. Circuits Syst. Video Technol. **32**(11), 7646–7661 (2022)

6. W. Gao, G. Liao, S. Ma, G. Li, Y. Liang, W. Lin, Unified information fusion network for multimodal RGB-d and RGB-t salient object detection. IEEE Trans. Circuits Syst. Video Technol. **32**(4), 2091–2106 (2021)
7. W. Gao, G. Li, H. Yuan, R. Hamzaoui, Z. Li, S. Liu, Apccpa'22: 1st international workshop on advances in point cloud compression, processing and analysis, in *Proceedings of the 30th ACM International Conference on Multimedia* (2022), pp. 7392–7393
8. W. Gao, G. Li, Point cloud compression, enhancement and applications: from 3d perception to large models, in *Proceedings of the 32nd ACM International Conference on Multimedia* (2024), pp. 11292–11293
9. H. Sun, G. Li, S. Chen, L. Li, W. Gao, Special topic on 3d point cloud processing and applications. ZTE Commun. **21**(4), 1 (2023)
10. W. Gao, W. Gao, X. Mu, C. Peng, G. Li, Overview and comparison of AVS point cloud compression standard. APSIPA Trans. Signal Inf. Process. **14**(2), 1–33 (2025)
11. W. Gao, S. Wang, X. Zhang, S. Kwong, Editorial for special issue on deep learning-based data compression. APSIPA Trans. Signal Inf. Process. **13**(6), 1–2 (2024)
12. L. Xie, X. Mu, G. Li, W. Gao, et al., PKU-DPCC: a new dataset for dynamic point cloud compression. APSIPA Trans. Signal Inf. Process. **13**(6), 1–23 (2024)
13. S. Sun, X. Liang, S. Fan, W. Gao, W. Gao, VE-bench: subjective-aligned benchmark suite for text-driven video editing quality assessment, in *Proceedings of the AAAI Conference on Artificial Intelligence* (2025)
14. Z. Guo, W. Gao, H. Wang, J. Wang, S. Fan, No-reference deep quality assessment of compressed light field images, in *2021 IEEE International Conference on Multimedia and Expo (ICME)* (IEEE, New York, 2021), pp. 1–6
15. B. Qu, X. Liang, S. Sun, W. Gao, Exploring AIGC video quality: a focus on visual harmony, video-text consistency and domain distribution gap, in *Proceedings of the IEEE/CVF Conference on Computer Vision and Pattern Recognition Workshops* (2024)
16. B. Qu, H. Li, W. Gao, Bringing textual prompt to ai-generated image quality assessment, in *2024 IEEE International Conference on Multimedia and Expo (ICME)* (IEEE, New York, 2024)
17. W. Gao, H. Ye, G. Li, H. Zheng, Y. Wu, L. Xie, Openpointcloud: an open-source algorithm library of deep learning based point cloud compression, in *Proceedings of the 30th ACM International Conference on Multimedia* (2022), pp. 7347–7350
18. Y. Zhang, W. Gao, G. Li, Openpointcloud-v2: a deep learning based open-source algorithm library of point cloud processing, in *Proceedings of the 1st International Workshop on Advances in Point Cloud Compression, Processing and Analysis* (2022), pp. 51–55
19. L. Xie, W. Gao, Learningpcc: a pytorch library for learning-based point cloud compression, in *Proceedings of the 32nd ACM International Conference on Multimedia* (2024), pp. 11234–11238
20. L. Xie, W. Gao, Pchmvision: an open-source library of point cloud compression for human and machine vision, in *Proceedings of the 32nd ACM International Conference on Multimedia* (2024), pp. 11239–11243
21. S. Fan, W. Gao, G. Li, Salient object detection for point clouds. arXiv preprint arXiv:2207.11889 (2022)
22. S. Luo, W. Gao, A general framework for rotation invariant point cloud analysis, in *ICASSP 2024-2024 IEEE International Conference on Acoustics, Speech and Signal Processing (ICASSP)* (IEEE, New York, 2024), pp. 3665–3669
23. X. Lu, W. Gao, Attentivenet: Detecting small objects for lidar point clouds by attending to important points, in *2023 IEEE International Conference on Visual Communications and Image Processing (VCIP)* (IEEE, New York, 2023), pp. 1–5
24. Z. Pan, N. Zhang, W. Gao, S. Liu, G. Li, Less is more: label recommendation for weakly supervised point cloud semantic segmentation, in *Proceedings of the AAAI Conference on Artificial Intelligence*, vol. 38(5) (2024), pp. 4397–4405

25. Z. Pan, G. Liu, W. Gao, T.H. Li, Epcontrast: effective point-level contrastive learning for large-scale point cloud understanding, in *2024 IEEE International Conference on Multimedia and Expo (ICME)* (IEEE, New York, 2024), pp. 1–6
26. N. Zhang, Z. Pan, T.H. Li, W. Gao, G. Li, Improving graph representation for point cloud segmentation via attentive filtering, in *Proceedings of the IEEE/CVF Conference on Computer Vision and Pattern Recognition* (2023), pp. 1244–1254
27. K. Wen, N. Zhang, G. Li, W. Gao, MPVNN: multi-resolution point-voxel non-parametric network for 3d point cloud processing, in *2024 IEEE International Conference on Multimedia and Expo (ICME)* (IEEE, New York, 2024), pp. 1–6
28. Z. Pan, N. Zhang, W. Gao, S. Liu, G. Li, Point cloud semantic segmentation with sparse and inhomogeneous annotations, in *Proceedings of the AAAI Conference on Artificial Intelligence* (2025)
29. R. Zhang, G. Li, W. Gao, S. Liu, A quantum-inspired framework in master-servant mode for large-scale multi-modal place recognition. IEEE Trans. Intell. Transp. Syst. **26**(2), 2027–2039 (2025)
30. D. Yang, W. Gao, Pointchd: a point cloud benchmark for congenital heart disease classification and segmentation. IEEE J. Biomed. Health Inform. **29**(4), 2683–2694 (2025)
31. S. Fan, W. Gao, G. Li, Point-MPP: point cloud self-supervised learning from masked position prediction. IEEE Trans. Neural Networks Learn. Syst. **36**(7), 12964–12976 (2025)
32. Z. Pan, W. Gao, G. Li, Distribution guidance network for weakly supervised point cloud semantic segmentation, in *Advances in Neural Information Processing Systems* (2024)
33. R. Zhang, G. Li, W. Gao, T.H. Li, Compoint: can complex-valued representation benefit point cloud place recognition? IEEE Trans. Intell. Transp. Syst. **25**(7), 7494–7507 (2024)
34. Y. Wu, L. Xie, S. Sun, W. Gao, Y. Yan, Adaptive intra period size for deep learning-based screen content video coding, in *2024 IEEE International Conference on Multimedia and Expo Workshops (ICMEW)* (IEEE, New York, 2024), pp. 1–6
35. S. Fan, W. Gao, Screen-based 3d subjective experiment software. arXiv preprint arXiv:2308.03698 (2023)
36. J. Wang, W. Gao, G. Li, Zoom to perceive better: no-reference point cloud quality assessment via exploring effective multiscale feature. IEEE Trans. Circuits Syst. Video Technol. **34**(7), 6334–6346 (2024)
37. K. Zheng, W. Gao, H. Zheng, Octree-based learned point cloud geometry compression: a lossy perspective, in *2025 Data Compression Conference (DCC)* (IEEE, New York, 2025)
38. G. Li, G. Wei, W. Gao, *Point Cloud Compression: Technologies and Standardization* (Springer, Berlin, 2024)
39. W. Gao, G. Li, *Deep Learning for 3D Point Clouds* (Springer, Berlin, 2024)
40. G. Li, W. Gao, W. Gao, MPEG video-based point cloud compression (V-PCC) standard, in *Point Cloud Compression: Technologies and Standardization* (Springer, Berlin, 2024), pp. 199–218
41. G. Li, W. Gao, W. Gao, MPEG geometry-based point cloud compression (G-PCC) standard, in *Point Cloud Compression: Technologies and Standardization* (Springer, Berlin, 2024), pp. 135–165
42. T. Qin, G. Li, W. Gao, S. Liu, Multi-grained point cloud geometry compression via dual-model prediction with extended octree. ACM Trans. Multimed. Comput. Commun. Appl. **20**(9), 1–30 (2024)
43. R. Zhang, W. Gao, G. Li, T.H. Li, Qinet: decision surface learning and adversarial enhancement for quasi-immune completion of diverse corrupted point clouds. IEEE Trans. Geosci. Remote Sens. **60**, 1–14 (2022)
44. R. Bao, Y. Ren, G. Li, W. Gao, S. Liu, Flow-based point cloud completion network with adversarial refinement, in *ICASSP 2022-2022 IEEE International Conference on Acoustics, Speech and Signal Processing (ICASSP)* (IEEE, New York, 2022), pp. 2559–2563
45. S. Sun, X. Liang, B. Qu, W. Gao, Content-rich AIGC video quality assessment via intricate text alignment and motion-aware consistency. arXiv preprint arXiv:2502.04076 (2025)

46. Y. Shao, W. Gao, S. Liu, G. Li, Advanced patch-based affine motion estimation for dynamic point cloud geometry compression. Sensors **24**(10), 3142 (2024)
47. Y. Shao, F. Song, W. Gao, S. Liu, G. Li, Texture-guided graph transform optimization for point cloud attribute compression. Appl. Sci. **14**(10), 4094 (2024)
48. Y. Shao, X. Yang, W. Gao, S. Liu, G. Li, 3d point cloud attribute compression using diffusion-based texture-aware intra prediction. IEEE Trans. Circuits Syst. Video Technol. **34**(10), 9633–9646 (2024)
49. J. Zhang, Y. Chen, G. Liu, W. Gao, G. Li, Efficient point cloud attribute compression framework using attribute-guided graph fourier transform, in *ICASSP 2024-2024 IEEE International Conference on Acoustics, Speech and Signal Processing (ICASSP)* (IEEE, New York, 2024), pp. 8426–8430
50. E. Alexious, A.M. Pinheiro, C. Duarte, D. Matković, E. Dumić, L.A. da Silva Cruz, L.G. Dmitrović, M.V. Bernardo, M. Pereira, T. Ebrahimi, Point cloud subjective evaluation methodology based on reconstructed surfaces, in *Applications of Digital Image Processing XLI*, vol. 10752 (SPIE, New York, 2018), pp. 160–173
51. M. Kazhdan, H. Hoppe, Screened poisson surface reconstruction. ACM Trans. Graph. (ToG) **32**(3), 1–13 (2013)
52. H. Yuan, W. Gao, W. Gao, Opensep: an open source subjective experiment platform, in *Proceedings of the 32nd ACM International Conference on Multimedia* (2024), pp. 11248–11251
53. S. Schwarz, M. Preda, V. Baroncini, M. Budagavi, P. Cesar, P.A. Chou, R.A. Cohen, M. Krivokuća, S. Lasserre, Z. Li, et al., Emerging MPEG standards for point cloud compression. IEEE J. Emerging Sel. Top. Circuits Syst. **9**(1), 133–148 (2018)
54. D. Tian, H. Ochimizu, C. Feng, R. Cohen, A. Vetro, Geometric distortion metrics for point cloud compression, in *2017 IEEE International Conference on Image Processing (ICIP)* (IEEE, New York, 2017), pp. 3460–3464
55. D. Tian, H. Ochimizu, C. Feng, R. Cohen, A. Vetro, Geometric distortion metrics for point cloud compression, in *Proceedings of IEEE International Conference on Image Processing (ICIP)* (IEEE, New York, 2017), pp. 3460–3464
56. E. Alexiou, T. Ebrahimi, Point cloud quality assessment metric based on angular similarity, in *Proceedings of IEEE International Conference on Multimedia and Expo (ICME)* (IEEE, New York, 2018), pp. 1–6
57. A. Javaheri, C. Brites, F. Pereira, J. Ascenso, Improving PSNR-based quality metrics performance for point cloud geometry, in *Proceedings of IEEE International Conference on Image Processing (ICIP)* (IEEE, New York, 2020), pp. 3438–3442
58. A. Javaheri, C. Brites, F. Pereira, J. Ascenso, A generalized Hausdorff distance based quality metric for point cloud geometry, in *2020 Twelfth International Conference on Quality of Multimedia Experience (QoMEX)* (IEEE, New York, 2020), pp. 1–6
59. A. Javaheri, C. Brites, F. Pereira, J. Ascenso, Mahalanobis based point to distribution metric for point cloud geometry quality evaluation. IEEE Signal Process Lett. **27**, 1350–1354 (2020)
60. G. Meynet, Y. Nehmé, J. Digne, G. Lavoué, PCQM: a full-reference quality metric for colored 3d point clouds, in *Proceedings of Twelfth International Conference on Quality of Multimedia Experience (QoMEX)* (IEEE, New York, 2020), pp. 1–6
61. R. Diniz, P.G. Freitas, M.C. Farias, Towards a point cloud quality assessment model using local binary patterns, in *Proceedings of Twelfth International Conference on Quality of Multimedia Experience (QoMEX)* (IEEE, New York, 2020), pp. 1–6
62. R. Diniz, P.G. Freitas, M.C. Farias, Local luminance patterns for point cloud quality assessment, in *Proceedings of IEEE 22nd International Workshop on Multimedia Signal Processing (MMSP)* (IEEE, New York, 2020), pp. 1–6
63. A. Chetouani, M. Quach, G. Valenzise, F. Dufaux, Convolutional neural network for 3d point cloud quality assessment with reference, in *Proceedings of IEEE 23rd International Workshop on Multimedia Signal Processing (MMSP)* (IEEE, New York, 2021), pp. 1–6
64. A. Chetouani, M. Quach, G. Valenzise, F. Dufaux, Deep learning-based quality assessment of 3d point clouds without reference, in *Proceedings of IEEE International Conference on Multimedia & Expo Workshops (ICMEW)* (IEEE, New York, 2021), pp. 1–6

65. W. Tao, G. Jiang, Z. Jiang, M. Yu, Point cloud projection and multi-scale feature fusion network based blind quality assessment for colored point clouds, in *Proceedings of the 29th ACM International Conference on Multimedia* (2021), pp. 5266–5272
66. Q. Liu, H. Yuan, H. Su, H. Liu, Y. Wang, H. Yang, J. Hou, PQA-net: deep no reference point cloud quality assessment via multi-view projection. IEEE Trans. Circuits Syst. Video Technol. **31**(12), 4645–4660 (2021)
67. Q. Yang, Y. Liu, S. Chen, Y. Xu, J. Sun, No-reference point cloud quality assessment via domain adaptation, in *Proceedings of the IEEE/CVF Conference on Computer Vision and Pattern Recognition* (2022), pp. 21179–21188
68. Y. Liu, Q. Yang, Y. Xu, L. Yang, Point cloud quality assessment: dataset construction and learning-based no-reference metric. ACM Trans. Multimed. Comput. Commun. Appl. **19**(2s), 1–26 (2023)
69. Z. Zhang, W. Sun, X. Min, Q. Wang, J. He, Q. Zhou, G. Zhai, MM-PCQA: multi-modal learning for no-reference point cloud quality assessment, in *Proceedings of the Thirty-Second International Joint Conference on Artificial Intelligence* (2023), pp. 1759–1767
70. Z. Zhang, W. Sun, X. Min, T. Wang, W. Lu, G. Zhai, No-reference quality assessment for 3d colored point cloud and mesh models. IEEE Trans. Circuits Syst. Video Technol. **32**(11), 7618–7631 (2022)
71. J. Wang, W. Gao, G. Li, Applying collaborative adversarial learning to blind point cloud quality measurement. IEEE Trans. Instrum. Meas. **72**, 1–15 (2023)
72. B. Mu, F. Shao, X. Chai, Q. Liu, H. Chen, Q. Jiang, Multi-view aggregation transformer for no-reference point cloud quality assessment. Displays **78**, 102450 (2023)
73. L. Xie, W. Gao, H. Zheng, G. Li, Roi-guided point cloud geometry compression towards human and machine vision. arXiv preprint arXiv:2504.14240 (2025)
74. X. Ding, W. Lin, Z. Chen, X. Zhang, Point cloud saliency detection by local and global feature fusion. IEEE Trans. Image Process. **28**(11), 5379–5393 (2019)
75. L. Itti, C. Koch, E. Niebur, A model of saliency-based visual attention for rapid scene analysis. IEEE Trans. Pattern Anal. Mach. Intell. **20**(11), 1254–1259 (1998)
76. A. Borji, Saliency prediction in the deep learning era: successes and limitations. IEEE Trans. Pattern Anal. Mach. Intell. **43**(2), 679–700 (2019)
77. W. Wang, Q. Lai, H. Fu, J. Shen, H. Ling, R. Yang, Salient object detection in the deep learning era: an in-depth survey. IEEE Trans. Pattern Anal. Mach. Intell. **44**(6), 3239–3259 (2021)
78. S. Bhatia, S.K. Chalup, et al., Segmenting salient objects in 3d point clouds of indoor scenes using geodesic distances. J. Signal Inf. Process. **4**(03), 102 (2013)
79. O. Akman, P. Jonker, Computing saliency map from spatial information in point cloud data, in *International Conference on Advanced Concepts for Intelligent Vision Systems* (Springer, Berlin, 2010), pp. 290–299
80. J. Leroy, N. Riche, M. Mancas, B. Gosselin, 3d saliency based on supervoxels rarity in point clouds, in *Hamburg, Germany* (2015)
81. E. Alexiou, P. Xu, T. Ebrahimi, Towards modelling of visual saliency in point clouds for immersive applications, in *2019 IEEE International Conference on Image Processing (ICIP)* (IEEE, New York, 2019), pp. 4325–4329
82. V.F. Figueiredo, G.L. Sandri, R.L. de Queiroz, P.A. Chou, Saliency maps for point clouds, in *2020 IEEE 22nd International Workshop on Multimedia Signal Processing (MMSP)* (IEEE, New York, 2020), pp. 1–5
83. Y. Guo, F. Wang, J. Xin, Point-wise saliency detection on 3d point clouds via covariance descriptors. Vis. Comput. **34**(10), 1325–1338 (2018)
84. R.B. Rusu, N. Blodow, M. Beetz, Fast point feature histograms (FPFH) for 3d registration, in *IEEE International Conference on Robotics and Automation* (IEEE, New York, 2009), pp. 3212–3217
85. A. Borji, Boosting bottom-up and top-down visual features for saliency estimation, in *IEEE Conference on Computer Vision and Pattern Recognition* (IEEE, New York, 2012), pp. 438–445

86. Y. Yuan, C. Li, J. Kim, W. Cai, D.D. Feng, Reversion correction and regularized random walk ranking for saliency detection. IEEE Trans. Image Process. **27**(3), 1311–1322 (2017)
87. F.P. Tasse, J. Kosinka, N. Dodgson, Cluster-based point set saliency, in *Proceedings of the IEEE International Conference on Computer Vision* (2015), pp. 163–171
88. C.R. Qi, L. Yi, H. Su, L.J. Guibas, Pointnet++: deep hierarchical feature learning on point sets in a metric space. Adv. Neural Inf. Proces. Syst. **30**, 5104–5114 (2017)
89. X. Wu, Y. Zhang, C. Fan, J. Hou, S. Kwong, Subjective quality database and objective study of compressed point clouds with 6DoF head-mounted display. IEEE Trans. Circuits Syst. Video Technol. **31**(12), 4630–4644 (2021)
90. Q. Yang, H. Chen, Z. Ma, Y. Xu, R. Tang, J. Sun, Predicting the perceptual quality of point cloud: a 3D-to-2D projection-based exploration. IEEE Trans. Multimedia **23**, 3877–3891 (2021)
91. W. Gao, *AI-based Image and Video Coding: Methods, Standards, and Applications* (Springer, Berlin, 2025)

Chapter 4
Deep Learning–Based Static 3D Point Cloud Geometry Coding

Abstract This chapter methodically examines static point cloud geometry compression techniques, encompassing both lossless and lossy approaches. It further organizes these approaches into three primary frameworks, including point-based compression, voxel-based compression, and octree-based compression. By analyzing the core mechanisms and distinguishing features of prominent algorithms in each category, the discussion evaluates their operational contexts and compression effectiveness. This in-depth investigation establishes foundational insights and methodological references to advance the development of static point cloud geometry coding technology.

Keywords Point cloud geometry coding · Voxel-based · Octree-based · Point-based · Sparse convolution · Compression efficiency

4.1 Overview of Lossless Geometry Coding

Deep learning–based image and video coding methods [1–7] have shown better performances and potentials than traditional non-learning-based coding methods [8–15]. Therefore, deep learning approaches [16–27] have been expected to work more efficiently for point cloud coding. In deep learning–based point cloud coding [28–34], lossless coding serves as a fundamental component, as some lossy coding techniques depend on it [35–42]. Therefore, we begin by introducing lossless coding. The lossless point cloud geometry coding (PCGC) techniques preserve full geometric fidelity. All lossless coding approaches share a common goal, i.e., they estimate the occupancy probability distribution of each element using deep learning models, based on existing information and arithmetic coding. The main distinctions of different methods lie in data representation and context generation [43–48].

W. Gao, *AI-based 3D Point Cloud Coding*,
https://doi.org/10.1007/978-981-95-0660-6_4

4.1.1 Data Representation

The compression target is a frame of point cloud data, which can be represented as a voxel frame after coordinates are quantized. The quantization process can introduce geometry distortion, but it is actually not a result of compression. Voxel-based methods directly compress the occupancy of each voxel. Additionally, because the coordinate space in voxel representation is composed of integers, a voxel frame can be organized in the form of an octree. Octree-based methods, in turn, compress the occupancy of each octree node.

After introducing the two types of data representation, it is important to clarify the concept of occupancy. In voxel space, an unknown voxel is termed a Probable Positively Occupied Voxel (P-POV) until it is determined to be occupied or unoccupied. Positively Occupied Voxel (POV) refers to occupied voxels, while Negatively Occupied Voxel (NOV) refers to unoccupied ones. In the encoder, the status of POVs and NOVs is known, but it remains unknown in the decoder. The encoder compresses the occupancy of each P-POV, while the decoder reconstructs POVs from P-POVs. POVs are assigned with the value of "1," while NOVs are assigned with the value of "0," representing the occupancy status of each voxel.

The cubic space is recursively divided into 8 equal-sized sub-cubes (octants). To describe the occupancy status of the 8 octants, an 8-bit occupancy code is used, where "1" represents a non-empty sub-cube and "0" represents an empty sub-cube. The distribution of 8-bit code will be predicted and sent into an arithmetic encoder for encoding as a binary file or decoding from a binary file.

4.1.2 Context Modeling

Context information can be extracted using sparse convolution and attention mechanisms, with the former commonly used in voxel-based methods and the latter in octree-based methods. Sparse convolution can directly process unstructured voxel data without requiring prior assumptions, such as tree structures or squeeze structures. It effectively aggregates and embeds spatial information from local neighborhoods across multiple scales, making it well-suited for compressing point clouds with arbitrary distributions in 3D space. This is why it is frequently used in voxel representations. In contrast, octree-based models construct a context window that includes the current node's ancestor nodes, sibling nodes, or the ancestor nodes of its siblings and rely on the context window to estimate the distribution of coding nodes.

4.2 Typical Methods of Lossless Geometry Coding

4.2.1 Voxel-Based Coding

Non-Up-and-Down-Scaling An effective approach for voxel-based lossless geometry compression involves estimating the occupancy probability of each voxel

[49, 50]. The pioneering work by Nguyen et al. [51] introduced an innovative voxel-domain compression technique where neural networks directly process geometric information through convolutional operations. The point cloud is voxelized on a $2^n \times 2^n \times 2^n$ grid, and the blocks are encoded by the octree-based encoder within the voxel domain. Nguyen et al. [51] denoted occupied voxel v_i as:

$$v_i = \begin{cases} 1, & \text{if } i\text{th voxel is occupied,} \\ 0, & \text{otherwise.} \end{cases} \tag{4.1}$$

Then, the voxelized point cloud is encoded by a context-adaptive binary arithmetic coding method. The probability model $p(v)$ for a specific block v composed by $d \times d \times d$ voxels is factorized as $p(v_i \mid v_{i-1}, \ldots, v_1)$ over the voxel volume:

$$p(v) = \prod_{i=1}^{d^3} p(v_i \mid v_{i-1}, v_{i-2}, \ldots, v_1), \tag{4.2}$$

where $p(v_i \mid v_{i-1}, \ldots, v_1)$ is estimated by using VoxelDNN [51]. The VoxelDNN is trained by CE loss, which can be expressed as:

$$H(p, \hat{p}) = \mathbb{E}_{v \sim p(v)} \left[\sum_{i=1}^{d^3} - \log \hat{p}(v_i) \right]. \tag{4.3}$$

VoxelDNN dynamically divides the point cloud into hierarchical voxel regions according to data characteristics, employing octree-based structure to represent spatial subdivisions. Nevertheless, the method's overly detailed probabilistic modeling introduces substantial redundancies during reconstruction, causing prolonged computational durations that hinder real-world deployment despite its theoretical compression advantages.

Up-and-Down-Scaling Building upon the original VoxelDNN framework, Nguyen et al. developed MSVoxelDNN [52], implementing a hierarchical multi-scale approach for lossless point cloud geometry coding. The methodology begins by segmenting the point cloud into octree representations at varying resolutions, enabling higher-level octree nodes to capture broader structural information while lower-level nodes preserve finer geometric details. MSVoxelDNN employs a conditional grouping mechanism that partitions octree nodes at each scale into distinct clusters, allowing parallel prediction of voxel occupancy across groups. At the finest resolution level, the system utilizes the conventional VoxelDNN architecture for voxel occupancy encoding. For coarser scales, the model learns to estimate voxel occupancy probabilities through an inverse max-pooling operation that maps features from lower to higher scales. This multi-scale design significantly reduces computational overhead during decoding compared to the baseline VoxelDNN implementation.

Existing approaches predominantly rely on standard convolution operations, yet sparse convolution demonstrates superior efficacy within 3D voxel representations. Wang et al. [53] introduced SparsePCGC, employing a hierarchical framework combined with sparse convolutional networks for compressing point cloud data. This technique specifically targets positively occupied voxels (POVs) through sparse convolution operations, effectively minimizing computational overhead. The hierarchical representation enables efficient compression of probable positively occupied voxels (P-POVs) by exploiting both inter-scale and intra-scale relationships. The neural network architecture, built upon sparse convolution principles, predicts occupancy probabilities through either single-phase cross-scale analysis or multi-phase neighbor-scale examination. This solution achieves cutting-edge results in lossless coding for both dense object models and sparse LiDAR datasets, while preserving computational efficiency. Furthermore, UniPCGC [32] enhances the original grouping strategy by implementing an adaptive nonuniform grouping mechanism, thereby improving reference information accessibility and boosting compression performance particularly for dense point cloud objects [54].

4.2.2 Octree-Based Coding

Octree structures provide an optimized approach for encoding geometric information in point clouds by efficiently organizing spatial coordinates within hierarchical nodes. Conventional point cloud coding standards have long employed this octree representation scheme for geometry encoding. More recently, novel deep learning approaches [30, 55–57] leveraging octree-based methodologies have demonstrated significant improvements in compression efficiency. This hierarchical data organization enables effective representation of 3D point cloud geometry while maintaining compact storage requirements. When the predicted probability distribution $\mathbb{E}_{\mathbf{x}\sim P}\left[-\log_2 Q(\mathbf{x})\right]$ better approximates the true distribution, the resulting bitrate approaches its theoretical minimum $\mathbb{E}_{\mathbf{x}\sim P}\left[-\log_2 P(\mathbf{x})\right]$ more precisely. Unlike conventional approaches that rely on handcrafted features for probability estimation, deep learning techniques offer superior performance advantages.

OctSqueeze The core principle of these methods is to predict the likelihood of occupancy of octree nodes that represent the geometry of point clouds and then perform lossless coding by arithmetic encoder, which requires for each octree node a distribution predicting the probability of all possible occupancy values. These methods, also called entropy models, can be several ways to utilize the contexts in the octree. When the predicted probability distribution $\mathbb{E}_{\mathbf{x}\sim P}\left[-\log_2 Q(\mathbf{x})\right]$ better approximates the true distribution, the resulting bitrate approaches its theoretical minimum $\mathbb{E}_{\mathbf{x}\sim P}\left[-\log_2 P(\mathbf{x})\right]$ more precisely. Compared with traditional methods, which estimate the probability based on manual features, deep learning–based methods provide greater benefits. OctSqueeze [58] is the first learning-based deep octree entropy model. Its framework is shown in Fig. 4.1.

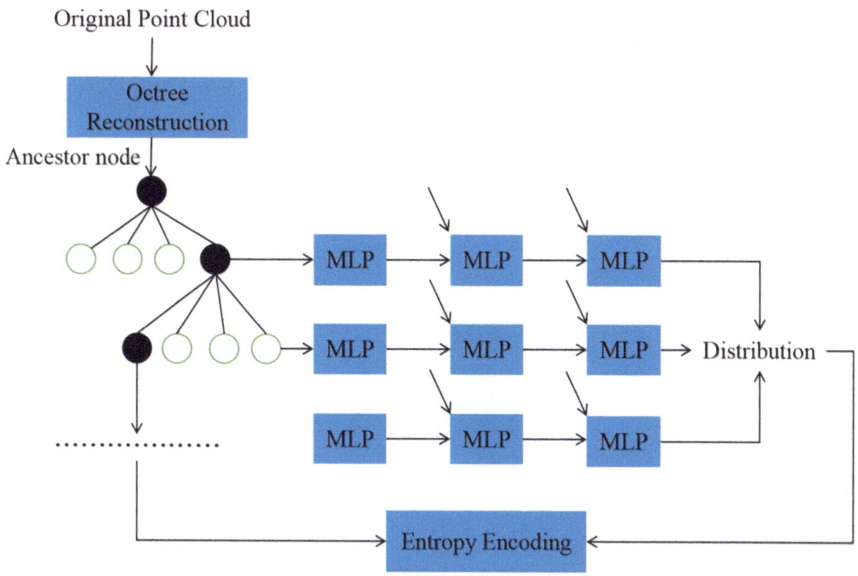

Fig. 4.1 The overall framework of OctSqueeze. Public-domain open-access image [55]

The point cloud is coded as octree after quantization, and the whole process is lossless except for this quantization. The tree-based entropy model predicts the occupancy of each node of the octree (occupancy code) by its bounding box coordinates, octant, level, and parent occupancy. The three-layer parental context features are aggregated by three shared MLPs. 256-dimensional vectors are output for each node in the current layer to estimate the probability distribution of its occupancy. Finally, serialized node occupancy is encoded losslessly by the arithmetic encoder. OctSqueeze achieves end-to-end encoding in real time. OctSqueeze was trained and tested on the SemanticKITTI [1] dataset [59]. Its performance is comparable with G-PCC [2] [60], which obtained a BD-rate of 10%–20% compared with Draco [61] and MPEG Anchor [62].

VoxelContext-Net VoxelContext-Net [63] predicts the occupancy using only the parent context in octree. It first extracts a local voxel representation with size as $9 \times 9 \times 9$ in parent LoD for each node and employs a 3D convolution network to predict occupancy probabilities. In addition, they propose a coordinate refinement module (CRM) for the post-process at the decoder side. While the approaches mentioned above maintain reasonable complexity, they fail to leverage the already decoded context within the current Level of Octree, which restricts their compression performance.

[1] https://semantic-kitti.org/.

[2] MPEG TMC13 v14.

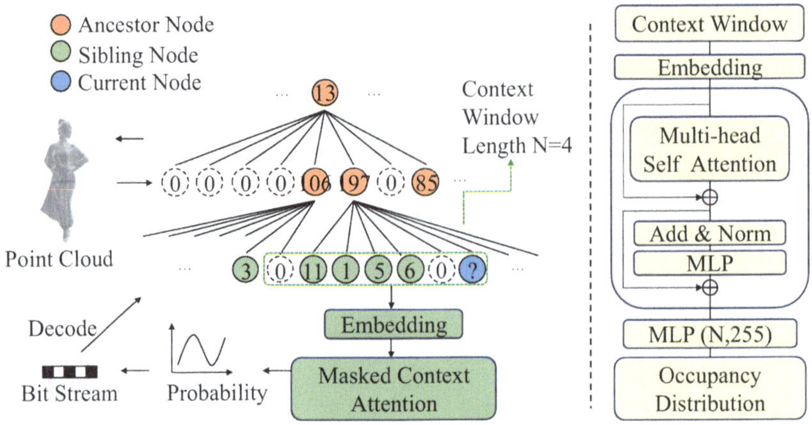

Fig. 4.2 The overall framework of OctAttention. Public-domain open-access image [30]

OctAttention Fu et al. [30] noticed this problem and argued that the scale of contexts in the local voxel representation is limited as octree depth increases. They proposed a method called OctAttention to take advantage of the context in the current context window, also known as the sibling node in the octree. As shown in Fig. 4.2, they gather information from $N - 1$ encoded siblings and their ancestor nodes in a fully auto-regressive manner by a context window and apply the self-attention mechanism to point cloud coding. OctAttention [30] factorizes estimated occupancy distribution $Q(\mathbf{x})$ as:

$$Q(\mathbf{x}) = \prod_i q_i \left(x_i \mid \boldsymbol{f}_{i-N+1}, \ldots, \boldsymbol{f}_k, \ldots, \boldsymbol{f}_i; \mathbf{w}\right), \tag{4.4}$$

in this formula, x_i is the occupancy symbol of the currently encoding node, ranging from 1 to 255 in the formula (4.4), with possible values spanning from 1 to 255, composed as high-dimensional vector $\boldsymbol{f}_k = [\boldsymbol{h}_k^{(0)}, \boldsymbol{h}_k^{(1)}, \boldsymbol{h}_k^{(2)}, \ldots, \boldsymbol{h}_k^{(K-1)}]$, combines the embedded characteristics of nodes. These features are determined by encoding their respective occupancy states, hierarchical levels, and spatial positions within the octant structure. Here, $\mathbf{w}$ refers to the learnable parameters of the context prediction model. It is important to highlight that $\boldsymbol{f}_i$ captures the feature representation of the current processing node, whose depth and octant position are known quantities during the decoding phase. The associated loss function, as presented in [30], can be mathematically expressed as:

$$\ell = -\sum_i \log q_i \left(x_i \mid \boldsymbol{f}; \mathbf{w}\right). \tag{4.5}$$

They also proposed a masking operation to speed up encoding and alleviate the time-consuming drawbacks of autoregression. OctAttention can acquire contextual information from more than 1000 sibling nodes and their parent nodes. However, the autoregressive context model greatly increases the decoding complexity. Many following methods focus on tackling this complexity problem caused by the autoregressive scheme.

Octformer Octformer [64] directly replaces the mask window in an autoregressive scheme with non-overlapping context windows to create octree node sequences. It then shares the results of a multihead self-attention operation across this sequence of nodes. In this way, sibling nodes are unavailable; therefore, only the ancestor nodes are utilized as context for coding. This method significantly accelerates the decoding speed, as one context window only takes one-time coding. However, the loss of sibling nodes results in a performance drop.

EHEM EHEM [65] introduces the checkerboard-like coding strategy, where half of the nodes are coded based on ancestor features and the rest are coded based on ancestor and former coded sibling features. This is quite similar to the checkerboard strategy [66] in image compression. This method balances the speed and performance, as one context window only takes two times coding, and half of the octree nodes' context is enriched with neighboring nodes.

ECM-OPCC ECM-OPCC [67] further expands the two-stage coding strategy to n-stage. The context window is evenly divided into n parts in a cross-checkerboard way, one context window takes n times coding, but node context is enriched more. This provides an option as a trade-off between coding speed and performance. The differences among OctAttention, Octformer, EHEM, and ECM-OPCC are shown in Fig. 4.3.

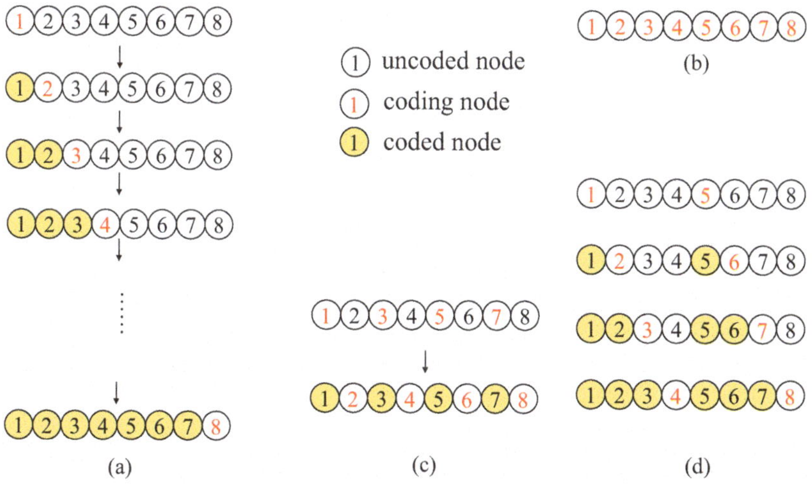

Fig. 4.3 Coding strategies of different methods. (**a**) OctAttention [30]. (**b**) Octformer [64]. (**c**) EHEM [65]. (**d**) ECM-OPCC [67], 4-stage. Source: Author

4.3 Overview of Lossy Geometry Coding

While lossless coding ensures that the original data can be perfectly reconstructed, it usually struggles to significantly reduce the data size, resulting in higher-bandwidth demands. In contrast, lossy coding reduces data size by sacrificing some precision and allows for flexible bitrate adjustment depending on the tolerable level of distortion, making it better suited for bandwidth-constrained scenarios. As a result, lossy coding has become an important method for substantially reducing point cloud data size while maintaining an acceptable quality of the reconstructed data [68–71].

The compression of static point clouds shares a similar framework with traditional image compression, involving three key steps: transformation, quantization, and entropy coding. In learning-based methods, the transformation is constructed by the deep network. Following this, quantization maps continuous values to discrete ones, reducing precision to achieve higher compression rates. Finally, entropy coding leverages the statistical distribution of the quantized data to further compress it, achieving a more efficient representation. Although this compression framework is widely applied to both point clouds and images, the 3D structure and spatial characteristics of point clouds introduce unique challenges that make point cloud coding a more complex problem.

4.4 Typical Methods of Lossy Geometry Coding

4.4.1 Point-Based Coding

Pcc_geo_cnn_v2 The pcc_geo_cnn_v2 framework, introduced in the work of Quach et al. [72], provides an in-depth exploration of advanced techniques for PCGC. Building upon the foundational architecture, this approach incorporates several key innovations to optimize compression performance. Notably, the system employs a scale hyperprior model to enhance entropy coding efficiency while utilizing deeper transformation layers for improved feature extraction. A specially calibrated balancing weight is integrated into the focal loss function to better handle imbalanced data distributions. The methodology further improves reconstruction quality through novel thresholding techniques during the decoding phase, complemented by a progressive model training strategy that sequentially refines network parameters. These combined advancements demonstrate significant improvements in both compression ratios and reconstruction fidelity compared to conventional approaches.

DALGC As the first autoencoder-based point cloud coding method that processes points, this approach demonstrates adaptation to unfamiliar media contents and formats, while maintaining competitive performance. The compression architecture [73] can be formulated as:

$$x' = D(Q(E(S(x)))), \tag{4.6}$$

where x is the original point cloud. x' represents the reconstructed point cloud in the decoder. S is a sampling layer [74], which is adopted to achieve the down-sampling step. In contrast to random sampling, the point set exhibits a more uniform point density, thereby preserving the shape characteristics of the original object more effectively. E is an encoder, Q is quantization approach, and D is decoder model. The encoder is employed for PointNet [75] to learn the compressive representation, while the decoder utilizes a fully connected layer to reconstruct the compressed point cloud representation. The quantization method employed in [73] is identical to the one utilized in [76], effectively reducing the redundancy significantly. Similar to learned image compression, rate and distortion are a trade-off. Entropy rate estimation is highly dependent on the actual probability model of quantized latent representation. The distortion is measured by the Chamfer distance, which effectively represents the reconstruction error. In summary, the rate–distortion loss function is shown as:

$$L\left[f_e, f_d, p_{\hat{z}}\right] = \lambda \mathbb{E}\left[d_{CH}(S1, S2)\right] + \mathbb{E}\left[-\log_2 p_{\hat{z}}\right], \tag{4.7}$$

where f_e represents the nonlinear transformation of the encoder, f_d represents the nonlinear transformation of the decoder, $p_{\hat{z}}$ represents the estimated probability model, λ is the hyperparameter aiming to control the RD loss, and d_{CH} denotes the Chamfer distance function. The proposed approach exhibits improved coding efficiency compared to existing codecs. It outperforms TMC13 and achieves an average BD-rate gain of 73.15%.

NGS On the basis of [73, 77] designs a three-step neural graph sampling (NGS) method. The architecture of the NGS method is shown in Fig. 4.4. First, the local graph for each point is constructed using its K nearest neighbors based on Euclidean distance. By aggregating the local geometric structure features and attribute features of the neighboring points, the KNN graph attributes and spatial features are derived for feature embedding. Second, a dynamic filter [78] is applied to each local graph to adaptively extract latent representations in the feature domain. Finally, to reduce redundant information in the point cloud KNN graph, a subset of points is selected to represent the input points. To minimize computational complexity, attention-based

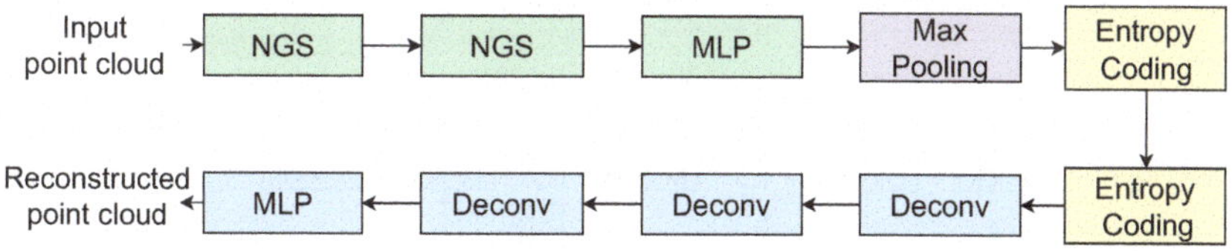

Fig. 4.4 The framework of three-step NGS. ©2021 IEEE. Reprinted, with permission, from Ref. [77]

pooling [79] is utilized, with the pooling output formulated as:

$$Q = \text{softmax}\left(\omega P^T\right). \tag{4.8}$$

The method surpasses the state-of-the-art point-based coding methods and achieves shorter coding time.

D-DPCC Point-based methods [80] handling interpret the point cloud as a collection of individual points, rather than a binary occupancy indication across a voxel grid. D-DPCC [81] adopts autoencoder fashion. The compression pipeline is shown in Fig. 4.5. Different from [73, 77], D-DPCC focuses on preserving local density information in order to represent point cloud local details. Within the encoder, the local geometry and density information is represented through three distinct embeddings: an embedding for density, one for local position, and another for ancestral relations. Thus, the encoder is called density-preserving encoder. Three embeddings are calculated to capture the geometry and density. The density embedding captures the number of points in the collapsed point set by using MLPs to map the down-sampling factor to a compact embedding. Secondly, the spatial distribution of the collapsed point set is captured by the local position embedding. As the local density and geometry are being calculated, it is essential to convey this information from earlier stages without significantly increasing the rate cost. Therefore, the point transformer layer [82] is used to combine the features from the earlier stage.

Traditionally, up-sampling methods at the decoder side have utilized multi-branch MLP architectures for feature augmentation. However, this method frequently results in the unwanted artifact of clustered points because of feature replication. To address this limitation, a new and effective operator known as sub-point convolution has been introduced, inspired by the sub-pixel convolution technique introduced in [83]. The approach addresses the issue of feature replication by first dividing the input feature into U groups. A convolutional layer is then applied to each group to expand the features into a space with high dimensions. To reshape the high-dimensional feature while preventing feature replication, a periodic shuffle operation is employed. The sub-point convolution plays a pivotal role in achieving this objective. In order to reconstruct the features with learnable scales, the authors introduce an up-sampling block that incorporates the adaptive scale concept based on the sub-point convolution. This adaptive scale enables us to tailor the feature reconstruction process according to the specific characteristics

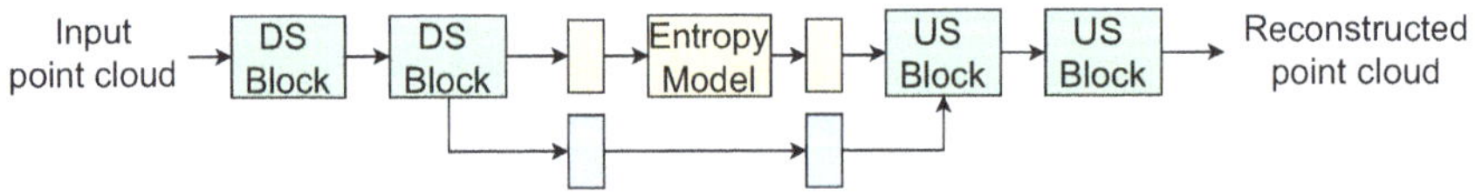

Fig. 4.5 The compression pipeline of D-DPCC. Public domain open access image [81]

of the point cloud data, resulting in more accurate and faithful representations. The work also adopts a rate–distortion loss function during training. Unlike [73, 77], a density term is incorporated to promote the restoration of local density, which is denoted as:

$$D_{den} = \sum_{s=0}^{S-1} \sum_{\hat{p} \in \hat{\mathcal{P}}_{s+1}} \frac{||\mathcal{C}(p)| - |\hat{\mathcal{C}}(\hat{p})|| + \gamma |\overline{\mathcal{C}(p)} - \overline{\mathcal{C}(\hat{p})}|}{\left|\hat{\mathcal{P}}_{s+1}\right|}. \tag{4.9}$$

The first term in the numerator of the equation calculates the difference in cardinality (number of points) between the two sets being compared. It quantifies the dissimilarity in the number of points between the ground truth set and the reconstructed point cloud. The second term computes the disparity between the average distances of all points in the sets to their respective central points, denoted as p and $\hat{p}$. This term captures the discrepancy in the average distances of points to their center points. The parameter γ represents the weight assigned to this term, controlling its influence on the overall loss.

Furthermore, to enhance density estimation, the authors incorporate an additional loss term for each stage s of the process. This loss term quantifies the discrepancy in cardinality (number of points) between the ground truth $\mathcal{P}_s$ and the reconstructed point cloud $\hat{p}_s$. It serves as a measure of the difference in the number of points between the original set and the reconstructed set at each stage. The specific formulation for this additional loss term is presented as:

$$D_{card} = \sum_{s=0}^{S-1} ||\mathcal{P}_s| - |\hat{\mathcal{P}}_s||. \tag{4.10}$$

In comparison to alternative approaches, the method outlined in [81] not only achieves the current best rate–distortion performance but also demonstrates superior accuracy in reconstructing local density.

ADL-PCC ADL-PCC [84] serves as a technical contribution to the MPEG standardization process, announcing the open-source implementation of a deep learning–driven PCGC framework. This development aligns with MPEG's ongoing Point Cloud Coding standardization efforts, particularly in advancing data-driven compression methodologies. The proposed system operates by dividing the point cloud into volumetric segments, then dynamically choosing the optimal neural compression model for each individual block. This adaptive selection mechanism enhances coding efficiency by matching model capabilities with local geometric properties. The architectural overview of ADL-PCC [84] is illustrated in Fig. 4.6 and the loss function can be described as:

$$\begin{aligned} &\text{Best DL mode } = \\ &= \underset{i \in \text{Models}}{\arg\min} \left(D_{MSE} \left(\text{inPC}, \ \text{recPC } C_i\right) + \lambda_{\text{mode}} \times R_i \right), \end{aligned} \tag{4.11}$$

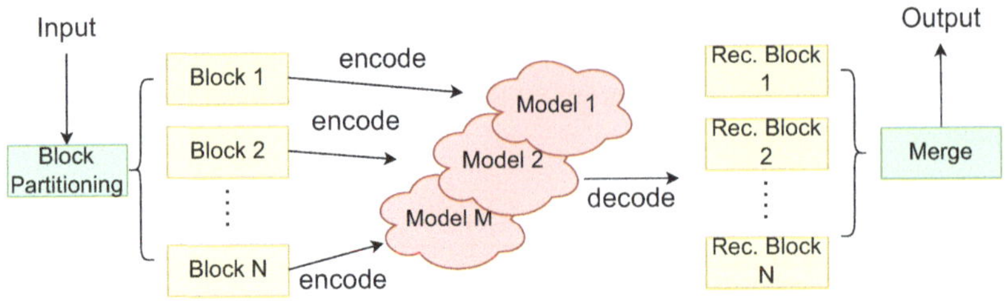

Fig. 4.6 The structure of ADL-PCC for lossy coding, ©2020 IEEE. Reprinted, with permission, from Ref. [84]

where inPC represents the input data block, recPC_i denotes its reconstructed version obtained using deep learning compression model i. The term D_{MSE} quantifies reconstruction error through MSE, R_i measures the required bitrate, and λ_{mode} serves as a balancing coefficient between these competing objectives. Extensive testing has shown that very low values of λ_{mode} yield better performance, indicating that distortion tends to dominate.

For adjusting Rate–Distortion (RD) performance, a conventional formulation utilizing a Lagrangian multiplier, λ_{train}, is employed for the training loss function:

$$\text{Loss Function} = \text{Distortion} + \lambda_{\text{Train}} \times \text{Coding rate}. \tag{4.12}$$

Within this framework, the study in [84] employs Binary Cross Entropy (BCE) as its distortion metric, a widely adopted measure for assessing prediction accuracy in binary classification scenarios. The BCE formulation can be expressed as:

$$BCE(v, u) = \begin{cases} -\log v, & u = 1 \\ -\log(1 - v), & u = 0 \end{cases} \tag{4.13}$$

where the variable u corresponds to the ground truth binary value of each voxel, while v indicates the predicted probability of voxel occupancy in the reconstruction. Due to the inherent class imbalance, the aggregation of losses across a complete block results in voxels with 0 labels contributing disproportionately to the overall loss, consequently causing suboptimal reconstruction quality for voxels marked as 1. To address this class imbalance, a variant of Binary Cross Entropy (BCE), known as Focal Loss (FL), is employed [84]. FL introduces weighting factors to mitigate this issue, and its loss function is defined as:

$$FL(v, u) = \begin{cases} -\alpha(1 - v)^{\gamma} \log v, & u = 1 \\ -(1 - \alpha)v^{\gamma} \log(1 - v), & u = 0 \end{cases} \tag{4.14}$$

where the coefficients γ and α serve as tunable hyperparameters that modulate the model's characteristics and ultimately impact the rate–distortion trade-off.

These parameters can be fine-tuned to optimize the compression efficiency while maintaining reconstruction quality.

4.4.2 *Voxel-Based Coding*

The advancement in point cloud geometry compression techniques has seen widespread adoption of voxel-based approaches for processing geometric data. This methodology demonstrates superior efficiency when handling densely populated point clouds, in contrast to alternative point-based compression strategies. The voxel-based approach leverages structured grid representations to efficiently encode spatial information, making it particularly well-suited for scenarios involving high point densities. Its computational effectiveness and ability to preserve geometric fidelity in dense environments set it apart from point-centric compression techniques, which may struggle with similar data configurations. By utilizing volumetric partitioning, this method ensures robust compression performance while maintaining critical geometric details, establishing it as a preferred solution for applications requiring efficient processing of densely sampled point cloud datasets.

Pcc_geo_cnn_v1 The pcc_geo_cnn_v1 approach presents an innovative geometry compression framework for static point clouds that utilizes data-driven convolutional transforms combined with uniform quantization techniques. This methodology differs from VoxelDNN's approach by adopting convolutional transforms and quantization strategies typically employed in neural image compression systems. The framework incorporates a balancing parameter to optimize the compromise between compression rate and reconstruction quality. While conventional octree-based techniques often exhibit limited performance at lower bitrates, this solution demonstrates the capability to maintain high-quality reconstructions even under significant rate constraints. The underlying neural architecture, depicted in the referenced figure, implements a 3D convolutional autoencoder structure that simultaneously handles both analysis and synthesis transformations.

During decoding, the task is formulated as a binary classification problem to determine the presence or absence of each voxel grid point. The overall optimization objective combines rate and distortion through the loss function $\lambda D + R$ [85], where the distortion term D employs a focal loss formulation for the reconstructed point cloud, mathematically expressed as:

$$FL(\tilde{x}) = \sum_{z \in S} -\alpha_z \left(1 - p_z^t\right)^{\gamma} \log\left(p_z^t\right), \tag{4.15}$$

where p_z^t indicates whether point z is occupied, α and γ are the hyper-parameters of focal loss.

PCGCv1 Wang et al. [86] presented a new learning approach for PCGC framework called PCGCv1. The PCGC framework is achieved through the utilization of

DNN and a variational autoencoder. The compression process begins by voxelizing and partitioning the PCG into non-overlapping 3D cubes. The term PCG, in this work, specifically refers to the volumetric representation of point cloud geometry unless stated otherwise. By using a volumetric model for PCG, the framework is able to capture correlations between voxels in a 3D space. The proposed method demonstrates notable compression improvements for sparse point cloud data while preserving excellent performance characteristics at lower bitrate conditions for dense point clouds. These cubic segments are processed through multiple stacked 3D convolutional layers to derive compressed latent features. The framework's core building block utilizes a Voxception-ResNet (VRN) architecture, which effectively captures critical information for compact representation. Moreover, the implementation benefits from employing reduced-size convolutional kernels, which offer computational advantages through lower-complexity requirements. These compact kernels demand fewer parameters and computational resources compared to their larger counterparts, thereby enhancing the framework's overall efficiency and practical deployment feasibility.

To improve the modeling capability of conditional probabilities, the architecture integrates a hyperprior mechanism that has become standard in neural image compression systems. Following prevalent practices in the field, the researchers employ a Lagrangian-based loss function during model training to achieve optimal balance between compression rate and reconstruction quality [86], formulated as:

$$J_{\text{loss}} = R + \lambda D, \tag{4.16}$$

where the λ is the hyper-parameter that balances the trade-off between the rate and distortion in the compression process in the loss function (4.16). By adjusting the value of λ, it can prioritize either achieving a higher compression rate or maintaining a higher level of distortion quality in the compressed point cloud representation [86]. The rate consumption in the framework is determined by the compressed representations of the point cloud, denoted as $\hat{y}$ and $\hat{z}$. The rate approximation of $\hat{y}$ and $\hat{z}$ in the framework [86] can be expressed as:

$$R_{\hat{y}} = \sum_i -\log_2\left(p_{\hat{y}_i|\hat{z}_i}\left(\hat{y}_i \mid \hat{z}_i\right)\right), \tag{4.17}$$

$$R_{\hat{z}} = \sum_i -\log_2\left(p_{\hat{z}_i|\psi^{(i)}}\left(\hat{z}_i \mid \psi^{(i)}\right)\right). \tag{4.18}$$

The rate–distortion trade-off seeks to optimize compression efficiency while maintaining reconstruction quality through careful parameter tuning. Distortion evaluation involves analyzing decoded voxel classifications across volumetric units. In point cloud representations, active voxels signify occupied spatial positions, conventionally encoded using normalized values ([0,1]). Occupancy is marked by a binary "1" or "TRUE" state, while "0" or "FALSE" denotes void space. Voxel classification depends on its numerical value—values exceeding a threshold are considered occupied (1), otherwise unoccupied (0). The training process incorporates Weighted Binary Cross-Entropy (WBCE) loss combined with dynamic threshold adjustment. This adaptive thresholding approach [86] is formulated as:

$$D_{\text{WBCE}} = \frac{1}{N_o}\sum^{N_o} - \log p_{\tilde{x}_o} + \alpha\frac{1}{N_n}\sum^{N_n} - \log\left(1 - p_{\tilde{x}_n}\right). \tag{4.19}$$

During the decoding phase, the reconstructed voxel values x in each volumetric block are represented as floating-point numbers between 0 and 1. To convert these continuous values into discrete binary classifications (1 for occupied, 0 for empty), an intelligent thresholding approach is introduced. This technique dynamically determines the classification boundary based on the density of occupied points in the original block, utilizing precomputed occupancy statistics stored as auxiliary data as shown in Fig. 4.7.

PCGCv2 Building upon the foundation established in [86], the subsequent work [87] presents further advancements in point cloud geometry compression. The proposed system utilizes a sparse convolution-based auto-encoder architecture specifically designed for compressing and reconstructing point cloud data, with the detailed structure illustrated in Fig. 4.8. This approach implements a progressive resampling mechanism to achieve hierarchical reconstruction of 3D point cloud

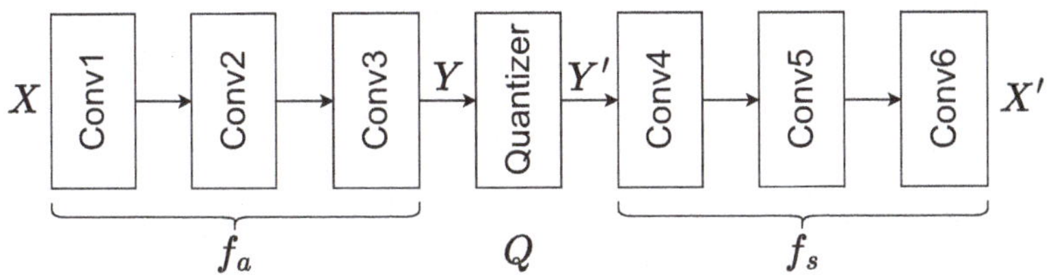

Fig. 4.7 The network architecture of pcc_geo_cnn_v1. Public-domain open-access image [85]

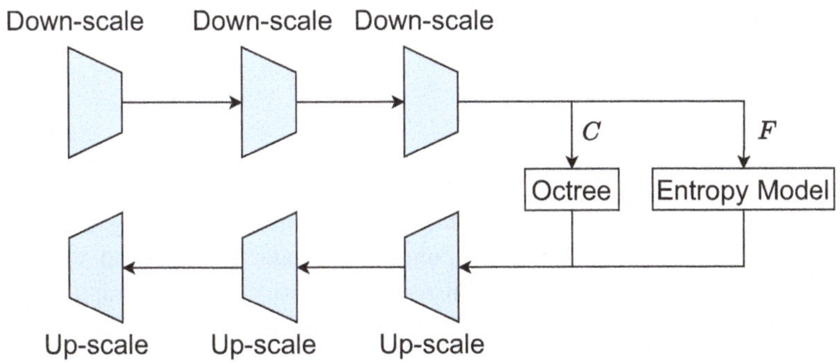

Fig. 4.8 The compression framework for multiscale point cloud geometry compression. Public-domain open-access image [87]

geometry. The auto-encoder incorporates an Inception-Residual Network as its fundamental building block for effective feature extraction. On the decoding side, the method adopts a multi-level refinement strategy that progresses from coarse to fine details to accurately restore geometric information. This is accomplished through a voxel classification process that eliminates incorrect voxels while preserving authentic occupied ones. The framework incorporates rate–distortion optimization techniques. For voxel occupancy determination, a binary classification approach is implemented, where sparse convolutional layers calculate occupancy probabilities after several convolution operations. The BCE loss function is formulated as:

$$L_{\mathrm{BCE}} = \frac{1}{N}\sum_{i} -\left(x_i \log\left(p_i\right) + \left(1 - x_i\right)\log\left(1 - p_i\right)\right), \tag{4.20}$$

where represents the ground truth occupancy status of each voxel, while x_i denotes the predicted occupancy probability p_i in the study [87]. This approach achieves substantial computational efficiency improvements while maintaining accuracy. The probability-based representation enables more efficient processing compared to traditional binary classification methods, as it better captures the underlying spatial relationships in point cloud data. Experiments demonstrate that this probabilistic modeling leads to faster convergence during training and reduced memory requirements during inference, making it particularly suitable for real-time applications.

SparsePCGC The SparsePCGC [53] exhibits superior performance in both lossless and lossy coding when applied to a diverse range of datasets, encompassing dense surface and sparse LiDAR point clouds. The researchers behind SparsePCGCv2 have enhanced the implementation of its predecessor while incorporating a novel neighborhood attention mechanism utilizing K-Nearest Neighbors (KNNs) for improved point aggregation. This approach demonstrates superior efficiency compared to conventional convolutional networks when processing sparse LiDAR datasets. The newly developed attention layer has been seamlessly integrated into the existing multi-scale and multi-stage architecture of SparsePCGC, maintaining the framework's structural integrity while boosting performance.

4.4.3 Hybrid-Based Coding

Most discussions on MPEG on learning-based point cloud coding (PCC) have focused on methods targeting solid point cloud data, typically up to 11 bits. The method pcc_geo_cnn_v2 [72] utilizes a hyperprior model to capture spatial correlations, while ADL-PCC [84] applies different models based on the content being encoded. PCGCv2 [87] employs sparse CNNs, which are particularly well-suited for feature analysis and aggregation of point cloud geometry. All these methods rely on voxelized point clouds processed by CNN-based backbones. While they perform well on dense point clouds, they struggle with sparser data.

GRASP-Net In contrast, Pang et al. [88] introduced an architecture that integrates both MLP and CNN backbones. Unlike CNN-based method, which implicitly assumes point cloud smoothness, the MLP backbone excels at capturing intricate geometric details, especially those represented as residuals. It leverages the MLP backbone in the proposed GRASP-Net to handle sparse point clouds more effectively, such as those with up to 12-bit precision. Additionally, previous MPEG discussions have explored post-processing techniques to refine decoded point clouds, enhancing lossy point cloud geometry compression without requiring additional coded information. However, the proposed method seeks to improve quality by incorporating side information.

The compression pipeline in [88] begins with a lossless coding of the downsampled point cloud version through G-PCC. Subsequently, geometric discrepancies between this simplified representation and the original point cloud are captured as per-point attributes using a PointNet [75] architecture. These residual features undergo encoding via sparse convolutional neural networks. During reconstruction, the decoder initially restores the base point cloud, then processes the encoded sparse features through corresponding sparse CNNs. The geometric offsets are subsequently reconstructed through fully connected layers and combined with the base point cloud to produce the final output. The complete encoding and decoding workflows are illustrated in Fig. 4.9. To perform training, we adopt the following loss function as:

$$L = D + \lambda R, \tag{4.21}$$

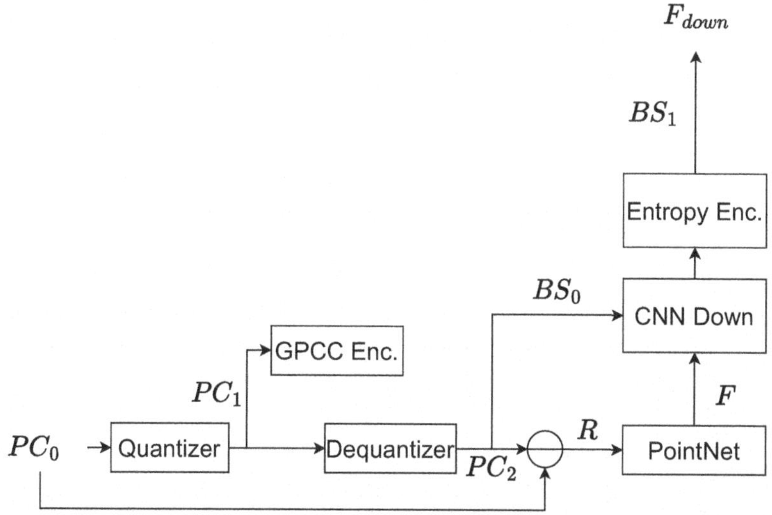

Fig. 4.9 The encoder structure of GRASP-Net for lossy coding. Public-domain open-access image [88]

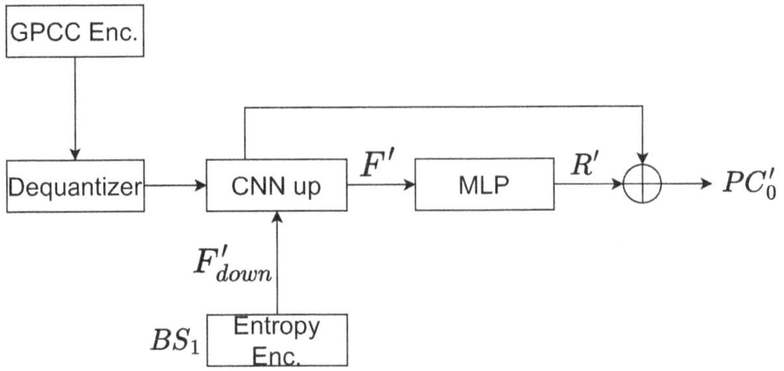

Fig. 4.10 The decoder structure of GRASP-Net for lossy coding. Public-domain open-access image [88]

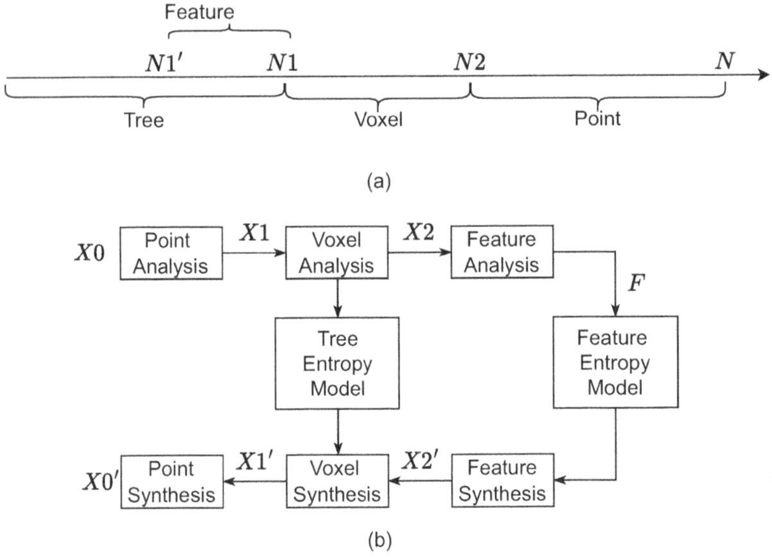

Fig. 4.11 (**a**) Tree, voxel, and point in bit-depth distribution, (**b**) Architecture of the PIVOT-Net. Public-domain open-access image [89]

where the distortion metric D represents the Chamfer distance between the reconstructed point set PC_0' and its source counterpart PC_0, with R denoting the predicted compression rate generated by the factorized probability model as shown in Fig. 4.10.

PIVOT-Net Furthermore, PIVOT-Net [89] unifies the three data formats—point, voxel, and tree—within a single point cloud framework. The distribution characteristics of point clouds are different under different bit depths, as shown in Fig. 4.11a. The point density varies significantly with bit-depth representation—lower bit depths yield more concentrated point distributions, whereas higher bit depths produce increasingly dispersed spatial arrangements. This characteristic directly impacts compression efficiency, as the data redundancy patterns differ substantially between these two regimes. For low-bit depth point clouds, tree-based encoding methods like octree can efficiently encode partition information. For medium-bit depth point clouds, voxel-based convolutional neural networks are suitable for extracting geometry features. For sparse, high-bit depth point clouds, point-based neural networks are effective at extracting local geometry features. The approach advances voxel-based processing through two novel components: a spatially adaptive up-sampling mechanism and a refined voxel transformer architecture. This dual-component system enables efficient compression of point cloud data across multiple bit-depth resolutions by capitalizing on voxel representation benefits. The developed PIVOT-Net demonstrates superior compression capabilities compared to existing methods when tested on diverse real-world point cloud datasets. The spatially adaptive up-sampling preserves structural details during reconstruction, while the optimized transformer architecture effectively models long-range spatial relationships in the voxel domain, contributing to the framework's exceptional performance.

Its encoder and decoder consist of three parts, as shown in Fig. 4.11b.

- **Point analysis network.** This neural architecture adopts a point-based approach comparable to PointNet++. It first generates a coarse point cloud representation $X1$ through uniform quantization, followed by geometric feature extraction for each point using PointNet's framework. This corresponds to encoding the last few bits, i.e., the bit range $[n2, n]$.
- **Voxel analysis network.** This is a sparse convolutional network used to down-sample and aggregate features of $X1$. It downsamples $X1$ by a factor to obtain $X2$ and extracts features of $X2$. This corresponds to encoding the bit range $[n1, n2]$.
- **Feature analysis network.** This is also a sparse convolutional network used to further down-sample the feature maps of $X2$. This corresponds to encoding the bit range $[n1', n1]$.
- **Tree-based encoder.** This part is responsible for lossless encoding of the occupancy state information of $X2$, corresponding to the bit range $[0, n1]$.

In summary, the three frameworks of PIVOT-Net adopt different encoding strategies for point clouds with different bit depth distribution characteristics, thereby achieving more efficient point cloud coding.

4.5 Comparative Analysis

A comparative analysis of various approaches for point cloud coding will be introduced in this section, encompassing both lossless and lossy techniques across different structural representations including point-based, voxel-based, octree-based, and hybrid configurations. The evaluation framework examines several key performance metrics: computational complexity during both encoding and decoding phases, compression efficiency measured by bitrate requirements for lossless methods, and the critical rate–distortion trade-off characteristic of lossy coding schemes. The analysis provides insights into the relative strengths and limitations of each methodology, offering practical guidance for selecting appropriate compression strategies based on specific application requirements and system constraints. Special attention is given to the distinctive characteristics of each representation format and their implications for compression performance across different point cloud datasets and usage scenarios.

Lossless Coding In voxel-based methods, it is found that VoxelDNN has excellent compression performance. However, its decoding time is quite long due to its autoregressive mechanism. On the other hand, MSVoxelDNN addresses the complex decoding issues associated with autoregression through a multi-scale approach, but its compression performance is not as good as that of VoxelDNN. In contrast, Lossless SparsePCGC achieves excellent performance in lossless point cloud coding while maintaining low computational complexity by utilizing an up-down-sampling mechanism, and an efficient grouping strategy, thus establishing its status as the SOTA. The summary of voxel-based lossless coding is shown in Table 4.1.

These novel learning-based PCGC techniques focus on enhancing compression efficiency and computational performance through sophisticated modeling of spatial relationships and hierarchical structures within octree representations. Various innovative methods have emerged in this domain: VoxelContext-Net leverages voxel-based contextual information for octree compression, OctAttention introduces an advanced entropy model with extensive contextual awareness incorporating both sibling and ancestral relationships, OctFormer implements non-overlapping context windows to create efficient node sequences that accelerate processing, EHEM develops a multi-level attention mechanism with grouped context architecture to enable parallel decoding capabilities, and ECM-OPCC utilizes a multi-stage grouped context framework to optimize the trade-off between compression quality and processing speed. Collectively, these cutting-edge deep learning methodologies showcase promising developments in the field of point cloud coding technology. The key characteristics of octree-based lossless coding approaches are summarized in Table 4.2.

Table 4.1 Summary of contributions of voxel-based lossless coding methods

Method name	Published in	Highlight
VoxelDNN [51]	ICASSP 21	Devises the first voxel-based lossless point cloud coding network, based on auto-regression.
MSVoxelDNN [52]	ICMEW 21	Improves VoxelDNN with multi-scale for reduction of decoding time.
SparsePCGC [53]	TPAMI 22	Designs the lossless point cloud coding network with group strategy and multi-scale.

Source: Author

Table 4.2 Summary of contributions of octree-based lossless coding methods

Method name	Published in	Highlight
OctSqueeze [58]	CVPR 20	Specifically designs the pioneering neural network architecture for octree-structured LiDAR point cloud coding.
VoxelContext-Net [63]	CVPR 21	Leverages spatial correlations within voxelized representations to efficiently encode octree-organized data, achieving superior compression ratios.
OctAttention [30]	AAAI 22	Incorporates an advanced conditional probability model featuring an expansive receptive field, which simultaneously captures both hierarchical dependencies and spatial relationships within the octree structure.
OctFormer [64]	AAAI 23	Utilizes non-overlapping context windows to construct octree node sequence, significantly reducing computation time.
EHEM [65]	CVPR 23	Devises a hierarchical attention model and a grouped context structure that enables parallel decoding and time saving.
ECM-OPCC [67]	ICASSP 24	Devises a n-stage grouped context structure to balance between compression performance and speed.

Source: Author

Lossy Coding Early point-based methods utilized structures similar to PointNet or PointNet++ for transformations. They achieved relatively good performance on small point clouds in ShapeNet.[3] However, the PointNet-based structures perform poorly on large-scale point clouds, resulting in longer encoding and decoding times and higher levels of distortion. Additionally, entropy models struggle to learn effective information from unstructured data, making it difficult to achieve a lower compression rate. However, point-based methods remain a milestone, opening a new chapter in deep point cloud coding. The summary of point-based lossy coding is shown in Table 4.3.

Voxel-based point cloud coding methods perform quite well on large-scale dense point clouds. Before sparse convolutions are used, their computational efficiency and performance are low. However, after the use of sparse convolutions, both computational efficiency and performance improve. PCGCv1 and PCC_Geo_CNN_v1 do not use sparse convolutions, resulting in low efficiency, while PCGCv2 and SparsePCGC (Lossy) use sparse convolutions, achieving good compression results for large-scale dense point clouds. The summary of voxel-based lossy coding is shown in Table 4.4.

Hybrid-based approaches integrate diverse methodologies by fusing tree-based, voxel-based, and point-based techniques into unified frameworks. GRASP-Net

[3] https://shapenet.org/.

Table 4.3 Summary of contributions of point-based lossy coding methods

Method name	Published in	Highlight
DALGC [73]	arXiv 19	Designs the first point-based point cloud coding network.
ADL-PCC [84]	JSTSP 20	Partitions a frame of the point cloud as some blocks, and finds the most suitable model for compression.
NGS [77]	ICIP 21	Utilizes K-NN for feature extraction and hyper-prior entropy model.
D-DPCC [81]	CVPR 22	Applies up-sampling and down-sampling as transformation, and define a D3-PSNR.

Source: Author

Table 4.4 Summary of contributions of voxel-based lossy coding methods

Method name	Published in	Highlight
pcc_geo_cnn [72, 85]	ICIP 19 / IMSPW 20	Jointly optimizes the bit-rate and distortion, and achieves efficient point cloud coding using unified quantization.
PCGCv1 [86]	TCSVT 21	Pioneers the application of hierarchical Variational AutoEncoder architectures employing stacked Deep Neural Networks for effective PCGC.
PCGCv2 [87]	DCC 21	Firstly Introduces sparse convolution in point cloud coding, which achieves a significant RD performance improvement.
SparsePCGC [53]	TPAMI 23	Introduces up-sampling and down-sampling strategies to lossy coding, with different distortion scales.

Source: Author

employs a dual-layer architecture where the foundational layer handles coarse point cloud coding, while the refinement layer leverages the structural coherence of this coarse representation to enhance geometric fidelity through sparse convolutional networks. Building upon this foundation, PIVOT-Net extends the framework by adaptively learning optimal combinations of tree, voxel, and point processing techniques, demonstrating superior performance across both dense and sparse point cloud datasets. The comparative analysis of hybrid compression techniques is presented in Table 4.5.

Table 4.5 Summary of contributions of hybrid-based lossy coding methods

Method name	Published in	Highlight
GRASP-Net [88]	APCCPA 22	Proposes two layers to compress coarse and fined point cloud representation.
PIVOT-Net [89]	3DVC 24	Firstly introduces point, voxel, and tree as a unified point cloud coding framework.

Source: Author

4.6 Summary

Deep learning approaches for static point cloud coding continue to encounter significant obstacles. A primary concern involves the generalization capability across different data types—current evidence indicates voxel-based techniques excel with dense point clouds, whereas octree-based methods prove more effective for sparse datasets. Developing a unified deep learning framework that effectively accommodates both representation schemes presents an ongoing research challenge. However, deep learning provides fundamental support for PCGC technologies. As a key component in point cloud processing, static compression utilizes deep neural networks to efficiently encode geometric structures, laying the groundwork for subsequent applications like dynamic point cloud coding and real-time transmission. Through innovative voxelization representations, octree structures, and attention-based context modeling, this technology significantly enhances compression efficiency. Particularly in precision-demanding scenarios, deep PCGC demonstrates superior performance. Its core algorithms and theoretical frameworks have become essential references for international standardization bodies organizations, such as MPEG, when establishing point cloud coding standards. For readers who are interested in the related technologies of AI-based image and video coding, please refer to [89, 90].

Exercises

1. What are the different categories of end-to-end point cloud coding approaches? Analyze and contrast various deep learning–based point cloud coding techniques.
2. Describe how deep learning techniques can enhance the compression performance of point cloud data.
3. Compare and contrast conventional point cloud coding approaches with learning-based alternatives.
4. Outline the fundamental processing stages in lossy point cloud coding systems.
5. For voxel-based compression approaches, what objective function is typically optimized during training?
6. What factors contribute to the exclusive use of lossless coding in current octree-based methods?
7. Define the key terms: octant, occupancy status, and depth level within octree compression frameworks.
8. What benefits do combined compression strategies offer compared to single-approach methods?
9. Identify primary obstacles in neural network-based point cloud coding systems, particularly regarding sparse and dense point distributions.

10. Discuss how AI-driven coding techniques enhance visual quality in point clouds and explain their practical importance.

References

1. Y. Wu, L. Xie, S. Sun, W. Gao, Y. Yan, Adaptive intra period size for deep learning-based screen content video coding, in *2024 IEEE International Conference on Multimedia and Expo Workshops (ICMEW)* (IEEE, New York, 2024), pp. 1–6
2. H. Zheng, W. Gao, End-to-end rgb-d image compression via exploiting channel-modality redundancy, in *Proceedings of the AAAI Conference on Artificial Intelligence*, vol. 38(7) (2024), pp. 7562–7570
3. L. Tao, W. Gao, G. Li, C. Zhang, Adanic: towards practical neural image compression via dynamic transform routing, in *Proceedings of the IEEE/CVF International Conference on Computer Vision* (2023), pp. 16879–16888
4. Y. Wu, W. Gao, End-to-end lossless compression of high precision depth maps guided by pseudo-residual, in *2022 Data Compression Conference (DCC)* (IEEE, New York, 2022), pp. 489–489
5. Y. Wu, Z. Qi, H. Zheng, L. Tao, W. Gao, Deep image compression with latent optimization and piece-wise quantization approximation, in *Proceedings of the IEEE/CVF Conference on Computer Vision and Pattern Recognition* (2021), pp. 1926–1930
6. W. Gao, L. Tao, L. Zhou, D. Yang, X. Zhang, Z. Guo, Low-rate image compression with super-resolution learning, in *Proceedings of the IEEE/CVF Conference on Computer Vision and Pattern Recognition Workshops* (2020), pp. 154–155
7. W. Gao, S. Sun, H. Zheng, Y. Wu, H. Ye, Y. Zhang, Opendmc: an open-source library and performance evaluation for deep-learning-based multi-frame compression, in *Proceedings of the 31st ACM International Conference on Multimedia* (2023), pp. 9685–9688
8. Z. Yang, W. Gao, G. Li, Y. Yan, Sur-driven video coding rate control for jointly optimizing perceptual quality and buffer control. IEEE Trans. Image Process. **32**, 5451–5464 (2023)
9. F. Shen, Z. Cai, W. Gao, An efficient rate control algorithm for intra frame coding in avs3, in *2021 IEEE International Conference on Systems, Man, and Cybernetics (SMC)* (IEEE, New York, 2021), pp. 3164–3169
10. H. Yuan, W. Gao, J. Wang, Dynamic computational resource allocation for fast inter frame coding in video conferencing applications, in *2021 IEEE International Conference on Multimedia and Expo (ICME)* (IEEE, New York, 2021), pp. 1–6
11. W. Gao, Q. Jiang, R. Wang, S. Ma, G. Li, S. Kwong, Consistent quality oriented rate control in hevc via balancing intra and inter frame coding. IEEE Trans. Industr. Inform. **18**(3), 1594–1604 (2021)
12. H. Yuan, W. Gao, A new coding unit partitioning mode for screen content video coding, in *Proceedings of the 2021 5th International Conference on Digital Signal Processing* (2021), pp. 66–72
13. W. Gao, On the performance evaluation of state-of-the-art rate control algorithms for practical video coding and transmission systems, in *Proceedings of the 2020 4th International Conference on Video and Image Processing* (2020), pp. 179–185
14. W. Gao, S. Kwong, Q. Jiang, C.-K. Fong, P.H. Wong, W.Y. Yuen, Data-driven rate control for rate-distortion optimization in HEVC based on simplified effective initial QP learning. IEEE Trans. Broadcast. **65**(1), 94–108 (2018)
15. W. Gao, A multi-objective optimization perspective for joint consideration of video coding quality, in *2019 Asia-Pacific Signal and Information Processing Association Annual Summit and Conference (APSIPA ASC)* (IEEE, New York, 2019), pp. 986–991

16. W. Liu, W. Gao, X. Mu, Fast inter-frame motion prediction for compressed dynamic point cloud attribute enhancement, in *Proceedings of the AAAI Conference on Artificial Intelligence*, vol. 38(4) (2024), pp. 3720–3728
17. Z. Yang, W. Gao, X. Lu, Danet: density-adaptive network for geometry-based point cloud compression artifacts removal, in *2023 IEEE International Conference on Visual Communications and Image Processing (VCIP)* (IEEE, New York, 2023), pp. 1–5
18. X. Fan, G. Li, D. Li, Y. Ren, W. Gao, T.H. Li, Deep geometry post-processing for decompressed point clouds, in *2022 IEEE International Conference on Multimedia and Expo (ICME)* (IEEE, New York, 2022), pp. 1–6
19. X. Zhang, G. Liao, W. Gao, G. Li, Tdrnet: transformer-based dual-branch restoration network for geometry based point cloud compression artifacts, in *2022 IEEE International Conference on Multimedia and Expo (ICME)* (IEEE, New York, 2022), pp. 1–6
20. Z. Li, G. Li, T.H. Li, S. Liu, W. Gao, Semantic point cloud upsampling. IEEE Trans. Multimedia **25**, 3432–3442 (2022)
21. S. Fan, W. Gao, G. Li, Salient object detection for point clouds, in *European Conference on Computer Vision* (Springer, Berlin, 2022), pp. 1–19
22. S. Luo, W. Gao, A general framework for rotation invariant point cloud analysis, in *ICASSP 2024-2024 IEEE International Conference on Acoustics, Speech and Signal Processing (ICASSP)* (IEEE, New York, 2024), pp. 3665–3669
23. X. Lu, W. Gao, Attentivenet: Detecting small objects for lidar point clouds by attending to important points, in *2023 IEEE International Conference on Visual Communications and Image Processing (VCIP)* (IEEE, New York, 2023), pp. 1–5
24. Z. Pan, N. Zhang, W. Gao, S. Liu, G. Li, Less is more: label recommendation for weakly supervised point cloud semantic segmentation, in *Proceedings of the AAAI Conference on Artificial Intelligence*, vol. 38(5) (2024), pp. 4397–4405
25. Z. Pan, G. Liu, W. Gao, T.H. Li, Epcontrast: effective point-level contrastive learning for large-scale point cloud understanding, in *2024 IEEE International Conference on Multimedia and Expo (ICME)* (IEEE, New York, 2024), pp. 1–6
26. S. Fan, W. Gao, Screen-based 3d subjective experiment software, in *Proceedings of the 31st ACM International Conference on Multimedia* (2023), pp. 9672–9675
27. J. Wang, W. Gao, G. Li, Zoom to perceive better: no-reference point cloud quality assessment via exploring effective multiscale feature. IEEE Trans. Circuits Syst. Video Technol. **34**(7), 6334–6346 (2024)
28. Y. Zhang, W. Gao, G. Li, Openpointcloud-v2: A deep learning based open-source algorithm library of point cloud processing, in *Proceedings of the 1st International Workshop on Advances in Point Cloud Compression, Processing and Analysis* (2022), pp. 51–55
29. Z. Qi, H. Liu, W. Gao, Variable-rate point cloud compression with channel-wise entropy modeling, in *2025 Data Compression Conference (DCC)* (IEEE, New York, 2025)
30. C. Fu, G. Li, R. Song, W. Gao, S. Liu, Octattention: Octree-based large-scale contexts model for point cloud compression. arXiv preprint arXiv:2202.06028 (2022)
31. C. Zhang, W. Gao, Adadpcc: adaptive rate control and rate-distortion-complexity optimization for dynamic point cloud compression, in *Proceedings of the AAAI Conference on Artificial Intelligence* (2025)
32. K. Wang, W. Gao, Unipcgc: towards practical point cloud geometry compression via an efficient unified approach, in *Proceedings of the AAAI Conference on Artificial Intelligence* (2025)
33. K. Zheng, W. Gao, H. Zheng, Octree-based learned point cloud geometry compression: a lossy perspective, in *2025 Data Compression Conference (DCC)* (IEEE, New York, 2025)
34. H. Zheng, W. Gao, Z. Yu, T. Zhao, G. Li, Viewpcgc: view-guided learned point cloud geometry compression, in *Proceedings of the 32nd ACM International Conference on Multimedia* (2024), pp. 7152–7161
35. T. Qin, G. Li, W. Gao, S. Liu, Multi-grained point cloud geometry compression via dual-model prediction with extended octree. ACM Trans. Multimed. Comput. Commun. Appl. **20**(9), 1–30 (2024)

36. Y. Shao, W. Gao, S. Liu, G. Li, Advanced patch-based affine motion estimation for dynamic point cloud geometry compression. Sensors **24**(10), 3142 (2024)
37. Y. Shao, F. Song, W. Gao, S. Liu, G. Li, Texture-guided graph transform optimization for point cloud attribute compression. Appl. Sci. **14**(10), 4094 (2024)
38. Y. Shao, X. Yang, W. Gao, S. Liu, G. Li, 3d point cloud attribute compression using diffusion-based texture-aware intra prediction. IEEE Trans. Circuits Syst. Video Technol. **34**(10), 9633–9646 (2024)
39. J. Zhang, Y. Chen, G. Liu, W. Gao, G. Li, Efficient point cloud attribute compression framework using attribute-guided graph fourier transform, in *ICASSP 2024-2024 IEEE International Conference on Acoustics, Speech and Signal Processing (ICASSP)* (IEEE, New York, 2024), pp. 8426–8430
40. W. Gao, H. Yuan, G. Li, Z. Li, H. Yuan, Low complexity coding unit decision for video-based point cloud compression. IEEE Trans. Image Process. **33**, 149–162 (2023)
41. Y. Shao, G. Li, Q. Zhang, W. Gao, S. Liu, Nonrigid registration-based progressive motion compensation for point cloud geometry compression. IEEE Trans. Geosci. Remote Sens. **61**, 1–14 (2023)
42. F. Song, G. Li, X. Yang, W. Gao, S. Liu, Block-adaptive point cloud attribute coding with region-aware optimized transform. IEEE Trans. Circuits Syst. Video Technol. **33**(8), 4294–4308 (2023)
43. W. Gao, H. Ye, G. Li, H. Zheng, Y. Wu, L. Xie, Openpointcloud: an open-source algorithm library of deep learning based point cloud compression, in *Proceedings of the 30th ACM International Conference on Multimedia* (2022), pp. 7347–7350
44. W. Gao, G. Li, H. Yuan, R. Hamzaoui, Z. Li, S. Liu, Apccpa'22: 1st international workshop on advances in point cloud compression, processing and analysis, in *Proceedings of the 30th ACM International Conference on Multimedia* (2022), pp. 7392–7393
45. W. Gao, G. Li, Point cloud compression, enhancement and applications: from 3d perception to large models, in *Proceedings of the 32nd ACM International Conference on Multimedia* (2024), pp. 11292–11293
46. H. Sun, G. Li, S. Chen, L. Li, W. Gao, Special topic on 3d point cloud processing and applications. ZTE Commun. **21**(4), 1 (2023)
47. W. Gao, W. Gao, X. Mu, C. Peng, G. Li, Overview and comparison of AVS point cloud compression standard. APSIPA Trans. Signal Inf. Process. **14**(2), 1–33 (2025)
48. W. Gao, S. Wang, X. Zhang, S. Kwong, Editorial for special issue on deep learning-based data compression. APSIPA Trans. Signal Inf. Process. **13**(6), 1–2 (2024)
49. G. Li, G. Wei, W. Gao, *Point Cloud Compression: Technologies and Standardization* (Springer, Berlin, 2024)
50. W. Gao, G. Li, *Deep Learning for 3D Point Clouds* (Springer, Berlin, 2024)
51. D.T. Nguyen, M. Quach, G. Valenzise, P. Duhamel, Learning-based lossless compression of 3d point cloud geometry, in *ICASSP 2021-2021 IEEE International Conference on Acoustics, Speech and Signal Processing (ICASSP)* (IEEE, New York, 2021), pp. 4220–4224
52. D.T. Nguyen, M. Quach, G. Valenzise, P. Duhamel, Multiscale deep context modeling for lossless point cloud geometry compression, in *2021 IEEE International Conference on Multimedia & Expo Workshops (ICMEW)* (2021), pp. 1–6
53. J. Wang, D. Ding, Z. Li, X. Feng, C. Cao, Z. Ma, Sparse tensor-based multiscale representation for point cloud geometry compression. IEEE Trans. Pattern Anal. Mach. Intell. **45**(7), 9055–9071 (2022)
54. L. Xie, W. Gao, H. Zheng, G. Li, Roi-guided point cloud geometry compression towards human and machine vision. arXiv preprint arXiv:2504.14240 (2025)
55. L. Huang, S. Wang, K. Wong, J. Liu, R. Urtasun, Octsqueeze: Octree-structured entropy model for lidar compression. arXiv preprint arXiv:2005.07178 (2020)
56. S. Biswas, J. Liu, K. Wong, S. Wang, R. Urtasun, MuSCLE: multi sweep compression of LiDAR using deep entropy models, in *Advances in Neural Information Processing Systems* (2020), pp. 22170–22181

57. Y. Zhou, O. Tuzel, Voxelnet: end-to-end learning for point cloud based 3d object detection, in *Proceedings of the IEEE Conference on Computer Vision and Pattern Recognition* (2018), pp. 4490–4499
58. L. Huang, S. Wang, K. Wong, J. Liu, R. Urtasun, Octsqueeze: Octree-structured entropy model for lidar compression, in *2020 IEEE/CVF Conference on Computer Vision and Pattern Recognition (CVPR)* (2020), pp. 1310–1320
59. J. Behley, M. Garbade, A. Milioto, J. Quenzel, S. Behnke, C. Stachniss, J. Gall, Semantickitti: A dataset for semantic scene understanding of lidar sequences, in *2019 IEEE/CVF International Conference on Computer Vision, ICCV 2019, Seoul, Korea (South), October 27–November 2, 2019* (IEEE, New York, 2019), pp. 9296–9306
60. MPEG, Mpeg g-pcc tmc13 (2021). https://github.com/MPEGGroup/mpeg-pcc-tmc13
61. Google, Draco 3d data compresison (2017). https://github.com/google/draco
62. R. Mekuria, K. Blom, P. César, Design, implementation, and evaluation of a point cloud codec for tele-immersive video. IEEE Trans. Circuits Syst. Video Techn. **27**(4), 828–842 (2017)
63. Z. Que, G. Lu, D. Xu, Voxelcontext-net: An octree based framework for point cloud compression. arXiv preprint arXiv:2105.02158 (2021)
64. M. Cui, J. Long, M. Feng, B. Li, H. Kai, Octformer: efficient octree-based transformer for point cloud compression with local enhancement, in *Proceedings of the AAAI Conference on Artificial Intelligence*, vol. 37(1) (2023), pp. 470–478
65. R. Song, C. Fu, S. Liu, G. Li, Efficient hierarchical entropy model for learned point cloud compression, in *Proceedings of the IEEE/CVF Conference on Computer Vision and Pattern Recognition* (2023), pp. 14368–14377
66. D. He, Y. Zheng, B. Sun, Y. Wang, H. Qin, Checkerboard context model for efficient learned image compression, in *Proceedings of the IEEE/CVF Conference on Computer Vision and Pattern Recognition* (2021), pp. 14771–14780
67. Y. Jin, Z. Zhu, T. Xu, Y. Lin, Y. Wang, ECM-OPCC: efficient context model for octree-based point cloud compression, in *ICASSP 2024-2024 IEEE International Conference on Acoustics, Speech and Signal Processing (ICASSP)* (IEEE, New York, 2024), pp. 7985–7989
68. H. Yuan, W. Gao, W. Gao, Opensep: an open source subjective experiment platform, in *Proceedings of the 32nd ACM International Conference on Multimedia* (2024), pp. 11248–11251
69. B. Qu, X. Liang, S. Sun, W. Gao, Exploring AIGC video quality: a focus on visual harmony, video-text consistency and domain distribution gap, in *Proceedings of the IEEE/CVF Conference on Computer Vision and Pattern Recognition Workshops* (2024)
70. B. Qu, H. Li, W. Gao, Bringing textual prompt to ai-generated image quality assessment, in *2024 IEEE International Conference on Multimedia and Expo (ICME)* (IEEE, New York, 2024)
71. S. Sun, X. Liang, S. Fan, W. Gao, W. Gao, Ve-bench: subjective-aligned benchmark suite for text-driven video editing quality assessment, in *Proceedings of the AAAI Conference on Artificial Intelligence* (2025)
72. M. Quach, G. Valenzise, F. Dufaux, Improved deep point cloud geometry compression, in *IEEE 22nd International Workshop on Multimedia Signal Processing* (IEEE, New York, 2020), pp. 1–6
73. W. Yan, Y. Shao, S. Liu, T.H. Li, Z. Li, G. Li, Deep autoencoder-based lossy geometry compression for point clouds. arXiv preprint arXiv:1905.03691 (2019)
74. C.R. Qi, L. Yi, H. Su, L.J. Guibas, Pointnet++: deep hierarchical feature learning on point sets in a metric space. Adv. Neural Inf. Proces. Syst. **30**, 5105–5114 (2017)
75. C.R. Qi, H. Su, K. Mo, L.J. Guibas, Pointnet: deep learning on point sets for 3d classification and segmentation, in *Proceedings of the IEEE Conference on Computer Vision and Pattern Recognition* (2017), pp. 652–660
76. J. Ballé, V. Laparra, E.P. Simoncelli, End-to-end optimized image compression. arXiv preprint arXiv:1611.01704 (2016)

77. L. Gao, T. Fan, J. Wan, Y. Xu, J. Sun, Z. Ma, Point cloud geometry compression via neural graph sampling, in *2021 IEEE International Conference on Image Processing (ICIP)* (IEEE, New York, 2021), pp. 3373–3377
78. X. Jia, B. De Brabandere, T. Tuytelaars, L.V. Gool, Dynamic filter networks. Adv. Neural Inf. Proces. Syst. **29**, 667–675 (2016)
79. M. Ilse, J. Tomczak, M. Welling, Attention-based deep multiple instance learning, in *International Conference on Machine Learning* (PMLR, New York, 2018), pp. 2127–2136
80. L. Xie, W. Gao, H. Zheng, End-to-end point cloud geometry compression and analysis with sparse tensor, in *Proceedings of the 1st International Workshop on Advances in Point Cloud Compression, Processing and Analysis* (2022), pp. 27–32
81. Y. He, X. Ren, D. Tang, Y. Zhang, X. Xue, Y. Fu, Density-preserving deep point cloud compression. arXiv preprint arXiv:2204.12684 (2022)
82. H. Zhao, L. Jiang, J. Jia, P.H. Torr, V. Koltun, Point transformer, in *Proceedings of the IEEE/CVF International Conference on Computer Vision* (2021), pp. 16259–16268
83. W. Shi, J. Caballero, F. Huszár, J. Totz, A.P. Aitken, R. Bishop, D. Rueckert, Z. Wang, Real-time single image and video super-resolution using an efficient sub-pixel convolutional neural network, in *Proceedings of the IEEE Conference on Computer Vision and Pattern Recognition* (2016), pp. 1874–1883
84. A.F. Guarda, N.M. Rodrigues, F. Pereira, Adaptive deep learning-based point cloud geometry coding. IEEE J. Sel. Top. Sign. Proces. **15**(2), 415–430 (2020)
85. M. Quach, G. Valenzise, F. Dufaux, Learning convolutional transforms for lossy point cloud geometry compression. arXiv preprint arXiv:1903.08548 (2019)
86. J. Wang, H. Zhu, H. Liu, Z. Ma, Lossy point cloud geometry compression via end-to-end learning. IEEE Trans. Circuits Syst. Video Technol. **31**(12), 4909–4923 (2021)
87. J. Wang, D. Ding, Z. Li, X. Feng, C. Cao, Z. Ma, Sparse Tensor-based Multiscale Representation for Point Cloud Geometry Compression. ArXiv Preprint ArXiv:2111.10633 (2021)
88. J. Pang, M.A. Lodhi, D. Tian, Grasp-net: geometric residual analysis and synthesis for point cloud compression. arXiv preprint arXiv:2209.04401 (2022)
89. J. Pang, K. Bui, D. Tian, Pivot-net: heterogeneous point-voxel-tree-based framework for point cloud compression. arXiv preprint arXiv:2402.07243 (2024)
90. W. Gao, *AI-based Image and Video Coding: Methods, Standards, and Applications* (Springer, New York, 2025)

Chapter 5
Deep Learning–Based Static 3D Point Cloud Attribute Coding

Abstract Point cloud representations encapsulate both spatial coordinates and associated feature data including RGB values and surface reflectance properties. Point cloud attribute coding aims to reduce data size by eliminating statistical redundancies in feature values. Point cloud attributes present greater compression challenges than geometry data due to their higher complexity and more intricate redundancy patterns. Contemporary attribute coding approaches utilizing conventional transformation and prediction techniques demonstrate competitive compression performance, while deep learning–based methods are constantly evolving and can have a great potential for optimization. This chapter provides a comprehensive review of the deep learning–based static point cloud attribute coding methods.

Keywords Point cloud attribute coding · Lossy coding · Lossless coding · Sparse convolution · Variable rate · Autoregressive · Entropy model

5.1 Introduction

In point cloud applications [1–10] , both geometry and attribute data play crucial roles across various fields [11–17]. For instance, digital museums rely on color attributes of point clouds, while LiDAR-based autonomous driving systems utilize reflectivity data. As the use of point clouds expands, traditional approaches to attribute coding have evolved. MPEG defines two standards of Point Cloud Compression (PCC) [18], including Video-based Point Cloud Compression (V-PCC) [19] and Geometry-based Point Cloud Compression (G-PCC) [20]. V-PCC projects the point cloud into a 2D plane, encoding both its geometry and attribute information, and then processes it using a 2D video encoder. However, this method becomes less efficient with sparse point clouds, necessitating alternative representation strategies. To overcome this limitation, G-PCC was developed, which directly processes 3D geometry structures for compression. In G-PCC, attribute coding techniques primarily fall into two categories, i.e., transform-based and prediction-based lifting methods. The first approach employs the Region Adaptive Hierarchical

W. Gao, *AI-based 3D Point Cloud Coding*,
https://doi.org/10.1007/978-981-95-0660-6_5

Transform (RAHT) [21], which decomposes point cloud color attributes into low-frequency and high-frequency components. By quantizing and encoding the high-frequency elements, this method reduces inter-point attribute redundancy. Alternatively, the prediction-based lifting scheme leverages Level of Details (LoD) [22] segmentation to partition the point cloud into layers of varying resolution. Subsequently, it applies predictive lifting to estimate attributes across these layers, effectively minimizing redundancy among different levels of detail.

Currently, learning-based point cloud attribute coding methods achieve good results [23–30], which are very similar to deep learning-based image and video coding methods [31–38]. Point cloud coding techniques can be categorized into point-based and voxel-based methods, depending on how the data are structured. Alternatively, these methods may be categorized as either lossy or lossless, based on whether they preserve the original signal integrity or permit controlled data reduction.

5.2 Overview of Lossless Attribute Coding

Point cloud lossless attribute coding aims to encode point cloud attributes while preserving complete data integrity. In the domain of lossless point cloud coding, machine learning methods commonly require fitting a probabilistic predictive entropy model in the point cloud attribute domain with a neural network.

5.2.1 Predict-Based Framework

Lossless Attribute Coding usually divides the point cloud coding procedure into multiple phases, with the different phases being coded sequentially to each other, with the phase that is coded first providing contextual information to the phase that is coded later. For example, some of these methods divide the point cloud into scales according to resolution, and then the smaller-scale point cloud is used to predict the probability distribution of attributes of a point cloud that is one scale larger. Another example is LoD-based prediction. This technique employs a multi-scale partitioning scheme, segmenting the point cloud into progressively refined clusters. Contextual modeling leverages already decoded points to forecast the probability distribution of remaining points. This approach leverages previously decoded points to improve prediction accuracy.

5.2.2 Data Structure in Compact Feature Representation

Voxel-Based Methods In voxel-represented point cloud coding, the primary step consists of quantizing spatial coordinates to align with a predefined grid system.

A voxel is a pixel-like representation of a picture, where the coordinates of the voxelized point cloud are on a grid, facilitating feature extraction from the point cloud using operators used for structured data such as convolution. The voxels are then organized using octree or sparse tensor approaches.

Sparse tensor is used for sparse convolution [39, 40], which is an improved convolution operation designed to deal with sparse data, i.e., matrices or tensors where most elements are zero. This approach improves computational efficiency, especially when dealing with high-dimensional data, such as 3D point clouds. Traditional convolution operations are performed on each localized region of the image or data matrix, and global computation is performed even if the data are sparse, which is inefficient in many application scenarios. Sparse convolution, on the other hand, greatly reduces computation and memory requirements by skipping the computation of zero elements or irrelevant regions and focusing on meaningful non-zero data parts. Choy et. al [39] organized the data into a set of coordinates $C = \{(x_i, y_i, z_i)\}_i$ and their corresponding attribute values $F = \{f_i\}_i$, and sparse convolution is implemented, restricting computations solely to occupied grid locations, and the convolution is defined as follows:

$$f_u^{\text{out}} = \sum_{i \in N^3(u, C^{\text{in}})} W_i f_{u+i}^{\text{in}}, \tag{5.1}$$

where C^{in} and C^{out} represent the input and output coordinates, $u \in C^{\text{out}}$, while f_u^{in} and f_u^{out} denote the feature vectors at input and output coordinate u. The 3D convolution kernel is defined as $N^3(u, C^{in}) = i|u + i \in C^{in}, i \in N^3$, which represents a set of locations centered at u, where the offsets i belong to C^{in}. The kernel value at a given offset i is denoted as W_i.

Octree is another method of organizing voxelized point clouds, which is a recursive spatial partitioning data structure that is mainly used in 3D space. Its basic idea is to recursively divide the space into eight sub-regions to form a tree-like structure. In an octree, each node represents a 3D cubic space. If the point cloud data in a node are dense, the tree continues to partition that node into smaller octets until a certain stopping condition is reached. The information contained in each node typically includes the spatial boundary represented by the current node and the point cloud data contained in the current node such as the position and the attribute of the point. The standard octree methodology adopts a top-down recursive prediction algorithm, encoding nodes progressively from the root to leaves.

Point-Based Methods The point-based methods take advantage of the raw, unquantized data, allowing them to maintain the highest level of detail and precision in representing the point cloud's attributes and geometry. Unlike voxel-based methods, which impose a grid structure, point-based methods treat each point independently, which is particularly useful when dealing with sparse or irregular point clouds where a voxel grid may introduce unnecessary complexity and redundancy.

Contemporary approaches employ advanced deep learning frameworks [41–47], particularly PointNet [48], PointNet++ [49] variants and Graph Neural Networks (GNNs) [50], to hierarchically extract multi-scale features from unstructured point data. These models capture both local geometry patterns, such as edges or surfaces, and global shapes, which are essential for high-quality reconstruction after decompression. Attribute redundancy among points is minimized using neural networks such as Multilayer Perceptrons (MLPs) or Transformers, which can model complex dependencies between points. Transformers, in particular, excel at capturing both short-range and long-range dependencies without being constrained by spatial locality. Self-attention mechanisms enable context-aware processing by computing pairwise point dependencies, yielding a more sophisticated representation of the global geometry.

5.3 Typical Methods of Lossless Attribute Coding

5.3.1 CNeT

The CNeT method [51] employs masked convolutional operations in an autoregressive framework to estimate the attribute probability distributions. The overall structure is shown in Fig. 5.1.

Let the feature set $F = \{f^0, f^1, f^2, f^3\}$ consist of four components, i.e., one occupancy feature f^0 and three color features f^1, f^2, f^3, which can represent attributes like Red, Green, and Blue channels. The probability distribution of the entire feature set is modeled as a product of conditional distributions. The corresponding formula in [51] is expressed as:

$$p(F) = p(f^0) \cdot p(f^1|f^0) \cdot p(f^2|f^1, f^0) \cdot p(f^3|f^2, f^1, f^0). \tag{5.2}$$

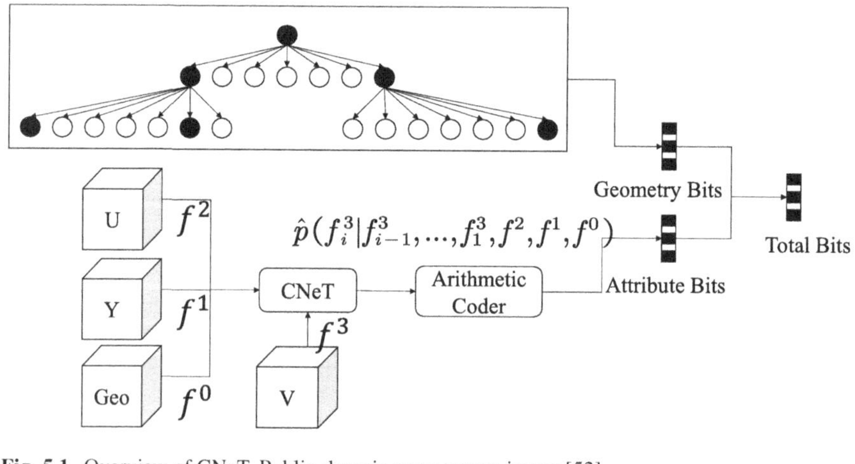

Fig. 5.1 Overview of CNeT. Public-domain open-access image [52]

This equation means that the probability of each feature is conditioned on the previously encoded features. The model first encodes the occupancy features f^0 and then encodes each color feature sequentially using the context from previously encoded features.

For the occupancy feature f^0, the probability distribution is further factorized in the spatial dimension. For a point cloud with d^3 voxels, the distribution over the voxels is written as:

$$p(f^0) = \prod_{i=1}^{d^3} p(f_i^0 | f_{i-1}^0, f_{i-2}^0, \ldots, f_1^0). \tag{5.3}$$

Occupancy prediction is performed conditionally, with each voxel's state determined in relation to its predecessors in the 3D raster-scan sequence. The model skips empty voxels and only processes the occupied ones, reducing redundancy and focusing on relevant parts of the point cloud. Nguyen et al. in [51] formulated this as:

$$p(f^1 | f^0) = \prod_{i=1}^{N} p(f_i^1 | f_{i-1}^1, f_{i-2}^1, \ldots, f_1^1, f^0), \tag{5.4}$$

where N represents the count of non-empty voxels in the volume. The probability of color feature depends on both previously encoded color features and the occupancy information f^0. This approach is applied to all color features.

The model uses neural networks to estimate the conditional probability distributions $p(f_i^0 | \ldots)$, $p(f_i^1 | \ldots)$, etc. The neural network architecture is designed with causal masks to ensure that each voxel's feature is predicted based only on previously encoded voxels, preserving the causality required for auto-regressive modeling. The context used for each prediction includes both spatial and feature-based dependencies. For example, when encoding a color feature f^2, the model uses the previously encoded color features f^1, f^0, utilizing spatial context to estimate the feature value probability distribution for the target voxel. Nguyen et al. in [51] formulated this as:

$$p(f^2 | f^1, f^0) = \prod_{i=1}^{N} p(f_i^1 | f_{i-1}^1, f_{i-2}^1, \ldots, f_1^1, f^1, f^0). \tag{5.5}$$

5.3.2 LPCAC-3C

Building upon multiscale frameworks previously used for geometry compression, LPCAC-3C [53] extends this approach to attribute coding. The method improves coding performance through comprehensive utilization of inter-scale, inter-group, and inter-channel attribute correlations for precise probability modeling.

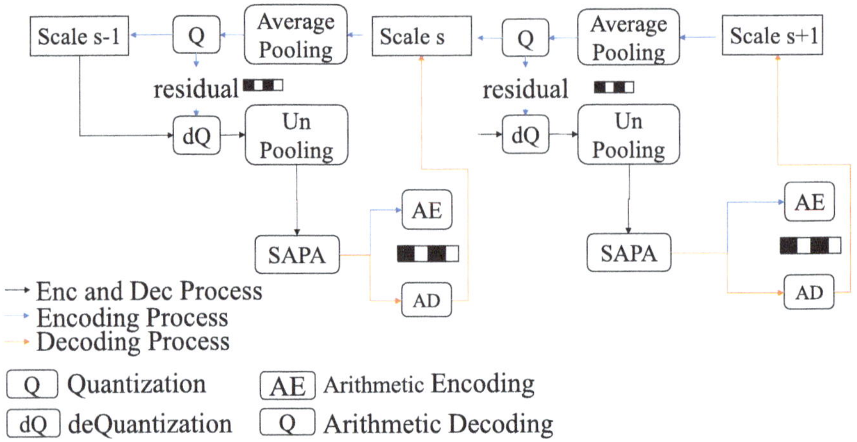

Fig. 5.2 Cross-scale prediction. Public-domain open-access image [54]

Cross-Scale Prediction Figure 5.2 demonstrates the cross-scale prediction mechanism. The encoder progressively constructs multi-resolution representations through average pooling operations. Lower-scale decoded attributes serve as predictors for current-scale attribute probabilities, while uniformly distributed quantization residuals (obtained via rounding-based quantization) are subsequently compressed. The Sparse Convolution-based Attribute Probability Approximation (SAPA) uses sparse convolution to effectively capture neighborhood correlations for probability estimation. SAPA takes the attributes from scale $s-1$, denoted as $\tilde{x}_i^{(s-1)}$, as input, and outputs the probability distributions for the attributes at scale s, which are modeled by a Laplacian distribution characterized by a mean μ_i and variance σ_i for each element in $\hat{x}_i^{(s)}$. Thus, the target probability can be derived through the integration of the Laplacian probability density function:

$$p\left(\left\{\hat{x}_i^{(s)}\right\}\right) = \prod_i \left(\mathcal{L}(\mu_i, \sigma_i) * \mathcal{U}\left(-\frac{1}{2}, \frac{1}{2}\right)\right)\left(\hat{x}_i^{(s)}\right) \qquad (5.6)$$

$$\text{with } \mu_i, \sigma_i = \text{SAPA}\left(\left\{\tilde{x}_i^{(s)}\right\}\right),$$

where $\mathcal{U}(-\frac{1}{2}, \frac{1}{2})$ is the uniform distribution ranging from $-\frac{1}{2}$ to $\frac{1}{2}$.

Cross-Group Prediction Cross-group prediction is illustrated in Fig. 5.3. A progressive prediction approach is applied to sequentially estimate the probability for the eight different groups. An iterative refinement step is incorporated at each level to enhance the attributes of the unprocessed Positively-Occupied Voxels (POVs), which are initially set using $\{\tilde{x}_i^{(s)}\}$, by leveraging the information from the previously processed POVs in the earlier groups. Specifically, this correction

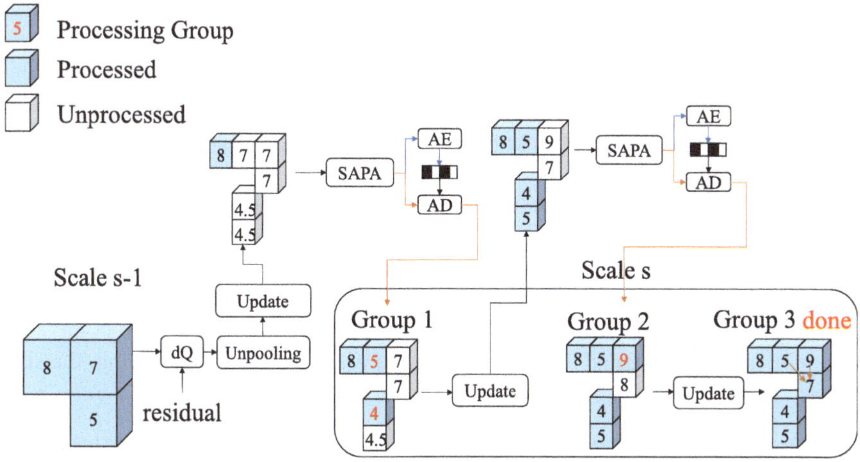

Fig. 5.3 Cross-group prediction. Public-domain open-access image [54]

is performed as:

$$\mathrm{U}\left(\hat{x}_i^{(s,m)}\right) = \frac{k \times x^{(s-1)} - \sum\left(\hat{x}^{(s,1)}, \hat{x}^{(s,2)}, \cdots, \hat{x}^{(s,g)}\right)}{k-g}, \tag{5.7}$$

where $g < m \leq 8$ and $\{\hat{x}^{(s,1)}, \hat{x}^{(s,2)}, \ldots, \hat{x}^{(s,g)}\}$ represent the groups that have already been processed, while $\{\hat{x}_i^{(s,m)} \mid m = g+1, \ldots, 8\}$ refer to the unprocessed groups. The values $x^{(s-1)}$ represent the group averages generated by the previously mentioned stride 2 average pooling, and k indicates the count of POVs within each 2^3 cube. This refinement process facilitates more accurate attribute initialization for subsequent processing stages. When a 2^3 cube contains just one remaining unprocessed POV, its exact value becomes uniquely determinable, eliminating the need for additional signaling overhead.

5.3.3 *Polo-PCAC*

The Polo-PCAC framework [55] introduces a lossless compression approach for point cloud attributes using point-based representations. It divides point cloud into different groups and utilizes KNN-based point transformer to achieve inter-group prediction. Since the point-based method operates directly on the geometry coordinates of the Euclidean space of the points and does not require voxelization, the method has good generalizability.

Progressive Random Grouping Strategy This approach fundamentally aims to achieve optimal segmentation of the point cloud into distinct clusters with minimal computational overhead. Each group is progressively formed with increasing sizes, allowing for coarse-to-fine context modeling. Given a point cloud with positions $X = \{x_1, x_2, \ldots, x_N\}$ and corresponding attributes $Y = \{y_1, y_2, \ldots, y_N\}$, the grouping function g splits the point cloud into M mutually exclusive groups, with each group containing a set of points s_i. The groups are represented as $\{X_i, Y_i\} = g(X, Y, \{s_i\}_{i=1}^{M})$, where X_i is the set of points in the i-th group, and Y_i is the corresponding attribute set. The number of points in the i-th group is denoted as s_i. The grouping process initiates by randomly selecting s_1 points from the input point cloud to construct the initial cluster. Subsequent groups are formed by iteratively sampling s_2 points from the residual point set until complete data partitioning is achieved. This ensures that each group is formed by sampling from the points that have not yet been assigned to a group. To achieve coarse-to-fine modeling, the size of each group increases progressively.

Group-Wise Autoregressive Modeling PoLo-PCAC uses a local context window for each point during the encoding process. For each point x_j in group i, the context window is constructed using its neighboring points, typically selected using a K-Nearest Neighbor (KNN) search. This neighborhood provides valuable context for predicting the attribute distribution of x_j. A neural network processes the contextual neighborhood features to estimate the target point's attributes. The neural architecture estimates the characteristic parameters governing a Laplacian probability distribution, which is used to model the attribute values of the point. The predicted parameters include the mean and scale of the Laplacian distribution. The context modeling is shown in Fig. 5.4, where $\mathcal{N}_x(x_j^i)$ and $\mathcal{N}_y(x_j^i)$ is the position and attribute of the K-nearest neighbor of target decoding point x_j^i. $\mu_{y_j^i}, b_{y_j^i}$ are the estimated local and scale parameters of the Laplacian distribution of x_j^i.

Spatial Normalization Point clouds have significant variability in terms of scale and density. Spatial normalization ensures that the local context around each point is scaled appropriately. This design ensures consistent contextual relationships and point interactions remain comparable across diverse point cloud datasets. This normalization helps the network to focus on relative distances rather than absolute distances, improving stability when handling point clouds of differing resolutions or point distributions. For each point x_j^i in the point cloud, the spatial normalization first shifts the coordinate of the KNN context x_k of x_j^i so that the target point x_j^i is at the origin. Following centralization, neighbor distances are scaled relative to the largest separation present in the local context region. This rescaling step ensures that all points within the window fall within a standard range, regardless of the original scale of the point cloud. The formula for rescaling formulated by You et al. in [55] is:

$$\hat{x}_k = \frac{x_k - x_j^i}{\max_{x_k' \in \mathcal{N}_x\left(x_j^i\right)} \left\{ \left\| x_k' - x_j^i \right\|_2 \right\}}, \quad x_k \in \mathcal{N}_x\left(x_j^i\right) \tag{5.8}$$

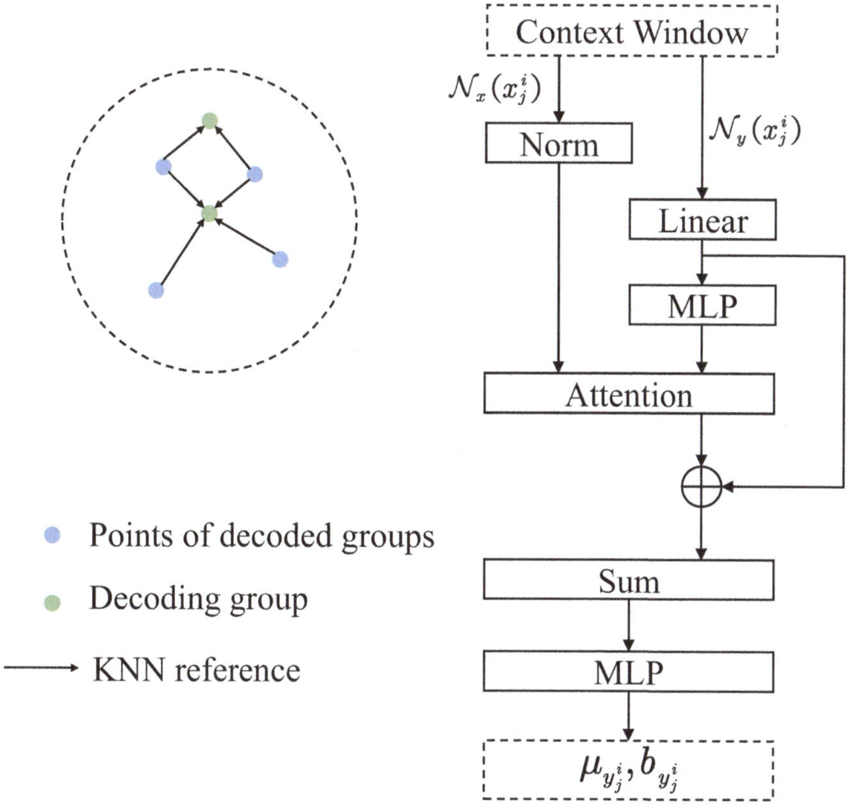

Fig. 5.4 Group-wise autoregressive modeling. Public-domain open-access image [55]

where $\mathcal{N}_x(x_j^i)$ represents the set of neighboring points in the context window, where the normalization factor corresponds to the greatest distance separating the target point x_j^i from any point within its contextual neighborhood. This ensures that the normalized coordinates are bounded within a fixed range.

5.4 Overview for Lossy Attribute Coding

The lossy compression of point cloud attributes mainly focuses on the compression of attribute information related to visual perception in point clouds, such as color or reflectance. These attributes possess substantial information density, making raw storage inefficient. However, strategic simplification enables considerable data reduction. The basic principle of lossy compression is to allow errors in the compression process, especially errors that are not easily noticeable visually or have a small impact on certain applications. The compression process can introduce minor inaccuracies in the reconstructed attribute data, but it can still maintain a high perceptual quality [41, 56–58].

The lossy attribute coding methods usually utilize the autoencoder-based [59–62] end-to-end framework. This end-to-end compression pipeline processes raw point cloud data through successive transformation stages to generate a compact feature encoding. The transformed features undergo entropy encoding via a learned probability model to generate the final compressed bit stream. On the decoding side, the stream is recovered into features by the entropy model, and the features are then reconstructed into point clouds by the decoder. A typical end-to-end compression framework comprises three core components: an encoder network, a probability model, and a decoder network. In this case, the coding network transforms the original point cloud with a transformation operation to reduce its redundant information and obtain a compact feature representation. The entropy model mines the remaining redundancy information between the quantized characters, and predicts the probability of each character, then encodes the characters into a binary stream using an arithmetic encoder. On the decoding side, the compact feature representation is inverted into the original point cloud by a neural network.

5.5 Typical Methods of Lossy Attribute Coding

5.5.1 3DAC

3DAC proposes a deep learning entropy model based on the RAHT transform, which utilizes learning-based methods to extract the contextual information of the high-frequency components generated by the RAHT transform and encode them with probabilistic prediction and entropy coding [63] as shown in Fig. 5.5.

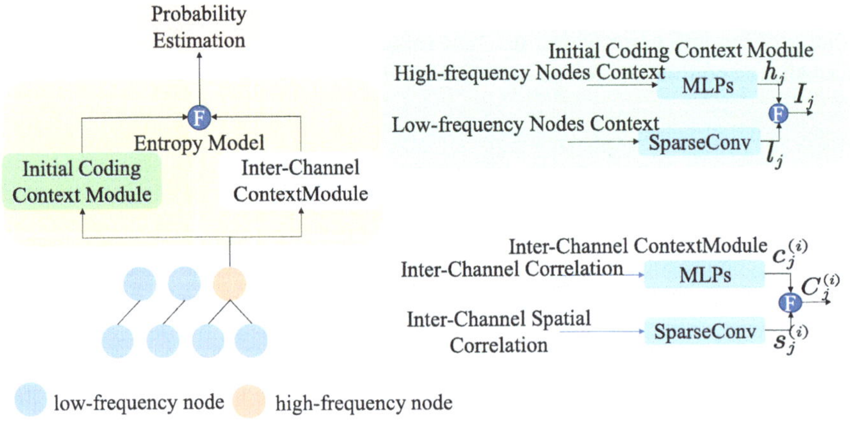

Fig. 5.5 The framework of 3DAC. Public-domain open-access image [64]

Initial Coding 3DAC [64] implements a deep learning–based entropy coding framework specifically optimized for the transform coefficients generated by RAHT [64], a point cloud-adapted version of the Haar wavelet transform. It enables the conversion of point cloud attributes into frequency-domain coefficients. The pipeline initiates by converting the unstructured point cloud into a voxel grid representation, followed by spectral decomposition of attributes into low- and high-frequency components. RAHT repeatedly transforms attributes into coefficients along three dimensions. The transformation is performed sequentially along the x-axis, followed by the y-axis and the z-axis. This process continues through the traversal and merging of all subspaces until the entire 3D space is transformed. To merge neighboring points, the subsequent transform formulated by Fang et al. in [64] is applied:

$$\begin{bmatrix} l_{d+1,x,y,z} \\ h_{d+1,x,y,z} \end{bmatrix} = \mathbf{T}_{w_1,w_2} \begin{bmatrix} l_{d,2x,y,z} \\ l_{d,2x+1,y,z} \end{bmatrix}. \tag{5.9}$$

The low-frequency coefficients of two neighboring points along the x-dimension are denoted as $l_{d,2x,y,z}$ and $l_{d,2x+1,y,z}$. On the other hand, $l_{d+1,x,y,z}$ and $h_{d+1,x,y,z}$ correspond to the low-pass and high-pass filtered components respectively at decomposition level $d+1$. The high-frequency components undergo quantization before being arranged into a symbol sequence following breadth-first ordering. The coefficients of the root level are serialized as h_2, while the coefficients of the second level are serialized as h_1. The serialization process ensures lossless representation, meaning that the attribute distortion only arises from the quantization step.

Overview of Entropy Model The entropy model estimates the statistical distribution of RAHT-transformed coefficients derived from 3D point cloud attributes. These coefficients include both low- and high-frequency components, but only the high-frequency components need to be transmitted after quantization. The entropy model is responsible for estimating the probability of these quantized high-frequency coefficients, which allows the use of entropy coding to compress the data efficiently. The entropy model fundamentally leverages spatial contextual information from the encoding phase along with cross-channel dependencies among attribute dimensions. This improves the accuracy of the probability estimates, leading to better compression performance. The deep entropy model is structured around Initial Coding Context Module and Inter-Channel Correlation Module.

Initial Coding Context Module The Initial Coding Context Module captures contextual features from all nodes in the RAHT hierarchy, including both approximation and detail coefficients. The contextual features encompass each node's hierarchical depth, child node count, low-band coefficients, and associated attribute values. A combination of these factors, processed through an MLP and sparse convolutions, creates a context feature for probability estimation.

Inter-Channel Correlation Module The Inter-Channel Correlation Module leverages the correlation between different attribute channels. The model leverages already-processed coefficients from parallel channels to capture cross-channel statistical dependencies. The spatial relationship between the coefficients of different points is captured through 3D sparse convolutions, creating a spatial embedding that further enhances the probability estimation.

5.5.2 TSC-PCAC

TSC-PCAC [65] proposes an end-to-end compression framework combining Transformer-Sparse Convolution hybrid modules with variational autoencoding [66] and cross-channel context modeling.

Two-Stage TSCM Block The TSCM Block employs a two-stage process for feature extraction. The initial processing phase emphasizes extraction of local geometry relationships and characteristic features from the point set. In the second stage, it extends its scope to gather global features by applying spatial and channel pooling over broader receptive fields. This dual approach allows for efficient extraction of both local and global inter-point relationships, effectively reducing information redundancy. The architecture further integrates a transformer network to dynamically adjust feature extraction across heterogeneous regions, overcoming sparse convolution's uniform parameter limitation. The TSCM Block is shown in Fig. 5.6.

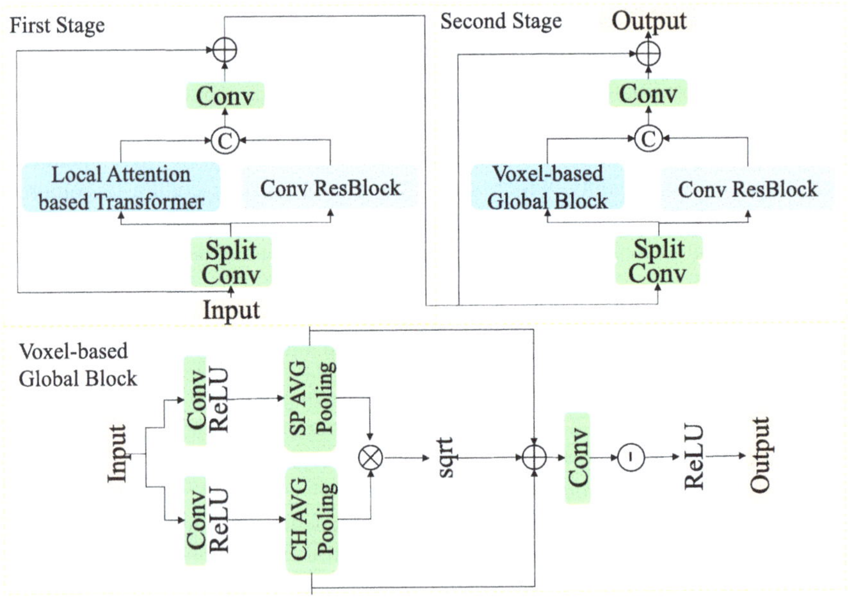

Fig. 5.6 The TSCM and its Voxel-based Global Block Module. Public-domain open-access image [65]

TSCM-Based Channel Context Module Similarity to [67], the TSCM Channel Context Module specifically targets cross-channel dependencies among latent representations for enhanced compression efficiency. It operates by dividing the quantized latent representation $\hat{y}$ into slices along the channel and predicting the mean, scale, and quantization error for each slice. Specifically, for each slice i (where $i \in 1, 2, 3, \ldots, C$), the mean μ_i, scale σ_i, and quantization error $y_{e,i}$ are estimated using information from previously decoded slices $\overline{y}_{<i}$ and the current slice $\hat{y}_i$. The mathematical expressions for these predictions formulated by Guo et al. in [65] are:

$$\begin{cases} \sigma_i = f_{TSCM_T}(\overline{y}_{<i}, \sigma'; \theta_{\sigma,i}) \\ \mu_i = f_{TSCM_T}(\overline{y}_{<i}, \mu'; \theta_{\mu,i}) \\ y_{e,i} = f_{TSCM_T}(\overline{y}_{<i}, \hat{y}_i, \mu'; \theta_{y,i}) \end{cases} \tag{5.10}$$

Here, σ_i and μ_i represent the refined scale and mean of $\hat{y}_i$, while $y_{e,i}$ is the estimated quantization error. The latent representation $\overline{y}i$ is refined as $\overline{y}_i = y_{e,i} + \hat{y}_i$. This process continues for all slices, and the mean μ_i and scale σ_i are used for entropy encoding and decoding. The TSCM-based transform, $f_{TSCM_T}(\cdot)$, applies different parameters $\theta_{\sigma,i}$, $\theta_{\mu,i}$, and $\theta_{y,i}$ for each slice.

5.5.3 *Scalable-PCAC*

Scalable-PCAC [68] implements a hybrid approach, employing G-PCC for base-layer compression of downsampled point clouds and a neural network at the enhancement layer for full-resolution reconstruction. The framework implements a hierarchical reconstruction strategy where the base layer provides fundamental geometry and the enhancement layer adds fine details. The base output serves as a critical prior that enhances the neural enhancement's performance. The overall structure is shown in Fig. 5.7.

Base Layer The base layer in Scalable-PCAC uses G-PCC to encode a downscaled version of the original large-scale point cloud. The down-sampled output constitutes a thumbnail representation that captures the essential structural characteristics at

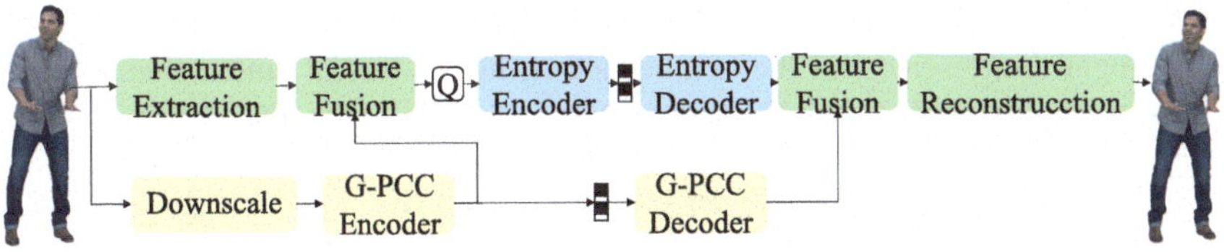

Fig. 5.7 The overall structure of ScalablePCAC. ©2023 IEEE. Reprinted, with permission, from ref. [68]

lower fidelity. The primary purpose of the base layer is to provide a low-quality, low-bitrate representation of the point cloud that can be transmitted efficiently over networks with limited bandwidth. By using G-PCC, the base layer remains compatible with existing point cloud coding standards, ensuring compliance with widely adopted formats. Two key parameters regulate base layer performance: the down-sampling ratio for spatial simplification and the Quantization Parameter (QP) value for coefficient quantization.

Enhancement Layer Scalable-PCAC's enhancement layer operates hierarchically upon the base layer output, employing neural networks to encode and reconstruct the complete high-resolution attribute set. The system utilizes the base layer's approximate reconstruction as a foundation for neural super-resolution, restoring the point cloud to its original resolution. The enhancement layer introduces additional features through deep learning techniques, such as a VAE [66] structure with sparse convolutions, to improve the attribute reconstruction. The framework implements an adaptive bit allocation mechanism across layers, dynamically tuning quality parameters to optimize the rate-distortion trade-off. The enhancement layer allows for improved detail restoration when network conditions allow for higher bandwidth transmission.

Together, the base layer provides a foundational, low-bitrate representation, while the enhancement layer enhances the quality by adding more refined details, allowing for scalable and efficient point cloud attribute coding adaptable to different network conditions.

5.5.4 YOGA

YOGA [69] proposes a framework for joint geometry and attribute coding. The system processes geometry data and attribute information through dedicated compression pipelines, each operating in an end-to-end manner. For the attribute coding part, they use the concept of the base layer and enhancement layer, where the base layer is compressed using G-PCC and the enhancement layer is compressed using neural networks, like [68]. At the same time, this joint compression framework also implements variable-rate coding with an adaptive transform.

In the YOGA framework, a variable-rate approach is employed using an adaptive transform to embed the rate control parameter λ into a quality vector $\vec{q}$ for controlling the quality at different bitrates. The rate control parameter λ is first transformed into a logarithmic scale and then embedded using sinusoidal embedding. This is followed by passing the result through an MLP to generate the quality vector $\vec{q}$:

$$\vec{q} = MLP(SinEmbed(ln(\lambda))). \tag{5.11}$$

Once the quality vector $\vec{q}$ is generated, it is mapped to two arguments, a_i and b_i, which are used to create an affine transformation. This affine transformation in [69] builds relationships between the feature maps at different quality levels:

$$F_i' = AT(F_i) = a_i \cdot F_i + b_i, \tag{5.12}$$

where F_i and F_i' represent the feature maps of the i-th point cloud slice before and after the transformation. The parameters a_i and b_i are derived from the quality vector $\vec{q}$, which is split into two parts, with the first part controlling the scaling a_i and the second part controlling the bias b_i for each feature map. This capability enables the YOGA framework to adaptively modulate compression fidelity according to target bitrate requirements. The quality vector is fed into the adaptive quantization layer within the Adaptive Quantization Enhanced Inception-Residual Network (AQ-IRN) block [69], where it controls the quantization of the transforming feature. This integration ensures that the model supports variable-rate coding, enabling it to adapt to different bandwidths while maintaining quality.

5.5.5 SPAC

SPAC [70] analyzes the frequency distribution of point cloud attributes and compresses the high- and low-frequency components separately. Given the distinct data distributions of these two components, it is logical to apply different compression methods to each. A frequency-aware partitioning mechanism is introduced to bifurcate the point cloud into low- and high-spectral components. Specialized end-to-end networks with frequency-optimized architectures subsequently process these distinct spectral components. The overall structure is shown in Fig. 5.8.

Frequency Sampling Module Let $\mathcal{P} = (G, C) = \{p_i = (G_i, C_i)\}_{i=1}^{M}$ represent the point cloud to be compressed, in which G_i and C_i represents the coordinates and the corresponding attributes of the point cloud $\mathcal{P}$. Then they serialize the points

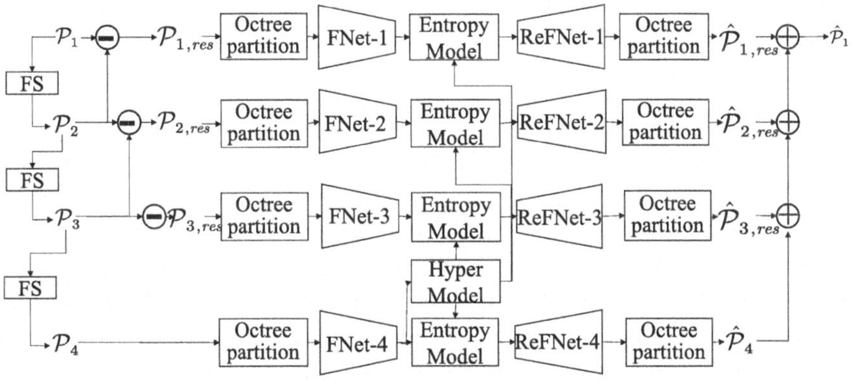

Fig. 5.8 The overall structure of SPAC. Public-domain open-access image [70]

into a 1D sequence and use the Fast Fourier Transform (FFT) to transform the 1D sequence into the frequency domain. Mao et al. [70] formulated this as:

$$\omega(n) = 0.54 - 0.46\cos\left(\frac{2\pi n}{N-1}\right), n = 0, 1, \ldots, N-1, \tag{5.13}$$

$$\mathbb{F}(C) = FFT(\omega \cdot C), \tag{5.14}$$

where $\omega(n)$ means a Hamming window function, $\mathbb{F}(C)$ indicates the frequency domain of the point cloud attributes. Then, the selected high-frequency points $\mathcal{P}_{high}$ can be attained by the following formula:

$$C'_{high} = IFFT(\mathbb{F}(C)_{high}), \tag{5.15}$$

$$\mathcal{P}_{high} = map(\mathcal{P}, C'_{high}) = (G_{high}, C_{high}), \tag{5.16}$$

where IFFT means Inverse Fast Fourier Transform. After obtaining the high-frequency points, the low-frequency points can be attained by excluding the high-frequency points in $\mathcal{P}$.

5.6 Comparative Analysis

This analysis concentrates on evaluating diverse approaches to both lossless and lossy compression, categorizing them by their fundamental representations (point-wise, voxel-based, octree-structured, and combined methodologies). The comparison will primarily be evaluated by the complexity of encoding and decoding, bitrate (for lossless methods) and rate-distortion performance (for lossy methods).

Lossless Coding Among the point cloud attribute lossless compression methods, CNeT has achieved good results with voxel autoregression. However, the autoregressive method also brings a large decoding time overhead; LPCAC-3C utilizes the cross-scale cross-grouping cross-channel prediction method, which makes full use of the multiscale relationship of the point cloud attributes. Polo-PCAC uses the point-based LoD grouping prediction method, which achieves good compression results for different types of point clouds. The summary of lossless compression is shown in Table 5.1

Lossy Coding In point cloud attribute lossy compression methods, 3DAC proposes an entropy model for RAHT based on deep learning. While the other methods are end-to-end compression methods based on autoencoder architecture. TSC-PCAC integrates a voxel transformer into the feature extraction framework and introduces a channel autoregressive entropy model. Scable-PCAC uses G-PCC as the base layer of the compression framework and learning-based neural network as the enhancement layer of the compression framework and achieves good RD performance with a simple network structure. The basic structure of YOGA

Table 5.1 Summary of contributions of point cloud attribute lossless coding. Source: Author

Method name	Paper title	Published in	Highlight
CNeT	Lossless Point Cloud Geometry and Attribute Coding Using a Learned Conditional Probability Model	TCSVT 23	Introduces a voxel-based autoregressive entropy model.
LPCAC-3C	Lossless Point Cloud Attribute Coding Using Cross-scale, Cross-group, and Cross-color Prediction	DCC 22	Introduces cross-scale, cross-group, cross-channel context model.
Polo-PCAC	PoLoPCAC: Efficient and Generic Point Model for Lossless Point Cloud Attribute Coding	arXiv 23	Introduces a point-based approach that is insensitive to the distribution of point cloud data.

and Scalable-PCAC is similar, but YOGA uses affine transformation to realize variable rate. SPAC does not simply input a whole point cloud into the end-to-end compression network, but uses a frequency sampling module to divide the point cloud into points with different attribute according to the frequency, and then inputs the point clouds with different attribute frequencies into the end-to-end compression network with different parameters and structures, respectively. The summary of lossy compression is shown in Table 5.2

Table 5.2 Summary of contributions of point cloud attribute lossy coding methods. Source: Author

Method name	Paper title	Published in	Highlight
3DAC	3DAC: Learning Attribute Coding for Point Clouds	CVPR 22	Introduces deep entropy model for RAHT.
TSC-PCAC	TSC-PCAC: Voxel Transformer and Sparse Convolution Based Point Cloud Attribute Coding for 3D Broadcasting	TBC 24	Introduces voxel transformer into autoencoder-based compression structure.
Scalable-PCAC	Scalable Point Cloud Attribute Coding	TMM 23	Introduces base layer and enhancement layer compression scheme into point cloud attribute coding.
YOGA	YOGA: Yet Another Geometry-based Point Cloud Compressor	MM 23	Introduces a variable-rate adapter into the auto encoder-based compression structure.
SPAC	SPAC: Sampling-based Progressive Attribute Coding for Dense Point Clouds	arXiv 24	Introduces frequency sampling module to compress the point cloud attributes of different frequencies using different compression structures.

5.7 Summary

This chapter presents an organized survey of learned compression techniques for point cloud attributes. Compressing these attributes poses a more significant challenge than compressing geometry data due to the complexity and redundancy present in the attributes. Traditional methods like transform-based and predictive coding-based approaches are widely used for point cloud coding, with techniques such as RAHT and predictive lifting methods. Contemporary neural approaches have demonstrated significant potential in this field, providing complete processing pipelines that transform raw point clouds into compact representations. These learned methods can be classified according to their underlying representations (point or voxel formats) and compression fidelity (exact or approximate reconstruction).

Lossless Coding Methods The chapter discusses various deep learning models such as LPCAC-3C and CNeT. CNeT employs autoregressive models with masked convolutions to predict point attributes, leveraging cross-dimensional dependencies to improve compression. The LPCAC-3C framework employs a multidimensional prediction approach, leveraging inter-scale, inter-group, and inter-channel correlations to enhance probability estimation for lossless encoding.

Lossy Coding Methods Several methods are explored for lossy coding of point cloud attributes, focusing on reducing storage space while maintaining perceptual quality. Techniques like 3DAC employ deep entropy models to effectively compress high-dimensional attribute data, leveraging sparse convolutional networks and multiscale strategies to minimize data loss while preserving key attributes. Additionally, more advanced frameworks such as TSC-PCAC introduce a combination of Transformer and Sparse Convolutional Modules to enhance compression efficiency and scalability. ScalablePCAC integrates G-PCC at a base layer with a learning-based enhancement layer for progressive quality improvement, while Yoga combines geometry and attribute coding with adaptive transforms to support variable-rate coding.

This chapter highlights the expanding capabilities of neural networks in compressing point cloud attributes. However, deep learning–based point cloud attribute coding methods still have many limitations. Current architectures demonstrate limited adaptability, struggling to effectively handle both high-density and low-density point distributions within a unified framework. The compression algorithm occupies too many resources, etc. Meanwhile, task-oriented deep point cloud attribute coding also needs to be paid attention to, and attribute coding algorithms for human eye perception and machine perception have great research value. For readers who are interested in the related technologies of AI-based image and video coding, please refer to [71].

Exercises

1. Please define point cloud attribute coding and explain its importance in point cloud applications.
2. Please describe the difference between Video-based Point Cloud Compression (V-PCC) and Geometry-based Point Cloud Compression (G-PCC).
3. What are the main differences between point-based and voxel-based methods for point cloud attribute coding? Provide examples of each.
4. Please explain the concept of Sparse Convolution in the context of voxel-based point cloud coding. How does it improve computational efficiency?
5. Please describe the end-to-end deep learning framework for point cloud attribute coding. What are the key components, and how do they work together?
6. Please discuss the CNeT approach to lossless point cloud attribute coding. How does it utilize autoregressive patterns and mask convolution for compression?
7. What is the purpose of cross-scale and cross-group prediction in the LPCAC-3C method, and how do these methods improve lossless compression efficiency?
8. What are the benefits and challenges of using point-based methods for point cloud attribute coding compared to voxel-based methods?
9. Please explain the concept of the adaptive transform in the YOGA framework. How does it help in achieving variable-rate coding for joint geometry and attribute coding?
10. What are the current limitations of deep learning–based point cloud attribute coding methods mentioned in the chapter? How can future research address these challenges?

References

1. W. Liu, W. Gao, X. Mu, Fast inter-frame motion prediction for compressed dynamic point cloud attribute enhancement, in *Proceedings of the AAAI Conference on Artificial Intelligence*, vol. 38(4) (2024), pp. 3720–3728
2. Z. Yang, W. Gao, X. Lu, Danet: density-adaptive network for geometry-based point cloud compression artifacts removal, in *2023 IEEE International Conference on Visual Communications and Image Processing (VCIP)* (IEEE, New York, 2023), pp. 1–5
3. X. Fan, G. Li, D. Li, Y. Ren, W. Gao, T.H. Li, Deep geometry post-processing for decompressed point clouds, in *2022 IEEE International Conference on Multimedia and Expo (ICME)* (IEEE, New York, 2022), pp. 1–6
4. X. Zhang, G. Liao, W. Gao, G. Li, Tdrnet: transformer-based dual-branch restoration network for geometry based point cloud compression artifacts, in *2022 IEEE International Conference on Multimedia and Expo (ICME)* (IEEE, New York, 2022), pp. 1–6
5. Z. Li, G. Li, T.H. Li, S. Liu, W. Gao, Semantic point cloud upsampling. IEEE Trans. Multimedia **25**, 3432–3442 (2022)
6. Z. Li, S. Liu, W. Gao, G. Li, G. Li, S4r: rethinking point cloud sampling via guiding upsampling-aware perception. IEEE Trans. Multimedia **27**, 6677–6689 (2025)

7. R. Zhang, W. Gao, G. Li, T.H. Li, Qinet: decision surface learning and adversarial enhancement for quasi-immune completion of diverse corrupted point clouds. IEEE Trans. Geosci. Remote Sens. **60**, 1–14 (2022)
8. R. Bao, Y. Ren, G. Li, W. Gao, S. Liu, Flow-based point cloud completion network with adversarial refinement, in *ICASSP 2022–2022 IEEE International Conference on Acoustics, Speech and Signal Processing (ICASSP)* (IEEE, New York, 2022), pp. 2559–2563
9. J. Chen, G. Li, R. Zhang, T.H. Li, W. Gao, Pointivae: invertible variational autoencoder framework for 3d point cloud generation, in *2022 IEEE International Conference on Image Processing (ICIP)* (IEEE, New York, 2022), pp. 3216–3220
10. R. Zhang, J. Chen, W. Gao, G. Li, T.H. Li, Pointot: interpretable geometry-inspired point cloud generative model via optimal transport. IEEE Trans. Circuits Syst. Video Technol. **32**(10), 6792–6806 (2022)
11. S. Fan, W. Gao, G. Li, Salient object detection for point clouds, in *European Conference on Computer Vision* (Springer, Berlin, 2022), pp. 1–19
12. S. Fan, W. Gao, G. Li, Point-MPP: point cloud self-supervised learning from masked position prediction. IEEE Trans. Neural Networks Learn. Syst. **36**(7), 12964–12976 (2025)
13. Z. Pan, W. Gao, G. Li, Distribution guidance network for weakly supervised point cloud semantic segmentation, in *Advances in Neural Information Processing Systems* (2024)
14. X. Zang, W. Gao, G. Li, H. Fang, C. Ban, Z. He, H. Sun, A baseline investigation: transformer-based cross-view baseline for text-based person search, in *Proceedings of the 31st ACM International Conference on Multimedia* (2023), pp. 7737–7746
15. G. Liao, W. Gao, G. Li, J. Wang, S. Kwong, Cross-collaborative fusion-encoder network for robust RGB-thermal salient object detection. IEEE Trans. Circuits Syst. Video Technol. **32**(11), 7646–7661 (2022)
16. W. Gao, G. Liao, S. Ma, G. Li, Y. Liang, W. Lin, Unified information fusion network for multi-modal RGB-D and RGB-T salient object detection. IEEE Trans. Circuits Syst. Video Technol. **32**(4), 2091–2106 (2021)
17. G. Liao, W. Gao, Q. Jiang, R. Wang, G. Li, MMNET: multi-stage and multi-scale fusion network for RGB-D salient object detection, in *Proceedings of the 28th ACM International Conference on Multimedia* (2020), pp. 2436–2444
18. G. Li, G. Wei, W. Gao, *Point Cloud Compression: Technologies and Standardization* (Springer, Berlin, 2024)
19. 3DG, V-PCC codec description. ISO/IEC JTC 1/SC 29/WG 7, MPEG N00100 (2022)
20. 3DG, G-PCC codec description v12. ISO/IEC JTC 1/SC 29/WG 7, MPEG N00271 (2022)
21. R.L. De Queiroz, P.A. Chou, Compression of 3d point clouds using a region-adaptive hierarchical transform. IEEE Trans. Image Process. **25**(8), 3947–3956 (2016)
22. K. Mammou, A. Tourapis, J. Kim, F. Robinet, V. Valentin, Y. Su, Proposal for improved lossy compression in TMC1. ISO/IEC JTC1/SC29/WG11 M42640, Tech. Rep. (2018)
23. Y. Shao, F. Song, W. Gao, S. Liu, G. Li, Texture-guided graph transform optimization for point cloud attribute compression. Appl. Sci. **14**(10), 4094 (2024)
24. Y. Shao, X. Yang, W. Gao, S. Liu, G. Li, 3d point cloud attribute compression using diffusion-based texture-aware intra prediction. IEEE Trans. Circuits Syst. Video Technol. **34**(10), 9633–9646 (2024)
25. F. Song, G. Li, X. Yang, W. Gao, S. Liu, Block-adaptive point cloud attribute coding with region-aware optimized transform. IEEE Trans. Circuits Syst. Video Technol. **33**(8), 4294–4308 (2023)
26. F. Song, G. Li, W. Gao, T.H. Li, Rate-distortion optimized graph for point cloud attribute coding. IEEE Signal Process Lett. **29**, 922–926 (2022)
27. F. Song, G. Li, X. Yang, W. Gao, T.H. Li, Fine-grained correlation representation for graph-based point cloud attribute compression, in *2022 IEEE International Conference on Multimedia and Expo (ICME)* (IEEE, New York, 2022), pp. 1–6
28. F. Shen, W. Gao, A rate control algorithm for video-based point cloud compression, in *2021 International Conference on Visual Communications and Image Processing (VCIP)* (IEEE, New York, 2021), pp. 1–5

29. F. Song, Y. Shao, W. Gao, H. Wang, T. Li, Layer-wise geometry aggregation framework for lossless lidar point cloud compression. IEEE Trans. Circuits Syst. Video Technol. **31**(12), 4603–4616 (2021)
30. Z. Cai, W. Gao, G. Li, W. Gao, Distortion propagation model-based V-PCC rate control for 3d point cloud broadcasting. IEEE Trans. Broadcast., **71**(1), 180–192 (2025)
31. Y. Wu, L. Xie, S. Sun, W. Gao, Y. Yan, Adaptive intra period size for deep learning-based screen content video coding, in *2024 IEEE International Conference on Multimedia and Expo Workshops (ICMEW)* (IEEE, New York, 2024), pp. 1–6
32. H. Zheng, W. Gao, End-to-end rgb-d image compression via exploiting channel-modality redundancy, in *Proceedings of the AAAI Conference on Artificial Intelligence*, vol. 38(7) (2024), pp. 7562–7570
33. L. Tao, W. Gao, G. Li, C. Zhang, Adanic: towards practical neural image compression via dynamic transform routing, in *Proceedings of the IEEE/CVF International Conference on Computer Vision* (2023), pp. 16879–16888
34. Y. Wu, W. Gao, End-to-end lossless compression of high precision depth maps guided by pseudo-residual, in *2022 Data Compression Conference (DCC)* (IEEE, New York, 2022), pp. 489–489
35. Y. Wu, Z. Qi, H. Zheng, L. Tao, W. Gao, Deep image compression with latent optimization and piece-wise quantization approximation, in *Proceedings of the IEEE/CVF Conference on Computer Vision and Pattern Recognition* (2021), pp. 1926–1930
36. W. Gao, L. Tao, L. Zhou, D. Yang, X. Zhang, Z. Guo, Low-rate image compression with super-resolution learning, in *Proceedings of the IEEE/CVF Conference on Computer Vision and Pattern Recognition Workshops* (2020), pp. 154–155
37. Y. Li, W. Gao, G. Li, S. Ma, Saliency segmentation oriented deep image compression with novel bit allocation. IEEE Trans. Image Process. **34**, 16–29 (2025)
38. C. Zhang, W. Gao, Learned rate control for frame-level adaptive neural video compression via dynamic neural network, in *European Conference on Computer Vision* (Springer, Berlin, 2024)
39. C. Choy, J. Gwak, S. Savarese, 4d spatio-temporal convnets: Minkowski convolutional neural networks, in *Proceedings of the IEEE/CVF Conference on Computer Vision and Pattern Recognition* (2019), pp. 3075–3084
40. B. Graham, Unsupervised learning with sparse space-and-time autoencoders. arXiv preprint arXiv:1811.10355 (2018)
41. W. Gao, G. Li, *Deep Learning for 3D Point Clouds* (Springer, New York, 2024)
42. W. Gao, G. Li, H. Yuan, R. Hamzaoui, Z. Li, S. Liu, Apccpa'22: 1st international workshop on advances in point cloud compression, processing and analysis, in *Proceedings of the 30th ACM International Conference on Multimedia* (2022), pp. 7392–7393
43. W. Gao, G. Li, Point cloud compression, enhancement and applications: from 3d perception to large models, in *Proceedings of the 32nd ACM International Conference on Multimedia* (2024), pp. 11292–11293
44. H. Sun, G. Li, S. Chen, L. Li, W. Gao, Special topic on 3d point cloud processing and applications. ZTE Commun. **21**(4), 1 (2023)
45. W. Gao, W. Gao, X. Mu, C. Peng, G. Li, Overview and comparison of AVS point cloud compression standard. APSIPA Trans. Signal Inf. Process. **33**(8), 4294–4308 (2024)
46. W. Gao, S. Wang, X. Zhang, S. Kwong, Editorial for special issue on deep learning-based data compression. APSIPA Trans. Signal Inf. Process. **13**(6), 1–2 (2024)
47. W. Gao, H. Ye, G. Li, H. Zheng, Y. Wu, L. Xie, Openpointcloud: an open-source algorithm library of deep learning based point cloud compression, in *Proceedings of the 30th ACM International Conference on Multimedia* (2022), pp. 7347–7350
48. C.R. Qi, H. Su, K. Mo, L.J. Guibas, Pointnet: deep learning on point sets for 3d classification and segmentation, in *Proceedings of the IEEE Conference on Computer Vision and Pattern Recognition* (2017), pp. 652–660
49. C.R. Qi, L. Yi, H. Su, L.J. Guibas, Pointnet++: deep hierarchical feature learning on point sets in a metric space. Adv. Neural Inf. Proces. Syst. **30**, 5105–5114 (2017)

50. W. Shi, R. Rajkumar, Point-gnn: Graph neural network for 3d object detection in a point cloud, in *Proceedings of the IEEE/CVF Conference on Computer Vision and Pattern Recognition* (2020), pp. 1711–1719
51. D.T. Nguyen, A. Kaup, Lossless point cloud geometry and attribute compression using a learned conditional probability model. IEEE Trans. Circuits Syst. Video Technol. **33**(8), 4337–4348 (2023)
52. D.T. Nguyen, A. Kaup, Lossless point cloud geometry and attribute compression using a learned conditional probability model. arXiv preprint arXiv:2303.06519 (2023)
53. J. Wang, D. Ding, Z. Ma, Lossless point cloud attribute compression using cross-scale, cross-group, and cross-color prediction, in *2023 Data Compression Conference (DCC)* (IEEE, New York, 2023), pp. 228–237
54. J. Wang, D. Ding, Z. Ma, Lossless point cloud attribute compression using cross-scale, cross-group, and cross-color prediction. arXiv preprint arXiv:2303.12917 (2023)
55. K. You, P. Gao, Z. Ma, Efficient and generic point model for lossless point cloud attribute compression. arXiv preprint arXiv:2404.06936 (2024)
56. J. Wang, W. Gao, G. Li, Zoom to perceive better: no-reference point cloud quality assessment via exploring effective multiscale feature. IEEE Trans. Circuits Syst. Video Technol. **34**(7), 6334–6346 (2024)
57. H. Li, W. Gao, Information exploration of projected views for point cloud quality measurement. IEEE Trans. Instrum. Meas. **74**, 1–14 (2025)
58. J. Wang, W. Gao, G. Li, Applying collaborative adversarial learning to blind point cloud quality measurement. IEEE Trans. Instrum. Meas. **72**, 1–15 (2023)
59. J. Ballé, V. Laparra, E.P. Simoncelli, End-to-end optimized image compression. arXiv preprint arXiv:1611.01704 (2016)
60. J. Ballé, D. Minnen, S. Singh, S.J. Hwang, N. Johnston, Variational image compression with a scale hyperprior. arXiv preprint arXiv:1802.01436 (2018)
61. D. He, Y. Zheng, B. Sun, Y. Wang, H. Qin, Checkerboard context model for efficient learned image compression, in *Proceedings of the IEEE/CVF Conference on Computer Vision and Pattern Recognition* (2021), pp. 14771–14780
62. J. Liu, H. Sun, and J. Katto, Learned image compression with mixed transformer-cnn architectures, in *Proceedings of the IEEE/CVF Conference on Computer Vision and Pattern Recognition* (2023), pp. 14388–14397
63. L. Xie, W. Gao, H. Zheng, G. Li, ROI-guided point cloud geometry compression towards human and machine vision. arXiv preprint arXiv:2504.14240 (2025)
64. G. Fang, Q. Hu, H. Wang, Y. Xu, Y. Guo, 3DAC: learning attribute compression for point clouds. arXiv preprint arXiv:2203.09931 (2022)
65. Z. Guo, Y. Zhang, L. Zhu, H. Wang, G. Jiang, TSC-PCAC: voxel transformer and sparse convolution based point cloud attribute compression for 3d broadcasting. arXiv preprint arXiv:2407.04284 (2024)
66. D.P. Kingma, Auto-encoding variational Bayes. arXiv preprint arXiv:1312.6114 (2013)
67. C. Ma, Z. Wang, R. Liao, Y. Ye, A cross channel context model for latents in deep image compression. arXiv preprint arXiv:2103.02884 (2021)
68. J. Zhang, J. Wang, D. Ding, Z. Ma, Scalable point cloud attribute compression. IEEE Trans. Multimedia **27**, 889–899 (2025)
69. J. Zhang, T. Chen, D. Ding, Z. Ma, Yoga: yet another geometry-based point cloud compressor, in *Proceedings of the 31st ACM International Conference on Multimedia* (2023), pp. 9070–9081
70. X. Mao, H. Yuan, T. Guo, S. Jiang, R. Hamzaoui, S. Kwong, SPAC: sampling-based progressive attribute compression for dense point clouds. arXiv preprint arXiv:2409.10293 (2024)
71. W. Gao, *AI-based Image and Video Coding: Methods, Standards, and Applications* (Springer, Berlin, 2025)

Chapter 6
Deep Learning–Based Dynamic 3D Point Cloud Coding

Abstract Dynamic point clouds are emerging as a critical technology for immersive applications, particularly in virtual reality (VR) and augmented reality (AR) systems. The growing demand for high-quality, real-time 3D visualization necessitates advanced coding techniques for efficient representation. While traditional dynamic point cloud coding (DPCC) approaches, such as MPEG V-PCC that employs 3D-to-2D projection to reduce temporal redundancy, demonstrate limitations when handling large-scale, complex dynamic scenes, deep learning–based methods have recently shown superior performance by effectively capturing both spatial and temporal correlations. This chapter systematically investigates deep learning approaches for DPCC, highlighting their potential to revolutionize compression efficiency and enable next-generation immersive experiences through innovative architectures and learning paradigms. The presented analysis demonstrates how these data-driven methods can significantly advance the state of the art in dynamic point cloud coding and transmission.

Keywords Dynamic point cloud coding · Motion estimation · Motion compensation · Point cloud reconstruction · Optical flow

6.1 Introduction

In previous chapters, we introduced the fundamental concepts and methods for static point cloud coding [1–13]. Similar to the relationship between image and video coding [14–20], dynamic point cloud is also very important for applications such as virtual reality (VR), augmented reality (AR), and immersive experiences [21–31]. As these technologies evolve, the demand for high-quality and real-time 3D data processing [32–40]continues to grow, necessitating the development of dynamic point cloud coding (DPCC) techniques that not only reduce data size but also preserve geometric and visual fidelity.

Traditional methods for DPCC, such as MPEG V-PCC [41], have been widely adopted for compressing 3D point cloud data. These methods often rely on tech-

W. Gao, *AI-based 3D Point Cloud Coding*,
https://doi.org/10.1007/978-981-95-0660-6_6

niques like 3D-2D projection to reduce temporal redundancy. While effective, they encounter limitations in terms of both coding efficiency and overall effectiveness when handling more complex, large-scale dynamic point clouds. The rise of deep learning has introduced new possibilities for point cloud coding [42, 43]. Neural networks, with their ability to learn and exploit spatial and temporal correlations, offer significant improvements over traditional methods [44, 45]. By using architectures such as MLPs [46], CNNs [11, 43], and transformers [47, 48], deep learning–based approaches can capture intricate patterns within the data, leading to more efficient compression and highly accurate reconstructions of dynamic point cloud.

Current deep learning–based compression techniques are typically categorized based on the underlying data structure (e.g., voxel-based, point-based, octree-based) [44, 45, 49–58], feature extraction strategies, inter-frame prediction mechanisms, and reconstruction techniques. This classification helps clarify the wide range of approaches in the field and highlights the innovations that have contributed to the recent progress in dynamic point cloud coding. In summary, the integration of deep learning into dynamic point cloud coding marks a substantial advancement in the ability to efficiently manage and transmit 3D data. This chapter aims to examine the latest developments and techniques in this field, providing insights into how deep learning is shaping the future of dynamic point cloud processing and compression.

6.2 Overview of Dynamic 3D Point Cloud Coding

6.2.1 Overall Framework

The dynamic point cloud coding (DPCC) framework [10, 59, 60] aims to achieve efficient compression of dynamic point cloud data—a temporal sequence of 3D point cloud frames. The primary objective of this framework is to minimize the amount of data needed to represent these frames while preserving crucial geometric and temporal information. To achieve this, the framework typically integrates three core components: Feature Extraction, Inter-frame Prediction, and Point Cloud Reconstruction, as shown in Fig. 6.1. Each of these components is essential to the compression process, collectively contributing to the overall goal of reducing data volume without significant quality loss. The DPCC framework generally follows

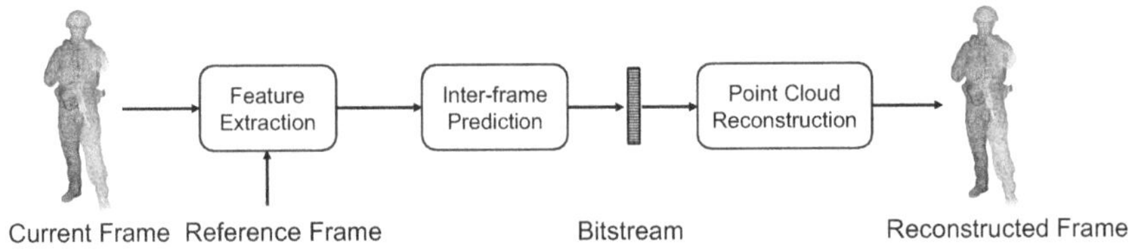

Fig. 6.1 Pipeline of dynamic point cloud coding (DPCC) (Source: Author)

a structured process, beginning with the raw point cloud data undergoing feature extraction. During this stage, relevant features are extracted from the data, providing a compact and informative representation that facilitates more efficient processing in subsequent steps. These features are vital for understanding the underlying structure and movement within the point cloud data, making the subsequent tasks of prediction and reconstruction more manageable.

Following feature extraction, the framework employs inter-frame prediction to exploit temporal coherence between consecutive frames. This step is crucial for identifying and encoding only the changes between frames, rather than redundantly encoding each frame independently. By focusing on the differences, or residuals, between frames, the framework achieves substantial data reduction, minimizing storage requirements and transmission bandwidth demands. This approach not only enhances compression efficiency but also maintains the continuity and dynamics of the original point cloud sequence. The final component of the DPCC framework is the point cloud reconstruction, which involves reconstructing the point cloud from the compressed data. The goal of this step is to ensure that the reconstructed point cloud closely matches the original sequence in both spatial and temporal fidelity. This requires sophisticated algorithms that can accurately decode and reassemble the compressed data into a coherent and high-quality point cloud sequence.

Throughout the entire compression process, the DPCC framework must balance the trade-offs between compression efficiency, computational complexity, and reconstruction quality [61–65]. Achieving this balance necessitates careful design and optimization of each component, along with the integration of advanced deep learning techniques that are capable of adapting to the unique challenges posed by dynamic point clouds. The modular nature of the framework also provides flexibility in selecting algorithms and methods, allowing for customization based on specific application requirements where data efficiency and accuracy are of paramount importance. In the following subsections, we will delve deeper into each component of the DPCC framework, examining the specific techniques and architectures that enable effective point cloud coding.

6.2.2 Feature Extraction

Feature extraction serves as a core component of the DPCC framework, transforming raw 3D point cloud data into a compressed yet information-rich latent representation. This stage reduces the dimensionality of the data and captures essential geometric structures, making it easier to perform subsequent tasks such as motion prediction and reconstruction. For dynamic point clouds, feature extraction must overcome distinct challenges arising from the inherent irregularity and sparsity of point cloud data. Unlike the structured grid arrangement of pixels in 2D images, point clouds comprise unstructured 3D point distributions characterized by nonuniform densities and intricate spatial relationships. To efficiently process such data, deep learning–based methods typically employ one or a combination of the following approaches.

Voxel-Based Networks One common approach to feature extraction in point clouds is to voxelize the data, converting the irregular point cloud into a structured 3D grid [60]. Each voxel in this grid represents a small region of space, and the presence or absence of points within each voxel can be encoded as binary values or other feature descriptors. Once the data are voxelized, traditional 3D CNNs can be applied to extract hierarchical features, similar to how they process 2D images. As an extension to traditional 3D CNNs, Sparse Convolutions are employed to improve efficiency by focusing computations only on non-empty voxels. This reduces the computational burden and memory usage by skipping operations on empty regions, which are common in sparse point cloud data. Sparse Convolutions make it feasible to work with large-scale point clouds while preserving detailed geometric information. The advantage of this approach is that it leverages the power of CNNs to learn spatial hierarchies, capturing both local and global geometric features. However, voxelization can introduce quantization errors, and the memory requirements can grow significantly with the resolution of the voxel grid, making this approach less efficient for very large point clouds.

Point-Based Networks Another approach is to directly operate on the raw point cloud data without converting it into a regular grid [59]. Point-based networks, such as PointNet and its extensions (e.g., PointNet + +), are designed to handle the unordered nature of point clouds. These networks typically use multi-layer perceptrons (MLPs) [46] to process each point individually, followed by global pooling operations to aggregate information across all points. Building on this, Transformer [47, 48] and Mamba [66] have been developed to effectively model long-range dependencies and large-scale spatial correlations in point cloud data. By using self-attention mechanisms, they can effectively model interactions between distant points, allowing for more robust feature extraction. Point-based networks are well-suited for capturing fine-grained geometric details and can be more efficient in terms of memory usage compared to voxel-based methods. They also allow for flexible processing of point clouds with varying densities. However, these networks may struggle to capture large-scale spatial relationships without additional hierarchical mechanisms, where transformers and Mamba excel.

Octree-Based Networks Octree-based methods represent point clouds using an octree structure, which recursively divides 3D space into eight octants at each level, creating a hierarchical representation of the data [67]. Each node in the octree corresponds to a specific region of space, with leaf nodes representing the smallest subdivisions that contain points. This hierarchical structure allows the network to adaptively partition space based on the density of points, focusing computational resources on regions with more geometric detail. The primary advantage of octree-based methods is their ability to efficiently manage varying point densities and maintain a compact representation of large-scale point clouds. This is particularly useful for processing scenes with sparse or unevenly distributed points, where voxel-based methods might become inefficient due to the large number of empty voxels. Octree-based networks can apply convolutional operations directly on the octree structure, capturing multi-scale geometric features through the hierarchical levels of the octree.

In practice, many DPCC frameworks employ a combination of the above methods to perform multi-scale feature extraction [68, 69]. By processing the point cloud at multiple scales, the framework can capture both fine-grained details and larger geometric structures. This process is typically implemented through sequential down-sampling and up-sampling operations, where feature resolution undergoes progressive reduction followed by hierarchical aggregation to construct a holistic representation of the point cloud. Multi-scale feature extraction allows the framework to handle the diverse range of geometric complexities present in dynamic point clouds, from small surface details to large object movements. The extracted features are then passed to the inter-frame prediction module, where they are used to estimate motion and predict future frames. The feature extraction module constitutes a critical component in DPCC frameworks, converting raw point cloud data into an optimized representation suitable for efficient processing by downstream pipeline stages. By leveraging deep learning techniques such as voxel-based, point-based, and octree-based networks, the framework can capture a rich representation of the point cloud, enabling effective compression and reconstruction. The selection of feature extraction methodologies is application-dependent, governed by two key factors, including the required level of geometric detail preservation and the available computational resources.

6.2.3 Inter-Frame Prediction

Inter-frame prediction [10, 60, 70] is a critical component in the DPCC framework, as it leverages temporal coherence between consecutive frames to reduce the amount of data that needs to be encoded. Dynamic point cloud consists of a sequence of 3D frames, where the changes between successive frames are often minimal. The framework achieves compression efficiency by predicting the current frame from preceding frames and encoding only the residual information—the discrepancy between predicted and actual frames. This inter-frame prediction mechanism comprises two core components: motion estimation and motion compensation (Fig. 6.2), which collectively predict point positions and attributes in the current frame through temporal analysis of previous frame(s).

Motion Estimation Motion estimation is the process of determining the movement of points from one frame to the next. In the context of dynamic point cloud, motion estimation must handle both rigid transformations (e.g., translations and rotations of entire objects) and non-rigid deformations (e.g., changes in the shape or position of individual points). Various motion estimation approaches can be

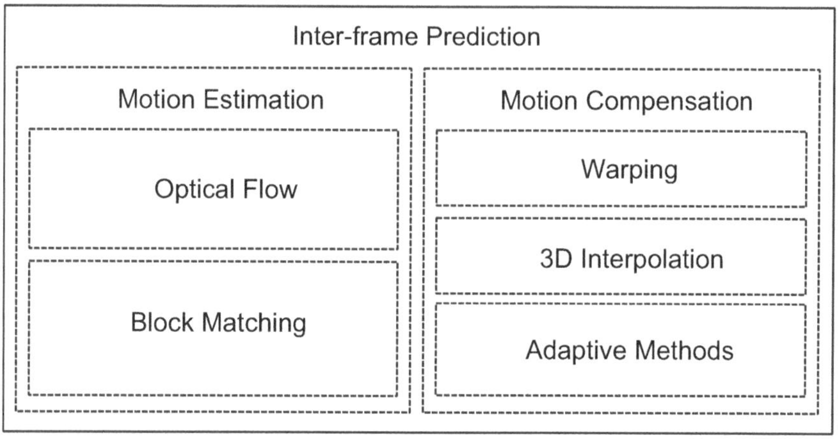

Fig. 6.2 Category of inter-frame prediction (Source: Author)

utilized, determined by the point cloud data characteristics and the target accuracy requirements.

- **Optical flow.** Optical flow methods estimate the motion of points between frames by computing the flow vectors that describe how points move from one frame to the next. In DPCC, optical flow can be used to predict the movement of points in 3D space, allowing the framework to align the previous frame with the current one. Deep learning–based optical flow networks can learn to estimate complex motion patterns, making them suitable for handling both rigid and non-rigid movements in dynamic point clouds.
- **Block matching.** Block matching divides the point cloud into blocks or regions and estimates the motion of each block between frames. This method is particularly effective for capturing large-scale movements, such as the translation of entire objects. Through block matching between consecutive frames, the framework derives motion estimates for corresponding regions, enabling predictive encoding. Block matching can be further enhanced by incorporating deep learning techniques that improve the accuracy of the matching process.

Motion Compensation After motion estimation, the framework performs motion compensation by applying the estimated motion vectors to align the reference frame with the current frame. This process minimizes the residual error, defined as the difference between the motion-compensated predicted frame and the actual current frame. In practice, motion compensation can be implemented in several ways.

- **Warping.** Warping techniques apply estimated motion vectors to transform points from the reference frame to their predicted locations in the target frame. This alignment process maximizes frame correspondence, thereby reducing the residual information requiring encoding.

- **3D interpolation.** In cases where the motion estimation is not perfectly accurate, 3D interpolation methods can be used to refine the predicted positions of points. By interpolating between the estimated positions and the actual positions, the framework can further reduce the residual error.
- **Adaptive methods.** Adaptive motion compensation methods dynamically adjust the level of compensation based on the complexity of the motion. For example, coarse motion compensation might be used for large-scale movements, while more precise methods are applied to areas with finer details or non-rigid deformations.

Hierarchical Inter-Frame Prediction Given the varying scales of motion in dynamic point clouds, a hierarchical approach to inter-frame prediction is often employed. This approach estimates motion at multiple resolutions, allowing the framework to capture both large-scale and fine-grained movements. The hierarchical process typically involves two stages:

- **Low-resolution prediction.** The first stage estimates coarse motion at a lower resolution. This captures the overall movement of large objects or regions within the point cloud, providing a rough alignment between frames. Low-resolution prediction is computationally efficient and serves as the foundation for more detailed motion estimation.
- **High-resolution refinement.** The second stage refines the motion estimation at a higher resolution. This stage focuses on finer details, such as small deformations or precise point movements, that were not captured in the low-resolution prediction. The high-resolution refinement improves the accuracy of the prediction, ensuring that the residual error is minimized.

The hierarchical approach allows the DPCC framework to balance accuracy and computational efficiency, adapting to different types of motion within the point cloud data. Inter-frame prediction is essential for reducing the data required to represent dynamic point clouds. By accurately estimating and compensating for motion between frames, the framework can focus on encoding only the differences between frames, leading to significant compression gains. The combination of motion estimation, motion compensation, and hierarchical processing enables the DPCC framework to handle a wide range of motions, from large-scale object translations to subtle point-level deformations.

6.2.4 Point Cloud Reconstruction

Point cloud reconstruction constitutes the final stage of the DPCC pipeline, decoding compressed data to reconstruct the original 3D point cloud sequence. The aim is to reconstruct the dynamic point cloud with minimal geometric and temporal loss, ensuring that the reconstructed frames are as close as possible to the original data. This process involves decoding compressed latent features, applying motion compensation, and up-sampling the decoded data to generate the final point cloud. These steps are crucial to maintaining the quality and accuracy of the reconstructed frames, especially when dealing with the trade-off between compression efficiency and reconstruction quality. Lossy compression techniques, while enabling higher compression ratios, must be balanced with a reconstruction module that minimizes the impact of information loss on the point cloud's visual and geometric fidelity.

The first step in reconstruction is decoding the compressed data generated during feature extraction and inter-frame prediction. This includes decompressing encoded residuals, motion vectors, and other compressed features. Decompression reverses the transformations applied during compression, restoring latent representations used for point cloud reconstruction. Deep learning methods, such as auto-encoders, are often employed for decoding, learning a mapping from the compressed latent space back to the original feature space to ensure accurate reconstructed features. After decoding, motion compensation is applied, aligning the reconstructed frame with previous ones using motion vectors estimated during inter-frame prediction. This reduces residual errors and ensures that the reconstructed frame reflects the actual motion between frames. Due to the complex and non-rigid nature of dynamic point cloud motion, advanced techniques like 3D warping or adaptive interpolation are used to refine motion compensation and improve reconstruction accuracy.

Following motion compensation, the next step is up-sampling the latent features to generate the final point cloud. During feature extraction, the point cloud may have been down-sampled for a compact representation, and this is reversed during reconstruction. Neural networks, such as transposed convolutions, are typically used for up-sampling, designed to handle the irregular and sparse nature of point cloud data, ensuring accurate spatial distribution of points. The process may also include refinement steps, such as filtering or pruning, to remove noise or outliers introduced during compression, enhancing the final reconstruction quality. The result of the reconstruction process is a dynamic point cloud frame that closely resembles the original in terms of geometry and motion, with minimal visible artifacts. Quality is assessed using metrics like point-to-point or point-to-plane distances, measuring fidelity compared to the original data. The reconstruction process plays a vital role in DPCC systems, achieving effective data recovery while maintaining an optimal balance between compression efficiency and reconstruction quality.

6.3 Typical Methods of Dynamic 3D Point Cloud Coding

6.3.1 D-DPCC

Feature Extraction As illustrated in Fig. 6.3, the D-DPCC framework processes input frames through its Feature Extraction module, which transforms the current frame x_t and reconstructed previous frame $\hat{x}_{t-1}$ into latent representations y_t and $\hat{y}_{t-1}$ via sparse convolutional encoding. This feature extraction pipeline sequentially applies two Down-sample Blocks to eliminate spatial redundancies

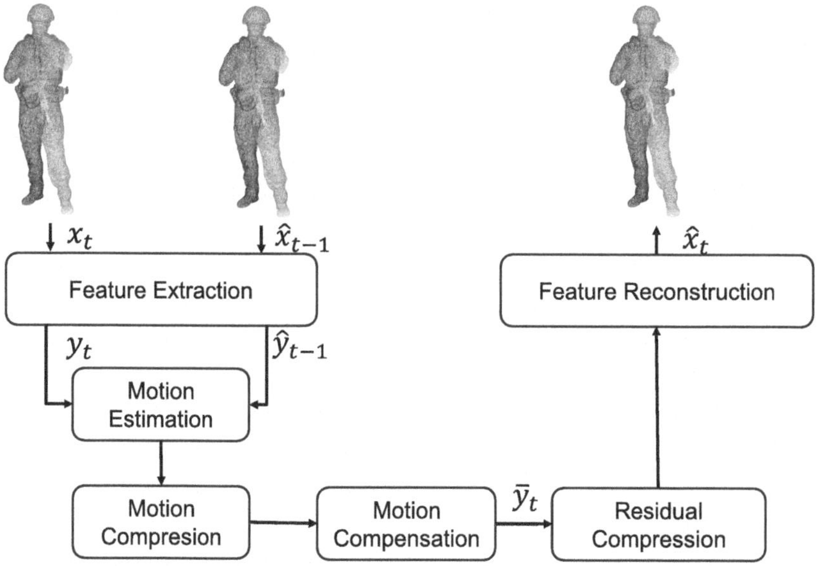

Fig. 6.3 Overall framework of the D-DPCC method (Public-domain open-access image [72])

hierarchically [71]. Each Down-sample Block combines a sparse convolution layer for dimensional reduction with multiple Inception-Residual Network (IRN) blocks performing local feature extraction and integration [72], ultimately generating compressed latent representations preserving the input frames' key characteristics:

$$y_t = \{C_{2x_t}, F_{y_t}\}, \tag{6.1}$$

where C_{2x_t} represents the coordinate matrix at different down-sampling scales, and F_{y_t} is the corresponding feature matrix.

Inter-Frame Prediction The Inter-frame Prediction module is responsible for predicting the current frame's feature representation $\bar{y}_t$ by analyzing the temporal correlation between the latent representations of the current frame y_t and the previous frame $\hat{y}_{t-1}$. This module integrates a Multi-scale Motion Fusion (MMF) module and a 3D Adaptively Weighted Interpolation (3DAWI) algorithm to enhance the accuracy of motion estimation and compensation. MMF first concatenates the latent representations y_t and $\hat{y}_{t-1}$ to form a combined feature map $y_{cat,t}$, which is used to estimate the motion flow between frames. This is achieved through a multi-scale approach, where coarse and fine-grained motion information is fused to produce robust motion embedding e_t [72]:

$$\bar{y}_{t,u} = \frac{\sum_{v\in\vartheta_{u'}} d_{u',v}^{-1} \cdot \hat{y}_{t-1,v}}{\max\left(\sum_{v\in\vartheta_{u'}} d_{u',v}^{-1}, \alpha\right)}, \tag{6.2}$$

where $\bar{y}_{t,u}$ represents the predicted feature vector at position u in the current frame, $\hat{y}_{t-1,v}$ represents the feature vector at position v in the previous frame, u' is the translated coordinate of u, and $\vartheta_{u'}$ denotes the 3-nearest neighbors of u' in $\hat{y}_{t-1}$. The term $d_{u',v} = \|u' - v\|_2^2$ denotes the squared Euclidean distance between coordinates u' and v, where α serves as a penalty coefficient regulating the impact of distant neighboring points. The 3DAWI algorithm further refines this process by adaptively weighting the contribution of each neighbor based on their spatial proximity. This ensures that the predicted feature vectors are more accurate, particularly in regions where the spatial distribution of points is sparse or irregular. The penalty coefficient α plays a crucial role in reducing the impact of distant neighbors that may otherwise introduce significant prediction errors.

Point Cloud Reconstruction To reconstruct the point cloud from the latent representation after inter-frame prediction and residual compression, this module mirrors the operations of the feature extraction process but in reverse. It uses two serially connected Up-sample Blocks to hierarchically reconstruct the point cloud, progressively increasing the resolution at each step. Each Up-sample Block incorporates a sparse transpose convolution layer for feature up-sampling, succeeded by refinement convolutions to enhance the voxel representation. These operations culminate in a final sparse convolution layer that predicts voxel occupancy probabilities, determining whether a voxel is part of the reconstructed point cloud. To maintain sparsity, an adaptive pruning mechanism [72] is employed to remove false positives based on the computed occupancy probability:

$$D = \frac{1}{K} \sum_{k=1}^{K} D_{BCE}^{(k)}, \tag{6.3}$$

where the loss function D is calculated as the average binary cross-entropy (BCE) loss over multiple scales k, where K denotes the total number of scales considered in the reconstruction process.

6.3.2 Predictor-Based DPCC

Feature Extraction The proposed deep learning–based inter-frame encoding scheme is shown in Fig. 6.4, which uses a hierarchical multi-scale 3D feature learning approach. The encoder utilizes sparse convolutions to capture geometric features from the input point cloud frames. For the current frame P_2, the encoder generates multiple down-sampled versions of the input, creating features at different scales, such as P_{0ds}, P_{1ds}, P_{2ds}, and P_{3ds}. These multi-scale features enable efficient spatial information encoding while retaining point cloud structural integrity. The point coordinates undergo progressive down-sampling to reduce point density and ensure computational tractability. Both the encoded features and subsampled coordinates serve as inputs to the inter-frame prediction network for

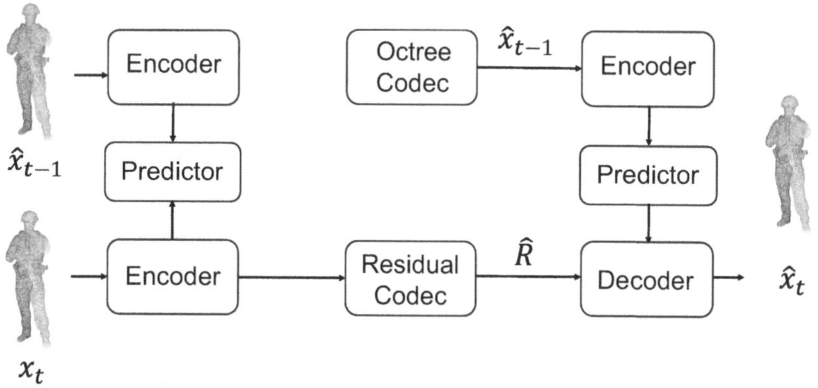

Fig. 6.4 Overall framework of the Predictor-based DPCC (Public-domain open-access image [73])

subsequent processing [73]:

$$y_t = E(x_t), \tag{6.4}$$

where y_t represents the feature embedding of the current frame x_t, and $E(\cdot)$ denotes the encoder function that applies sparse convolutions.

Inter-Frame Prediction This module generates predictions for the current frame's feature embedding $\hat{F}_{2,3ds}$ by processing the decoded feature embedding from the preceding frame $\hat{P}_1$. The prediction network implements a coordinate-targeted convolution operation that projects latent features from $\hat{P}_1$ onto the down-sampled coordinate space of $C_{2,3ds}$. The network architecture integrates multi-scale features from $\hat{P}_1$ with the 3× down-sampled coordinates from P_2 to produce the predicted embedding $\hat{F}_{2,3ds}$ [73]:

$$\hat{F}_{2,3ds} = P(C_{2,3ds}, P_{1,0ds}, P_{1,1ds}, P_{1,2ds}, P_{1,3ds}), \tag{6.5}$$

where $P(\cdot)$ denotes the prediction network transforming multi-scale features and coordinates from the preceding frame to the current frame. The residual features $R_{2,3ds}$ are obtained by computing the difference between the original features $F_{2,3ds}$ and predicted features $\hat{F}_{2,3ds}$ [73]:

$$R_{2,3ds} = F_{2,3ds} - \hat{F}_{2,3ds}. \tag{6.6}$$

The residual features subsequently undergo compression via a learned probabilistic entropy model.

Point Cloud Reconstruction This module reconstructs the current frame from the encoded residual features and the previously decoded frame. The decoder network, which mirrors the encoder architecture, progressively up-samples the down-sampled point cloud tensor $\tilde{P}_{2,3ds}$ to reconstruct the full-resolution point cloud $\tilde{P}_2$ [73]:

$$\tilde{P}_2 = D(\tilde{P}_{2,3ds}), \tag{6.7}$$

where $D(\cdot)$ represents the decoder function that upscales the point cloud tensor to reconstruct the original frame. The reconstruction process involves hierarchical rescaling of the point cloud, where each up-sampling step is followed by a pruning layer to remove false voxels and retain true occupied voxels. This hierarchical reconstruction ensures that the point cloud is reconstructed with high fidelity while maintaining computational efficiency. The combined framework efficiently compresses dynamic point clouds by leveraging temporal correlations between consecutive frames, reducing the bitrate required for transmission while maintaining high reconstruction quality.

6.3.3 Inter-Conditional-Based DPCC

Feature Extraction The overall framework is shown in Fig. 6.5, where the feature extraction process begins by utilizing an extended Multi-scale Sparse Representation (MSR) framework, originally designed for static point cloud geometry compression. The Encoder, or Extractor, applies sparse convolutions and nonlinear activations to downscale the resolution of the input point cloud, aggregating local

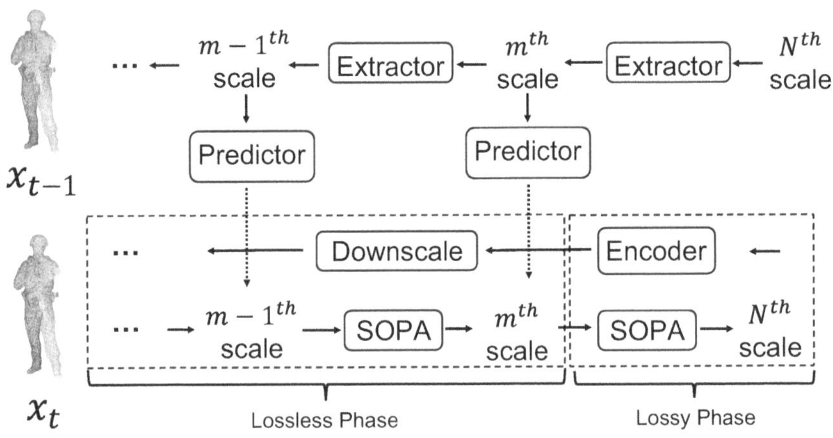

Fig. 6.5 Overall framework of the Inter-Conditional-based DPCC method (Public-domain open-access image [69])

neighborhood information to form spatial intra-frame or temporal inter-frame priors. These extracted features serve as the basis for encoding. Specifically, the encoder employs a convolutional voxel down-sampling layer, followed by Inception-ResNet (IRN) blocks for deep feature aggregation. Each IRN block consists of multiple convolutional layers with a kernel size of $3 \times 3 \times 3$, which helps capture both fine and coarse geometric details across different scales [69]. The feature extraction process is expressed as:

$$y_t = E(x_t), \tag{6.8}$$

where y_t denotes the feature representation of the current frame x_t, and $E(\cdot)$ represents the encoder function that processes the input through multiple scales.

Inter-Frame Prediction The inter-frame prediction module leverages the temporal correlation between consecutive point cloud frames by incorporating multi-scale temporal priors from the previously reconstructed frame. This mapping is implemented through a Predictor network that executes coordinate-targeted convolutions to transfer features between consecutive frames. The prediction network utilizes a one-layer sparse convolution to adaptively transfer information from the temporal reference frame to the current frame. This approach involves downscaling the previous frame's features and then using these features as temporal priors, which are concatenated with spatial priors from the current frame for better occupancy probability approximation [69]. The Inter-frame Prediction process is expressed as:

$$\hat{F}_t = P(C_t, y_{t-1}). \tag{6.9}$$

In this formulation, $\hat{F}_t$ denotes the predicted feature embedding for frame t, C_t corresponds to the current frame's coordinates, and y_{t-1} represents the previous frame's features. The residual features R_t are computed as [69]:

$$R_t = F_t - \hat{F}_t, \tag{6.10}$$

where R_t denotes the residual features, F_t is the actual feature embedding of the current frame, and $\hat{F}_t$ is the predicted embedding. The residuals are encoded using a learned probabilistic entropy model for efficient compression.

Point Cloud Reconstruction This module is designed to reconstruct the point cloud geometry using both spatial and temporal priors. The decoder progressively upscales the down-sampled point cloud tensor to reconstruct the original frame, employing a multi-stage Sparse Occupancy Probability Approximation (SOPA) model. The SOPA model, operating at multiple scales, uses both the spatial priors from the current frame and temporal priors from the reference frame to accurately estimate voxel occupancy, thereby improving the quality of the reconstructed point cloud. The reconstruction involves applying transposed convolutional layers and an adaptive feature concatenation strategy [69], allowing the model to leverage both intra-frame and inter-frame information for enhanced geometric fidelity:

$$\tilde{P}_t = D(R_t, \hat{P}_{t-1}), \tag{6.11}$$

where $\tilde{P}_t$ is the reconstructed point cloud for the current frame, $D(\cdot)$ represents the decoder function, R_t are the encoded residuals, and $\hat{P}_{t-1}$ is the reconstructed previous frame. The framework ensures efficient compression by combining the strengths of multi-scale feature extraction, temporal prediction, and hierarchical reconstruction.

6.3.4 Hierarchical-Based DPCC

Feature Extraction The complete framework architecture, illustrated in Fig. 6.6, employs a feature extraction module comprising cascaded down-sampling blocks and IRNs to hierarchically eliminate spatial redundancies in input point cloud frames. The encoder simultaneously processes both the current frame x_t and the reconstructed previous frame $\hat{x}_{t-1}$, encoding them into multi-scale latent features, denoted as y_t and y_{t-1}, respectively. The process involves down-sampling the point cloud data to extract coarse-to-fine geometric features. This hierarchical approach enables the encoder to effectively capture spatial structures and relevant geometric information across different scales. The down-sampled features are

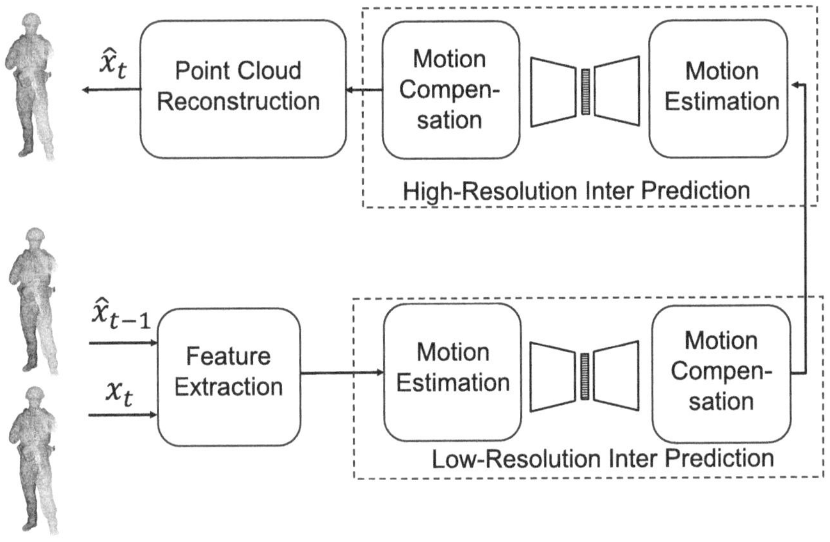

Fig. 6.6 Overall framework of the Hierarchical-based DPCC method (Public-domain open-access image [68])

further processed to support subsequent inter-frame prediction tasks [68]:

$$y_t = E(x_t), \tag{6.12}$$

where y_t represents the latent feature embedding of the current frame x_t, and $E(\cdot)$ denotes the encoding function involving sparse convolutions and down-sampling operations.

Inter-Frame Prediction The inter-frame prediction module introduces a hierarchical motion estimation and motion compensation (Hie-ME/MC) framework, which performs inter-prediction through adaptive granularity selection of optical flows. The motion estimation network uses a KABM approach to determine the potential corresponding points between frames based on geometry and feature correlation. The KABM network is designed to enhance the accuracy of optical flow estimation by leveraging both local geometry and feature similarities. The inter-prediction process begins with a low-resolution inter-prediction that generates a coarse optical flow $\mathbf{e}_{t,l}$ from the 3x down-sampled latent features $y_{t-1}^{3\downarrow}$ and $y_t^{3\downarrow}$. The coarse optical flow captures large movements between blocks, providing a base prediction for the higher-resolution inter-prediction stage [68]:

$$\mathbf{e}_{t,l} = P_{low}\left(y_{t-1}^{3\downarrow}, y_t^{3\downarrow}\right), \tag{6.13}$$

where $P_{low}(\cdot)$ denotes the low-resolution motion prediction function. This coarse optical flow is up-sampled and refined in the high-resolution inter-prediction stage to generate a fine-grained optical flow $\mathbf{e}_{t,h}$ [68], which is used to predict finer motion details:

$$\mathbf{e}_{t,h} = P_{high}\left(\mathbf{e}_{t,l}, y_{t-1}^{2\downarrow}, y_t^{2\downarrow}\right). \tag{6.14}$$

The combined optical flows $\mathbf{e}_{t,l}$ and $\mathbf{e}_{t,h}$ are used to generate a final motion-compensated prediction $\hat{y}_t$ of the current frame's latent features.

Point Cloud Reconstruction This module utilizes both predicted latent features and residual information to reconstruct point cloud frames. Mirroring the encoder's architecture, the decoder employs cascaded up-sampling blocks to progressively restore the original point cloud resolution. The reconstruction pipeline initiates by decoding the low-resolution optical flow $\mathbf{e}_{t,l}$ and high-resolution optical flow $\mathbf{e}_{t,h}$, which are then used to derive motion-compensated features. These features are then combined with the decoded residuals to produce the final reconstructed latent features $\tilde{y}_t$. The decoder's up-sampling operations mirror the encoder's down-sampling steps [68], using transpose convolutions to upscale the point cloud data back to its original resolution:

$$\tilde{x}_t = D(\tilde{y}_t), \tag{6.15}$$

where $\tilde{x}_t$ is the reconstructed point cloud frame, and $D(\cdot)$ denotes the decoding function that involves up-sampling and feature refinement. The hierarchical inter-frame block matching strategy employed in this framework allows for effective compression by accurately capturing both coarse and fine-grained motions, yielding significant enhancements in reconstructed dynamic point cloud fidelity.

6.3.5 Diverse Context Model-Based DPCC

Feature Extraction The overall framework architecture, illustrated in Fig. 6.7, incorporates an octree-based feature extraction module for efficient dynamic point cloud representation. The octree structure partitions the 3D space hierarchically through cubic bounding boxes, where each node encodes occupancy status as an 8-bit binary value, enabling compact and progressive point cloud encoding. Feature extraction is augmented through multi-frame, multi-scale context integration, combining localized detail preservation with global sparse context utilization. To achieve this, the encoder network integrates a series of transformer-based modules designed

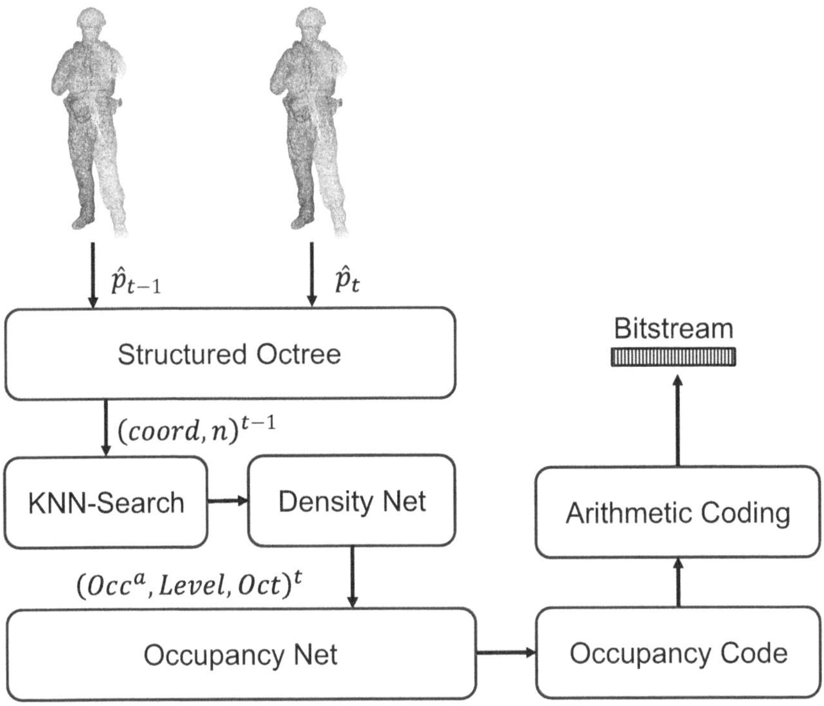

Fig. 6.7 Overall framework of DCM method (©2023 IEEE. Reprinted, with permission, from ref. [67])

to handle different types of contexts effectively. These modules include a density network for inter-frame context extraction and a two-stream occupancy network for intra-frame context handling. The dense context stream captures detailed local information, while the sparse context stream focuses on large-scale geometric features, ensuring a comprehensive feature extraction process [67]. The feature extraction process is expressed as:

$$E_{inter} = [e(0), e(1), \ldots, e(y)], \tag{6.16}$$

where E_{inter} represents the inter-frame node embeddings aggregated from y nearest neighbor nodes found using the kNN algorithm in the previous frame, enhancing temporal context awareness.

Inter-Frame Prediction The inter-frame prediction module employs a transformer-based density network to capture temporal context through analysis of co-positioned node densities across consecutive frames. This process utilizes kNN search to aggregate contextual information from topologically similar nodes in preceding frames. Specifically, for each node in the current frame, the algorithm identifies the y closest neighbors within the corresponding octree level of the previous frame. The density of a node is represented by the number of its child nodes, and this density information is used as a proxy for the inter-frame context. The embeddings of these neighboring nodes are then concatenated to form the inter-frame node embeddings, which are processed by the transformer encoder to generate the inter-frame density context [67]. The Inter-frame Prediction process is expressed as:

$$F_{Inter} = \text{InterEncoder}(E_{inter}), \tag{6.17}$$

where F_{Inter} is the output of the inter-frame density context, and InterEncoder denotes the transformer encoder applied to the concatenated embeddings.

Point Cloud Reconstruction The point cloud reconstruction module reconstructs the point cloud geometry by combining the intra-frame and inter-frame contexts extracted by the two-stream occupancy network. This network employs separate streams for dense and sparse context extraction, followed by a fusion encoder that merges the features from both streams. The dense context stream utilizes a sliding context window to capture detailed local information within a small spatial extent, while the sparse context stream employs a longer sliding window and a dilated mask to gather large-scale sparse context. The fusion encoder integrates these diverse contexts to predict the occupancy probability distribution of octree nodes, which is crucial for accurate point cloud reconstruction. The final reconstructed point cloud is obtained by applying arithmetic coding to the predicted occupancy probabilities, ensuring efficient compression [67]:

$$Q(X_i) = \prod_k q_k(x_k | f_k^F; \theta), \tag{6.18}$$

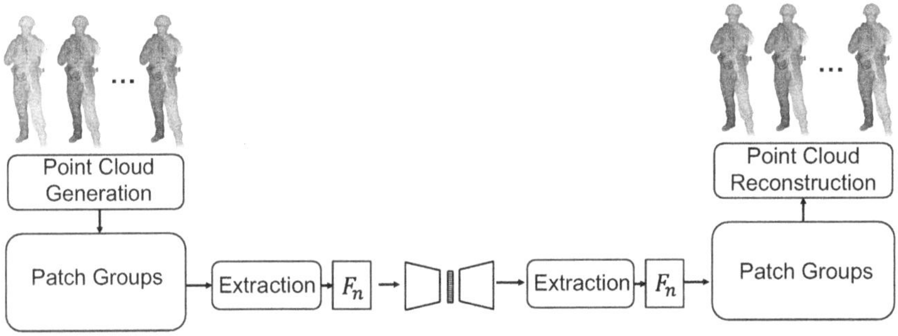

Fig. 6.8 Overall framework of the patchDPCC method (Public-domain open-access image [59])

where $Q(X_i)$ represents the estimated probability distribution of the occupancy codes, f_k^F is the concatenated feature from both dense and sparse streams, and θ denotes the parameters of the occupancy network. This diverse context model effectively balances the extraction of local and large-scale geometric features, significantly improving the compression efficiency for dynamic point clouds.

6.3.6 PatchDPCC

Feature Extraction The overall framework architecture, illustrated in Fig. 6.8, incorporates a point-based deep learning approach within its feature extraction module, eliminating voxelization requirements while preserving point cloud geometric accuracy. This design avoids voxel-induced artifacts by directly processing raw point data. The extraction pipeline initiates by partitioning the point cloud into uniformly sized patches, which are designated as I-patches for I-frames and P-patches for P-frames, through an iterative algorithm guaranteeing consistent point counts per patch, facilitating uniform processing in the subsequent steps. The I-patch from the I-frame serves as a reference for generating corresponding patches in the P-frames using Iterative Closest Point (ICP) alignment, preserving spatial consistency across frames. This process extracts point-wise features, which are then used for entropy coding, ensuring efficient compression and fast reconstruction speeds [59].[1] The feature extraction process is expressed as:

$$F = E(C), \tag{6.19}$$

where F represents the extracted features and $E(\cdot)$ denotes the encoding function applied to the patch coordinates C.

[1] https://ojs.aaai.org/index.php/AAAI/article/view/28238

Inter-Frame Prediction This module utilizes a feature transfer mechanism to exploit the temporal correlation between consecutive frames. By applying a point-wise feature transfer, the features extracted from an I-patch are adapted and transferred to the corresponding P-patches in subsequent frames. This process involves a series of steps where features from the I-patch are first concatenated with the coordinates of the P-patches, followed by an MLP that refines the features. The feature transfer module uses kNN search to align points from the P-patch with those in the transformed I-patch, capturing local geometric variations while maintaining temporal coherence. This approach enhances the quality of the features used for compression by ensuring that the inter-frame similarities are effectively leveraged, reducing redundancy and improving compression efficiency [59]. The inter-frame prediction process is expressed as:

$$F_i = T(F_{i-1}, C_i, C_{i-1}), \tag{6.20}$$

where F_i is the feature of the i-th P-patch, $T(\cdot)$ represents the feature transfer function, and C_i, C_{i-1} denote the coordinates of the current and previous patches, respectively.

Point Cloud Reconstruction This module performs reconstruction of dynamic point cloud frames from their compressed feature representations. This module employs a coordinate reconstruction strategy that combines both the transferred features and the original features from the I-patches. The reconstruction process begins by decoding the quantized features back into point-wise coordinates. A refinement stage subsequently applies self-attention mechanisms to optimize point positioning accuracy, ensuring that the reconstructed points closely match their original positions in the point cloud. The attention mechanism captures long-range dependencies within the patch, allowing the network to correct any deviations caused during the compression and feature transfer processes. This results in a high-fidelity reconstruction that retains the original geometric structure of the point cloud while achieving significant compression [59]. The point cloud reconstruction process is expressed as:

$$\hat{C} = R(F), \tag{6.21}$$

where $\hat{C}$ denotes the reconstructed coordinates, and $R(\cdot)$ is the reconstruction function applied to the decoded features F. The patchDPCC framework's patch-based approach and efficient feature transfer mechanism significantly improve compression performance by reducing redundancy across frames while maintaining high reconstruction quality. Experimental results demonstrate patchDPCC's superior performance over state-of-the-art compression methods, achieving higher compression ratios and faster decoding speeds.

6.4 Comparative Analysis

This section provides a comprehensive comparative analysis of deep learning–based DPCC methodologies. We systematically categorize these methods to provide a clear view of their structural and functional components. We classify these methods along five critical dimensions, i.e., data structure, feature extraction, inter-prediction, reconstruction, and the time of publication, as shown in Table 6.1.

The term "data structure" denotes the fundamental representation format employed by point cloud processing algorithms. Three primary categories are identified: point-based, voxel-based, and octree-based representations. This classification helps to understand the foundational data representation upon which the compression algorithms operate. The "feature extraction component" encompasses the methodologies for deriving rich features from point cloud data, which are essential for achieving efficient compression and accurate reconstruction. Next, we explore the "inter-prediction" strategies, which examine how temporal information between consecutive frames is utilized to enhance compression. This dimension highlights diverse methods such as feature transfer modules, multi-scale feature prediction, KNN-attention block-matching (KABM), and inter-frame density context. These strategies illustrate the varying ways algorithms exploit temporal correlations to achieve higher compression efficiency. The "reconstruction" dimension delves into the methodologies used to reconstruct the original point cloud from its compressed representation. Lastly, the "time" dimension provides a chronological context, indicating the year and conference where each method was introduced. This timeline allows us to understand the progression and evolution of dynamic point cloud coding methods in recent years.

Table 6.1 Various dynamic point cloud coding methods and their components (Source: Author)

Method	Published in	Data structure	Feature extraction	Inter-prediction	Reconstruction
patchDPCC [59]	AAAI 24	Point	MLP	Feature Transfer Module	MLP
Predictor-based DPCC [70]	TIP 24	Voxel	Down-sample Block	Multi-scale feature prediction	Up-sample Block
Hierarchical-based DPCC [68]	MM 23	Voxel	Down-sample Block	KABM	Up-sample Block
Inter Conditional-based DPCC [69]	arXiv 23	Voxel	Down-sample Block	Feature Concatenation	SOPA
DCM [67]	VCIP 23	Octree	Two-stream Occupancy Network	Inter-frame density context	/
D-DPCC [60]	IJCAI 22	Voxel	Down-sample Block	3DAWI	Up-sample Block

This systematic analysis provides detailed insights into deep learning–based dynamic point cloud coding approaches, examining their data structure implementations, feature extraction methods, inter-frame prediction mechanisms, and reconstruction techniques.

6.5 Summary

This chapter provides an in-depth exploration of dynamic point cloud coding techniques, emphasizing the role of deep learning in advancing this field. We examine a variety of methods and their applications, highlighting the progress made in optimizing compression efficiency while maintaining high fidelity in 3D data representation. The discussion includes detailed overviews of several key approaches, such as patch-based and voxel-based methods, as well as innovative strategies like feature transfer and multi-scale prediction. Throughout the chapter, we analyze the critical components that define deep learning–based dynamic point cloud coding, including feature extraction, temporal prediction, and point cloud reconstruction. We discuss how different methods utilize these components to achieve efficient compression, focusing on the diverse strategies employe to handle spatial and temporal information in dynamic environments. The evolution of these techniques is also outlined, showcasing the advancements in neural network design and their impact on the capabilities of compression algorithms.

Looking ahead, the future of dynamic point cloud coding lies in further enhancing these techniques to meet the growing demands of applications like augmented reality, autonomous navigation, and 3D video conferencing. Continued research is necessary to develop models that are not only more efficient but also capable of generalizing across varied datasets and scenarios. The incorporation of emerging technologies and advanced computational architectures is anticipated to address existing challenges, enabling more robust and scalable dynamic point cloud coding solutions. In conclusion, deep learning–based dynamic point cloud coding represents a rapidly evolving area of study, with significant potential to transform how 3D data are managed and transmitted across different platforms. As the field advances, it will open up new possibilities for more immersive and interactive digital experiences, driven by the need for high-quality and real-time 3D data processing. For readers who are interested in the related technologies of AI-based image and video coding, please refer to [74].

Exercises

1. Please explain the main differences between traditional point cloud coding methods and deep learning–based approaches. What are the primary advantages of using deep learning for dynamic point cloud coding?

2. Please describe how temporal prediction is utilized in deep learning–based dynamic point cloud coding. What are the benefits and challenges of implementing effective temporal prediction?
3. In the context of dynamic point cloud coding, what additional criteria could be used to evaluate the performance of deep learning models beyond compression ratio and reconstruction quality? Provide at least two examples.
4. Please explain the concept of feature extraction in deep learning–based dynamic point cloud coding. What role does it play, and what are some common methods used?
5. Please propose a potential future direction for research in deep learning-based dynamic point cloud coding. Justify why this direction would be valuable to explore.
6. What are the key challenges associated with reconstructing high-quality point clouds in deep learning–based compression methods?
7. Please discuss how feature transfer mechanisms improve the efficiency of dynamic point cloud coding. Provide an example of a feature transfer method mentioned in the chapter.
8. Why is the choice of data structure important in deep learning–based point cloud coding methods? Compare the use of point-based and voxel-based data structures.
9. What are the advantages of using attention mechanisms in deep learning models for dynamic point cloud coding?
10. How do deep learning–based methods handle the trade-off between compression efficiency and computational complexity in dynamic point cloud coding?

References

1. H. Zheng, W. Gao, Z. Yu, T. Zhao, G. Li, ViewPCGC: view-guided learned point cloud geometry compression, in *Proceedings of the 32nd ACM International Conference on Multimedia* (2024), pp. 7152–7161
2. L. Xie, W. Gao, H. Zheng, G. Li, ROI-guided point cloud geometry compression towards human and machine vision, in *Proceedings of the 32nd ACM International Conference on Multimedia* (2024), pp. 3741–3750
3. L. Xie, W. Gao, H. Zheng, G. Li, SPCGC: scalable point cloud geometry compression for machine vision, in *2024 IEEE International Conference on Robotics and Automation (ICRA)* (IEEE, Piscataway, 2024), pp. 17 272–17 278
4. L. Xie, W. Gao, H. Zheng, H. Ye, Semantic-aware visual decomposition for point cloud geometry compression, in *2024 Data Compression Conference (DCC)* (IEEE, Piscataway, 2024), pp. 595–595
5. Z. Qi, W. Gao, Variable-rate point cloud geometry compression based on feature adjustment and interpolation, in *2024 Data Compression Conference (DCC)* (IEEE, Piscataway, 2024), pp. 63–72
6. Z. Yu, W. Gao, When dynamic neural network meets point cloud compression: computation-aware variable rate and checkerboard context, in *2024 Data Compression Conference (DCC)* (IEEE, Piscataway, 2024), pp. 600–600

7. L. Xie, W. Gao, S. Fan, Z. Yao, PDNet: parallel dual-branch network for point cloud geometry compression and analysis, in *2024 Data Compression Conference (DCC)* (IEEE, Piscataway, 2024), pp. 596–596
8. L. Xie, W. Gao, H. Zheng, End-to-end point cloud geometry compression and analysis with sparse tensor, in *Proceedings of the 1st International Workshop on Advances in Point Cloud Compression, Processing and Analysis* (2022), pp. 27–32
9. C. Fu, G. Li, R. Song, W. Gao, S. Liu, Octattention: Octree-based large-scale contexts model for point cloud compression. Proc. AAAI Conf. Artif. Intell. **36**(1), 625–633 (2022)
10. C. Zhang, W. Gao, AdaDPCC: Adaptive rate control and rate-distortion-complexity optimization for dynamic point cloud compression, in *Proceedings of the AAAI Conference on Artificial Intelligence* (2025)
11. K. Wang, W. Gao, UniPCGC: towards practical point cloud geometry compression via an efficient unified approach, in *Proceedings of the AAAI Conference on Artificial Intelligence* (2025)
12. K. Zheng, W. Gao, H. Zheng, Octree-based learned point cloud geometry compression: A lossy perspective, in *2025 Data Compression Conference (DCC)* (IEEE, Piscataway, 2025)
13. Z. Qi, H. Liu, W. Gao, Variable-rate point cloud compression with channel-wise entropy modeling, in *2025 Data Compression Conference (DCC)* (IEEE, Piscataway, 2025)
14. Y. Wu, L. Xie, S. Sun, W. Gao, Y. Yan, Adaptive intra period size for deep learning-based screen content video coding, in *2024 IEEE International Conference on Multimedia and Expo Workshops (ICMEW)* (IEEE, Piscataway, 2024), pp. 1–6
15. H. Zheng, W. Gao, End-to-end RGB-D image compression via exploiting channel-modality redundancy. Proc. AAAI Conf. Artif. Intell. **38**(7), 7562–7570 (2024)
16. L. Tao, W. Gao, G. Li, C. Zhang, AdaNIC: towards practical neural image compression via dynamic transform routing, in *Proceedings of the IEEE/CVF International Conference on Computer Vision* (2023), pp. 16 879–16 888
17. Y. Wu, W. Gao, End-to-end lossless compression of high precision depth maps guided by pseudo-residual, in *2022 Data Compression Conference (DCC)* (IEEE, Piscataway, 2022), pp. 489–489
18. Y. Wu, Z. Qi, H. Zheng, L. Tao, W. Gao, Deep image compression with latent optimization and piece-wise quantization approximation, in *Proceedings of the IEEE/CVF Conference on Computer Vision and Pattern Recognition* (2021), pp. 1926–1930
19. W. Gao, L. Tao, L. Zhou, D. Yang, X. Zhang, Z. Guo, Low-rate image compression with super-resolution learning, in *Proceedings of the IEEE/CVF Conference on Computer Vision and Pattern Recognition Workshops* (2020), pp. 154–155
20. Y. Li, W. Gao, G. Li, S. Ma, Saliency segmentation oriented deep image compression with novel bit allocation. IEEE Trans. Image Proces. **34**, 16–29 (2025)
21. S. Fan, W. Gao, G. Li, Salient object detection for point clouds, in *European Conference on Computer Vision* (Springer, Berlin, 2022), pp. 1–19
22. S. Luo, W. Gao, A general framework for rotation invariant point cloud analysis, in *ICASSP 2024-2024 IEEE International Conference on Acoustics, Speech and Signal Processing (ICASSP)* (IEEE, Piscataway, 2024), pp. 3665–3669
23. X. Lu, W. Gao, AttentiveNet: detecting small objects for lidar point clouds by attending to important points, in *2023 IEEE International Conference on Visual Communications and Image Processing (VCIP)* (IEEE, Piscataway, 2023), pp. 1–5
24. Z. Pan, N. Zhang, W. Gao, S. Liu, G. Li, Less is more: label recommendation for weakly supervised point cloud semantic segmentation. Proc. AAAI Conf. Artif. Intell. **38**(5), 4397–4405 (2024)
25. Z. Pan, G. Liu, W. Gao, T.H. Li, EPContrast: effective point-level contrastive learning for large-scale point cloud understanding, in *2024 IEEE International Conference on Multimedia and Expo (ICME)* (IEEE, Piscataway, 2024), pp. 1–6
26. N. Zhang, Z. Pan, T.H. Li, W. Gao, G. Li, Improving graph representation for point cloud segmentation via attentive filtering, in *Proceedings of the IEEE/CVF Conference on Computer Vision and Pattern Recognition* (2023), pp. 1244–1254

27. K. Wen, N. Zhang, G. Li, W. Gao, MPVNN: multi-resolution point-voxel non-parametric network for 3D point cloud processing, in *2024 IEEE International Conference on Multimedia and Expo (ICME)* (IEEE, Piscataway, 2024), pp. 1–6
28. Z. Pan, N. Zhang, W. Gao, S. Liu, G. Li, Point cloud semantic segmentation with sparse and inhomogeneous annotations, in *Proceedings of the AAAI Conference on Artificial Intelligence* (2025)
29. R. Zhang, G. Li, W. Gao, S. Liu, A quantum-inspired framework in leader-servant mode for large-scale multi-modal place recognition. IEEE Trans. Intell. Transport. Syst. **26**(2), 2027–2039 (2025)
30. D. Yang, W. Gao, PointCHD: a point cloud benchmark for congenital heart disease classification and segmentation. IEEE J. Biomed. Health Inf. **29**(4), 2683–2694 (2025)
31. S. Fan, W. Gao, G. Li, Point-MPP: point cloud self-supervised learning from masked position prediction. IEEE Trans. Neural Netw. Learn. Syst. **36**(7), 12964–12976 (2025)
32. W. Gao, G. Li, H. Yuan, R. Hamzaoui, Z. Li, S. Liu, Apccpa'22: 1st international workshop on advances in point cloud compression, processing and analysis, in *Proceedings of the 30th ACM International Conference on Multimedia* (2022), pp. 7392–7393
33. W. Gao, G. Li, Point cloud compression, enhancement and applications: from 3D perception to large models, in *Proceedings of the 32nd ACM International Conference on Multimedia* (2024), pp. 11 292–11 293
34. H. Sun, G. Li, S. Chen, L. Li, W. Gao, Special topic on 3D point cloud processing and applications. ZTE Commun **21**(4), 1 (2023)
35. W. Gao, W. Gao, X. Mu, C. Peng, G. Li, Overview and comparison of AVS point cloud compression standard. APSIPA Trans. Signal Inf. Proces. **14**(2), 1–33 (2025)
36. W. Gao, S. Wang, X. Zhang, S. Kwong, Editorial for special issue on deep learning-based data compression. APSIPA Trans. Signal Inf. Proces. **13**(6), 1–2 (2024)
37. W. Gao, H. Ye, G. Li, H. Zheng, Y. Wu, L. Xie, Openpointcloud: an open-source algorithm library of deep learning based point cloud compression, in *Proceedings of the 30th ACM International Conference on Multimedia* (2022), pp. 7347–7350
38. Y. Zhang, W. Gao, G. Li, Openpointcloud-v2: a deep learning based open-source algorithm library of point cloud processing, in *Proceedings of the 1st International Workshop on Advances in Point Cloud Compression, Processing and Analysis* (2022), pp. 51–55
39. L. Xie, W. Gao, LearningPCC: a pytorch library for learning-based point cloud compression, in *Proceedings of the 32nd ACM International Conference on Multimedia* (2024), pp. 11 234–11 238
40. L. Xie, W. Gao, PCHMVision: an open-source library of point cloud compression for human and machine vision, in *Proceedings of the 32nd ACM International Conference on Multimedia* (2024), pp. 11 239–11 243
41. S. Schwarz, M. Preda, V. Baroncini, M. Budagavi, P. César, P.A. Chou, R.A. Cohen, M. Krivokuca, S. Lasserre, Z. Li, J. Llach, K. Mammou, R. Mekuria, O. Nakagami, E. Siahaan, A.J. Tabatabai, A.M. Tourapis, V. Zakharchenko, Emerging MPEG standards for point cloud compression. IEEE J. Emerg. Sel. Topics Circuits Syst. **9**(1), 133–148 (2019)
42. M. Quach, G. Valenzise, F. Dufaux, Learning convolutional transforms for lossy point cloud geometry compression, in *IEEE International Conference on Image Processing* (2019), pp. 4320–4324
43. J. Wang, D. Ding, Z. Li, Z. Ma, Multiscale point cloud geometry compression, in *Data Compression Conference*, ed. by A. Bilgin, M.W. Marcellin, J. Serra-Sagristà, J.A. Storer (2021), pp. 73–82
44. G. Li, W. Gao, W. Gao, *Point Cloud Compression: Technologies and Standardization* (Springer, Berlin, 2024)
45. W. Gao, G. Li, *Deep Learning for 3D Point Clouds* (Springer, Berlin, 2024)
46. T. Huang, Y. Liu, 3D point cloud geometry compression on deep learning, in *ACM International Conference on Multimedia*, ed. by L. Amsaleg, B. Huet, M.A. Larson, G. Gravier, H. Hung, C. Ngo, W.T. Ooi (2019), pp. 890–898

47. C. Fu, G. Li, R. Song, W. Gao, S. Liu, Octattention: octree-based large-scale contexts model for point cloud compression, in *AAAI* (2022), pp. 625–633
48. R. Song, C. Fu, S. Liu, G. Li, Efficient hierarchical entropy model for learned point cloud compression, in *IEEE/CVF Conference on Computer Vision and Pattern Recognition (CVPR)*, Vancouver, BC, Canada, 2023, pp. 14368–14377. https://doi.org/10.1109/CVPR52729.2023.01381
49. W. Liu, W. Gao, X. Mu, Fast inter-frame motion prediction for compressed dynamic point cloud attribute enhancement. Proc. AAAI Conf. Artif. Intell. **38**(4), 3720–3728 (2024)
50. Z. Yang, W. Gao, X. Lu, Danet: density-adaptive network for geometry-based point cloud compression artifacts removal, in *2023 IEEE International Conference on Visual Communications and Image Processing (VCIP)* (IEEE, Piscataway, 2023), pp. 1–5
51. X. Fan, G. Li, D. Li, Y. Ren, W. Gao, T.H. Li, Deep geometry post-processing for decompressed point clouds, in *2022 IEEE International Conference on Multimedia and Expo (ICME)* (IEEE, Piscataway, 2022), pp. 1–6
52. X. Zhang, G. Liao, W. Gao, G. Li, TDRNet: transformer-based dual-branch restoration network for geometry based point cloud compression artifacts, in *2022 IEEE International Conference on Multimedia and Expo (ICME)* (IEEE, Piscataway, 2022), pp. 1–6
53. Z. Li, G. Li, T.H. Li, S. Liu, W. Gao, Semantic point cloud upsampling. IEEE Trans Multimedia **25**, 3432–3442 (2023)
54. Z. Li, S. Liu, W. Gao, G. Li, G. Li, S4r: rethinking point cloud sampling via guiding upsampling-aware perception. IEEE Trans. Multimedia **27**, 6677–6689 (2025)
55. R. Zhang, W. Gao, G. Li, T.H. Li, Qinet: decision surface learning and adversarial enhancement for quasi-immune completion of diverse corrupted point clouds. IEEE Trans. Geosci. Remote Sens. **60**, 1–14 (2022)
56. R. Bao, Y. Ren, G. Li, W. Gao, S. Liu, Flow-based point cloud completion network with adversarial refinement, in *ICASSP 2022-2022 IEEE International Conference on Acoustics, Speech and Signal Processing (ICASSP)* (IEEE, Piscataway, 2022), pp. 2559–2563
57. J. Chen, G. Li, R. Zhang, T.H. Li, W. Gao, Pointivae: invertible variational autoencoder framework for 3D point cloud generation, in *2022 IEEE International Conference on Image Processing (ICIP)* (IEEE, Piscataway, 2022), pp. 3216–3220
58. R. Zhang, J. Chen, W. Gao, G. Li, T.H. Li, PointOT: interpretable geometry-inspired point cloud generative model via optimal transport. IEEE Trans. Circuits Syst. Video Technol. **32**(10), 6792–6806 (2022)
59. Z. Pan, M. Xiao, X. Han, D. Yu, G. Zhang, Y. Liu, patchDPCC: a patchwise deep compression framework for dynamic point clouds, in *AAAI* (2024), pp. 4406–4414
60. T. Fan, L. Gao, Y. Xu, Z. Li, D. Wang, D-DPCC: deep dynamic point cloud compression via 3d motion prediction, in *IJCAI*, ed. by L.D. Raedt (2022), pp. 898–904
61. S. Fan, W. Gao, Screen-based 3D subjective experiment software, in *Proceedings of the 31st ACM International Conference on Multimedia* (2023), pp. 9672–9675
62. J. Wang, W. Gao, G. Li, Zoom to perceive better: no-reference point cloud quality assessment via exploring effective multiscale feature. IEEE Trans. Circuits Syst. Video Technol. **34**(7), 6334–6346 (2024)
63. J. Wang, W. Gao, G. Li, Applying collaborative adversarial learning to blind point cloud quality measurement. IEEE Trans. Instrum. Measure. **72**, 1–15 (2023)
64. H. Li, W. Gao, Information exploration of projected views for point cloud quality measurement. IEEE Trans. Instrum. Measure. **74**, 1–14 (2025)
65. S. Fan, W. Gao, Z. Chen, G. Li, G. Liu, Q. Wang, Stochasticity-aware no-reference point cloud quality assessment, in *International Joint Conference on Artificial Intelligence* (2025)
66. A. Gu, T. Dao, Mamba: linear-time sequence modeling with selective state spaces (2024). [Online]. Available: https://arxiv.org/abs/2312.00752
67. D. Zuo, P. Yu, R. Huang, Y. Huang, W. Sun, F. Liang, Diverse context model for large-scale dynamic point cloud compression, in *VCIP* (2023), pp. 1–5
68. S. Xia, T. Fan, Y. Xu, J. Hwang, Z. Li, Learning dynamic point cloud compression via hierarchical inter-frame block matching, in *ACM International Conference Multimedia*, ed.

by A. El-Saddik, T. Mei, R. Cucchiara, M. Bertini, D.P.T. Vallejo, P.K. Atrey, M.S. Hossain (2023), pp. 7993–8003
69. J. Wang, D. Ding, H. Chen, Z. Ma, Dynamic point cloud geometry compression using multiscale inter conditional coding. arXiv preprint arXiv:2301.12165 (2023)
70. A. Akhtar, Z. Li, G.V.D. Auwera, Inter-frame compression for dynamic point cloud geometry coding. IEEE Trans. Image Process. **33**, 584–594 (2024)
71. L. Xie, W. Gao, H. Zheng, G. Li, ROI-guided point cloud geometry compression towards human and machine vision. arXiv preprint arXiv:2504.14240 (2025)
72. T. Fan, L. Gao, Y. Xu, Z. Li, D. Wang, D-DPCC: deep dynamic point cloud compression via 3D motion prediction. arXiv preprint arXiv:2205.01135 (2022)
73. A. Akhtar, Z. Li, G. Van der Auwera, Inter-frame compression for dynamic point cloud geometry coding. arXiv preprint arXiv:2207.12554 (2022)
74. W. Gao, *AI-based Image and Video Coding: Methods, Standards, and Applications* (Springer, Berlin, 2025)

Chapter 7
Human and Machine Perception Oriented 3D Point Cloud Coding

Abstract This chapter discusses human and machine perception oriented point cloud coding technology, focusing on how to meet the needs of human visual perception and machine vision perception with the restricted bandwidth. Traditional point cloud coding techniques primarily optimize signal fidelity and human visual perception. However, as machine vision tasks become increasingly prevalent, new methods have been developed to optimize the machine perception performance. This chapter provides a detailed overview of several innovative point cloud coding frameworks, which enhance compression performance and task efficiency through techniques like octree depth prediction, semantic information extraction, and dual-branch architectures. It also explores how adaptive coding strategy can better support real-time processing for specific application scenarios, such as LiDAR point cloud coding in autonomous driving. Overall, this chapter summarizes the latest advancements in the field of point cloud coding and proposes potential future research directions.

Keywords Human and machine perception oriented coding · Point cloud coding · Machine vision · Human visual experience · Semantic-aware compression · Feature-based compression · Region of interest (RoI)

7.1 Introduction

To address the challenge of point cloud coding, researchers have focused on enhancing human visual quality metrics [1–11] under constrained bit rates, aiming to achieve reconstructed outputs that closely match the original data fidelity. This field has evolved through two principal methodologies: (1) Conventional approaches employing established image and video compression techniques including discrete cosine transform (DCT), motion estimation, predictive coding, quantization, and entropy coding. (2) Modern deep learning–based techniques that leverage neural architectures for perceptual quality preservation. The emergence of deep learning has introduced various neural network-based solutions [12] specifically designed for

W. Gao, *AI-based 3D Point Cloud Coding*,
https://doi.org/10.1007/978-981-95-0660-6_7

accurate geometric and textural reconstruction of compressed point cloud data [13–22].

However, for machine vision tasks, the necessity of fully decoding the point cloud beforehand limits compression efficiency. Machine vision applications commonly involve point cloud classification, object detection, and object segmentation [23–32]. While decoding high-quality point clouds can lead to substantial computational overhead, decoding lower quality point clouds may undermine feature extraction, ultimately impairing analysis performance.

7.2 Overview of Perception Oriented 3D Point Cloud Coding

Like image and video coding [33–43], the development of point cloud coding algorithms for machine vision continues to evolve to cater to its varied practical requirements. These techniques generally fall into two main types. The first type involves compressing the point cloud and subsequently utilizing this compressed data for downstream machine vision tasks [24–26, 31, 44–46], as depicted in Fig. 7.1. Typically, the encoding-decoding process in this type employs either a heuristic region-of-interest (RoI) bit allocation method or a dual optimization approach that integrates point cloud reconstruction with targeted task optimizations. However, this type faces certain limitations. The reconstruction of the point cloud imposes additional computational demands, as the intelligent analysis is only carried out after this reconstruction phase. Furthermore, the reconstructed point cloud often experiences significant quality distortion, compromising both signal fidelity and visual quality.

The second branch, the Intelligent Compression Module (ICM) framework, adopts a feature-based method tailored to specific tasks, which reduces transmission costs by only compressing the features extracted from the point cloud, as illustrated in Fig. 7.2. This allows for direct intelligent analysis from the reconstructed features in downstream tasks. However, this method faces challenges in widespread practical use, because it is designed to support only particular intelligent tasks, which restricts its adaptability across different tasks or application environments. Given the importance of collaboration between human and machine in compression, as emphasized in various studies [1, 23, 47–55], the International Organization

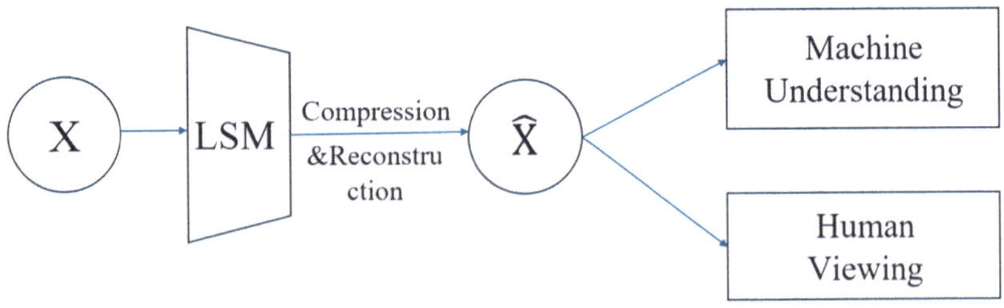

Fig. 7.1 The first branch of point cloud coding in machine vision. Source: Author

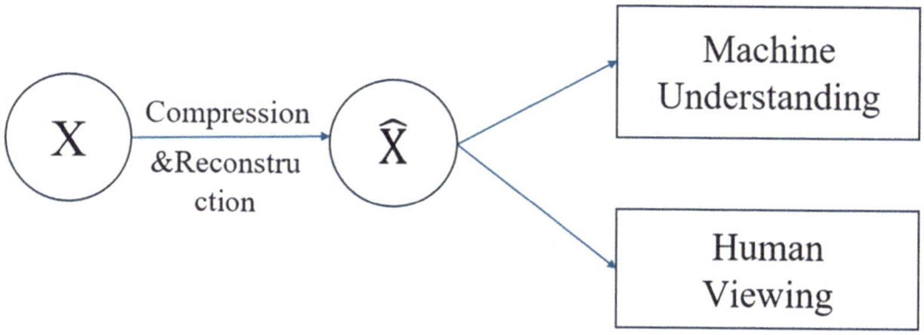

Fig. 7.2 The second branch of point cloud coding in machine vision. Source: Author

for Standardization (ISO) has developed standards relevant to point cloud coding technologies. To systematically tackle Point Cloud Compression (PCC), the Moving Picture Experts Group (MPEG) initiated standardization efforts in 2017, culminating in the establishment of the first PCC standard in 2021. MPEG has since introduced three PCC test models, including TMC1, TMC2 [56], and TMC3. Given the similarities in geometry compression methods between TMC1 and TMC3, they were merged into a unified platform, TMC13 [57], in 2018. The primary aspects of PCC involve geometry encoding, which compresses the 3D coordinates of the points, and attribute encoding, which focuses on compressing associated attributes like color and reflectivity.

7.3 Typical Methods of Perception Oriented Coding

In the domain of point cloud coding, to satisfy the requirements of both human and machine vision, numerous innovative approaches have been developed by researchers. These strategies aim to enhance the compression efficiency of point cloud data and simultaneously optimize the efficacy of machine vision tasks, ensuring superior visual quality is maintained. Notable techniques include scalable point cloud coding frameworks, semantic-aware compression methods, and parallel dual-branch networks. Such techniques are extensively utilized in sectors like autonomous vehicles, intelligent surveillance, and virtual reality. By merging geometric and semantic information, these methods substantially improve the effectiveness of both point cloud coding and analysis while also managing to lower the bitrate.

7.3.1 SPC-Net

SPC-Net [58] is a novel scalable point cloud coding framework designed to simultaneously support both machine vision and human vision tasks, as shown

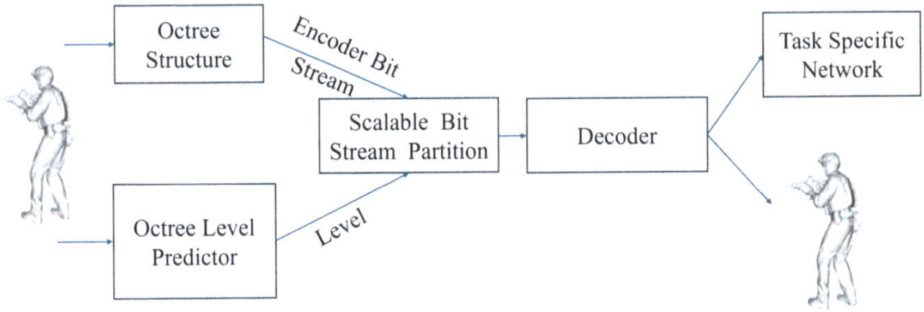

Fig. 7.3 The overall structure of SPC-Net network. Public domain open access image [58]

in Fig. 7.3. This framework describes point clouds using a scalable bitstream to enable efficient compression and transmission across different tasks. SPC-Net [58] is the first innovative approach that applies octree-based point cloud coding to both machine and human visual perception tasks. Its uniqueness lies in integrating the octree compression module into downstream machine perception tasks, distinguishing it from other point cloud encoding methods that are primarily designed for joint human-machine perception friendliness. A key innovation of SPC-Net is the introduction of the octree depth prediction module, which selects the optimal octree depth based on the specific downstream task. This adaptive selection mechanism allows SPC-Net to optimize the compression bitrate for different tasks, enhancing compression efficiency while maintaining effective encoding for each use case. By enabling the selection of different depth levels for machine and human vision tasks, SPC-Net achieves a scalable and efficient compression scheme, significantly reducing bandwidth and storage costs while preserving perception accuracy across tasks [33, 52].

SPC-Net can be widely applied in fields that require efficient point cloud data processing. This framework ensures high visual quality for human observers while optimizing the efficiency of machine vision tasks, making it a significant innovation in the field of point cloud coding.

7.3.2 HM-PCGC

Human-Machine Balanced Point Cloud Geometry Compression (HM-PCGC) [59] is a point cloud geometry compression framework designed to balance both human and machine vision, as shown in Fig. 7.4. This approach aims to meet the needs for visual fidelity and semantic fidelity in different application scenarios by combining geometric structure information with semantic information, enabling efficient point cloud coding.

The innovation of HM-PCGC lies in the introduction of a novel Learned Semantic Mining (LSM) module to better address the gap between signal reconstruction

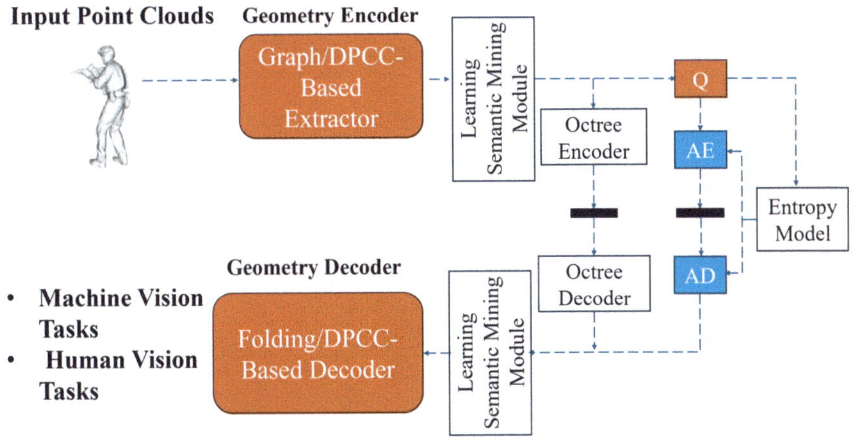

Fig. 7.4 The overall structure of HM-PCGC network. © 2023 IEEE. (Reprinted, with permission, from [59])

and machine perception, HM-PCGC provides more flexibility in balancing human visual perception and machine perception. Specifically, the LSM module adaptively extracts and aggregates geometric and semantic information, organically combining signal reconstruction with machine vision analysis to effectively balance signal distortion and semantic distortion during point cloud geometry compression. In traditional point cloud encoding methods, the focus is mainly on signal reconstruction, often overlooking the importance of semantic information for machine vision tasks. This limitation hampers performance in tasks like point cloud classification and segmentation. However, HM-PCGC's LSM module, by integrating multi-head attention mechanisms and multitask learning techniques, effectively extracts and integrates task-relevant multitask feature information, ensuring these features are preserved during compression. This not only improves compression efficiency but also ensures that downstream tasks are not adversely affected by compression. By leveraging the LSM module, HM-PCGC can dynamically allocate more bandwidth to semantic information that is more crucial for machine perception tasks while achieving highly efficient compression of geometric details required for human visual tasks. As a result, HM-PCGC excels in signal reconstruction tasks and significantly improves performance in machine vision tasks like classification and segmentation.

In summary, the innovation of HM-PCGC compared to other point cloud coding methods is that, through the introduction of the LSM module, it can better balance signal distortion and semantic distortion, thereby achieving more efficient geometric compression while meeting both machine vision needs. This makes it a leading solution in the field of point cloud encoding, designed to be friendly for both human and machine perception tasks.

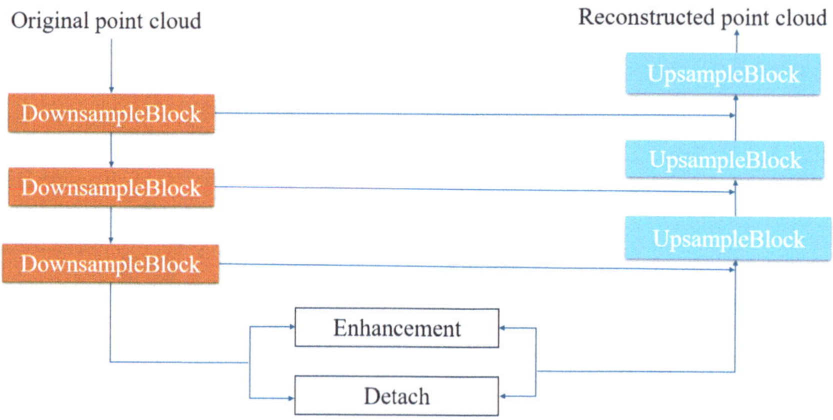

Fig. 7.5 The overall structure of Scalable Human-Machine Point Cloud Compression. Public domain open access image [60]

7.3.3 SM-PCC

Scalable Human-Machine Point Cloud Compression SM-PCC [60] introduces a novel architecture called the scalable human-machine point cloud codec, designed to simultaneously support machine tasks (such as classification) and human tasks (such as visual reconstruction), as shown in Fig. 7.5.

The SM-PCC codec improves upon other point cloud encoding schemes designed for joint human-machine perception in areas such as scalability, encoding structure, downstream task networks, and task-specific processing. In terms of scalability, the codec achieves this by utilizing two bitstreams: a base bitstream and an enhancement bitstream. The base bitstream primarily supports machine tasks (such as point cloud classification, etc.), while the enhancement bitstream is used to enhance the quality of the input reconstruction for human viewing. Regarding encoding structure, the input point cloud is first processed by a downsampling block, gradually reducing the point cloud data to a smaller feature representation. These feature representations are then compressed to generate the bitstreams, which are subsequently reconstructed using an upsampling block. For downstream applications, the codec utilizes the PointNet++ architecture, which is an advanced deep hierarchical method for analyzing point cloud data. In task-oriented processes, the codec splits the latent space into two segments: a foundational layer and an enhancement layer. The foundational layer supports machine-based tasks such as classification, while the enhancement layer, when merged with the foundational layer, assists in reconstructing the input. This configuration permits the transmission of only the foundational layer bitstream when there's no need for human visualization, thereby conserving bandwidth.

The scalable human-machine point cloud codec proposes a novel scalable point cloud coding architecture that enables flexible switching between machine analysis and human viewing tasks by separating task processing. This approach saves bandwidth while meeting the needs of different tasks, providing an effective solution for point cloud coding and multi-task processing.

7.3.4 SA-PCC

LiDAR has found extensive applications in autonomous vehicles, robotics, and terrain mapping, as it produces 3D point cloud data through laser emission and measurement of reflected signals. This point cloud data contains rich geometric information, but it is usually very large, making real-time processing and transmission challenging. Traditional LiDAR point cloud coding methods primarily focus on maintaining data fidelity during compression, without fully considering the specific needs of the decoder when performing tasks such as localization or scene understanding.

Compared to other current point cloud encoding methods designed for human-machine perception, the Real-Time Scene-Aware LiDAR Point Cloud Compression Using Semantic Prior Representation's [61] (SA-PCC) approach not only focuses on data fidelity but also adaptively adjusts according to the needs of the decoder, achieving better results in downstream machine perception tasks, as shown in Fig. 7.6. The core of the Real-Time Scene-Aware method is the introduction of a compression technique called Semantic Prior Representation (SPR). During the encoding stage, information about moving objects can be removed, thereby improving compression efficiency and enhancing the accuracy of machine perception tasks, such as localization. At the same time, SPR offers greater flexibility compared to other point cloud encoding methods designed for human-machine perception, making subsequent processing tasks simpler and better meeting real-

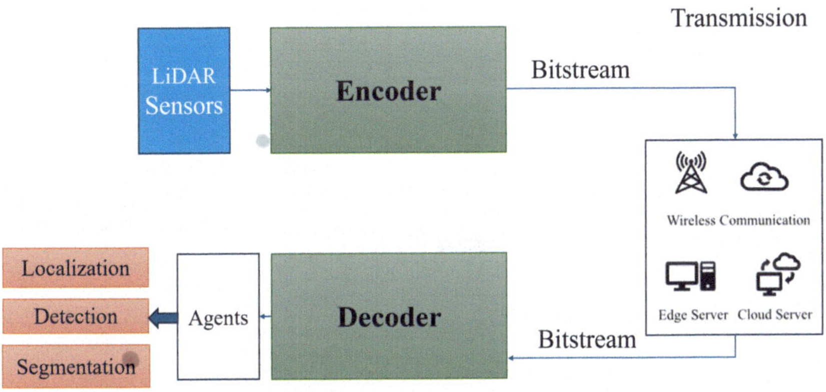

Fig. 7.6 Overall architecture of the machine and human eye perception network. © 2020 IEEE. (Reprinted, with permission, from [61])

time requirements. For instance, using SPR, points of noise that could impact localization accuracy at the decoder stage can be effectively eliminated during encoding.

The advantage of this point cloud coding system lies in its combination of semantic information with geometric compression, significantly improving the compression efficiency and real-time performance of LiDAR point clouds. This method is not only suitable for general point cloud coding but can also be directly applied to scenarios requiring high precision and real-time scene perception, such as autonomous driving.

7.3.5 Parallel Dual-branch Network

Parallel Dual-branch Network (PDNet) [62] is an innovative approach designed for lossy point cloud geometry compression and analysis, addressing the conflict between the compact data representation required for compression and the rich semantic retention needed for analysis, as shown in Fig. 7.7. The network flow in Fig. 7.7 is as follows: The process begins with inputs from "Human" and "Machine," each connected to their respective "Multilayer Perception (MLP)" modules. The information then passes through the "Token Learning Block (TLB)" and "Self-Attention (SA)," followed by multiple iterations of the "Transformer No Position Embedding (TNPE)" module. During the feature processing stage, the data flows through "Deconvolution" and "Feature Aggregation (FA)" to form a unified representation. It then proceeds through "Quantization (Q)" into the "Arithmetic Encoding (AE)" and "Arithmetic Decoding (AD)" modules, and finally reaches the "Entropy Model". Key modules such as "Multilayer Perception (MLP)" and "Transformer No Position Embedding (TNPE)" appear multiple times throughout the flow.

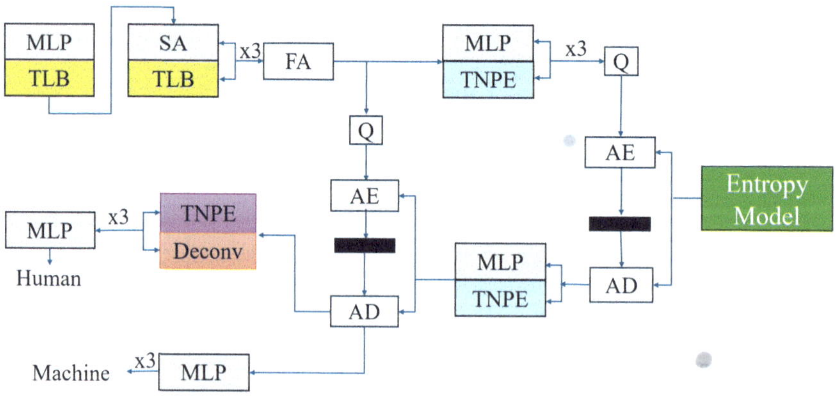

Fig. 7.7 The overall structure of PDNet structure. © 2024 IEEE. (Reprinted, with permission, from [62])

Some components are highlighted in different colors to emphasize their importance, and arrows indicate the direction of data flow, forming a complete multi-stage processing pipeline. Compared with other point cloud encoding methods designed for human-machine perception, PDNet employs a parallel dual-branch architecture where one branch focuses on compression while the other supports analysis. This design ensures that the compressed data remains practical for subsequent tasks, such as point cloud classification [63]. Utilizing a Transformer-based encoder-decoder framework, PDNet handles both local and global attention mechanisms to achieve precise latent representations of point cloud data. The encoder integrates a Multi-Scale Local-Global Feature Extraction (MLGF) module to effectively capture essential features, while the decoder and hyper-prior modules use a Transformer without Positional Embeddings (TNPE) for accurate reconstruction without relying on positional information. PDNet demonstrates significant improvements over existing methods, achieving nearly a 40% improvement in BD-Rate compared to G-PCC and other point-based compression techniques, and a 26% increase in instance classification accuracy when using the compressed bitstream for analysis. Overall, PDNet represents a major advancement in point cloud data processing by ensuring data effectiveness in analysis tasks while maintaining compression efficiency.

7.3.6 SAVD-PCGC

In the study of point cloud encoding, how to allocate more bitstream to the ROI has become a key area of research. The foreground ROI in point cloud data typically contains rich and critical geometric information, which is essential for applications such as autonomous driving, robot navigation, and virtual reality, as these areas are crucial for decision-making and recognition. However, previous point cloud coding methods generally apply uniform processing to the entire point cloud data, failing to differentiate between regions based on their actual importance. This approach often overlooks the significance of the ROI in practical applications, resulting in the loss of some critical information during compression, which in turn affects the performance and accuracy of downstream tasks involving point cloud data.

Therefore, a novel Semantic-Aware Visual Decomposition Point Cloud Geometry Compression [64] (SAVD-PCGC) strategy is proposed, as shown in Fig. 7.8. This strategy is based on intelligent decomposition and first performs precise identification and separation of the foreground and background regions in point cloud data. Through this segmentation process, the system can flexibly adjust bitstream allocation to ensure that higher-resolution geometric data is available for key areas processed by machine vision. Additionally, by controlling the parameters of the compression model, the SAVD-PCGC method can dynamically adjust the compression rate, allocating more bitrate to the foreground region to improve its fidelity after compression. Meanwhile, the background region can be compressed more efficiently while maintaining a certain level of precision, thus conserving bitstream and improving overall compression efficiency.

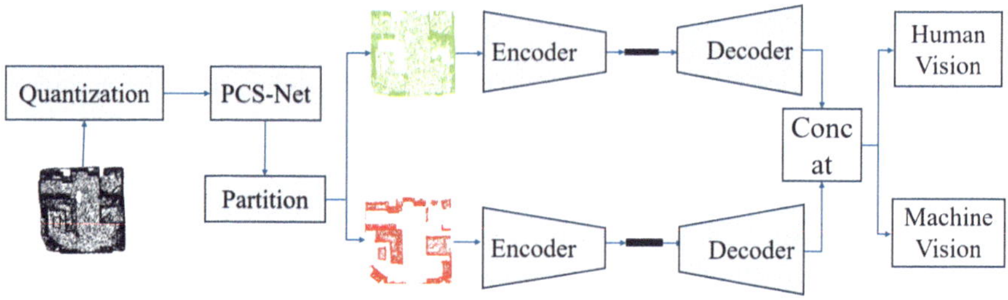

Fig. 7.8 The overall structure of SAVD-PCGC. © 2024 IEEE. (Reprinted, with permission, from [64])

In summary, the proposed SAVD-PCGC framework addresses the limitations of traditional uniform compression by introducing a semantic-aware decomposition mechanism that prioritizes critical foreground regions. By intelligently allocating more bitstream to regions of interest, the method not only preserves essential geometric details for key applications such as autonomous driving and robotics but also maintains high compression efficiency for less important background areas. This balance between precision and efficiency ensures improved fidelity in important regions while supporting the accuracy and reliability of downstream machine vision tasks.

7.3.7 SPCGC

With the widespread use of sensor devices, the application of 3D data in multimedia is becoming increasingly prevalent, and point clouds have become a widely used and intuitive representation of 3D data. However, point cloud data typically involves a large volume, posing significant challenges for storage and transmission, and much semantic information is often lost during transmission. This creates a challenge in maintaining perceptual quality for human vision while also meeting the requirements for machine vision tasks. To address this issue, the Scalable Point Cloud Geometry Compression (SPCGC) [65] framework was proposed, aiming to compress point cloud data effectively while preserving as much semantic information as possible for machine vision.

The SPCGC framework consists of a two-tier encoding structure: a base layer and an enhancement layer, as shown in Fig. 7.9. The base layer primarily encodes the geometric data of the point cloud, providing the fundamental structural information, while the enhancement layer utilizes semantic-guided residual data to encode finer details, preserving more semantic information. This framework incorporates Sparse Tensor-based Feature Analysis and Synthesis Modules (denoted as SFAM and SFSM) to capture and encode residual features, while also integrating losses from downstream tasks like classification and segmentation into the rate-distortion (RD)

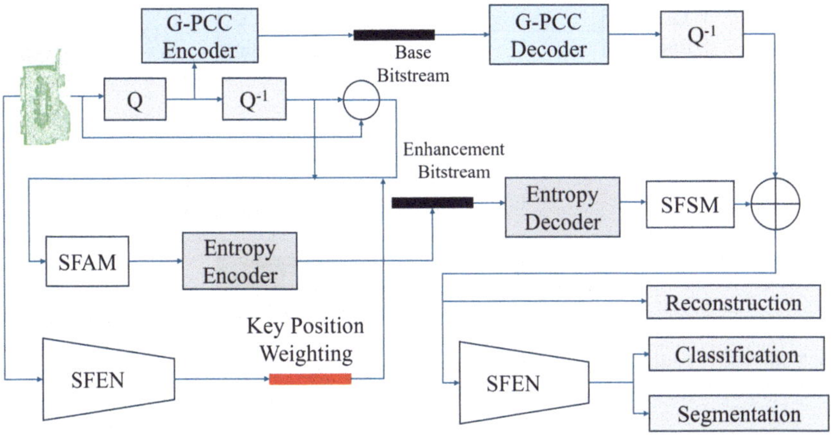

Fig. 7.9 The overall structure of SPCGC. © 2024 IEEE. (Reprinted, with permission, from [65])

optimization process to enhance performance in machine vision applications. The SPCGC framework successfully achieves scalable compression of point cloud data, maintaining compression efficiency while significantly enhancing the performance of machine vision tasks. Experimental results demonstrate that SPCGC surpasses current learning-based point cloud coding techniques in classification accuracy and semantic segmentation at lower bitrates, providing an efficient solution for utilizing point cloud data in machine perception tasks.

7.3.8 RPCGC

Point cloud data, which represents 3D objects and environments, is widely used in areas. However, the sheer volume of point cloud data poses significant challenges for effective storage and transmission. Conventional compression approaches primarily emphasize preserving data fidelity, often overlooking crucial semantic content. Therefore, it is crucial to propose a compression method that not only effectively compresses point cloud data but also retains essential geometric and semantic information during compression. The framework of RPCGC is shown in Fig. 7.10.

The RPCGC method adopts a dual-branch parallel framework, consisting of a Base Layer (BL) and an Enhancement Layer (EL). The base layer is responsible for encoding and decoding the geometric data of the point cloud, while the enhancement layer refines the geometric details to improve both visual and semantic fidelity. The method incorporates an ROI Prediction Network (RPN) to generate mask information, which is used to prioritize the encoding of key regions. Additionally, the RPCGC framework includes a Multi-Scale Feature Extraction Module (MSFEM) and a Semantic-Aware Attention Module (SAM), which further enhance the capture of local details and semantic information in the point cloud. During

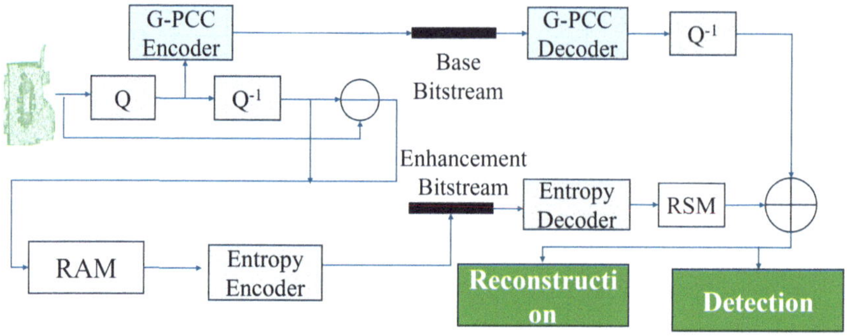

Fig. 7.10 The overall structure of RPCGC. Public domain open access image [63]

the RD optimization process, each point is weighted using the mask information, allowing the compression to focus more on critical areas, ultimately improving the performance of tasks like detection.

In summary, the RPCGC framework addresses the inherent challenges of point cloud data compression by adopting a dual-branch parallel structure consisting of a Base Layer (BL) and an Enhancement Layer (EL). By utilizing an ROI Prediction Network (RPN) to prioritize critical regions, and integrating both a Multi-Scale Feature Extraction Module (MSFEM) and a Semantic-Aware Attention Module (SAM), RPCGC effectively balances geometric accuracy with semantic preservation. This targeted approach ensures significant data reduction while maintaining essential geometric details and semantic information, ultimately improving the performance of downstream tasks such as detection and analysis.

7.4 Metric-Driven Human-Machine Co-Optimized Coding

7.4.1 *Problem Definition*

When optimizing compression methods specifically for human perception, the primary goal is to maintain high visual quality at a minimized bitrate. In other words, the compression process aims to balance image fidelity and efficient data transmission. This optimization objective [63] can be mathematically expressed as:

$$L_{human} = min(D(\boldsymbol{x}, \widehat{\boldsymbol{x}}) + \lambda R), \tag{7.1}$$

where R denotes the total number of bits required for transmission within the bitstream, λ acts as a balance parameter, and D evaluates the distortion between the original point cloud x and its reconstructed version $\widehat{x}$ following compression.

For a series of N machine vision tasks with associated labels $Y = \{Y_1, Y_2, \ldots, Y_N\}$, we represent the features extracted from the point cloud x as

$F = \{F_1, F_2, \ldots, F_N\}$, and the prediction for task i as $\widehat{Y}_i$. This chapter define the loss for task i as $L_i(\widehat{Y}_i, Y_i)$, which is influenced by the features $\widehat{F}_i$ and labels $\widehat{Y}_i$ extracted from the decoded point cloud. To optimize the compression for machine vision tasks, this chapter aim to minimize the loss associated with each specific task while considering the overall bitrate for transmission. This objective is formulated by incorporating both the task-specific losses and the bitrate into an unified optimization function:

$$L_{\text{machine}} = min(\lambda R + \sum_{i=1}^{N} \omega_i L_i), \tag{7.2}$$

where ω_i is the weight parameter utilized to balance the significance of each task. R denotes the bitrate of the image or video features. The overall objective function [63] integrates both human and machine centric losses:

$$L = L_{human} + L_{machine} = min(\omega_0 D(\boldsymbol{x}, \widehat{\boldsymbol{x}}) + \lambda R + \sum_{i=1}^{N} \omega_i L_i). \tag{7.3}$$

7.4.2 Compression Performance Metric

Perceptual evaluation metrics focus on assessing how humans perceive the visual quality of compressed point clouds. These metrics are essential for verifying that the compressed data maintains visual appeal. PSNR [66], despite its limitations, is commonly utilized as an engineering metric to quantify the relationship between peak signal strength and the level of noise present in the data. Typically, after compression, the output image will differ from the original image to some extent. To analyze the visual outcome of the image after processing, this chapter refer to the PSNR value to determine whether a certain processing method is satisfactory. In other words, PSNR is a traditional method for image evaluation. With the development of multimedia technology, point clouds, as a new media form, have gradually begun to be used in immersive media, gaming, autonomous driving, digital museums, and other fields. Like audio and images, point clouds also require effective quality evaluation methods. Given the application of PSNR in audio and image quality evaluation, PSNR has naturally been applied to point cloud quality evaluation as well.

In machine vision analysis, evaluating the performance of algorithms on point cloud processing tasks typically involves employing task-specific evaluation metrics. In addition to general perceptual metrics like PSNR, task-specific evaluation metrics are critical to provide a more granular understanding of algorithm performance. For instance, in point cloud classification, accuracy, precision, recall, and F1-score are commonly used to assess the correctness of predicted labels compared to ground truth. For segmentation tasks, metrics such as Intersection over Union (IoU) and Dice coefficient are employed to evaluate the overlap between predicted and true regions at the object or part level. For point cloud registration and alignment tasks, metrics like Chamfer Distance (CD), Earth Mover's Distance (EMD), and Root Mean Square Error (RMSE) of corresponding points are often used to quantify the alignment accuracy between source and target point clouds. Similarly, in reconstruction tasks, geometric similarity measures and visual fidelity evaluations are critical to ensure that the reconstructed point cloud preserves the structural integrity and appearance of the original scene. Furthermore, in dynamic or streaming scenarios, temporal consistency metrics are considered to ensure smooth transitions and coherence across frames. The choice of metric depends on the characteristics of the data and the specific goals of the application. Therefore, a comprehensive evaluation often integrates both perceptual and task-specific metrics to provide a more holistic view of algorithm effectiveness in real-world settings.

In summary, different point cloud processing tasks require tailored combinations of evaluation metrics to scientifically and comprehensively reflect the algorithm's performance and suitability in real-world applications.

7.5 Comparative Analysis

When targeting human receivers, the compression technique is focused on solving the rate-distortion optimization issue. There are multiple well-known point cloud coding datasets available, including SemanticKITTI,[1] ShapeNet,[2] Ford,[3] and ModelNet.[4] SemanticKITTI,[5] a publicly available autonomous driving dataset, consists of 21,351 scans from a Velodyne HDL-64 sensor, amassing over 4.5 billion points. This dataset, which also encompasses dense point set annotations across 25 categories, has been used to assess the efficacy of downstream tasks. It is crucial to acknowledge the substantial differences in scene composition and sensor setups (like sensor height, self-occlusion, beam angles, etc.) between SemanticKITTI and KITTI.[6]

The ShapeNet dataset is commonly used in point cloud tasks, particularly for part segmentation tasks, where both large and small parts of the point cloud data are segmented. It includes 16 major categories, each of which can be divided into several subcategories (for example, an aeroplane can be divided into wings, body, etc.), with a total of 50 subcategories. ShapeNet has widespread applications in

[1] https://semantic-kitti.org/

[2] https://shapenet.org/

[3] https://avdata.ford.com/

[4] https://modelnet.cs.princeton.edu/

[5] https://semantic-kitti.org/

[6] https://www.cvlibs.net/datasets/kitti/

the field of 3D shape understanding and generation, advancing research in 3D recognition, shape completion, 3D Generative Adversarial Networks (GANs), and 3D shape retrieval.

The Ford dataset is a multimodal dataset released by the Ford Motor Company for autonomous driving and robotics research. It contains high-resolution sensor data collected in urban roads and highway environments, primarily used for research on perception and localization tasks in autonomous vehicles. This dataset has been widely used in the development and evaluation of various autonomous driving algorithms, including object detection, object tracking, map building, and path planning.

The ModelNet dataset stands as a key benchmark in the realm of 3D shape analysis and is extensively utilized in studies focused on the classification and recognition of point cloud data. ModelNet40, a subset of this dataset, encompasses 40 object categories and includes 12,311 3D models, representing a diverse range of common objects. This dataset enables researchers to develop, train, and test point cloud processing algorithms, including tasks like classification, segmentation, and 3D shape retrieval. Its contribution has been pivotal in propelling the use and development of advanced technologies such as deep learning and graph convolutional networks in the processing of point cloud data.

As summarized in Table 7.1, these research directions together constitute a comprehensive strategy for enhancing the performance of compression frameworks in machine vision tasks. By enabling multi-task optimization, dynamically adapting compression strategies, incorporating advanced model architectures, strengthening semantic understanding, leveraging zero-shot learning, and improving energy efficiency, this chapter presents a cohesive approach that significantly boosts the effectiveness and scalability of point cloud coding technologies in real-world applications.

7.6 Summary

This chapter presents a comprehensive overview of perception oriented 3D point cloud coding, emphasizing the dual optimization of human visual quality and machine vision performance. While traditional methods focus on preserving visual fidelity after compression, modern applications require maintaining critical semantic information to support downstream tasks such as classification and segmentation. To address this, recent approaches balance geometric reconstruction and semantic preservation, leading to two main strategies: reconstruction-based and feature-based compression. Several representative frameworks, including SPC-Net, HM-PCGC, and PDNet, exemplify these advancements, enabling efficient and adaptive compression for real-world applications such as autonomous driving and virtual reality. For readers who are interested in the related technologies of AI-based image and video coding, please refer to [72].

Table 7.1 Summary of selected point cloud coding methods for different vision tasks. Source: Author

Category	Name	Publish	Highlight
Classification	PCGC-AST [67]	MM 22	A lossy point cloud coding method for computer vision tasks is proposed, utilizing a multi-scale channel attention mechanism to enhance compression efficiency, while integrating semantic information to effectively maintain classification accuracy
	LPCC-C [68]	MMSP 23	A point cloud codec specifically designed for classification tasks is proposed, achieving a high compression ratio while preserving classification performance, outperforming general-purpose point cloud codecs
	PDNet [62]	DCC 24	A Transformer-based lossy point cloud coding framework is proposed, enabling compact representation and effective preservation of semantic information, allowing classification tasks directly from the compressed bitstream
	SHM-PCC [60]	arXiv 24	A scalable codec tailored for classification on edge devices is introduced, achieving lower bitrates without sacrificing inference performance, while still meeting human visual perception needs
Detection	R-PCC [69]	ICRA 22	A range image-based method is proposed, effectively reducing data volume while preserving critical depth information
	PCHM-Net [70]	ICME 23	An integrated compression approach is introduced to efficiently serve both visual perception and machine-based interpretation, enhancing rate-distortion performance and supporting accurate classification
	JOPCC-OD [71]	ICIP 23	A learning-driven point cloud coding framework is proposed, tailored for object detection, which incorporates gradient bridging for end-to-end optimization and adopts a progressive training approach
	SAVD [64]	DCC 24	A semantic-guided visual decomposition approach is proposed to improve point cloud coding by prioritizing foreground areas, which helps boost object detection accuracy
Segmentation	RSPCC-SPR [61]	TCSVT 22	An efficient point cloud coding method is proposed, introducing semantic prior representations to optimize compression performance
	HM-PCGC [59]	ICIP 23	By integrating multi-task features, it balances human visual needs with machine vision task performance
	SPCGC [65]	ICRA 24	A scalable compression framework is proposed, which compresses point cloud data while preserving semantic information, enhancing visual task performance, and maintaining data fidelity

Exercises

1. Please describe the primary focus of human-machine friendly Point Cloud Coding (PCC).
2. Please describe the main challenges of traditional point cloud coding methods in the context of machine vision tasks.
3. Please clarify what SPC-Net is and how it improves point cloud coding for both human and machine vision tasks.
4. Please discuss how Human-Machine Balanced Point Cloud Geometry Compression (HM-PCGC) achieves a balance between human and machine vision.
5. Please identify what makes the Scalable Human-Machine Point Cloud Compression framework unique.
6. Please explain the role of Semantic Prior Representation (SPR) in Real-Time Scene-Aware LiDAR Point Cloud Compression.
7. Please describe how PCHM-Net addresses the limitations of existing point cloud coding methods.
8. Please outline the innovations that PDNet introduces in point cloud coding and analysis.
9. Please explain the significance of semantic-aware visual decomposition in SAVD-PCGC.
10. Please discuss some of the potential future research directions in human-machine collaborative point cloud coding mentioned in the document.

References

1. W. Gao, W. Gao, X. Mu, C. Peng, G. Li, Overview and comparison of avs point cloud compression standard. APSIPA Trans. Signal Inf. Process. **14**(2), 1–33 (2025)
2. S. Sun, X. Liang, B. Qu, W. Gao, Content-rich aigc video quality assessment via intricate text alignment and motion-aware consistency (2025). arXiv preprint arXiv:2502.04076
3. S. Sun, B. Qu, X. Liang, S. Fan, W. Gao, Ie-bench: Advancing the measurement of text-driven image editing for human perception alignment (2025). arXiv preprint arXiv:2501.09927
4. J. Wang, W. Gao, G. Li, Zoom to perceive better: No-reference point cloud quality assessment via exploring effective multiscale feature. IEEE Trans. Circuits Syst. Video Technol. **34**(7), 6334–6346 (2024)
5. J. Wang, W. Gao, G. Li, Applying collaborative adversarial learning to blind point cloud quality measurement. IEEE Trans. Instrum. Measur. **72**(2), 1–15 (2023)
6. H. Li, W. Gao, Information exploration of projected views for point cloud quality measurement. IEEE Trans. Instrum. Measur. **74**, 1–14 (2025)
7. H. Yuan, W. Gao, G. Li, Z. Li, Rate-distortion-guided learning approach with cross-projection information for v-pcc fast cu decision, in *Proceedings of the 30th ACM International Conference on Multimedia* (2022), pp. 3085–3093
8. F. Song, G. Li, W. Gao, T. H. Li, Rate-distortion optimized graph for point cloud attribute coding. IEEE Signal Process. Lett. **29**, 922–926 (2022)
9. F. Song, G. Li, X. Yang, W. Gao, T. H. Li, Fine-grained correlation representation for graph-based point cloud attribute compression, in *2022 IEEE International Conference on Multimedia and Expo (ICME)* (IEEE, 2022), pp. 1–6

10. F. Shen, W. Gao, A rate control algorithm for video-based point cloud compression, in *2021 International Conference on Visual Communications and Image Processing (VCIP)* (IEEE, 2021), pp. 1–5
11. F. Song, Y. Shao, W. Gao, H. Wang, T. Li, Layer-wise geometry aggregation framework for lossless lidar point cloud compression. IEEE Trans. Circuits Syst. Video Technol. **31**(12), 4603–4616 (2021)
12. K. Wang, W. Gao, Unipcgc: Towards practical point cloud geometry compression via an efficient unified approach, in *Proceedings of the AAAI Conference on Artificial Intelligence* (2025)
13. W. Liu, W. Gao, X. Mu, Fast inter-frame motion prediction for compressed dynamic point cloud attribute enhancement, in *Proceedings of the AAAI Conference on Artificial Intelligence*, vol. 38(4), pp. 3720–3728 (2024)
14. Z. Yang, W. Gao, X. Lu, Danet: Density-adaptive network for geometry-based point cloud compression artifacts removal, in *2023 IEEE International Conference on Visual Communications and Image Processing (VCIP)* (IEEE, 2023), pp. 1–5
15. X. Fan, G. Li, D. Li, Y. Ren, W. Gao, T. H. Li, Deep geometry post-processing for decompressed point clouds, in *2022 IEEE International Conference on Multimedia and Expo (ICME)* (IEEE, 2022), pp. 1–6
16. X. Zhang, G. Liao, W. Gao, G. Li, Tdrnet: Transformer-based dual-branch restoration network for geometry based point cloud compression artifacts, in *2022 IEEE International Conference on Multimedia and Expo (ICME)* (IEEE, 2022), pp. 1–6
17. Z. Li, G. Li, T. H. Li, S. Liu, W. Gao, Semantic point cloud upsampling. IEEE Trans. Multimedia **25**, 3432–3442 (2023)
18. Z. Li, S. Liu, W. Gao, G. Li, G. Li, S4r: Rethinking point cloud sampling via guiding upsampling-aware perception. IEEE Trans. Multimedia **27**, 6677–6689 (2025)
19. R. Zhang, W. Gao, G. Li, T. H. Li, Qinet: Decision surface learning and adversarial enhancement for quasi-immune completion of diverse corrupted point clouds. IEEE Trans. Geosci. Remote Sens. **60**, 1–14 (2022)
20. R. Bao, Y. Ren, G. Li, W. Gao, S. Liu, Flow-based point cloud completion network with adversarial refinement, in *ICASSP 2022-2022 IEEE International Conference on Acoustics, Speech and Signal Processing (ICASSP)* (IEEE, 2022), pp. 2559–2563
21. J. Chen, G. Li, R. Zhang, T. H. Li, W. Gao, Pointivae: Invertible variational autoencoder framework for 3d point cloud generation, in *2022 IEEE International Conference on Image Processing (ICIP)* (IEEE, 2022), pp. 3216–3220
22. R. Zhang, J. Chen, W. Gao, G. Li, T. H. Li, Pointot: Interpretable geometry-inspired point cloud generative model via optimal transport. IEEE Trans. Circuits Syst. Video Technol. **32**(10), 6792–6806 (2022)
23. W. Gao, G. Li, *Deep Learning for 3D Point Clouds* (Springer, 2024)
24. Z. Pan, N. Zhang, W. Gao, S. Liu, G. Li, Less is more: label recommendation for weakly supervised point cloud semantic segmentation, in *Proceedings of the AAAI Conference on Artificial Intelligence*, vol. 38(5), pp. 4397–4405 (2024)
25. Z. Pan, G. Liu, W. Gao, T. H. Li, Epcontrast: Effective point-level contrastive learning for large-scale point cloud understanding, in *2024 IEEE International Conference on Multimedia and Expo (ICME)* (IEEE, 2024), pp. 1–6
26. N. Zhang, Z. Pan, T. H. Li, W. Gao, G. Li, Improving graph representation for point cloud segmentation via attentive filtering, in *Proceedings of the IEEE/CVF Conference on Computer Vision and Pattern Recognition*, pp. 1244–1254 (2023)
27. K. Wen, N. Zhang, G. Li, W. Gao, Mpvnn: Multi-resolution point-voxel non-parametric network for 3d point cloud processing, in *2024 IEEE International Conference on Multimedia and Expo (ICME)* (IEEE, 2024), pp. 1–6
28. R. Zhang, G. Li, W. Gao, S. Liu, A quantum-inspired framework in leader-servant mode for large-scale multi-modal place recognition. IEEE Trans. Intell. Transport. Syst. **26**(2), 2027–2039 (2025)

29. D. Yang and W. Gao, Pointchd: A point cloud benchmark for congenital heart disease classification and segmentation. IEEE J. Biomed. Health Inf. **29**(4), 2683–2694 (2025)
30. S. Fan, W. Gao, G. Li, Point-mpp: Point cloud self-supervised learning from masked position prediction. IEEE Trans. Neural Networks Learn. Syst. **36**(7), 12964–12976 (2025)
31. Z. Pan, W. Gao, G. Li, Distribution guidance network for weakly supervised point cloud semantic segmentation, in *Advances in Neural Information Processing Systems* (2024)
32. R. Zhang, G. Li, W. Gao, T. H. Li, Compoint: Can complex-valued representation benefit point cloud place recognition? IEEE Trans. Intell. Transport. Syst. **25**(7), 7494–7507 (2024)
33. Y. Wu, L. Xie, S. Sun, W. Gao, Y. Yan, Adaptive intra period size for deep learning-based screen content video coding, in *2024 IEEE International Conference on Multimedia and Expo Workshops (ICMEW)* (IEEE, 2024), pp. 1–6
34. H. Zheng, W. Gao, End-to-end rgb-d image compression via exploiting channel-modality redundancy, in *Proceedings of the AAAI Conference on Artificial Intelligence*, vol. 38(7), pp. 7562–7570 (2024)
35. L. Tao, W. Gao, G. Li, C. Zhang, Adanic: Towards practical neural image compression via dynamic transform routing, in *Proceedings of the IEEE/CVF International Conference on Computer Vision*, pp. 16879–16888 (2023)
36. C. Zhang, W. Gao, Learned rate control for frame-level adaptive neural video compression via dynamic neural network, in *European Conference on Computer Vision* (Springer, 2024)
37. Y. Wu, Z. Qi, H. Zheng, L. Tao, W. Gao, Deep image compression with latent optimization and piece-wise quantization approximation, in *Proceedings of the IEEE/CVF Conference on Computer Vision and Pattern Recognition*, pp. 1926–1930 (2021)
38. Y. Li, W. Gao, G. Li, S. Ma, Saliency segmentation oriented deep image compression with novel bit allocation. IEEE Trans. Image Process. **34**, 16–29 (2025)
39. H. Yuan, W. Gao, S. Ma, Y. Yan, Divide-and-conquer-based rdo-free cu partitioning for 8k video compression. ACM Trans. Multimedia Comput. Commun. Appl. **20**(4), 1–20 (2024)
40. L. Tao, W. Gao, A hardware implementation of entropy encoder for 8k video coding, in *2022 IEEE International Conference on Multimedia and Expo (ICME)* (IEEE, 2022), pp. 1–6
41. Y. Guo, W. Gao, S. Ma, G. Li, Accelerating transform algorithm implementation for efficient intra coding of 8k uhd videos. ACM Trans. Multimedia Comput. Commun. Appl. (TOMM) **18**(4), 1–20 (2022)
42. Z. Cai, W. Gao, Efficient fast algorithm and parallel hardware architecture for intra prediction of avs3, in *2021 IEEE International Symposium on Circuits and Systems (ISCAS)* (IEEE, 2021), pp. 1–5
43. W. Gao, H. Yuan, Y. Guo, L. Tao, Z. Cai, G. Li, Openhardwarevc: An open source library for 8k uhd video coding hardware implementation, in *Proceedings of the 30th ACM International Conference on Multimedia*, pp. 7339–7342 (2022)
44. S. Fan, W. Gao, G. Li, Salient object detection for point clouds, in *European Conference on Computer Vision* (Springer, 2022), pp. 1–19
45. S. Luo, W. Gao, A general framework for rotation invariant point cloud analysis, in *ICASSP 2024-2024 IEEE International Conference on Acoustics, Speech and Signal Processing (ICASSP)* (IEEE, 2024), pp. 3665–3669
46. X. Lu, W. Gao, Attentivenet: Detecting small objects for lidar point clouds by attending to important points, in *2023 IEEE International Conference on Visual Communications and Image Processing (VCIP)* (IEEE, 2023), pp. 1–5
47. G. Li, G. Wei, W. Gao, *Point Cloud Compression: Technologies and Standardization* (Springer, 2024)
48. W. Gao, G. Li, H. Yuan, R. Hamzaoui, Z. Li, S. Liu, Apccpa'22: 1st international workshop on advances in point cloud compression, processing and analysis, in *Proceedings of the 30th ACM International Conference on Multimedia*, pp. 7392–7393 (2022)
49. W. Gao, G. Li, Point cloud compression, enhancement and applications: From 3d perception to large models, in *Proceedings of the 32nd ACM International Conference on Multimedia*, pp. 11292–11293 (2024)

50. H. Sun, G. Li, S. Chen, L. Li, W. Gao, Special topic on 3d point cloud processing and applications. ZTE Commun. **21**(4), 1 (2023)
51. W. Gao, S. Wang, X. Zhang, S. Kwong, Editorial for special issue on deep learning-based data compression. APSIPA Trans. Signal Inf. Process. **13**(6), (2024)
52. W. Gao, H. Ye, G. Li, H. Zheng, Y. Wu, L. Xie, Openpointcloud: An open-source algorithm library of deep learning based point cloud compression, in *Proceedings of the 30th ACM international conference on multimedia*, pp. 7347–7350 (2022)
53. Y. Zhang, W. Gao, G. Li, Openpointcloud-v2: A deep learning based open-source algorithm library of point cloud processing, in *Proceedings of the 1st International Workshop on Advances in Point Cloud Compression, Processing and Analysis*, pp. 51–55 (2022)
54. L. Xie, W. Gao, Learningpcc: A pytorch library for learning-based point cloud compression, in *Proceedings of the 32nd ACM International Conference on Multimedia*, pp. 11234–11238 (2024)
55. L. Xie, W. Gao, Pchmvision: An open-source library of point cloud compression for human and machine vision, in *Proceedings of the 32nd ACM International Conference on Multimedia*, pp. 11239–11243 (2024)
56. MPEG, Mpeg g-pcc tmc2 (2020)
57. MPEG, Mpeg g-pcc tmc13 (2021). https://github.com/MPEGGroup/mpeg-pcc-tmc13
58. L. Liu, Z. Hu, Z. Chen, Towards point cloud compression for machine perception: A simple and strong baseline by learning the octree depth level predictor (2024). arXiv preprint arXiv:2406.00791
59. X. Ma, Y. Xu, X. Zhang, L. Tang, K. Zhang, L. Zhang, Hm-pcgc: A human-machine balanced point cloud geometry compression scheme, in *2023 IEEE International Conference on Image Processing (ICIP)* (IEEE, 2023), pp. 2265–2269
60. M. Ulhaq, I. V. Bajić, Scalable human-machine point cloud compression (2024). arXiv preprint arXiv:2402.12532
61. L. Zhao, K.-K. Ma, Z. Liu, Q. Yin, J. Chen, Real-time scene-aware lidar point cloud compression using semantic prior representation. IEEE Trans. Circuits Syst. Video Technol. **32**(8), 5623–5637 (2022)
62. L. Xie, W. Gao, S. Fan, Z. Yao, Pdnet: parallel dual-branch network for point cloud geometry compression and analysis, in *2024 Data Compression Conference (DCC)* (IEEE, 2024), pp. 596–596
63. L. Xie, W. Gao, H. Zheng, G. Li, Roi-guided point cloud geometry compression towards human and machine vision (2025). arXiv preprint arXiv:2504.14240
64. L. Xie, W. Gao, H. Zheng, H. Ye, Semantic-aware visual decomposition for point cloud geometry compression, in *2024 Data Compression Conference (DCC)* (IEEE, 2024), pp. 595–595
65. L. Xie, W. Gao, H. Zheng, G. Li, Spcgc: scalable point cloud geometry compression for machine vision, in *2024 IEEE International Conference on Robotics and Automation (ICRA)* (IEEE, 2024), pp. 17272–17278
66. A. Hore, D. Ziou, Image quality metrics: Psnr vs. ssim, in *2010 20th International Conference on Pattern Recognition* (IEEE, 2010), pp. 2366–2369
67. L. Xie, W. Gao, H. Zheng, End-to-end point cloud geometry compression and analysis with sparse tensor, in *Proceedings of the 1st International Workshop on Advances in Point Cloud Compression, Processing and Analysis*, pp. 27–32 (2022)
68. M. Ulhaq, I. V. Bajić, Learned point cloud compression for classification, in *2023 IEEE 25th International Workshop on Multimedia Signal Processing (MMSP)* (IEEE, 2023), pp. 1–6
69. S. Wang, J. Jiao, P. Cai, L. Wang, R-pcc: A baseline for range image-based point cloud compression, in *2022 International Conference on Robotics and Automation (ICRA)* (IEEE, 2022), pp. 10055–10061
70. L. Liu, Z. Hu, J. Zhang, Pchm-net: A new point cloud compression framework for both human vision and machine vision, in *2023 IEEE International Conference on Multimedia and Expo (ICME)* (IEEE, 2023), pp. 1997–2002

71. B. Liu, S. Li, X. Sheng, L. Li, D. Liu, Joint optimized point cloud compression for 3d object detection, in *2023 IEEE International Conference on Image Processing (ICIP)* (IEEE, 2023), pp. 1185–1189
72. W. Gao, *AI-based Image and Video Coding: Methods, Standards, and Applications* (Springer, 2025)

Chapter 8
Compression Artifacts Removal for 3D Point Cloud Coding

Abstract 3D point cloud technology have grown significantly recently, and its compression technology enables real-time transmission in bandwidth-constrained environments. However, compression artifacts affect signal fidelity and visual quality, further limiting the performances of downstream point cloud tasks. To tackle this challenge, deep learning-based artifact removal techniques have shown remarkable promise, particularly in enhancing geometry accuracy and attribute quality. This chapter delves into deep learning-based methods for geometry and attribute artifacts removal, analyzing their advantages in point cloud data organization, feature extraction paradigms, inference forms, and loss functions, while showcasing their adaptability to varying sparsity levels of point clouds. Specifically, it first categorizes and compares point cloud geometry and attributes artifact removal techniques, highlighting the performance and applicability of methods such as sparse convolution, 3D convolution, and graph convolution in feature extraction. Second, it summarizes and compares representative methods, including U-Net, Grnet, MS-GAT, and GPCC++, outlining their strengths, limitations, and applicable scenarios. Afterward, it examines the uniqueness and challenges of joint geometry and attribute artifact removal tasks, introducing innovative frameworks like GPCC++ for handling hybrid distortions.

Keywords Point cloud coding · Geometry restoration · Attribute restoration · Motion estimation · Sparse convolution · Residual learning · Position offset

8.1 Introduction

Point clouds have become a versatile technology with broad applications across diverse fields [1–8]. Meanwhile, 3D technologies bring great challenges to point cloud storage and transmission [9–17]. Similar with the data compression problem of image and video [18–27], it is also necessary to develop highly efficient point cloud coding technology. Recently, MPEG has proposed G-PCC framework for point cloud coding [28–38]. Octree-based and trisoup-based algorithms are

W. Gao, *AI-based 3D Point Cloud Coding*,
https://doi.org/10.1007/978-981-95-0660-6_8

widely adopted for geometry compression under the G-PCC framework. Though the trisoup-based methods have huge potential in geometry coding, octree-based geometry coding methods are the most popular so far. Therefore, the following discussion about compression artifact removal will focus on an octree-based algorithm. Geometry compression artifact mainly comes from the change of point number and the position offset of original points. Correspondingly, Predlift and RAHT were proposed to compress point cloud attribute. However, distortion of geometry and attribute information inevitably occurs in the quantization process under lossy compression mode, such as blockiness and blurriness.

Geometry distortion and attribute distortion are common issues in point cloud coding, manifesting in different forms and categories. Geometry distortion includes changes in the number of points (e.g., downsampling or simplification during compression) and positional offsets (e.g., in octree compression, where points within leaf nodes are quantized to the center, leading to precision loss). Attribute distortion primarily appears as color distortion (e.g., blurred or inaccurate RGB information) and texture blurring (loss of details after quantizing high-resolution point clouds). While geometry distortion significantly affects the spatial structure of point clouds, attribute distortion mainly impacts visual quality and nongeometric information. Both require targeted methods for correction, as their characteristics and effects vary under different compression modes.

For the compression distortion of images and videos, a lot of related research has been proposed to improve visual quality [39–51] in a post-processing manner. However, little research has been conducted on post-processing restoration for compressed point clouds. Similar to CNN-based image or video restoration methods, more and more learning-based methods were proposed to remove geometry or attribute artifacts for point clouds. In this subsection, existing methods are briefly introduced and summarized. We will describe the post-processing restoration methods from both geometry and attribute perspectives.

For a clearer understanding of current leading methods, we systematically divide these approaches as reported in Table 8.1.

8.2 Geometry Restoration

Geometry compression artifact mainly comes from the change of point number and the position offset of original points. To be specific, every point in the original point clouds will be recorded as the center of its belonging leaf nodes of the octree during compression. However, the leaves node at the deepest level of the octree may contain more than one point, and these points may not lie in the center of its belonging leaf node. In other words, the max depth of the octree decides the granularity of compressed point clouds. Most geometry restoration methods try to solve these problems to enhance the point cloud quality. To vividly describe the subjective experience of geometry restoration, we choose the static point cloud *RedandBlack* in the MPEG PCC common test condition. Geometry compressed

Table 8.1 Summarization of leading restoration methods. Source: Author

Meth.	Published In	Info.	Struct.	Feat.	Cat.	Loss
Akhtar et al. [52]	VCIP 20	xyz	sparse	SPC	gen.	BCE
Borges et al. [53]	TIP 22	xyz & rgb	octree	NNI	gen.	–
Zhang et al. [50]	ICME 22	xyz	point	transformer	gen.	CD
Fan et al. [49]	ICME 22	xyz	voxel	3DCNN	gen.	BCE
Sheng et al. [54]	TIP 22	xyz & rgb	point	GNN	res.	MSE
Zhang et al. [55]	MM 23	xyz & rgb	sparse	SPC	gen. & res.	BCE & MSE
Liu et al. [56]	TVCG 24	xyz	sparse	SPC & Transformer	gen. & res.	BCE & MSE
Liu et al. [47]	AAAI 24	xyz & rgb	sparse	SPC	res.	MSE

point cloud post-processing aims to reduce the artifact brought by compression. Related methods include the traditional methods [53] and the deep learning-based methods [49, 50, 52, 56].

For the deep-learning-based methods, Fan et al. [49] proposed a U-Net framework to restore the decompressed point clouds. By dividing the point clouds into multiple small patches, the proposed network refines the point clouds by classifying the occupancy of each patch. The output patches will be concatenated to generate the repaired point clouds. To effectively utilize multi-scale features, Fan et al. [49] proposed the coarse-to-fine skip connection. The features at high level will be upsampled and added to low-level features. The summation of features is used to classify the occupancy. The corresponding framework is shown in Fig. 8.1.

Current methods focus on dense object point clouds, whereas autonomous driving LiDAR data mainly contains sparse point clouds of vehicles and pedestrians. It is difficult to extract features from highly sparse LiDAR point clouds using point cloud organization approaches implemented with the sparse convolution. In this regard, Liu et al. [56] proposed an alternative geometry quality enhancement framework (Grnet). As shown in Fig. 8.2, the framework implements a tri-category density classification, including solid, dense, and sparse point clouds. Direct expansion

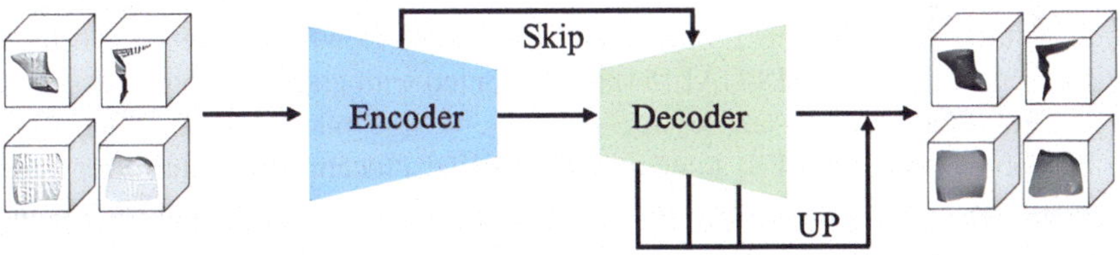

Fig. 8.1 Illustration of geometry restoration. Public domain open-access image [49]

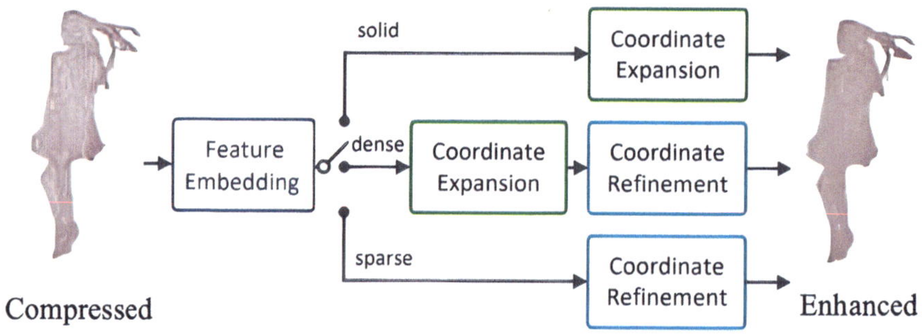

Fig. 8.2 Illustration of Grnet. © 2024 IEEE. (Reprinted, with permission, from [56])

implemented with sparse convolution is applied to the first category to fully increase the number of points. The second category of point clouds adds fine-tuning of geometry coordinates on the basis of expansion to further improve the quality. The last category only learns geometry coordinate offsets. Table 8.2 summarizes the leading methods.

8.3 Attribute Restoration

The attribute restoration algorithm is usually performed after the geometry restoration. Therefore, the existing methods for attribute artifact reduction are based on the assumption of geometry lossless. Given the compressed geometry coordinates $X = \{x_1, x_2, \cdots, x_n\}$ and the corresponding attributes $Y = \{y_1, y_2, \cdots, y_n\}$ with n points, where $x_i, y_i \in \mathbb{R}^3$, attribute restoration methods [54] aim to obtain restored point cloud attribute $\hat{Y} = \left\{\hat{y}_1, \hat{y}_2, \cdots, \hat{y}_n\right\}$:

$$\hat{Y} = \Phi(X, Y \mid \theta), \tag{8.1}$$

where Φ represents the restoration function and θ are the corresponding trainable parameters in the framework of the learning-based method.

Unlike images and videos, points are sparse and irregularly distributed in the point cloud. Therefore, existing compression quality enhancement methods for images and videos cannot be directly transferred to the point cloud coding artifact removal task. Sheng et al. proposed the first point cloud attribute compression artifact removal method MS-GAT [54] implemented with graph convolutions shown in Fig. 8.3. It first downsamples the point cloud into multiple scales using the farthest point sampling (FPS) strategy. The adaptive allocation of quantization steps $Q = \{q_1, q_2, ..., q_n\}, q_i \in R$ results in inconsistent distortion levels at each point. Hence, the quantization steps Q are considered as prior information to participate in compression artifact removal. GNNs are considered an effective learning paradigm

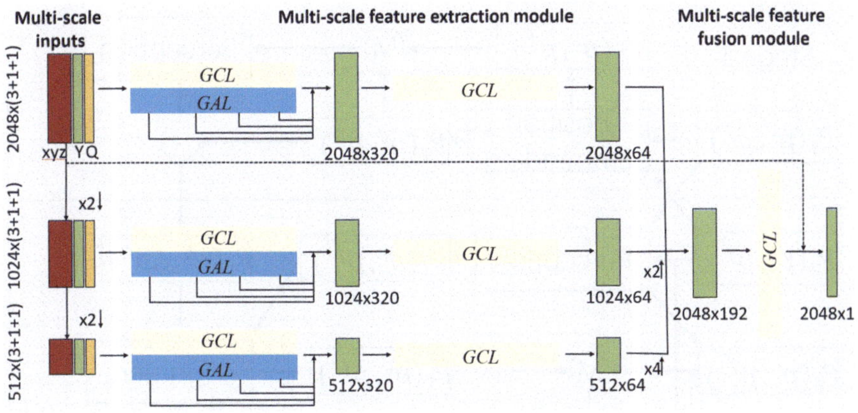

Fig. 8.3 Illustration of MS-GAT. Public domain open-access image [57]

for point cloud processing. MS-GAT adopts the framework of graph convolution. The obtained multi-scale features are fed to the fusion unit.

In MS-GAT, multi-scale feature extraction (MSFE) is designed to capture the correlations between points, which helps the model to effectively extract local and nonlocal features of point cloud attributes. To build connections between points, they construct an undirected graph $G = \{V, E\}$ to model all points. The graph Laplacian matrix L calculated by the connection matrix A and the degree matrix D is generally used to model the information propagation between graph nodes. The basis U and corresponding eigenvalues Λ of the Laplacian matrix L are computed by eigenvalue decomposition. The graph signals $H = \{h_1, h_2, \ldots, h_n\}, h_i \in \mathbb{R}^{C_{in}}$ is calculated as

$$H' = g_\theta(L)H = g_\theta\left(U\Lambda U^T\right)H = Ug_\theta(\Lambda)U^T H, \tag{8.2}$$

where $H' = \{h'_1, h'_2, \ldots, h'_n\}, h'_i \in \mathbb{R}^{C_{\text{out}}}$ and g_θ represent the eigenvalue function of the Laplacian matrix L. The eigenvalue decomposition of the Laplacian matrix L brings a huge computational overhead to node information propagation and aggregation. Hence, the truncated Chebyshev polynomial $Z_k(L)$ of the k-th order is used to replace the spectral filtering. We formulate the K-ordered filtering operation [54] as

$$H' = g_\theta(L)H = \sum_{k=0}^{K-1} Z_k(L)H\Theta_k, \tag{8.3}$$

where Θ_k is the k-th Chebyshev coefficient matrix.

For compressed static point clouds, this method improves the compression quality of single-frame attributes. Similar to quality enhancement tasks in image

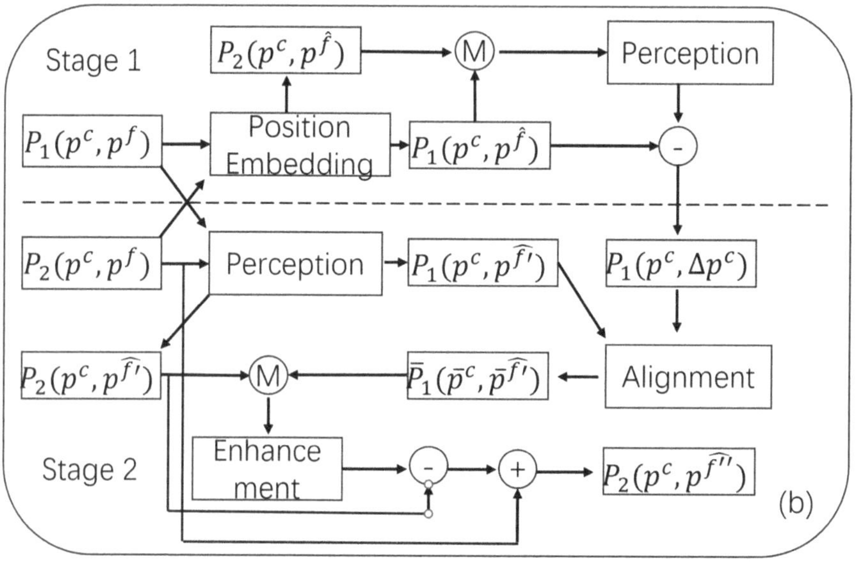

Fig. 8.4 The overall architecture of DAE. Public domain open-access image [47]

and video compression, the removal of attribute distortion of dynamic point clouds has become a research trend. Liu et al. [47][1] proposed a dynamic attribute quality enhancement method (DAE) based on fast inter-frame motion estimation. The corresponding framework is shown in Fig. 8.4. Inspired by temporal feature extraction in videos, this method uses a sparse convolution framework to achieve fast and accurate inter-frame motion prediction. Next, the attribute features of the reference frame are explicitly aligned with the inter-frame motion. Finally, the aligned inter-frame features and the features of the target frame are fused to predict the residual features of the attributes. Table 8.3 summarizes the leading methods.

8.4 Joint Geometry and Attribute Restoration

In the above sections, we introduce the characteristics of geometry or attribute artifacts of point clouds and related enhancement methods. Generally speaking, hybrid distortions are more common in real-world applications. Depending on the type of point cloud information considered, it includes geometry distortion, attribute distortion, and joint geometry and attribute distortion. At the same time, different point cloud coding standards and algorithms [18, 58] further expand the above distortion types. The joint distortion of geometry and attribute presents a more

[1] https://ojs.aaai.org/index.php/AAAI/article/view/28162

severe subjective experience than single-type distortion. As a result, enhancement methods for joint distortion of geometry and attribute are worth learning and bring new challenges.

GPCC++ [55] enhances point cloud quality through joint geometry and attribute restoration by using generative sparse convolution to generate candidate geometric points and applying k-nearest neighbor weighting to transfer attribute information from the compressed point cloud. Subsequently, the geometry enhancement branch (GeoNet) and attribute enhancement branch (AttNet) refine the geometry and attribute information, respectively, while a hybrid loss function integrates geometry and attribute errors. This method effectively addresses joint distortions in geometry and attributes but has high computational complexity due to dual processing, making it unsuitable for real-time applications [59].

To estimate point-to-point attribute errors resulting from mismatched geometries in the raw and enhanced point clouds, GPCC++ introduced a score-based loss function. This function takes into account both geometry and attribute distortions [55]. Given a raw point cloud $P' = \{G', S'\}$, where $G' = \left\{g'_j = \left(x'_j, y'_j, z'_j\right), j \in [0, M-1]\right\}$ and $S' = \left\{s'_j = \left(r'_j, g'_j, b'_j\right), j \in [0, M-1]\right\}$, the raw score $C_{o\to o}$ as the MSE loss between s'_j and its k nearest neighbors s''_j is calculated by

$$C_{o\to o} = \frac{\sum_{j=1}^{M} \sum_{l=1}^{k} \left\| s'_j - s''^{l}_j \right\|_2^2}{M}. \tag{8.4}$$

8.5 Comparative Analysis

This section provides a comprehensive comparative analysis of the compression artifacts removal methods for 3D point cloud coding, focusing on their key features, advantages, and limitations. The comparison is organized into three categories, including Geometry Restoration (shown in Table 8.2), Attribute Restoration (shown in Table 8.3), and Joint Geometry and Attribute Restoration (shown in Table 8.4).

The trade-offs between accuracy and computational efficiency are particularly evident in advanced methods like GPCC++ [55] and MS-GAT [54]. While these approaches achieve state-of-the-art performance in artifact removal—GPCC++ [54] through generative sparse convolution and joint geometry-attribute optimization, and MS-GAT [54] via multi-scale graph convolutions—their reliance on complex operations (e.g., spectral filtering, k-nearest neighbor weighting) results in significant computational overhead. For instance, GPCC++'s [55] dual-branch architecture (GeoNet and AttNet) demands high memory and processing power, making it impractical for real-time applications such as autonomous driving or live 3D streaming. Similarly, MS-GAT's [54] eigenvalue decomposition for graph

Table 8.2 Comparison of geometry restoration methods. Source: Author

Method	Published In	Advantages	Limitations
Traditional methods [53]	TIP 22	(1) Simple implementation; (2) Lower computational requirements	(1) Limited in handling complex geometries; (2) Less effective for high compression levels
U-Net [49]	ICME 22	(1) Effective coarse-to-fine feature aggregation; (2) Good for dense point clouds	(1) Less effective for LiDAR-like sparse data; (2) High computational cost
Grnet [56]	TVCG 24	(1) Adapts to sparse/dense/solid clouds; (2) Improved sparse area quality	(1) High processing power required; (2) Complexity from per-density processing
MS-GAT [54]	TIP 22	(1) Effective point relationship modeling; (2) Multi-scale feature fusion	(1) Spectral filtering overhead; (2) Requires connectivity modeling
GPCC++ [55]	MM 23	(1) Joint geometry-attribute restoration; (2) Generative sparse convolution	(1) High complexity; (2) Limited real-time use

Table 8.3 Comparison of attribute restoration methods. Source: Author

Method	Published In	Advantages	Limitations
MS-GAT [54]	TIP 22	(1) Effective attribute extraction via multi-scale graph convolution; (2) Adapts to irregular point distributions	(1) High complexity from multi-scale processing; (2) Spectral filtering limitations
DAE [47]	AAAI 24	(1) Accurate motion prediction for dynamic clouds; (2) Optimized sparse convolution for fast processing	(1) Restricted to dynamic clouds with motion data; (2) Challenging real-time feature alignment
GPCC++ [55]	MM 23	(1) Joint geometry-attribute enhancement; (2) Effective k-nearest neighbor weighting	(1) High load from joint processing; (2) Unsuitable for real-time scenarios

Table 8.4 Comparison of joint geometry and attribute restoration methods. Source: Author

Method	Published In	Advantages	Limitations
GPCC++ [55]	MM 23	(1) Joint geometry-attribute enhancement; (2) Effective k-nearest neighbor interpolation with Gaussian weighting	(1) High computational load from dual processing; (2) Limited scalability for complex/large point clouds
Hybrid Loss Function [55]	MM 23	(1) Unified geometry-attribute error integration; (2) Improved accuracy via score-based MSE loss	(1) Demands large training datasets; (2) Computationally intensive loss calculations

Laplacian matrices scales poorly with large point clouds, limiting its deployment in resource-constrained environments.

In contrast, methods like Grnet [56] and MS-GAT [54] demonstrate superior adaptability to sparse or irregular point clouds, a common challenge in LiDAR data and outdoor scenes. Grnet's [56] tri-category density classification (solid, dense, sparse) allows targeted processing—expanding solid regions, fine-tuning dense areas, and adjusting offsets for sparse points—which preserves structural integrity even with low point density. MS-GAT's [54] graph-based paradigm inherently handles irregular distributions by modeling point relationships dynamically, though its computational cost remains a bottleneck. On the other hand, U-Net-based approaches [49] excel with dense point clouds (e.g., VR/AR objects) due to their hierarchical feature aggregation, but their fixed grid assumptions struggle with the inherent sparsity of LiDAR scans, often producing artifacts in empty regions.

The distinction between dynamic and static point cloud processing is another critical factor. DAE [47] addresses temporal artifacts in dynamic sequences (e.g., motion-blurred LiDAR frames) by integrating sparse convolution for fast inter-frame motion estimation and feature alignment. This is essential for applications like autonomous navigation, where temporal consistency matters. However, DAE's [47] performance hinges on the availability of motion data and may underperform for static scenes where methods like GPCC++ [55] or MS-GAT [54] are more suitable.

For hybrid distortions (combined geometry and attribute artifacts, joint restoration frameworks like GPCC++ [55] offer a unified solution but sacrifice efficiency. Its generative sparse convolution and hybrid loss function (combining geometry Chamfer Distance and attribute MSE) improve fidelity but require iterative refinement, increasing latency. In comparison, single-modality approaches (e.g., U-Net [49] for geometry, MS-GAT [54] for attributes) are more efficient but may introduce inconsistencies when applied sequentially. For example, geometry restoration errors can propagate to attribute correction, degrading overall quality.

8.6 Summary

This chapter introduces deep learning-based methods for removing compression artifacts in 3D point clouds, focusing on both geometry and attribute restoration. It categorizes and compares techniques such as sparse convolution, 3D convolution, and graph convolution, highlighting their applications and limitations. The chapter also explores joint restoration frameworks like GPCC++ for addressing hybrid distortions and discusses challenges in handling dynamic and sparse point clouds. Key advancements and practical scenarios are summarized to provide a comprehensive overview of the field. For readers who are interested in the related technologies of AI-based image and video coding, please refer to [60].

Exercises

1. What are the classification standards for existing point cloud compression artifact removal methods?
2. What are the representative methods for point cloud compression artifact removal?
3. What are the differences between point-based organization and 3D convolution-based organization in artifact removal?
4. How does sparse convolution work for highly sparse LiDAR point clouds?
5. How can point clouds be organized to support both geometry and attribute restoration?
6. What is the difference between compression artifact removal and general enhancement tasks?
7. Is there a general quality enhancement framework applicable to different point cloud coding algorithms?
8. What are the practical application scenarios of LiDAR point cloud compression and artifact removal?
9. What additional challenges do dynamic point clouds pose compared to static ones in artifact removal?
10. What are the potential future applications of dense object point clouds beyond virtual reality games?

References

1. S. Fan, W. Gao, G. Li, Salient object detection for point clouds, in *European Conference on Computer Vision* (Springer, 2022), pp. 1–19
2. S. Luo, W. Gao, A general framework for rotation invariant point cloud analysis, in *ICASSP 2024-2024 IEEE International Conference on Acoustics, Speech and Signal Processing (ICASSP)* (IEEE, 2024), pp. 3665–3669
3. X. Lu, W. Gao, Attentivenet: Detecting small objects for lidar point clouds by attending to important points, in *2023 IEEE International Conference on Visual Communications and Image Processing (VCIP)* (IEEE, 2023), pp. 1–5
4. Z. Pan, N. Zhang, W. Gao, S. Liu, G. Li, Less is more: label recommendation for weakly supervised point cloud semantic segmentation, in *Proceedings of the AAAI Conference on Artificial Intelligence*, vol. 38(5), pp. 4397–4405 (2024)
5. G. Li, G. Wei, W. Gao, *Point Cloud Compression: Technologies and Standardization* (Springer, 2024)
6. W. Gao, G. Li, *Deep Learning for 3D Point Clouds* (Springer, 2024)
7. Z. Pan, G. Liu, W. Gao, T. H. Li, Epcontrast: Effective point-level contrastive learning for large-scale point cloud understanding, in *2024 IEEE International Conference on Multimedia and Expo (ICME)* (IEEE, 2024), pp. 1–6
8. N. Zhang, Z. Pan, T.H. Li, W. Gao, G. Li, Improving graph representation for point cloud segmentation via attentive filtering, in *Proceedings of the IEEE/CVF Conference on Computer Vision and Pattern Recognition*, pp. 1244–1254 (2023)

9. W. Gao, G. Li, H. Yuan, R. Hamzaoui, Z. Li, S. Liu, Apccpa'22: 1st international workshop on advances in point cloud compression, processing and analysis, in *Proceedings of the 30th ACM International Conference on Multimedia*, pp. 7392–7393 (2022)
10. W. Gao, G. Li, Point cloud compression, enhancement and applications: From 3d perception to large models, in *Proceedings of the 32nd ACM International Conference on Multimedia*, pp. 11292–11293 (2024)
11. H. Sun, G. Li, S. Chen, L. Li, W. Gao, Special topic on 3d point cloud processing and applications. ZTE Commun. **21**(4), 1 (2023)
12. W. Gao, W. Gao, X. Mu, C. Peng, G. Li, Overview and comparison of avs point cloud compression standard. APSIPA Trans. Signal Inf. Process. **14**(2), 1–33 (2025)
13. W. Gao, S. Wang, X. Zhang, S. Kwong, Editorial for special issue on deep learning-based data compression. APSIPA Trans. Signal Inf. Process. **13**(6), 1–2 (2024)
14. T. Qin, G. Li, W. Gao, S. Liu, Multi-grained point cloud geometry compression via dual-model prediction with extended octree. ACM Trans. Multimedia Comput. Commun. Appl. **20**(9), 1–30 (2024)
15. Y. Shao, W. Gao, S. Liu, G. Li, Advanced patch-based affine motion estimation for dynamic point cloud geometry compression. Sensors **24**(10), 3142 (2024)
16. L. Xie, W. Gao, Learningpcc: A pytorch library for learning-based point cloud compression, in *Proceedings of the 32nd ACM International Conference on Multimedia*, pp. 11234–11238 (2024)
17. L. Xie, W. Gao, Pchmvision: An open-source library of point cloud compression for human and machine vision, in *Proceedings of the 32nd ACM International Conference on Multimedia*, pp. 11239–11243 (2024)
18. Y. Wu, L. Xie, S. Sun, W. Gao, Y. Yan, Adaptive intra period size for deep learning-based screen content video coding, in *2024 IEEE International Conference on Multimedia and Expo Workshops (ICMEW)* (IEEE, 2024), pp. 1–6
19. H. Zheng, W. Gao, End-to-end rgb-d image compression via exploiting channel-modality redundancy, in *Proceedings of the AAAI Conference on Artificial Intelligence*, vol. 38(7), pp. 7562–7570 (2024)
20. L. Tao, W. Gao, G. Li, C. Zhang, Adanic: Towards practical neural image compression via dynamic transform routing, in *Proceedings of the IEEE/CVF International Conference on Computer Vision*, pp. 16879–16888 (2023)
21. Y. Wu, W. Gao, End-to-end lossless compression of high precision depth maps guided by pseudo-residual, in *2022 Data Compression Conference (DCC)* (IEEE, 2022), pp. 489–489
22. Y. Wu, Z. Qi, H. Zheng, L. Tao, W. Gao, Deep image compression with latent optimization and piece-wise quantization approximation, in *Proceedings of the IEEE/CVF Conference on Computer Vision and Pattern Recognition*, pp. 1926–1930 (2021)
23. W. Gao, L. Tao, L. Zhou, D. Yang, X. Zhang, Z. Guo, Low-rate image compression with super-resolution learning, in *Proceedings of the IEEE/CVF Conference on Computer Vision and Pattern Recognition Workshops*, pp. 154–155 (2020)
24. W. Gao, S. Sun, H. Zheng, Y. Wu, H. Ye, Y. Zhang, Opendmc: An open-source library and performance evaluation for deep-learning-based multi-frame compression, in *Proceedings of the 31st ACM International Conference on Multimedia*, pp. 9685–9688 (2023)
25. W. Gao, H. Zheng, C. Zhang, K. Zheng, Z. Yu, Y. Li, H. Ye, Y. Zhang, Opendic: An open-source library and performance evaluation for deep-learning-based image compression, in *Proceedings of the 32nd ACM International Conference on Multimedia*, pp. 11202–11205 (2024)
26. Y. Li, W. Gao, G. Li, S. Ma, Saliency segmentation oriented deep image compression with novel bit allocation. IEEE Trans. Image Process. **34**, 16–29 (2025)
27. C. Zhang, W. Gao, Learned rate control for frame-level adaptive neural video compression via dynamic neural network, in *European Conference on Computer Vision* (Springer, 2024)
28. Y. Shao, F. Song, W. Gao, S. Liu, G. Li, Texture-guided graph transform optimization for point cloud attribute compression. Appl. Sci. **14**(10), 4094 (2024)

29. Y. Shao, X. Yang, W. Gao, S. Liu, G. Li, 3d point cloud attribute compression using diffusion-based texture-aware intra prediction. IEEE Trans. Circuits Syst. Video Technol. **34**(10), 9633–9646 (2024)
30. J. Zhang, Y. Chen, G. Liu, W. Gao, G. Li, Efficient point cloud attribute compression framework using attribute-guided graph fourier transform, in *ICASSP 2024-2024 IEEE International Conference on Acoustics, Speech and Signal Processing (ICASSP)* (IEEE, 2024), pp. 8426–8430
31. W. Gao, H. Yuan, G. Li, Z. Li, H. Yuan, Low complexity coding unit decision for video-based point cloud compression. IEEE Trans. Image Process. **33**, 149–162 (2023)
32. Y. Shao, G. Li, Q. Zhang, W. Gao, S. Liu, Nonrigid registration-based progressive motion compensation for point cloud geometry compression. IEEE Trans. Geosci. Remote Sens. **61**, 1–14 (2023)
33. F. Song, G. Li, X. Yang, W. Gao, S. Liu, Block-adaptive point cloud attribute coding with region-aware optimized transform. IEEE Trans. Circuits Syst. Video Technol. **33**(8), 4294–4308 (2023)
34. Y. An, Y. Shao, G. Li, W. Gao, S. Liu, A fast motion estimation method with hamming distance for lidar point cloud compression, in *2022 IEEE International Conference on Visual Communications and Image Processing (VCIP)* (IEEE, 2022), pp. 1–5
35. H. Yuan, W. Gao, G. Li, Z. Li, Rate-distortion-guided learning approach with cross-projection information for v-pcc fast cu decision, in *Proceedings of the 30th ACM International Conference on Multimedia*, pp. 3085–3093 (2022)
36. F. Song, G. Li, W. Gao, T.H. Li, Rate-distortion optimized graph for point cloud attribute coding. IEEE Signal Process. Lett. **29**, 922–926 (2022)
37. F. Song, G. Li, X. Yang, W. Gao, T. H. Li, Fine-grained correlation representation for graph-based point cloud attribute compression, in *2022 IEEE International Conference on Multimedia and Expo (ICME)* (IEEE, 2022), pp. 1–6
38. F. Shen, W. Gao, A rate control algorithm for video-based point cloud compression, in *2021 International Conference on Visual Communications and Image Processing (VCIP)* (IEEE, 2021), pp. 1–5
39. H. Yuan, W. Gao, W. Gao, Opensep: An open source subjective experiment platform, in *Proceedings of the 32nd ACM International Conference on Multimedia*, pp. 11248–11251 (2024)
40. J. Wang, W. Gao, G. Li, Zoom to perceive better: No-reference point cloud quality assessment via exploring effective multiscale feature. IEEE Trans. Circuits Syst. Video Technol. **34**(7), 6334–6346 (2024)
41. J. Wang, W. Gao, G. Li, Applying collaborative adversarial learning to blind point cloud quality measurement. IEEE Trans. Instrum. Measur. **72**, 1–15 (2023)
42. H. Li, W. Gao, Information exploration of projected views for point cloud quality measurement. IEEE Trans. Instrum. Measur. **74**, 1–14 (2025)
43. B. Qu, X. Liang, S. Sun, W. Gao, Exploring aigc video quality: A focus on visual harmony, video-text consistency and domain distribution gap, in *Proceedings of the IEEE/CVF Conference on Computer Vision and Pattern Recognition Workshops* (2024)
44. B. Qu, H. Li, W. Gao, Bringing textual prompt to ai-generated image quality assessment, in *2024 IEEE International Conference on Multimedia and Expo (ICME)* (IEEE, 2024)
45. S. Sun, X. Liang, S. Fan, W. Gao, W. Gao, Ve-bench: Subjective-aligned benchmark suite for text-driven video editing quality assessment, in *Proceedings of the AAAI Conference on Artificial Intelligence* (2025)
46. Z. Guo, W. Gao, H. Wang, J. Wang, S. Fan, No-reference deep quality assessment of compressed light field images, in *2021 IEEE International Conference on Multimedia and Expo (ICME)* (IEEE, 2021), pp. 1–6
47. W. Liu, W. Gao, X. Mu, Fast inter-frame motion prediction for compressed dynamic point cloud attribute enhancement, in *Proceedings of the AAAI Conference on Artificial Intelligence*, vol. 38(4), pp. 3720–3728 (2024)

48. Z. Yang, W. Gao, X. Lu, Danet: Density-adaptive network for geometry-based point cloud compression artifacts removal, in *2023 IEEE International Conference on Visual Communications and Image Processing (VCIP)* (IEEE, 2023), pp. 1–5
49. X. Fan, G. Li, D. Li, Y. Ren, W. Gao, T.H. Li, Deep geometry post-processing for decompressed point clouds (2022). arXiv preprint arXiv:2204.13952
50. X. Zhang, G. Liao, W. Gao, G. Li, Tdrnet: Transformer-based dual-branch restoration network for geometry based point cloud compression artifacts, in *2022 IEEE International Conference on Multimedia and Expo (ICME)* (IEEE, 2022), pp. 1–6
51. Z. Li, G. Li, T. H. Li, S. Liu, W. Gao, Semantic point cloud upsampling. IEEE Trans. Multimedia **25**, 3432–3442 (2023)
52. A. Akhtar, W. Gao, X. Zhang, L. Li, Z. Li, S. Liu, Point cloud geometry prediction across spatial scale using deep learning, in *2020 IEEE International Conference on Visual Communications and Image Processing (VCIP)* (IEEE, 2020), pp. 70–73
53. T.M. Borges, D.C. Garcia, R.L. De Queiroz, Fractional super-resolution of voxelized point clouds. IEEE Trans. Image Process. **31**, 1380–1390 (2022)
54. X. Sheng, L. Li, D. Liu, Z. Xiong, Attribute artifacts removal for geometry-based point cloud compression. IEEE Trans. Image Process. **31**, 3399–3413 (2022)
55. J. Zhang, T. Chen, D. Ding, Z. Ma, G-pcc++: Enhanced geometry-based point cloud compression, in *Proceedings of the 31st ACM International Conference on Multimedia*, pp. 1352–1363 (2023)
56. G. Liu, R. Xue, J. Li, D. Ding, Z. Ma, Grnet: Geometry restoration for g-pcc compressed point clouds using auxiliary density signaling. IEEE Trans. Visual. Comput. Graph. **30**(10), 6740–6753 (2024)
57. X. Sheng, L. Li, D. Liu, Z. Xiong, Attribute artifacts removal for geometry-based point cloud compression (2021). arXiv preprint arXiv:2112.00560
58. K. Wang, W. Gao, Unipcgc: Towards practical point cloud geometry compression via an efficient unified approach, in *Proceedings of the AAAI Conference on Artificial Intelligence* (2025)
59. L. Xie, W. Gao, H. Zheng, G. Li, Roi-guided point cloud geometry compression towards human and machine vision (2025). arXiv preprint arXiv:2504.14240
60. W. Gao, *AI-based Image and Video Coding: Methods, Standards, and Applications* (Springer, 2025)

Chapter 9
AI-Based 3D Point Cloud Coding Standards

Abstract As the utilization of 3D visual sensors becomes more widespread, the volume of point cloud data continues to escalate, imposing significant demands on hardware storage and transmission. This surge in data has markedly influenced the processing speed and efficiency of 3D visual systems. As a result, there is a growing necessity for effective technologies in point cloud coding. The rise of deep learning has driven the development of numerous neural network-based coding methods, which have achieved remarkable success in image and video coding through end-to-end training optimization and more accurate entropy modeling. In recent years, this trend has gradually extended to point cloud coding, yielding extensive research advancements. However, deep learning-based point cloud coding methods face dual challenges. First, at the data level, point cloud data exhibits a massive scale compared to image and video, while deep learning models heavily rely on large-scale and high-quality training data. Second, at the methodological level, the diversity of deep learning coding approaches leads to a lack of unified standard framework and strategy, resulting in challenges for practical applications. Therefore, establishing standards is crucial for the development and application of deep learning-based point cloud coding. Furthermore, such standards can guide research directions to better promote the practical applications of point cloud coding technologies for data communications. This chapter provides a detailed discussion on AI-based point cloud coding standards, which have been investigated by the representative multimedia coding standardization groups during the past few years.

Keywords Standard · MPEG · JPEG · AVS · Point cloud geometry coding · Point cloud attribute coding

9.1 Introduction

In recent years, artificial intelligence has achieved significant breakthroughs, especially in the research and application of deep learning [1–6]. Similar to the case for image and video coding [7–14], one application of deep learning that has gained

W. Gao, *AI-based 3D Point Cloud Coding*,
https://doi.org/10.1007/978-981-95-0660-6_9

increasing attention is the compression of point clouds [15–25]. Point clouds are 3D data representations commonly used in various industries, such as autonomous driving, virtual reality, and robotics, which can also work in cooperatively with image and video data [26–30]. With the increasing size and complexity of point cloud data, there is an urgent demand for effective compression methods to lower storage and transmission expenses and bring better visual quality [31–41] experience and machine analysis performance [42–48]. This chapter aims to examine the significance of developing a standardized AI-based point cloud coding method [1, 2] and analyze the existing compression standards, including the MPEG AI-3DGC compression standard, the JPEG Point Cloud compression standard and AVS Point Cloud compression standard. By understanding the strengths and limitations of these standards, we can identify areas that warrant further research and improvement.

The adoption of a standardized AI-based point cloud coding standard offers several advantages. First, it ensures interoperability and compatibility between different systems and platforms. This enables seamless data exchange and facilitates collaboration among stakeholders working on point cloud-based applications. Second, a standardized approach enhances efficiency in storage and transmission, as it allows for optimized algorithms and techniques specifically designed for point cloud coding. Lastly, with a well-defined standard, it becomes easier to compare different compression methods, thus enabling researchers to identify the most effective solutions. In conclusion, developing a standardized AI-based point cloud coding framework is crucial for meeting the increasing need for efficient storage and transmission solutions. Analyzing existing compression standards, such as MPEG AI-3DGC and JPEG Point Cloud, highlights their strengths and limitations, paving the way for further research and improvement. By leveraging deep learning techniques and exploring new methods, we can decrease the limits of point cloud coding and unlock new possibilities for various industries. Next, we will provide details and explanations of the MPEG AI-3DGC, JPEG and AVS point cloud coding standards.

9.2 Overview of International Standards

The current international standards for deep learning point cloud coding mainly consist of three: the MPEG AI-3DGC compression standard, the JPEG Point Cloud compression standard, and the AVS Point Cloud compression standard.

MPEG has consistently promoted the development of multiple video and audio compression standards, and AI-3DGC is their latest effort for 3D data. The standard encompasses the creation of codecs designed to efficiently handle large-scale point cloud data, such as GRASP-Net [49], NF-PCAC [50], SparsePCGC [51], among others.

JPEG Point Cloud was proposed a compression standard for point cloud data, proposed by the Joint Photographic Experts Group. It primarily focuses on the point cloud data compression, which typically contains location information and attributes like color or reflectance. For example, at the 90th meeting, two scalable PCGC methods, RS-DLPCC [52] and QS-DLPCC [53], were proposed; at the 96th meeting, the IT-DL-PCC-G network, which compresses only the geometry information, and the IT-DL-PCC-GC network, which compresses both geometry and attribute information, were introduced.

AVS PCC is a point cloud coding standard proposed by the Audio Video Coding Standard Working Group of China. To ensure the secure development of China's digital media-related industries, AVS has also established a point cloud working group and released the country's first point cloud compression reference model, the Point Cloud Reference Model (PCRM), in December 2019. The content of this chapter primarily introduces AVS and presents experimental results of some proposals for deep learning point cloud coding, due to the lack of proposals for deep learning point cloud coding in AVS, so as to provide readers with a general understanding of AVS.

In summary, these standards each propose different solutions for point cloud coding tailored to varying needs and applications, and they are all evolving to meet growing performance and efficiency demands. As artificial intelligence technologies continue to develop and improve, these standards are expected to be further refined, offering more robust support for point cloud data compression.

9.3 MPEG AI-3DGC Standard

In January 2021, the Moving Picture Experts Group (MPEG) of the International Organization for Standardization (ISO) established an AI-3DGC working group during its 136th MPEG meeting. This working group is dedicated to researching point cloud coding techniques and standards based on deep learning. AI-3DGC has developed numerous compression solutions tailored to different scenarios and data types, such as PCGCv2 [54] and VoxelContentNet [55]. The aim is to propel the advancement of neural network-based point cloud coding algorithms. In this section, we will present an overview of significant proposals and standards introduced during the 137th to 146th MPEG meetings, as shown in Fig. 9.1.

9.3.1 MPEG 137th Meeting

In the MPEG 137th meeting, there are six important proposals proposed, as shown in Table 9.1.

m58780 (D-DPCC: A Deep Dynamic Point Cloud Geometry Compression Framework for AI-based PCC) In m58780 [56], they proposed a Deep Dynamic Point Cloud Compression (D-DPCC) framework. The proposed framework focuses

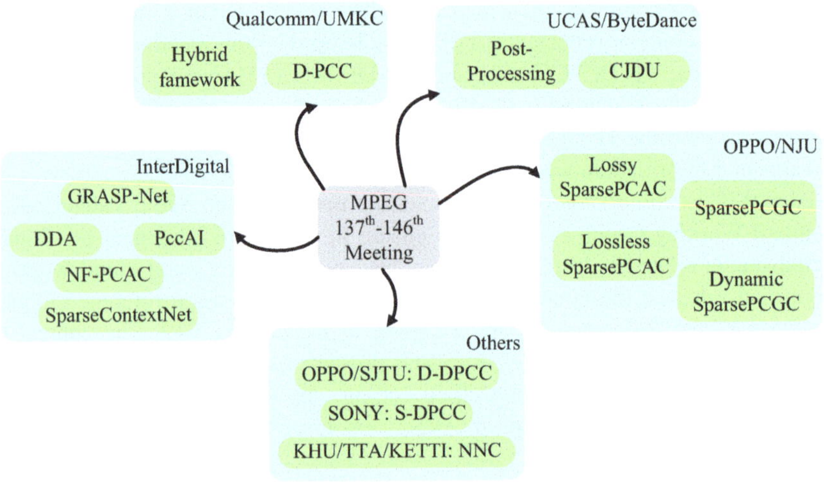

Fig. 9.1 The AI-3DGC proposals presented in the MPEG 137th–146th conferences. Source: Author

Table 9.1 MPEG 137th meeting

Proposal	Description	Organization
m58780	Proposes D-DPCC framework	SJTU, OPPO
m58961	Proposes PccAI framework	InterDigital
m58962	Proposes GRASP-Net framework	InterDigital
m58965	Summarizes OctSequeece and VCN, and proposes PCN framework	InterDigital
m59035	Proposes SparsePCGC framework	NJU, OPPO
m59037	Proposes lossy SparsePCAC framework	NJU, OPPO

Source: Author

on dynamic density point cloud geometry compression. Figure 9.2 depicts the architectural layout of D-DPCC. Consider two consecutive point cloud frames, $x_t = \{C_{x_t}, F_{x_t}\}$ and $\hat{x}_{t-1} = \{C_{x_{t-1}}, F_{x_{t-1}}\}$, where C_{x_t} and $C_{x_{t-1}}$ represent the coordinate matrices, and F_{x_t} and $F_{x_{t-1}}$ refer to corresponding feature matrices that include unit vectors to denote voxel occupancy. The current frame x_t and $\hat{x}_{t-1}$ will be used together as input data for the model. These inputs undergo an encoding process by a feature extraction module to yield latent representations y_t and $\hat{y}_{t-1}$. Subsequently, these encodings are processed by an inter prediction module that produces the current frame's predicted feature set $\overline{y}_t$. The residual between y_t and $\overline{y}_t$, denoted as r_t, will be compressed by residual module. The final reconstruction $\hat{x}_t$ is achieved by summing the restored residual $\hat{r}_t$ with the predicted feature set $\hat{y}_t$ and manipulating the result through a point cloud reconstruction module.

m58961 (PccAI: A Software Framework for AI-based PCC) Due to the current point cloud encoding frameworks based on deep learning not being uniform, there are various frameworks such as PyTorch, TensorFlow, etc. To address this issue,

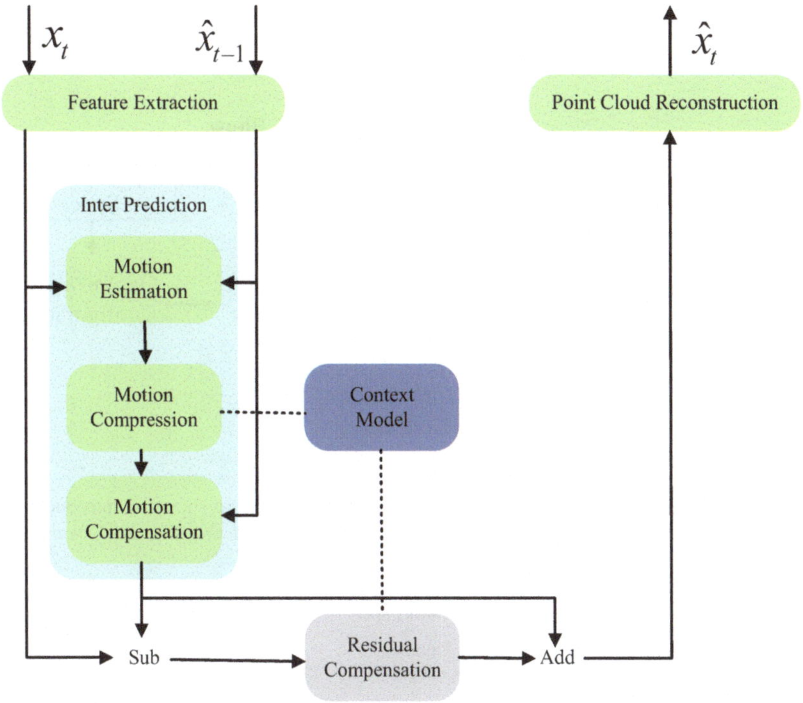

Fig. 9.2 The network structure of D-DPCC. The figure shown is introduced with MPEG open-access (OA) work under CC BY License (Copyright © 1988–2025, www.mpeg.org) [56]

m58961 [57] proposed PccAI, a software framework designed to serve as a unified test bed for researching AI-based PCC in MPEG 3DG. The process within PccAI is demonstrated in Fig. 9.3. The initial step involves setting up the neural network, data loader, and optimization parameters to align with predefined user requirements. After successfully establishing these components, they launch the training phase. Conversely, the workflow for encoding and decoding with PccAI is detailed in Fig. 9.4. This process begins with the initialization of the neural network and subsequent configuration of the encoder/decoder as per user specifications. Once configured, the framework is equipped to handle the encoding or decoding tasks for the supplied point cloud inputs.

m58962 (GRASP-Net: Geometric Residual Analysis and Synthesis for PCC) In m58962 [58], the authors introduce an innovative algorithm for lossy compression of point cloud geometry. Their two-tiered method features a base and an enhancement layer to refine point cloud geometry capture. Before using GRASP-Net for compression, the basic geometry part needs to be encoded using G-PCC to obtain a low-resolution point cloud. Following this, it leverages a PointNet architecture [59] to discern the geometry discrepancies—essentially, the fine-grained details between this simplified form and the full-resolution original. These differences, termed

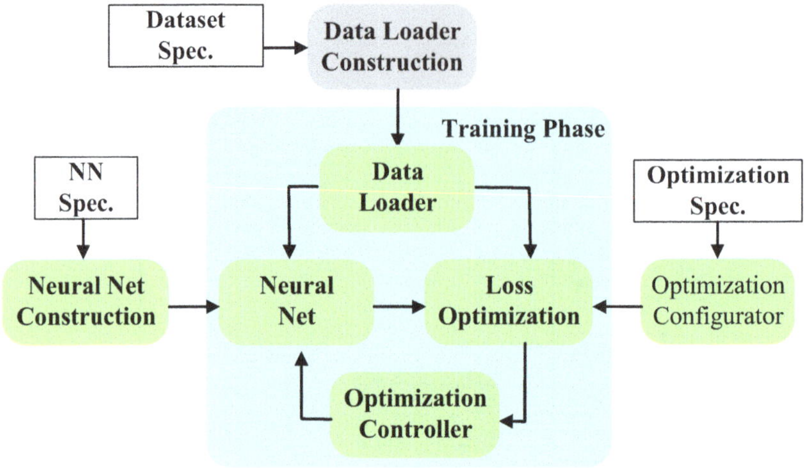

Fig. 9.3 The structure of neural net training with PccAI. The figure shown is introduced with MPEG open-access (OA) work under CC BY License (Copyright © 1988–2025, www.mpeg.org) [57]

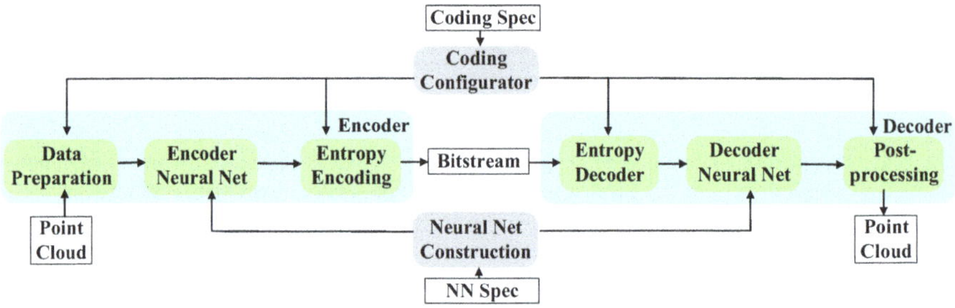

Fig. 9.4 The structure of encoding/decoding with PccAI. The figure shown is introduced with MPEG open-access (OA) work under CC BY License (Copyright © 1988–2025, www.mpeg.org) [57]

geometry residuals, are then quantified as a series of point-level features on the coarse point cloud, which a sparse CNN then encodes, as shown in Fig. 9.5. On the flip side, the GRASP-Net decoder performs its functions in reverse. It starts with the reconstructed coarse point cloud and decodes the point-level features via a sparse CNN. Multilayer perceptron (MLP) layers are then invoked to decode the geometry residuals from these features. Finally, by reincorporating these residuals into the coarse version, a high-fidelity approximation of the original point cloud emerges, as shown in Fig. 9.6. Additionally, GRASP-Net introduces a "skip mode" refinement process in the decoder operations. This permits refinement of the PC_2 coarse point cloud independently, without necessitating supplementary data from the BS_1 bitstream, as presented in Fig. 9.7.

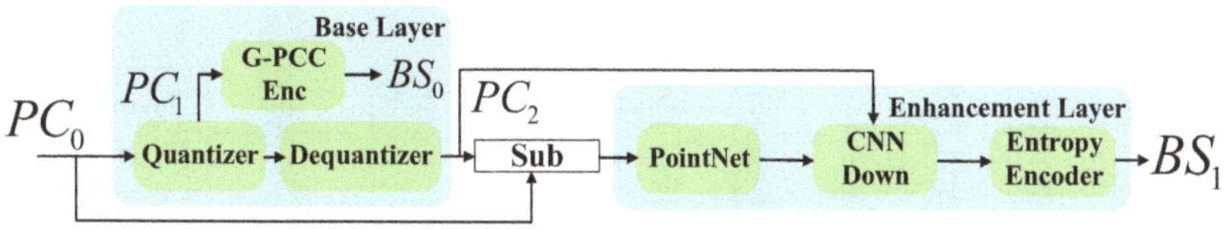

Fig. 9.5 Encoder architecture of GRASP-Net. The figure shown is introduced with MPEG open access (OA) work under CC BY License (Copyright © 1988–2025, www.mpeg.org) [58]

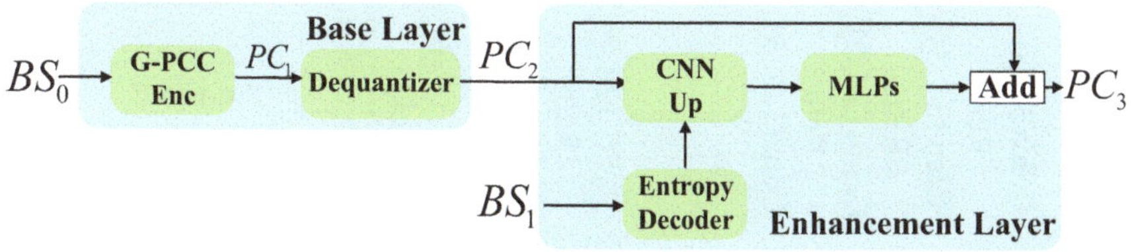

Fig. 9.6 Decoder architecture of GRASP-Net. The figure shown is introduced with MPEG open-access (OA) work under CC BY License (Copyright © 1988–2025, www.mpeg.org) [58]

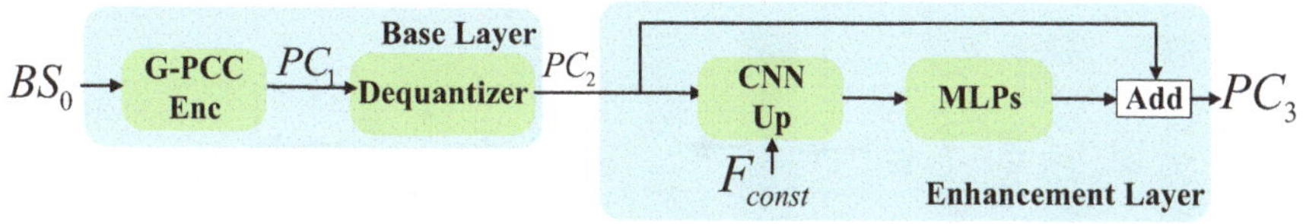

Fig. 9.7 Decoder architecture under skip mode of GRASP-Net. The figure shown is introduced with MPEG open-access (OA) work under CC BY License (Copyright © 1988–2025, www.mpeg.org) [58]

m58965 (VCN and PCN: Point Cloud Geometry Compression Using Learned Octree Entropy Coding) In the m58965 [60], they studied a point cloud coding method based on deep entropy coding of octree representation, named PointContestNet (PCN), which is a branch of learning-based point cloud coding techniques. The document firstly discusses two models for point cloud coding: OctSqueeze [61] and VoxelContextNet (VCN) [55]. OctSqueeze is introduced first, but it is noted that it has certain limitations, such as not taking advantage of the spatial relationships between nodes at the same depth level. To address these issues, VCN is presented as an alternative. Unlike OctSqueeze, VCN uses a voxelized representation of the point cloud and focuses on the local neighborhood of each node within this representation. This approach allows VCN to better capture the spatial context, which is beneficial for predicting the probability distribution of the data. Furthermore, VCN introduces a coordinate refinement module (CRM), which is designed to refine the positions of points after the octree structure has been decoded. The CRM is also depicted in Fig. 9.8. They proposed a point-based local info extractor, namely, PCN. The method is devised to establish a locally normalized point neighborhood by utilizing the normalized coordinates of points within a given vicinity, as opposed to relying

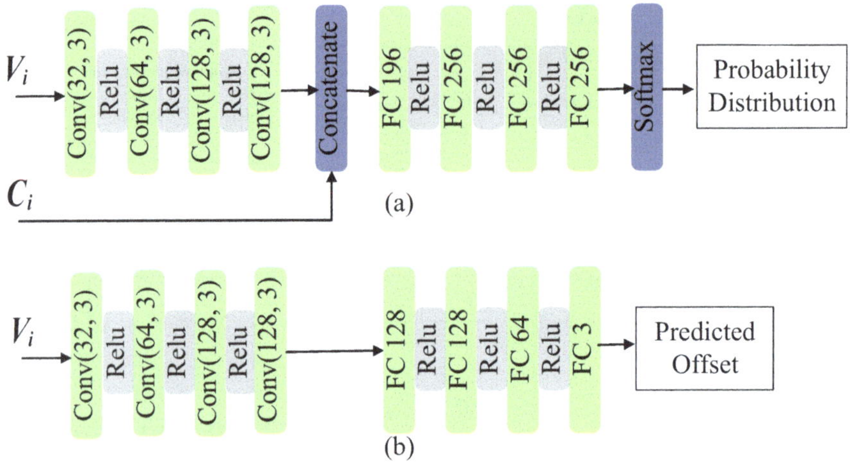

Fig. 9.8 The structure of VoxelContextNet network. The figure shown is introduced with MPEG open-access (OA) work under CC BY License (Copyright © 1988–2025, www.mpeg.org) [60]

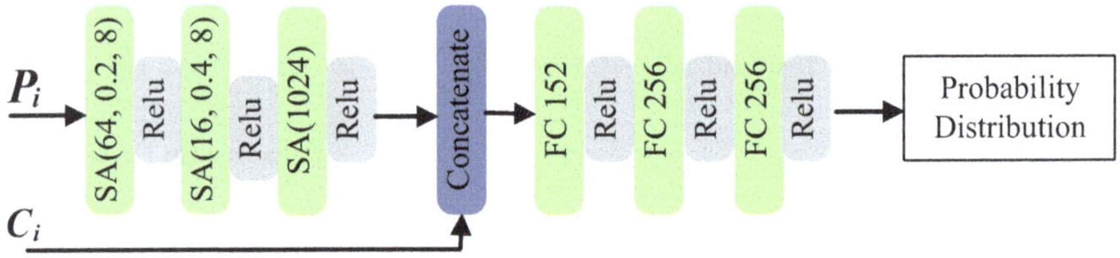

Fig. 9.9 Network architecture for PointContextNet. The figure shown is introduced with MPEG open-access (OA) work under CC BY License (Copyright © 1988–2025, www.mpeg.org) [60]

on a voxelized framework. This normalization process is conducted with respect to the node size at the corresponding level, ensuring that the point locations within the normalized neighborhood are directly aligned with the positions of the occupied voxels as delineated by the VCN model. Acknowledging the limitations of employing mere MLPs for this task, the authors advocate for a more sophisticated network architecture inspired by PointNet++ [62], which is better suited to capture the intricate features and relationships inherent in the point cloud data, as shown in Fig. 9.9.

m59035 (SparsePCGC: Point Cloud Geometry Compression Using Sparse Tensor-Based Multiscale Representation) In m59035 [63], they proposed a framework, namely, SparsePCGC, as depicted in Fig. 9.10. It is related to the work in [51]. The SparsePCGC framework utilizes dyadic voxel sampling at a $2 \times 2 \times 2$ ratio, integrated with SparseCNN, to facilitate resampling and multiscale representation, as depicted in Fig. 9.10. This approach ensures consistent processing across scales, exemplified by a two-scale example. Each voxel is subdivided into eight MP-POVs for occupancy status compression and POV reconstruction. Occu-

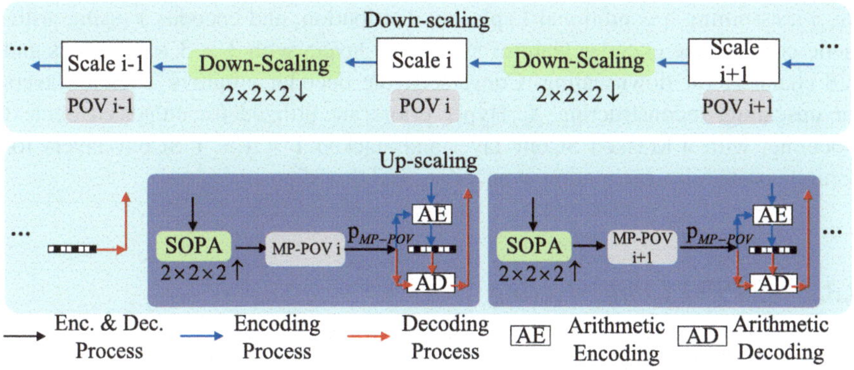

Fig. 9.10 Network architecture for SparsePCGC (lossless mode). The figure shown is introduced with MPEG open-access (OA) work under CC BY License (Copyright © 1988–2025, www.mpeg.org) [63]

pancy probabilities are estimated using a shared context model, while the SOPA mechanism enhances cross-scale context modeling, leveraging decoded POVs to calculate the occupancy probability p. Furthermore, the authors introduce a lossy mode for SparsePCGC, which employs a probabilistic threshold, denoted as th, to determine the binary occupancy status. For instance, an MP-POV is classified as a POV if $p > th$, and as an NOV if it falls below this threshold. The value of th is adaptively set based on the count of POVs at the given scale. It is evident that this methodology can lead to distortion as a result of misclassification.

m59037 (SparsePCAC: Point Cloud Attribute Compression Using Sparse Tensor-Representation) In m59037 [64], they present a point cloud attribute compression (PCAC) method based on sparse tensor representation and corresponding sparse tensor network. It is related to the work in [51].

Figure 9.11 showcases a SparsePCAC framework comprising two segments: an Encoder-Decoder pair for input transformation into a quantized latent representation $\hat{Y}$ and a probabilistic model for entropy coding. This model integrates autoregressive neighbors with hyper priors from a Hyper Encoder-Decoder to compute parameters

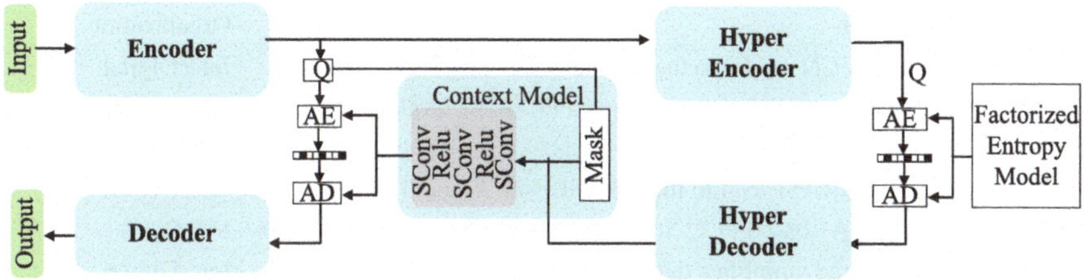

Fig. 9.11 Network architecture for SparsePCAC. The figure shown is introduced with MPEG open-access (OA) work under CC BY License (Copyright © 1988–2025, www.mpeg.org) [64]

(μ, σ), assuming a conditional Laplacian distribution, and encodes $\hat{Y}$ using arithmetic coding. The encoder features six SConv layers with $3 \times 3 \times 3$ kernels and 128 channels for downscaling. Conversely, the decoder employs TSConv layers for upscaling, reconstructing $\hat{X}$. Hyper priors are utilized for enhanced context modeling, with a Masked SConv layer and stacked $1 \times 1 \times 1$ SConv layers for accurate probability estimation in encoding and decoding.

9.3.2 MPEG 138th Meeting

In MPEG 138th meeting, there are seven important proposals proposed, as shown in Table 9.2.

m59552 (SparsePCGCv2: Improved SparsePCGC with Attention Mechanism) In m59552 [65], an enhanced SparsePCGC framework, termed SparsePCGCv2, is introduced, incorporating a neighborhood attention layer that significantly improves LiDAR point cloud coding. The promising results underscore the potential of the proposed techniques. Drawing on the flexibility of transformer models over CNNs, a transformer-based network forms the backbone of the deep models. The transformer layer's architecture, depicted in Fig. 9.12, includes a self-attention layer and a linear layer, each with residual connections and layer normalization. Unlike the original SparsePCGC's reliance on three stacked Inception-ResNets, SparsePCGCv2 employs a combination of three stacked ResNets and Transformers. Experimentally, hidden layers maintain 32 channels, with k set to 16.

m59617 (D-PCC: Dynamic Point Cloud Geometry Compression Using Sparse Convolutions) In m59617 [66], they introduce a lossy geometry compression scheme that outperforms G-PCC and V-PCC in terms of compression efficacy on dense point clouds and encoding/decoding efficiency. The framework is depicted in Fig. 9.13. The novel inter-frame approach employs encoder and decoder networks akin to PCGC, supplemented by a prediction network for feature embedding from the preceding frame. The method computes the residual between predicted and

Table 9.2 MPEG 138th meeting

Proposal	Description	Organization
m59529	Modifies VCN model to the SparseVCN model	InterDigital
m59552	Modifies SparsePCGC to the SparsePCGCv2 model	NJU, OPPO
m59617	Proposes D-PCC framework	Qualcomm, UMKC
m59623	Modifies GRASP-Net to the GRASP-Net-2 model	InterDigital
m59628	Discusses AI-based PCC Standardization efforts and directions	SONY
m59652	Improves and simplifies the PccAI framework	InterDigital
m59685	Modifies the D-DPCC framework and introduces more details	SJTU, OPPO

Source: Author

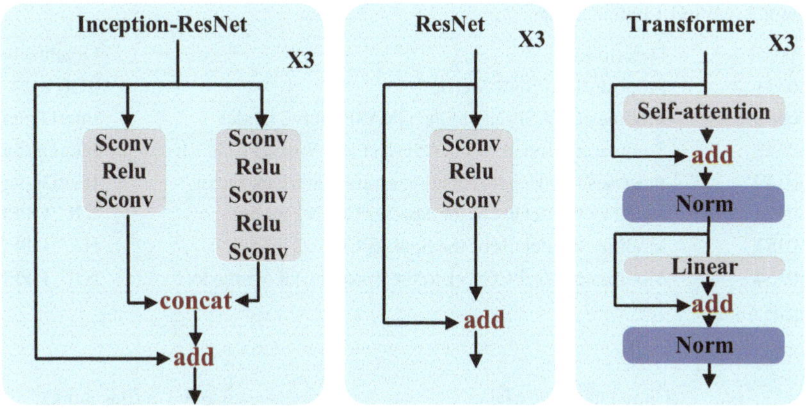

Fig. 9.12 Network architecture for SparsePCGCv2. The figure shown is introduced with MPEG open-access (OA) work under CC BY License (Copyright © 1988–2025, www.mpeg.org) [65]

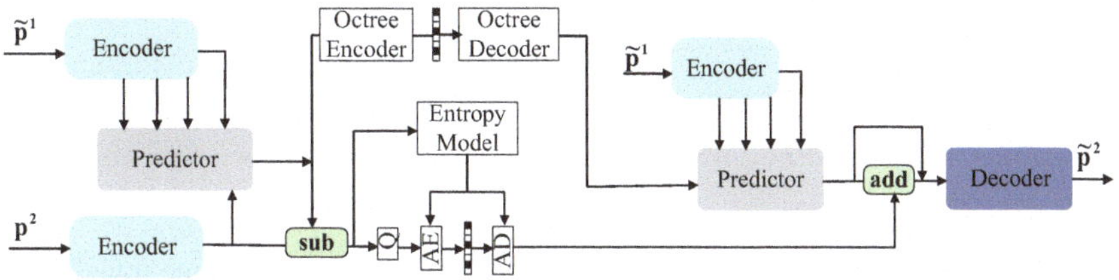

Fig. 9.13 Network architecture for D-PCC. The figure shown is introduced with MPEG open-access (OA) work under CC BY License (Copyright © 1988–2025, www.mpeg.org) [66]

actual features, transmitting this residual alongside thrice downsampled coordinates. These coordinates are losslessly encoded via G-PCC TMC13 octree codec [67], while the residual features undergo lossy encoding through a factorized entropy model for arithmetic coding probability distribution.

9.3.3 MPEG 139th Meeting

In the MPEG 139th meeting, there are seven important proposals proposed, as shown in Table 9.3.

m60342 (GRASP-NetV2: Improved Geometric Residual Analysis and Synthesis for PCC) In m60342 [68], the integration of transformer blocks within the Conv Up module is proposed to enhance feature aggregation capabilities. The refined Conv Up module is demonstrated in Fig. 9.14. Figure 9.14a is the original design, and Fig. 9.14b is the updated design. There are the following two key enhancement methods.

Table 9.3 MPEG 139th meeting

Proposal	Description	Organization
m60331	Proposes D3 PSNR Metric	SONY
m60342	Modifies GRASP-Net to the GRASP-Netv2 model	InterDigital
m60343	Summarizes report of GRASP-Net and SparsePCGCv1	InterDigital
m60349	Proposes the deep distribution aware feature extractor	InterDigital
m60352	Modifies the details of the SparsePCGCv1 model	NJU, OPPO
m60353	Modifies the details of the SparsePCGCv2 model	NJU, OPPO
m60354	Modifies SparsePCGCv1 to the SparsePCGCv3 model	NJU, OPPO

Source: Author

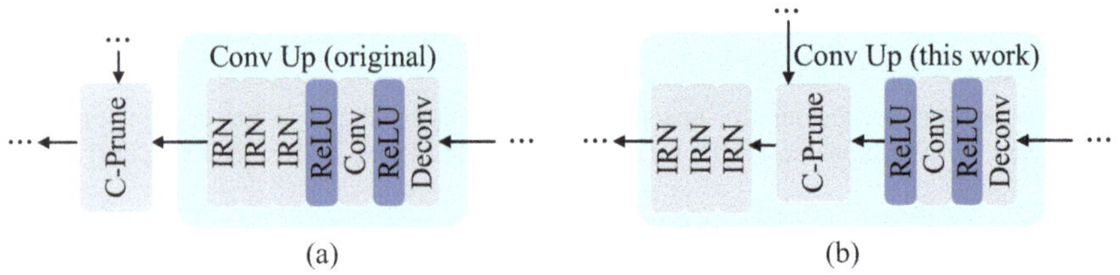

Fig. 9.14 Two key enhancements for GRASP-Netv2. The figure shown is introduced with MPEG open-access (OA) work under CC BY License (Copyright © 1988–2025, www.mpeg.org) [68]

- Replacement of the three Inception-ResNet (IRN) blocks with three transformer blocks.
- Incorporation of the Coordinate-Pruning module (C-Prune) directly into the Conv Up module, specifically before the transformer blocks. This strategic placement aims to eliminate superfluous voxels at an early stage, thereby streamlining feature aggregation and curtailing computational and memory demands.

m60349 (DDA: Deep Distribution Aware Point Feature Extractor for AI-based PCC) In m60349 [69], they explore alternative design strategies for point analysis and synthesis, focusing on leveraging a deeper residual network and distribution-aware processing. Experimental evidence suggests that incorporating a sophisticated feature extractor, such as the proposed Distribution and Detail Aware (DDA) architecture, can significantly enhance point cloud reconstruction fidelity. The DDA framework is bifurcated into two synergistic networks: one for distribution analysis and another for residual processing. Figure 9.15 showcases an exemplar of the encoder architecture within the DDA paradigm.

m60352 (SparsePCGCv1 Update: Improvements on Dense/Sparse/LiDAR Point Clouds) The m60352 [70] proposal introduces significant improvements for processing dense, sparse surface, and LiDAR point clouds, focusing on two main enhancements. First, the kernel size has been augmented from 3 to 5, which serves to streamline the model by reducing its size and computational overhead. Second, the adoption of the top (k+1) algorithm for point selection has refined the selection

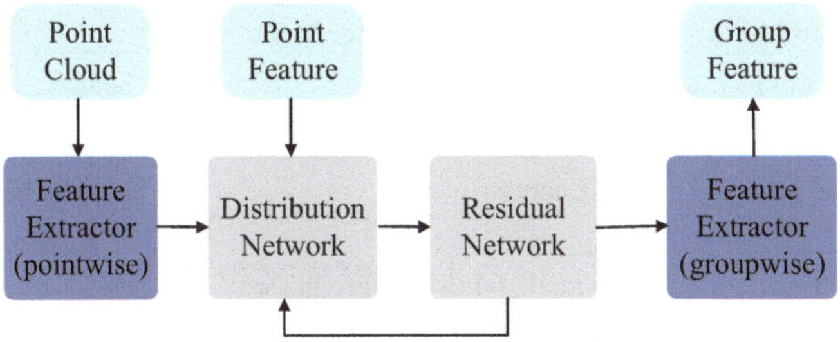

Fig. 9.15 Network architecture for DDA. The figure shown is introduced with MPEG open-access (OA) work under CC BY License (Copyright © 1988–2025, www.mpeg.org) [69]

process. This involves initially identifying the most probable voxel from a group of eight, followed by the selection of subsequent points from the remaining voxels. These strategic modifications have culminated in a performance that surpasses the original SparsePCGC model across various types of point clouds, including dense, sparse, and LiDAR datasets.

m60353 (SparsePCGCv2 Update: Multihead Neighborhood Point Attention for Sparse Point Cloud) In m60353 [71], enhancements to SparsePCGCv2 are introduced. The Singlehead neighborhood point attention (NPA) is evolved into a Multihead NPA, adhering to the principles established for conventional transformers, to more effectively harness correlations across diverse representation subspaces. Additionally, the lossy phase now incorporates an NPA&SparseCNN-based local embedding block, which interlaces stacked NPA with Inception-ResNet (IRN) blocks. This configuration is designed to compress and decompress latent features, thereby bolstering the capabilities of the SparseCNN-based Occupancy Probability Approximation (SOPA) engine. The empirical outcomes of these methodologies demonstrate notable improvements over the G-PCC standard, particularly with 12-bit sparse and LiDAR point clouds.

m60354 (SparsePCGCv3: Dynamic SparsePCGC with Inter Frame Prediction) In m60354 [72], to model inter-frame relationships in dynamic point clouds, the authors propose a target conv module based on neural networks. This module can applicable to both lossless and lossy compression. The architecture is depicted in Fig. 9.16. During compression, the objective is to reconstruct scale i from scale $i-1$, denoted as x_t and y_t, respectively. In the intra-frame mode (SparsePCGCv1), various upscaling models serve as decoders, such as one-stage or multistage SOPA, with or without SparseCNN-based Local Neighborhood Embedding (SLNE), tailored to different compression modes. In the inter-frame mode, the preceding frame's information, PC_{t-1}, is utilized as a reference for the current frame's reconstruction. Given x_{t-1} and y_{t-1} as the reference frame's scales i and $i-1$, an encoder network initially extracts geometry features from x_{t-1}, embedding them into y_{t-1} feature attributes using sparse convolution layers. A predictor then translates features from the previous frame y_{t-1} to the current frame y_t, employing target coordinate

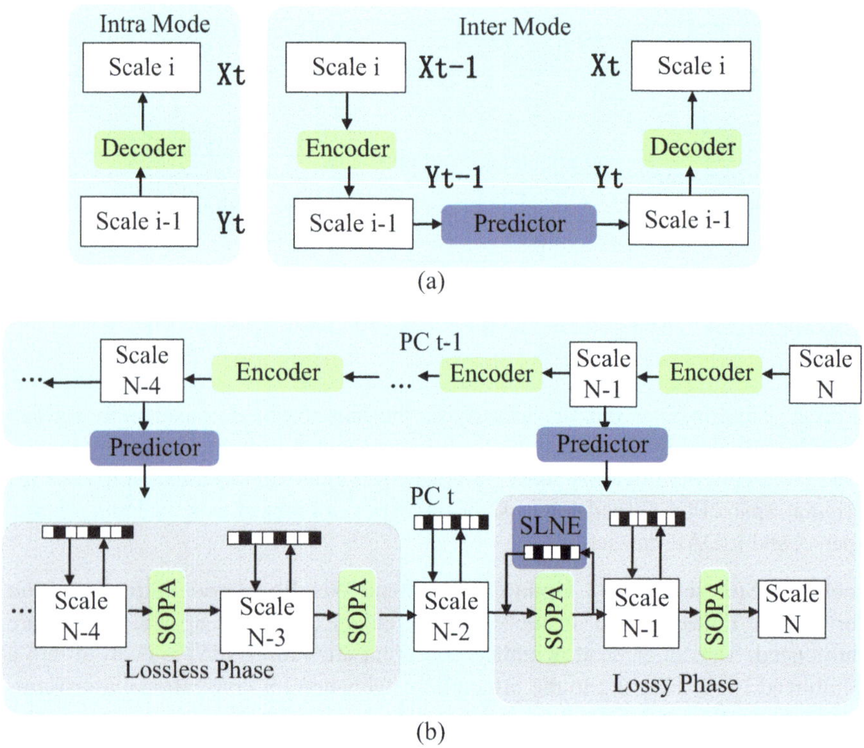

Fig. 9.16 Network architecture for SparsePCGCv3. The figure shown is introduced with MPEG open-access (OA) work under CC BY License (Copyright © 1988–2025, www.mpeg.org) [72]

convolutions for mapping, with a convolutional kernel size of $9 \times 9 \times 9$. Alternative compensation methods are also explored. The final step involves upscaling the predicted feature via the decoder to reconstruct x_t, paralleling the intra-frame reconstruction process. The experimental outcomes affirm the proposed method's enhanced compression efficacy.

9.3.4 MPEG 140th Meeting

In the MPEG 140th meeting, there are eight important proposals proposed, as shown in Table 9.4.

m61006 (Dynamic PCGC Update) The m61006 [73] proposal updates the dynamic SparsePCGC framework, elucidating enhancements in two pivotal areas as illustrated in Fig. 9.17. Initially, the document delves into the Encoder/Extractor Scale-Octree Probability Adaptive (SOPA) Models and Predictor modules, which

Table 9.4 MPEG 140th meeting

Proposal	Description	Organization
m61006	Modifies SparsePCGCv3 to the Dynamic PCGC model	NJU, OPPO
m61007	Proposes the lossless SparsePCAC model	NJU, OPPO
m61142	Proposes the NF-PCAC network	InterDigital
m61195	Modifies DDA to the enhanced DDA-Net	InterDigital
m61212	Discusses SGD optimizer in PCGCv2	KHU, ETRI
m61214	Discusses focal loss in PCGCv2	KHU, ETRI
m61218	Proposes the SparseContextNet framework	InterDigital
m61219	Modifies GRASP-NetV2 to the GRASP-Netv3 model	InterDigital

Source: Author

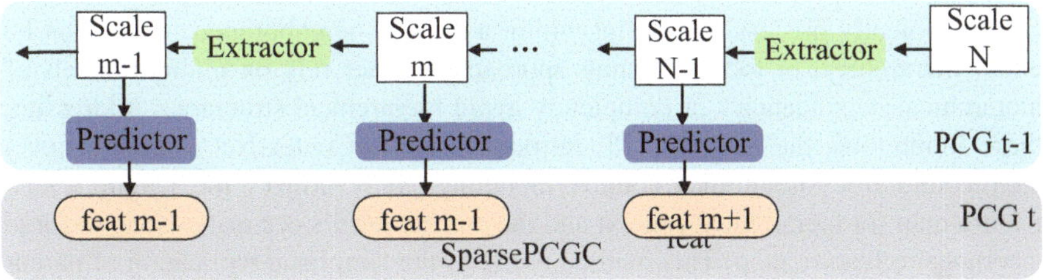

Fig. 9.17 Network architecture for Dynamic PCGC. The figure shown is introduced with MPEG open-access (OA) work under CC BY License (Copyright © 1988–2025, www.mpeg.org) [73]

harness Sparse Convolutions (Sconv) of $9^3 \times 32$. Subsequently, the Inter Conditional Coding phase leverages the reconstructed reference ($\hat{x}_{t-1}$) to generate scale-wise temporal priors. This methodology ensures the full utilization of temporal reference data for compressing (y_t), enabling the codec to adaptively discern and exploit pertinent information for occupancy probability estimation. In the lossless domain, this translates to a bitstream with diminished bitrate requirements, whereas, in the lossy realm, it contributes to the reconstruction of geometry with minimal distortion.

m61142 (NF-PCAC: Deep Point Cloud Attribute Compression with Normalizing Flow) The m61142 [74] introduces a pioneering normalizing flow (NF) architecture designed for point cloud attributes compression, alongside strategies to facilitate its implementation, as depicted in Fig. 9.18. Traditional variational autoencoder (VAE) models, which map data to a lower-dimensional latent space, inherently incur some information loss during decoding. To address this, the NF model is utilized, featuring dual mappings that preserve the dimensionality of the latent space, matching that of the original attribute space. Furthermore, to account for the inherent sparsity of point clouds, a novel squeeze layer is proposed, which applies averaging within the voxel shuffling process. This method achieves comparable performance to the G-PCC version 14 on select test models.

m61218 (SparseContextNet: Point Cloud Geometry Compression with Hierarchical Feature Propagation) Contemporary deep entropy models for point cloud

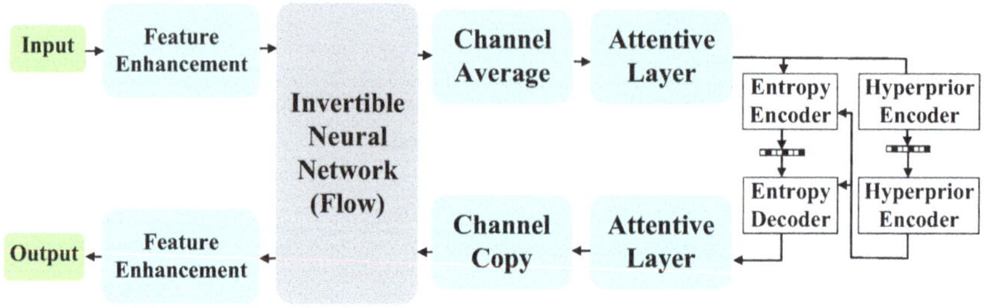

Fig. 9.18 Network architecture for NF-PCAC. The figure shown is introduced with MPEG open-access (OA) work under CC BY License (Copyright © 1988–2025, www.mpeg.org) [74]

coding typically process each point within a defined neighborhood, which can be either hierarchical or local. Existing approaches either rely on multiple levels of hierarchical dependencies or completely avoid hierarchical structures. Addressing these limitations, the m61218 [75] introduces SparseContextNet (SCN), a novel architecture that streamlines context modeling. SCN utilizes the parent level's feature map for hierarchical context and the current level's occupancy map to forge a composite feature map. This method eschews the simplistic replication of parent node features across their offspring. Instead, it advocates for upsampling the parent feature map in its entirety, thereby deriving unique features for each child node. The block diagram of this innovative architecture is presented in Fig. 9.19, illustrating the strategic integration of hierarchical and local contexts for enhanced point cloud coding.

9.3.5 *MPEG 141st Meeting*

In the MPEG 141st meeting, there are eight important proposals proposed, as shown in Table 9.5.

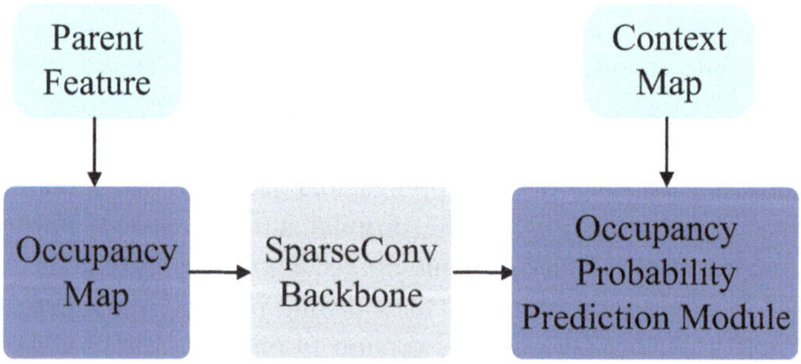

Fig. 9.19 Network architecture for SparseContextNet. The figure shown is introduced with MPEG open-access (OA) work under CC BY License (Copyright © 1988–2025, www.mpeg.org) [75]

Table 9.5 MPEG 141st meeting

Proposal	Description	Organization
m61979	Modifies the D3-PSNR metric	InterDigital
m62076	Summarizes results of the D-PCC model	Qualcomm, UMKC
m62077	Summarizes report of AI-Based Dynamic PC Coding	G. Van der Auwera
m62066	Modifies D-PCC to the S-DPCC model	SONY
m62099	Modifies the GRASP-Netv3 model	InterDigital
m62102	Introduces more details of the SparseContextNet	InterDigital
m62177	Modifies the Dynamic SparsePCGC model	NJU, OPPO
m62180	Proposes the hybrid framework	Qualcomm, UMKC

Source: Author

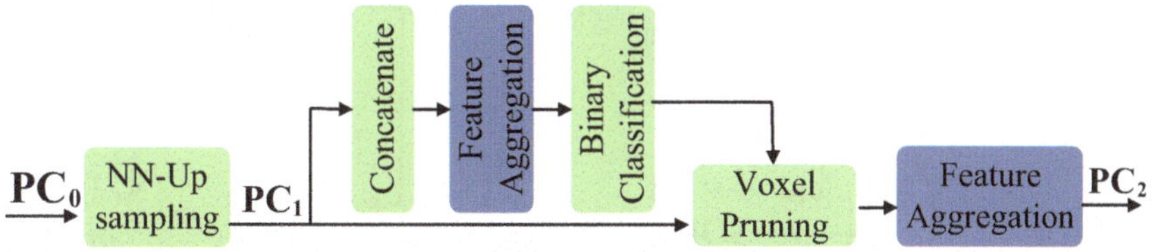

Fig. 9.20 Network architecture for GRASP-Netv3. The figure shown is introduced with MPEG open-access (OA) work under CC BY License (Copyright © 1988–2025, www.mpeg.org) [76]

m62099 (GRASP-Netv3: Improved Geometric Residual Analysis and Synthesis for PCC) In m62099 [76], they present their continued efforts to improve GRASP-Netv3. Specifically, first is the addition of a Feature Aggregation (FA) to enhance performance. Subsequently, due to having three FA modules, the author removed the FA module after upsampling and shared parameters between the remaining two FA modules. Finally, the author also reduced the feature dimensions for additional simplification, as shown in Fig. 9.20.

m62177 (SparsePCGCv3: Dynamic Point Cloud Geometry Compression for LiDAR Point Cloud with Ego-Motion Compensation) The m62177 [77] details the advancements in LiDAR point cloud coding, building upon SparsePCGCv3 [72], as depicted in Fig. 9.21. In autonomous driving contexts, motion pose information is readily available, typically sourced directly from IMU sensors or deduced via registration and odometry algorithms. The authors utilize pose data provided by the dataset, expressed as a Rotation vector Ro_{t-1}^{t} and a Translation vector Tr_{t-1}^{t}. This information facilitates the transformation of points from the $t-1$ frame to the t frame coordinate system. The incorporation of this ego-motion compensation allows the neural network to (1) disregard the ego-motion, focusing instead on the movement of other entities within the scene and (2) more effectively discern the spatial correlation of static objects post-compensation. This method is substantiated on the KITTI [78] dataset sequences.

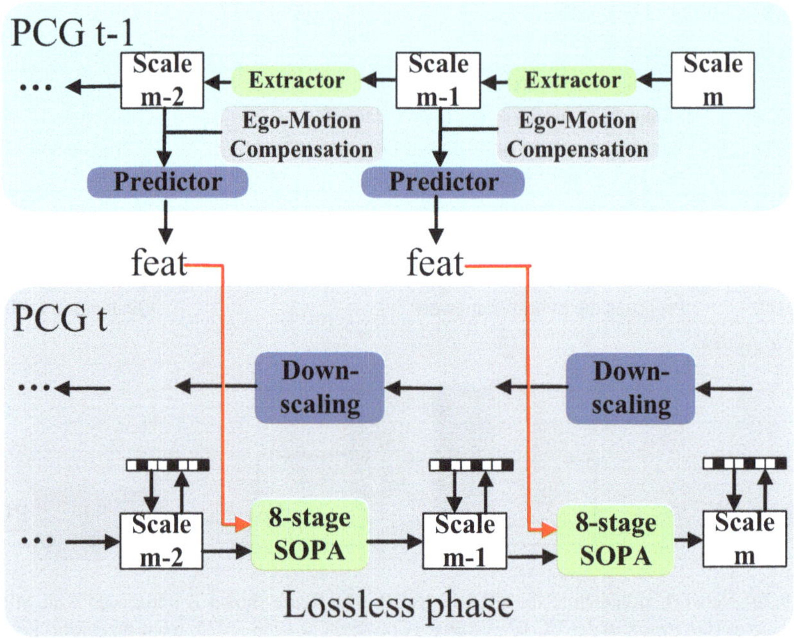

Fig. 9.21 Network architecture for SparsePCGCv3. The figure shown is introduced with MPEG open-access (OA) work under CC BY License (Copyright © 1988–2025, www.mpeg.org) [77]

m62180 (Update on Baseline Attribute Compression for ML-Based PCC) In m62180 [79], it shows that deep learning-based PCC methods exhibit strong performance in geometry compression but encounter challenges in attribute compression. With this consideration, a framework has been introduced that integrates deep learning-based geometry compression with G-PCC's attribute compression. As shown in Figs. 9.22 and 9.23, the framework utilizes G-PCC's recoloring scheme

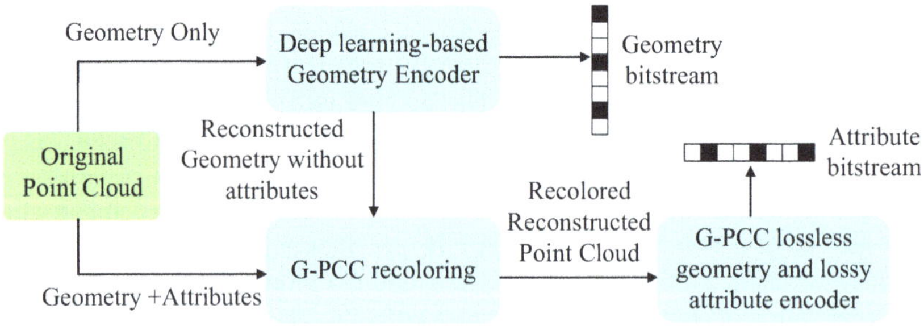

Fig. 9.22 Network framework for hybrid framework encoding. The figure shown is introduced with MPEG open-access (OA) work under CC BY License (Copyright © 1988–2025, www.mpeg.org) [79]

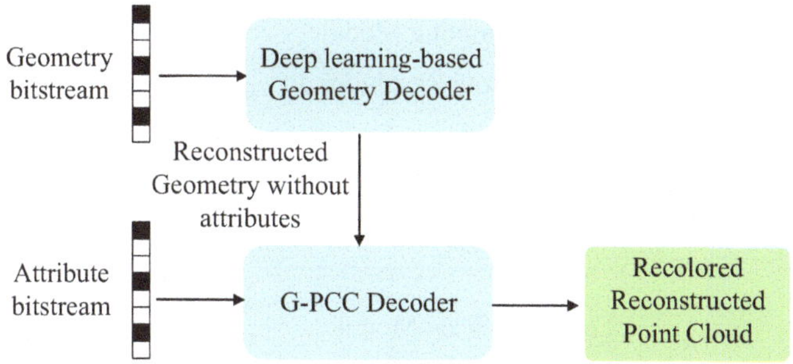

Fig. 9.23 Network framework for hybrid framework decoding. The figure shown is introduced with MPEG open-access (OA) work under CC BY License (Copyright © 1988–2025, www.mpeg.org) [79]

to accomplish attribute compression and is adaptable to any deep learning-based geometry compression method. Results indicate that the framework surpasses G-PCC and V-PCC on D1-PSNR. Regarding attributes, the framework performs comparably to G-PCC trisoup, and the results for attribute compression are on par with V-PCC.

9.3.6 MPEG 142nd Meeting

In the MPEG 142nd meeting, there are seven important proposals, as shown in Table 9.6.

m63059 (CJDU: Collaborative Joint Downsampling and Upsampling for Geometry Compression) In m63059 [80], the authors introduce a synergistic preprocessing and post-processing framework, termed Collaborative Joint Downsampling and Upsampling (CJDU), as illustrated in Fig. 9.24. This approach enhances point cloud geometry coding efficiency by concurrently training the downsampling and upsampling networks. The methodology commences with a

Table 9.6 MPEG 142nd meeting

Proposal	Description	Organization
m62965	Modifies the D3-PSNR metric	InterDigital
m62966	Modifies the D3-PSNR metric	InterDigital
m63059	Proposes the CJDU framework	UCAS, ByteDance
m63061	Proposes a post-processing framework	UCAS, ByteDance
m63246	Modifies the SparseContextNet model	InterDigital
m63248	Summarizes the SparsePCGCv1 and GRASP-NetV2 model	InterDigital
m63255	Modifies the hybrid framework	Qualcomm/UMKC

Source: Author

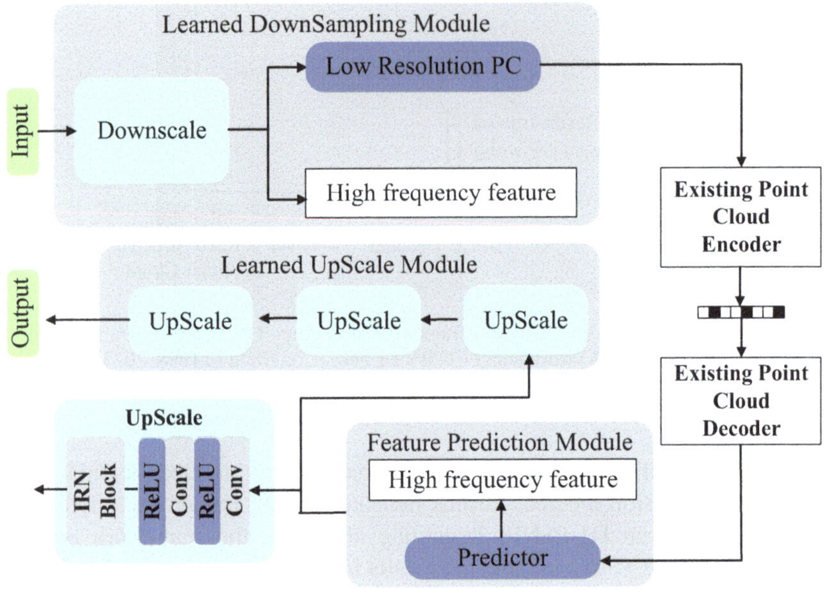

Fig. 9.24 Network architecture for CJDU. The figure shown is introduced with MPEG open-access (OA) work under CC BY License (Copyright © 1988–2025, www.mpeg.org) [80]

U-Net-based Predictor, which processes low-bit representations to produce high-bit outputs. The crux of this proposal is the collaborative training strategy, which unfolds in three phases: (1) stabilizing the Predictor's parameters while training the downsampling and upsampling networks; (2) fixing the downsampling parameters to refine the Predictor and upsampling networks; and (3) jointly optimizing the downsampling, Predictor, and upsampling networks. This structured training scheme is pivotal for achieving the method's efficacy.

m63061 (A Post-Processing Network: Compression Oriented Geometry Post-Processing of Point Clouds) The m63061 [81] focusing on geometry post-processing. This technique refines compressed lossy point clouds, restoring them to their original resolution or even enhancing them to a higher resolution, thereby improving the objective quality. The compression-centric geometry post-processing framework for point clouds is illustrated in Fig. 9.25, which is designed to optimize the geometry of compressed point clouds through a two-part framework, i.e., a structural context building module and a multi-stage point restoration module. Initially, the network leverages the structural context module to augment point cloud features. Subsequently, it employs a progressive reconstruction strategy, prioritizing structurally significant points and methodically upsampling to achieve the refined point cloud.

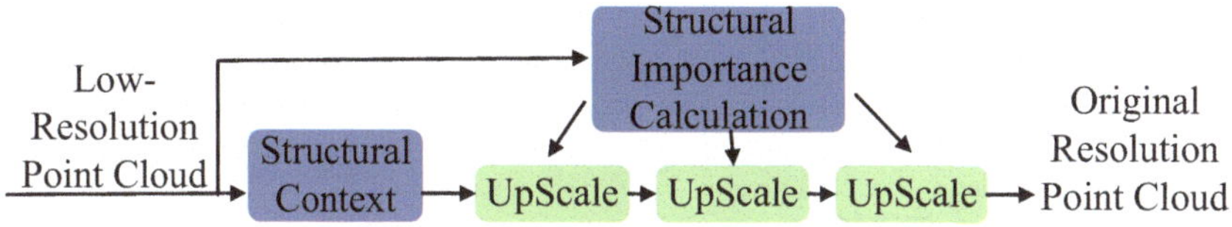

Fig. 9.25 Network architecture for post-processing. The figure shown is introduced with MPEG open-access (OA) work under CC BY License (Copyright © 1988–2025, www.mpeg.org) [81]

Table 9.7 MPEG 143rd–146th meetings

Proposal	Description	Organization
m64110	Modifies the D-DPCC network with Hie-ME/MC	SJTU, OPPO
m64308	Summarizes report of deep octree coding	InterDigital
m64315	Proposes the NNC framework	KHU/TTA/KETTI
m64329	Summarizes the SparsePCGCv1 and GRASP-NetV2 model	InterDigital
m64418	Validates the efficiency of SparsePCGCv3 on LiDAR	NJU, OPPO
m64438	Summarizes the hybrid framework for AI-PCC	Qualcomm
m64439	Summarizes the AI-based dynamic PC coding	Qualcomm
m64441	Releases software for the hybrid framework	Qualcomm
m64700	Introduces the FlyingThings3D dataset	InterDigital
m65061	Modifies results of D-DPCC network with Hie-ME/MC	SJTU, OPPO
m65519	Summarizes the AI-based dynamic PC coding	Qualcomm
m65520	Summarizes the hybrid framework for AI-PCC	Qualcomm
m65521	Summarizes the dataset selection for AI-PCC	Qualcomm
m66178	Proposes the MS-PCAC framework	SDU, OPPO
m66184	Proposes the ER-OctAttention framework	SDU, OPPO
m67523	Proposes a DPCC framework based via temporal contextual pyramid	SYSU, TCL

Source: Author

9.3.7 MPEG 143rd–146th Meetings

In the MPEG 143rd–146th meeting, there are 16 important proposals proposed, as shown in Table 9.7.

m64110 (D-DPCC with Hie-ME/MC: Learning Dynamic Point Cloud Compression via Hierarchical Inter-frame Block Matching) The m64110 [82] presents a dynamic point cloud coding method, featuring a novel hierarchical block-matching inter-prediction module. The authors introduce a Hierarchical Motion Estimation and Motion Compensation (Hie-ME/MC) scheme for adaptive inter-prediction. This approach selectively adjusts the granularity of optical flow to capture motion information with high fidelity. The framework comprises five modules, as illustrated in Fig. 9.26. The Hie-ME/MC employs a two-stage process: Initially, the low-resolution module estimates a coarse motion flow between $y_t^{3\downarrow}$

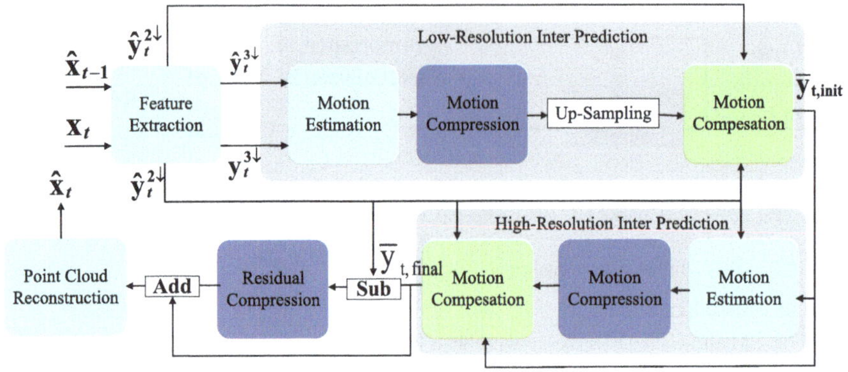

Fig. 9.26 Network architecture for D-DPCC with Hie-MEMC. The figure shown is introduced with MPEG open-access (OA) work under CC BY License (Copyright © 1988–2025, www.mpeg.org) [82]

and $\hat{y}_{t-1}^{3\downarrow}$, representing significant movements. This yields an initial prediction $\bar{y}_{t,ini}$ for $y_t^{2\downarrow}$, capturing the primary motion. Subsequently, the high-resolution module refines this prediction by extracting detailed movements, resulting in the final prediction $\bar{y}_{t,final}$ for $y_t^{2\downarrow}$. Enhancing motion estimation efficiency, a KNN-Attention Block Matching (KABM) network is designed to evaluate the relevance of potential correspondences through geometry and feature correlations. The residual and optical flows are then compressed using a deep learning-based entropy model.

m64315 (NNC: Compressed AI-PCC Decoder Transmission with NNC) This m64315 [83] identifies a constraint associated with employing AI-PCC as a codec, notably the requirement for clients to maintain multiple decoders. To circumvent this issue, the authors propose leveraging Neural Network Coding (NNC), as depicted in Fig. 9.27. Initially, point cloud is encoded using the AI-PCC codec, resulting in a compressed bitstream. Next, the AI-PCC model, specifically the decoder component utilized in the compression process, is itself encoded via the NNC encoder—this step is crucial as the client necessitates only the decoder. The bitstreams of both the compressed point cloud and the AI-PCC model are then multiplexed and dispatched to the client. Upon reception, the client first decodes the AI-PCC model bitstream to reconstruct the AI-PCC decoder. Thereafter, the compressed point cloud bitstream is decoded using this freshly reconstructed decoder, culminating in the restoration of the original point cloud.

m66178 (Harnessing Multiscale Network for Enhanced 3D Point Cloud Attribute Compression with Geometry-Assisted Learning) The m66178 [84] introduces an innovative deep learning framework called MS-PCAC. This framework features a frequency-based sampling module that focuses on preserving high-frequency color attribute areas, similar to the RAHT method's balance of high and low-frequency coefficients. Additionally, it implements a multiscale

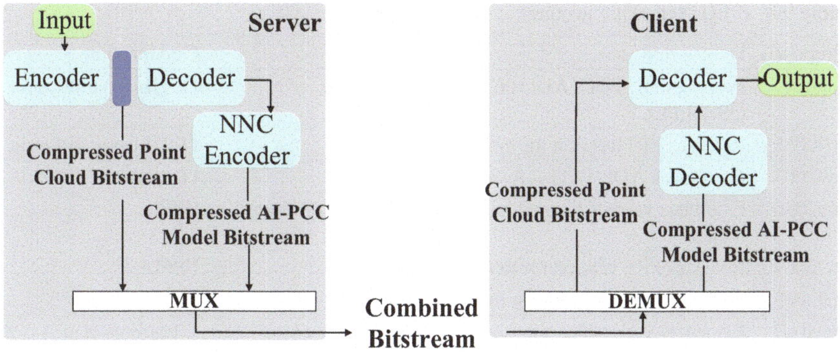

Fig. 9.27 Network architecture for NNC. The figure shown is introduced with MPEG open-access (OA) work under CC BY License (Copyright © 1988–2025, www.mpeg.org) [83]

compression strategy designed to capture and decode attribute features across various frequencies and resolutions.

m66184 (Enhancing Context Models for Point Cloud Geometry Compression with Context Feature Residuals) The m66184 [85] leverages context feature residuals to enhance context models for compressing point cloud geometry. The key improvement is in emphasizing the distinctions between contexts of different nodes within an octree. Their method is validated by demonstrating improved performance on OctAttention using the MPEG 8i datasets.

m67523 (Efficient Dynamic Point Cloud Compression via Temporal Contextual Pyramid) The m67523 [86] introduces a Dynamic Point Cloud Compression framework using a Temporal Contextual Pyramid (TCP) to perform cross-frame context fusion at multiple scales. A Temporal Codec Unit (TCU) is proposed for aggregating temporal context. This unit employs sparse convolution on target coordinates for context fusion, effectively modeling temporal context with minimal computational cost. The focus of this proposal is solely on point cloud geometry compression. Compared to V-PCC, their method achieves a 72.19% increase in D1 PSNR, and it also achieves faster encoding/decoding speeds compared to existing methods.

9.4 JPEG Point Cloud Coding Standard

In this section, we will provide an explanation of the JPEG standard for deep learning point cloud coding. To better illustrate this, they will continue to follow the order of the meetings, introducing proposals that made significant contributions and suggestions in each meeting.

Table 9.8 JPEG 90th–95th meetings

Proposal	Description	Organization
m90019	Proposes DL-PCC, ADL-PCC, RS-DLPCC and QS-DLPCC	IT, ULisboa, IPLeiria
m90085	Releases PPT version for m90019	IT, ULisboa, IPLeiria
m92003	Introduces ADL-PCC software coding	IT, ULisboa, IPLeiria
m92040	Evaluates various learned-based methods using different metrics	EPFL
m92069	Releases PPT version for m92040	EPFL
m93043	Releases paper version for m92040	EPFL
m95047	Evaluates various learning-based methods	J. Prazeres et al.

Source: Author

9.4.1 JPEG 90th–95th Meetings

In the JPEG 90th–95th meeting, there are seven important proposals proposed, as shown in Table 9.8.

m90019 (IT/IST/IPLeiria Response to the Call for Evidence on JPEG Pleno Point Cloud Coding) In the JPEG standard document m90019 [87], the research team initially developed two non-scalable point cloud geometry coding schemes: deep learning-based Point Cloud Geometry Coding (DL-PCC) and its adaptive version (ADL-PCC) [88]. To address the scalability limitations, subsequent research introduced two enhanced approaches: Resolution-Scalable DLPCC (RS-DLPCC) [52] supporting resolution-level transmission and Quality-Scalable DLPCC (QS-DLPCC) [53] enabling progressive quality transmission.

DL-PCC Framework The DL-PCC framework operates as follows: First, the point cloud is partitioned into blocks, enabling independent encoding within each block. The overall architecture is illustrated in Fig. 9.28. This process is similar to the transform coding approach in traditional methods but employs convolution

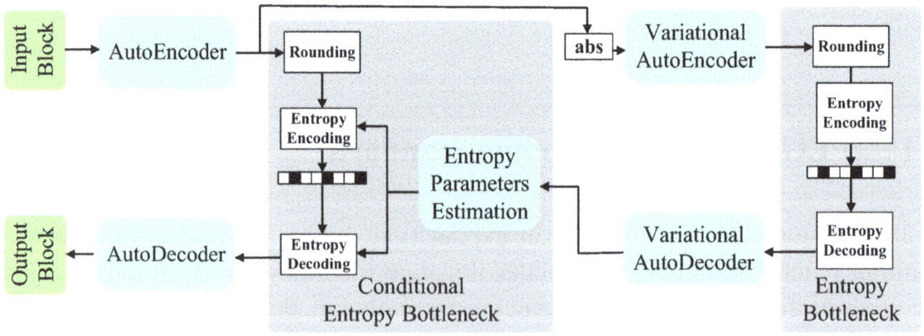

Fig. 9.28 Network architecture for DL-PCC. The figure shown is introduced with JPEG open-access (OA) work under CC BY License (Copyright © 1988–2025, www.jpeg.org) [87]

to learn a nonlinear transform, enabling the extraction of feature information. The resulting latent representation is a set of fractional coefficients, which first undergo processing. During inference, the coefficients are quantized through rounding, while during training, uniform noise is added to ensure gradient backpropagation. At the decoder side, each block undergoes independent decoding before being reassembled into a complete point cloud based on their global positional information.

ADL-PCC Framework The overall architecture is the same as that of DL-PCC, with the addition of a DL Coding Model Selection module, as shown in Fig. 9.29. The module aims to optimize encoding parameters and reduce bitstream size by dynamically selecting the most suitable encoding model.

RS-DLPCC Framework The design is showcased in Fig. 9.30. The framework implements a novel two-stage partitioning strategy: First, the complete point cloud is divided into nonoverlapping macro blocks, and then each macro block is further subdivided into eight micro blocks through sampling. This hierarchical partitioning structure enables both progressive encoding and multi-resolution encoding by dynamically selecting the number of transmitted micro blocks, significantly enhancing coding flexibility.

QS-DLPCC Framework The proposed architecture is delineated in Fig. 9.31. The point cloud is first partitioned into blocks, within which independent encoding operations are performed. The core of this framework is a feature-level multilayer auto-encoder, which transforms the latent representation to be encoded into multiple sets of feature maps, thereby enabling sequential entropy encoding of each feature group. This achieves a progressive and scalable encoding framework.

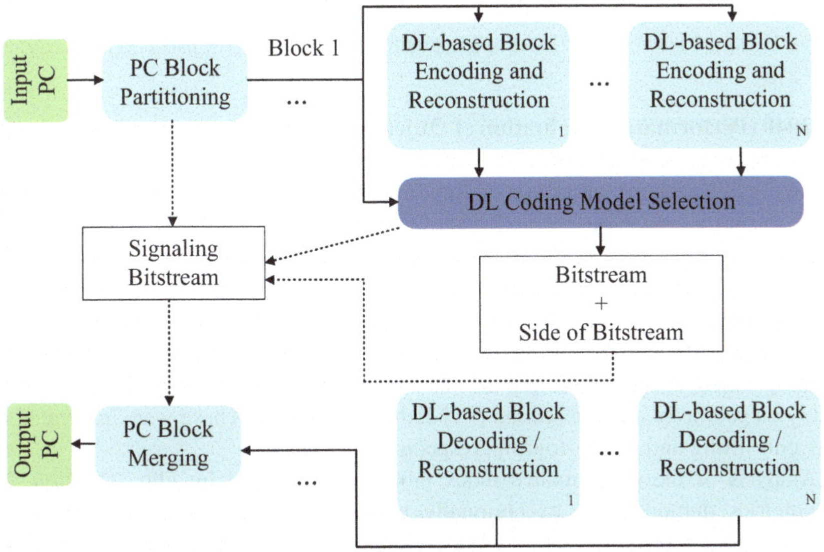

Fig. 9.29 Network architecture for ADL-PCC. The figure shown is introduced with JPEG open-access (OA) work under CC BY License (Copyright © 1988–2025, www.jpeg.org) [87]

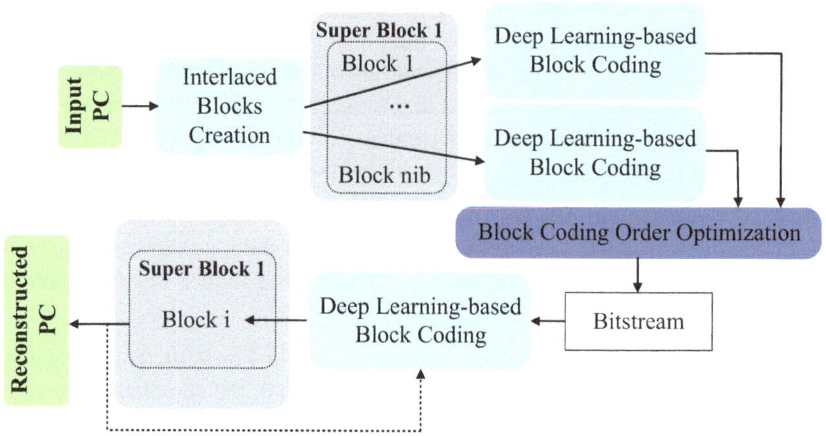

Fig. 9.30 Network architecture for RS-DLPCC. The figure shown is introduced with JPEG open-access (OA) work under CC BY License (Copyright © 1988–2025, www.jpeg.org) [87]

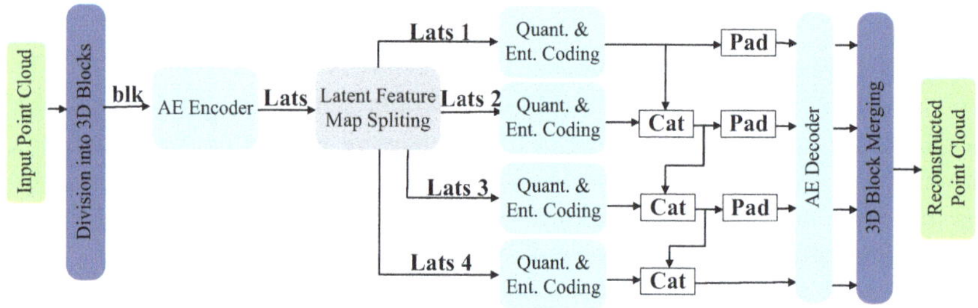

Fig. 9.31 Network architecture for QS-DLPCC. The figure shown is introduced with JPEG open-access (OA) work under CC BY License (Copyright © 1988–2025, www.jpeg.org) [87]

m92040 (Performance Evaluation of Objective Quality Metrics on Point Clouds Distorted with Learning-Based Codecs) The m92040 [89] presents a comprehensive evaluation of objective quality metrics vis-à-vis subjective assessments derived from a crowdsourced analysis of point clouds, which were modified using learning-based algorithms. Reference anchors were produced using both G-PCC and V-PCC standards. Given that G-PCC utilizes two distinct geometry coding modules (Octree and Trisoup) and two color coding techniques (RAHT and lifting), the study employed the octree-lifting and trisoup-lifting combinations. Two specialized learning-based compression algorithms were examined: the first [90] focusing solely on geometry and the second [91] dedicated to color. These were integrated as geo_cnn-lifting and octree-folding, respectively.

Analysis of the performance index table yields several insights: (1) None of the metrics demonstrated exceptionally high performance, with no correlation surpassing 0.9 across the dataset. (2) PCQM emerged as the top-performing metric, outperforming others in all indices within the full dataset and maintaining robust performance across individual codecs. (3) PointSSIM ranked as the second most effective metric, showcasing consistent results across all codecs.

9.4.2 JPEG 96th Meeting

In the JPEG 96th meeting, there are eight important proposals proposed, as shown in Table 9.9.

m96005 (IT/IST/IPLeiria Response to the Call for Proposals on JPEG Pleno Point Cloud Coding) The m96005 [92] proposal includes (1) IT Deep Learning-based Point Cloud Codec for Geometry only (IT-DL-PCC-G) and (2) IT Deep Learning-based Point Cloud Codec for Geometry and Color (IT-DL-PCC-GC).

IT-DL-PCC-G The codec under discussion encodes geometry using binary 3D blocks and incorporates two distinct deep learning models: one for block-based encoding and another for Advanced Block-based Upsampling (ABU). The DL model is tripartite, encompassing the generation of latent, entropy coding, and subsequent decoding. Adaptive downsampling is employed as necessary to adjust for the PC's density during encoding. The ABU model enhances the density and quality of the reconstructed PC without incurring additional bitrate, thereby optimizing the RD efficiency. The architecture is depicted in Fig. 9.32.

IT-DL-PCC-GC This model advances the capabilities of the IT-DL-PCC-G, by incorporating joint encoding capability for both geometry and three-channel 8-bit color components (RGB). This model employs the same coding model and architecture as its predecessor, which was originally designed for geometry alone, but now it optimizes the coding of both geometry and color in tandem. Additionally, the optional Advanced Block-based Upsampling (ABU) model is enhanced to support four channels, thereby elevating the quality of both geometry and color without increasing the bitrate.

Table 9.9 JPEG 96th meeting

Proposal	Description	Organization
m96005	Proposes IT-DL-PCC-G and IT-DL-PCC-GC	IT, ULisboa, IPLeiria
m96010	Releases PPT version for m96005	IT, ULisboa, IPLeiria
m96017	Releases Additional test PC for m96005	IT, ULisboa, IPLeiria
m96011	Proposes a geometry and attribute compression framework	USTC
m96012	Releases PPT version for m96011	USTC
m96018	Proposes Geometry-only encoder, Full geometry and color encoder	EPFL
m96076	Releases extend description for the m96018	EPFL
m96095	Releases PPT version for m96018 and m96076	EPFL

Source: Author

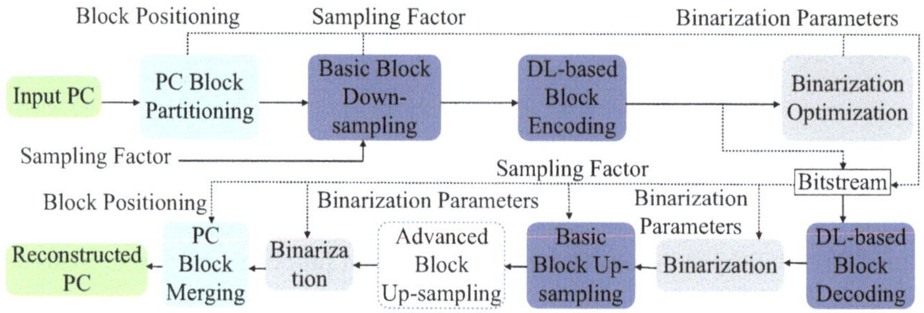

Fig. 9.32 Network architecture for IT-DL-PCC-G. The figure shown is introduced with JPEG open-access (OA) work under CC BY License (Copyright © 1988–2025, www.jpeg.org) [92]

m96018 and m96076 (EPFL Response to the Call for Proposals on JPEG Pleno Point Cloud Coding) The m96018 [93] describes the compression algorithm for PC compression. The m96076 [94] extends the description of color coding module.

In the geometry-only encoder, the latent representations y are divided channel-wise into N slices $\{y_1, y_2, \ldots, y_N\}$, each with $\frac{K}{N}$ channels, before entropy coding. Each slice y_i undergoes quantization to produce $\hat{y}_i$, which is then entropy coded based on an assumed normal distribution characterized by mean μ_i and scale σ_i. The parameters μ_i and σ_i are of identical dimensions to $\hat{y}_i$ and are derived from a convolutional layer block known as the slice transform.

The proposed codec employs a geometry-color compression scheme, where the geometry is encoded using the existing geometry coding algorithm while incorporating dedicated optimization for color compression. During color attribute encoding, the system first encodes and decodes the geometry to generate distorted geometry information, ensuring synchronization between the encoder and decoder. Subsequently, color attributes are assigned based on this distorted geometry, thereby enabling geometry-assisted color compression that references the distorted geometry information. The entire procedure is depicted in Fig. 9.33.

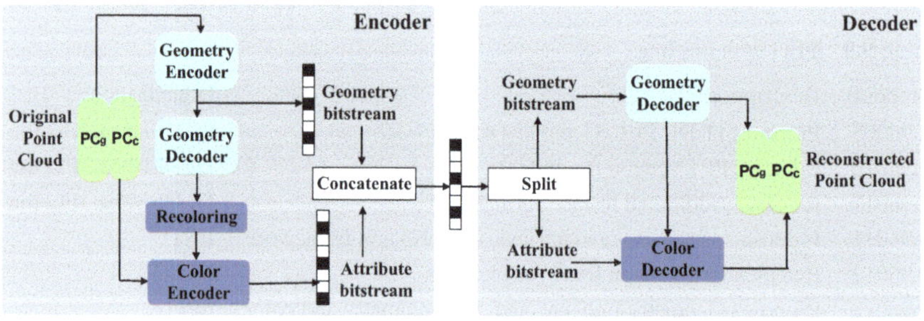

Fig. 9.33 Network architecture for pcc-geo-slicing-color. The figure shown is introduced with JPEG open-access (OA) work under CC BY License (Copyright © 1988–2025, www.jpeg.org) [93]

Table 9.10 JPEG 97th–101st meetings

Proposal	Description	Organization
m97049	Releases report on JPEG Pleno Point Cloud Test Set v2	S. Perry
m98062	Proposes a framework for compression artifact removal	HNU, NJU
m99100	Releases report the RD performance of m96018 with other networks	IT, IST, IPLeiria
m99102	Discusses adding attention models to the geometry JPEG PCC VM	IT, IST, IPLeiria
m100108	Introduces more details for m99102 and discuss using sparse convolutions	IT, IST, IPLeiria
m100113	Uses sparse convolutions in the VM and verify its performance	IT, IST, IPLeiria
m101077	Validates the new point cloud dataset	EPFL

Source: Author

9.4.3 JPEG 97th–101st Meetings

In the JPEG 97th–101st meeting, there are seven important proposals proposed, as shown in Table 9.10.

m99102 (Attention Models in the Geometry JPEG PCC VM: Performance and Core Experiment Proposal) The m99102 [95] proposal is dedicated to examining the rate-distortion (RD) performance and the complexity implications of incorporating attention mechanisms into the existing JPEG Pleno Point Cloud Coding (PCC) Verification Model (VM). A series of comprehensive experiments were conducted to address four key inquiries: the selection of an attention model, the quantity of attention mechanisms to implement, their placement within the architecture, and the consideration of removing the intra-block residual (IRB) structure. The findings indicate that attention mechanisms can enhance the RD efficiency of point cloud coding. The most effective configuration identified involves the integration of a single Cheng Attention Model (AttM), as illustrated in Fig. 9.34, positioned before the final (4th) CNN layer of the JPEG PCC VM. Relative to the

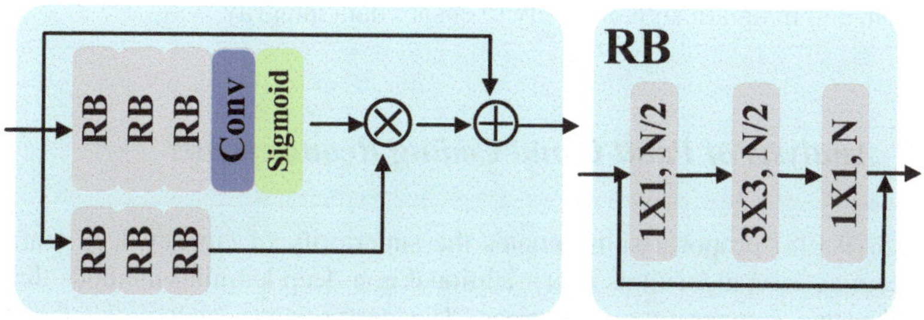

Fig. 9.34 Network architecture for cheng attention model. The figure shown is introduced with JPEG open-access (OA) work under CC BY License (Copyright © 1988–2025, www.jpeg.org) [95]

baseline VM, this setup achieves a rate reduction of 3.9% for PSNR D1 and 4.1% for PSNR D2, while the model complexity, in terms of the number of weights, increases by 23%, and the training duration per epoch extends by 10%.

9.5 AVS AI-Based Point Cloud Coding Standard

To ensure the secure development of China's digital media-related industries, AVS has also established a point cloud working group and released the country's first point cloud compression reference model, the Point Cloud Reference Model (PCRM), in December 2019. In this section, due to space constraints, they will only introduce some proposals of deep learning point cloud coding.

9.5.1 Demand for Point Cloud Compression Technology

The m7820 [96] and m7932 [97] proposals jointly call for establishing standardized deep learning-based point cloud coding technologies to accommodate the rapid development of artificial intelligence. Deep learning methods demonstrate superior compression potential compared to non-deep approaches through their end-to-end optimization and adaptive entropy modeling capabilities.

The proposal outlines demands for 3D modeling and metaverse applications, emphasizing the need for rendering and interaction with point cloud data, support for progressive layering like Level of Detail (LoD), and maintaining signal fidelity in lossless compression. For cultural heritage and digital art, it calls for high-fidelity depiction of point clouds, support for diverse compression needs from lossy to lossless, and progressive layering to facilitate hierarchical processing and retrieval.

The compression capabilities for large 3D point clouds must support real-time processing for datasets with millions of points, offer multiple grades for various applications and platforms, ensure signal fidelity in lossy compression with adjustable bitrates [18], provide limited lossy compression with controllable distortion, and maintain signal fidelity to ensure data integrity.

9.5.2 Analysis of Point Cloud Coding Requirements

The m7879 [98] proposal substantiates the superiority of current deep learning-based compression algorithms over traditional non-deep learning methods through comprehensive comparative evaluations. The performance evaluation of lossless geometry compression on the MPEG dataset yields the following ranking: SparsePCGC > OctAttention > VoxelDNN > G-PCC > AVS PCRM. This hierarchy indicates that deep learning-oriented point cloud coding schemes offer greater user convenience in the context estimation module design and superior accuracy in probability estimation for densely populated point clouds.

Regarding lossy point cloud coding, performance assessments on the MPEG dense point cloud dataset position the algorithms in the following order: SparsePCGC > PCGCv2 > G-PCC > AVS PCRM. Deep learning approaches demonstrate a marked reduction in bit rates coupled with elevated PSNR values, signifying their distinct performance benefits in lossy compression scenarios, particularly when factoring in rate-distortion (RD) performance optimization.

In high bit rate environments and tasks with a ten-bit width, classification performance is sequenced as SparsePCGC > G-PCC > AVS PCRM > PCGCv2, with deep learning methods maintaining a more compressed bit rate range (PointNet++). For segmentation tasks, the rankings diverge between deep learning approaches: PCGCv2 > SparsePCGC and non-deep learning methods—G-PCC > AVS PCRM (PointNet++), reflecting a stark contrast in their bit rate alignment capabilities. Nonetheless, it is generally observed that segmentation performance on distorted point clouds is markedly improved when utilizing deep learning-based methods.

9.6 Comparative Analysis

In the field of deep learning-based point cloud coding, many related proposals have been put forth by both MPEG, JPEG, and AVS. These proposals cover datasets, metrics, specific frameworks, and more. The frameworks include various network structures for geometry coding, attribute coding, static point cloud coding, and dynamic point cloud coding. These standards play a significant role in guiding the subsequent research on point clouds. As Table 9.11 shown, the proposals can be analyzed comparatively as follows. MPEG primarily utilizes GRASP-Net and SparsePCGC, etc., while JPEG focuses on frameworks like ADL-PCC, QS-DLPCC, and IT-DL-PCC-G, etc. Then, regarding the hybrid method for point cloud encoding that involves both geometry and attributes, the MPEG has put forward an approach that combines AI-based Geometry with traditional methods like G-PCC Attribute Coding or V-PCC Attribute Coding. On the other hand, JPEG has

Table 9.11 Comparative analysis of AI-based point cloud compression proposals

Aspect	MPEG	JPEG
Frameworks	GRASP-Net, SparsePCGC, etc.	ADL-PCC, QS-DLPCC, IT-DL-PCC-G, etc.
Hybrid Methods	AI-based Geometry + G-PCC/V-PCC Attribute Coding	AI-based Geometry + AI-based Attribute Coding
Dynamic Point Cloud	Several proposals	Nearly no proposals

Source: Author

proposed the combination of AI-based Geometry with AI-based Attribute Coding. Both approaches utilize different modes for compressing attributes. In the real world, especially with the ongoing development of autonomous driving and general artificial intelligence, dynamic point cloud coding represents a very tangible and highly applicable challenge. However, JPEG has almost no related proposals, while MPEG, despite having a number of proposals for dynamic point clouds, still has many areas that could be improved. Last but not least, for the datasets and metrics, there is an array of datasets currently available for point clouds, yet existing frameworks still have a voracious need for more point cloud datasets to be proposed and incorporated into standards. Overall, current deep learning-based point cloud coding still presents substantial research potential, which makes standardization efforts particularly crucial.

9.7 Summary

This chapter systematically elaborates on the standardization efforts for deep learning-based point cloud coding, focusing on detailed explanations of the proposals by MPEG, JPEG, and AVS. Through the introductions provided, the current development status of the standards has been clarified, and these standards offer guidance on the research directions for point cloud coding. Additionally, in the ongoing development of these standards, it is essential to address more complex tasks in point cloud coding, such as joint optimization of geometry and attributes, as well as bitrate allocation in geometry and attribute joint compression. It is believed that as the standards become increasingly detailed, the tasks associated with point cloud coding will become more regulated from a research perspective, and the practical application of deep learning point cloud coding will draw closer to actual implementation. For readers who are interested in the related technologies of AI-based image and video coding, please refer to [99].

Exercises

1. Please explain what the current AI-based point cloud coding standards are.
2. Please describe what the main aspects of the current point cloud proposal are.
3. Please explain what network frameworks are proposed in the MPEG AI-3DGC proposals.
4. Please explain what network frameworks are proposed in the JPEG AI Point Cloud proposals.
5. Please explain which evaluation metric is highlighted in the MPEG AI-3DGC proposals.
6. Please describe what the updates for SparsePCGC in the MPEG m60352 proposal are.

7. Please explain which two scalable PCGC methods are proposed in the JPEG m90019 proposal.
8. Please describe what important modules are adopted in the proposed IT-DL-PCC-G in the JPEG m96010 proposal.
9. Please explain what the main issues discussed in the JPEG m99102 proposal are.
10. Please describe what other aspects you think are worth discussing and studying for the point cloud coding proposal.

References

1. W. Gao, G. Li, *Deep Learning for 3D Point Clouds* (Springer, Berlin, 2024)
2. G. Li, G. Wei, W. Gao, *Point Cloud Compression: Technologies and Standardization* (Springer, Berlin, 2024)
3. W. Gao, G. Li, Point cloud compression, enhancement and applications: from 3d perception to large models, in *Proceedings of the 32nd ACM International Conference on Multimedia* (2024), pp. 11292–11293
4. H. Sun, G. Li, S. Chen, L. Li, W. Gao, Special topic on 3d point cloud processing and applications. ZTE Commun. **21**(4), 1 (2023)
5. W. Gao, W. Gao, X. Mu, C. Peng, G. Li, Overview and comparison of AVS point cloud compression standard. APSIPA Trans. Signal Inf. Process. **14**(2), 1–33 (2025)
6. W. Gao, S. Wang, X. Zhang, S. Kwong, Editorial for special issue on deep learning-based data compression. APSIPA Trans. Signal Inf. Process. **13**(6), 1–2 (2024)
7. Y. Wu, L. Xie, S. Sun, W. Gao, Y. Yan, Adaptive intra period size for deep learning-based screen content video coding, in *2024 IEEE International Conference on Multimedia and Expo Workshops (ICMEW)* (IEEE, New York, 2024), pp. 1–6
8. H. Zheng, W. Gao, End-to-end rgb-d image compression via exploiting channel-modality redundancy, in *Proceedings of the AAAI Conference on Artificial Intelligence*, vol. 38(7) (2024), pp. 7562–7570
9. H. Yuan, W. Gao, S. Ma, Y. Yan, Divide-and-conquer-based RDO-free CU partitioning for 8k video compression. ACM Trans. Multimed. Comput. Commun. Appl. **20**(4), 1–20 (2024)
10. Y. Wu, W. Gao, End-to-end lossless compression of high precision depth maps guided by pseudo-residual, in *2022 Data Compression Conference (DCC)* (IEEE, New York, 2022), pp. 489–489
11. Y. Wu, Z. Qi, H. Zheng, L. Tao, W. Gao, Deep image compression with latent optimization and piece-wise quantization approximation, in *Proceedings of the IEEE/CVF Conference on Computer Vision and Pattern Recognition* (2021), pp. 1926–1930
12. W. Gao, L. Tao, L. Zhou, D. Yang, X. Zhang, Z. Guo, Low-rate image compression with super-resolution learning, in *Proceedings of the IEEE/CVF Conference on Computer Vision and Pattern Recognition Workshops* (2020), pp. 154–155
13. Y. Li, W. Gao, G. Li, S. Ma, Saliency segmentation oriented deep image compression with novel bit allocation. IEEE Trans. Image Process. **34**, 16–29 (2025)
14. C. Zhang, W. Gao, Learned rate control for frame-level adaptive neural video compression via dynamic neural network, in *European Conference on Computer Vision* (Springer, Berlin, 2024)
15. Z. Yu, W. Gao, When dynamic neural network meets point cloud compression: computation-aware variable rate and checkerboard context, in *2024 Data Compression Conference (DCC)* (IEEE, New York, 2024), pp. 600–600
16. C. Fu, G. Li, R. Song, W. Gao, S. Liu, Octattention: octree-based large-scale contexts model for point cloud compression, in *Proceedings of the AAAI Conference on Artificial Intelligence*, vol. 36(1) (2022), pp. 625–633

17. C. Zhang, W. Gao, Adadpcc: adaptive rate control and rate-distortion-complexity optimization for dynamic point cloud compression, in *Proceedings of the AAAI Conference on Artificial Intelligence* (2025)
18. K. Wang, W. Gao, Unipcgc: towards practical point cloud geometry compression via an efficient unified approach, in *Proceedings of the AAAI Conference on Artificial Intelligence* (2025)
19. H. Zheng, W. Gao, Z. Yu, T. Zhao, G. Li, Viewpcgc: view-guided learned point cloud geometry compression, in *Proceedings of the 32nd ACM International Conference on Multimedia* (2024), pp. 7152–7161
20. K. Wang, S. Li, Q. Yi, W. Gao, A novel benchmark and dataset for efficient 3d gaussian splatting with gaussian point cloud compression. arXiv preprint arXiv:2505.18197 (2025)
21. L. Xie, W. Gao, H. Zheng, G. Li, SPCGC: scalable point cloud geometry compression for machine vision, in *2024 IEEE International Conference on Robotics and Automation (ICRA)* (IEEE, New York, 2024), pp. 17272–17278
22. W. Gao, H. Ye, G. Li, H. Zheng, Y. Wu, L. Xie, Openpointcloud: an open-source algorithm library of deep learning based point cloud compression, in *Proceedings of the 30th ACM International Conference on Multimedia* (2022), pp. 7347–7350
23. Y. Zhang, W. Gao, G. Li, Openpointcloud-v2: a deep learning based open-source algorithm library of point cloud processing, in *Proceedings of the 1st International Workshop on Advances in Point Cloud Compression, Processing and Analysis* (2022), pp. 51–55
24. L. Xie, W. Gao, Learningpcc: a pytorch library for learning-based point cloud compression, in *Proceedings of the 32nd ACM International Conference on Multimedia* (2024), pp. 11234–11238
25. L. Xie, W. Gao, Pchmvision: an open-source library of point cloud compression for human and machine vision, in *Proceedings of the 32nd ACM International Conference on Multimedia* (2024), pp. 11239–11243
26. S. Sun, B. Qu, X. Liang, S. Fan, W. Gao, IE-bench: advancing the measurement of text-driven image editing for human perception alignment. arXiv preprint arXiv:2501.09927 (2025)
27. Y. Ye, W. Gao, LLM-PCGC: large language model-based point cloud geometry compression. arXiv preprint arXiv:2408.08682 (2024)
28. S. Fan, W. Gao, Z. Chen, G. Li, G. Liu, Q. Wang, Stochasticity-aware no-reference point cloud quality assessment, in *International Joint Conference on Artificial Intelligence (IJCAI)* (2025)
29. Z. Yao, W. Gao, G. Li, T. Zhao, Collaborating constrained and unconstrained encodings for cross-modal salient object detection. IEEE Trans. Emerging Top. Comput. Intell. **9**(6), 3895–3909 (2025)
30. Q. Xu, L. Meng, G. Zhang, W. Gao, G. Li, Coding-free multiscale latent variables for lossless point cloud attribute compression, in *2025 IEEE International Conference on Multimedia and Expo (ICME)* (2025)
31. H. Yuan, W. Gao, W. Gao, Opensep: an open source subjective experiment platform, in *Proceedings of the 32nd ACM International Conference on Multimedia* (2024), pp. 11248–11251
32. H. Li, W. Gao, Information exploration of projected views for point cloud quality measurement. IEEE Trans. Instrum. Meas. **74**, 1–14 (2025)
33. B. Qu, X. Liang, S. Sun, W. Gao, Exploring aigc video quality: a focus on visual harmony, video-text consistency and domain distribution gap, in *Proceedings of the IEEE/CVF Conference on Computer Vision and Pattern Recognition Workshops* (2024)
34. B. Qu, H. Li, W. Gao, Bringing textual prompt to AI-generated image quality assessment, in *2024 IEEE International Conference on Multimedia and Expo (ICME)* (IEEE, New York, 2024)
35. S. Sun, X. Liang, S. Fan, W. Gao, W. Gao, VE-bench: subjective-aligned benchmark suite for text-driven video editing quality assessment, in *Proceedings of the AAAI Conference on Artificial Intelligence* (2025)
36. W. Liu, W. Gao, X. Mu, Fast inter-frame motion prediction for compressed dynamic point cloud attribute enhancement, in *Proceedings of the AAAI Conference on Artificial Intelligence*, vol. 38(4) (2024), pp. 3720–3728

37. Z. Yang, W. Gao, X. Lu, Danet: density-adaptive network for geometry-based point cloud compression artifacts removal, in *2023 IEEE International Conference on Visual Communications and Image Processing (VCIP)* (IEEE, New York, 2023), pp. 1–5
38. X. Fan, G. Li, D. Li, Y. Ren, W. Gao, T.H. Li, Deep geometry post-processing for decompressed point clouds, in *2022 IEEE International Conference on Multimedia and Expo (ICME)* (IEEE, New York, 2022), pp. 1–6
39. X. Zhang, G. Liao, W. Gao, G. Li, TDRNET: transformer-based dual-branch restoration network for geometry based point cloud compression artifacts, in *2022 IEEE International Conference on Multimedia and Expo (ICME)* (IEEE, New York, 2022), pp. 1–6
40. Z. Li, G. Li, T.H. Li, S. Liu, W. Gao, Semantic point cloud upsampling. IEEE Trans. Multimedia **25**, 3432–3442 (2022)
41. Z. Li, S. Liu, W. Gao, G. Li, G. Li, S4R: rethinking point cloud sampling via guiding upsampling-aware perception. IEEE Trans. Multimedia **27**, 6677–6689 (2025)
42. S. Fan, W. Gao, G. Li, Salient object detection for point clouds, in *European Conference on Computer Vision* (Springer, Berlin, 2022), pp. 1–19
43. S. Luo, W. Gao, A general framework for rotation invariant point cloud analysis, in *ICASSP 2024-2024 IEEE International Conference on Acoustics, Speech and Signal Processing (ICASSP)* (IEEE, New York, 2024), pp. 3665–3669
44. Z. Pan, W. Gao, G. Li, Distribution guidance network for weakly supervised point cloud semantic segmentation, in *Advances in Neural Information Processing Systems* (2024)
45. R. Zhang, G. Li, W. Gao, T.H. Li, Compoint: can complex-valued representation benefit point cloud place recognition? IEEE Trans. Intell. Transp. Syst. **25**(7), 7494–7507 (2024)
46. Z. Pan, N. Zhang, W. Gao, S. Liu, G. Li, Less is more: label recommendation for weakly supervised point cloud semantic segmentation, in *Proceedings of the AAAI Conference on Artificial Intelligence*, vol. 38(5) (2024), pp. 4397–4405
47. Z. Pan, G. Liu, W. Gao, T.H. Li, Epcontrast: effective point-level contrastive learning for large-scale point cloud understanding, in *2024 IEEE International Conference on Multimedia and Expo (ICME)* (IEEE, New York, 2024), pp. 1–6
48. N. Zhang, Z. Pan, T.H. Li, W. Gao, G. Li, Improving graph representation for point cloud segmentation via attentive filtering, in *Proceedings of the IEEE/CVF Conference on Computer Vision and Pattern Recognition* (2023), pp. 1244–1254
49. J. Pang, M.A. Lodhi, D. Tian, GRASP-net: geometric residual analysis and synthesis for point cloud compression, in *Proceedings of the 1st International Workshop on Advances in Point Cloud Compression, Processing and Analysis* (2022), pp. 11–19
50. R.B. Pinheiro, J.-E. Marvie, G. Valenzise, F. Dufaux, NF-PCAC: normalizing flow based point cloud attribute compression, in *ICASSP 2023-2023 IEEE International Conference on Acoustics, Speech and Signal Processing (ICASSP)* (IEEE, New York, 2023), pp. 1–5
51. J. Wang, D. Ding, Z. Li, X. Feng, Sparse tensor-based multiscale representation for point cloud geometry compression. IEEE Trans. Pattern Anal. Mach. Intell. **45**(7), 9055–9071 (2022)
52. A.F. Guarda, N.M. Rodrigues, F. Pereira, Deep learning-based point cloud geometry coding with resolution scalability, in *2020 IEEE 22nd International Workshop on Multimedia Signal Processing (MMSP)* (IEEE, New York, 2020), pp. 1–6
53. A.F. Guarda, N.M. Rodrigues, F. Pereira, Point cloud geometry scalable coding with a single end-to-end deep learning model, in *2020 IEEE International Conference on Image Processing (ICIP)* (IEEE, New York, 2020), pp. 3354–3358
54. J. Wang, D. Ding, Z. Li, Z. Ma, Multiscale point cloud geometry compression, in *2021 Data Compression Conference (DCC)* (IEEE, New York, 2021), pp. 73–82
55. Z. Que, G. Lu, D. Xu, Voxelcontext-net: an octree based framework for point cloud compression, in *Proceedings of the IEEE/CVF Conference on Computer Vision and Pattern Recognition* (2021), pp. 6042–6051
56. Y. Xu, T. Fan, L. Gao, L. Hou, V. Zakharchenko, H. Wei, D. Wang, A Deep Dynamic Point Cloud Geometry Compression Framework for AI-based PCC. ISO/IEC JTC 1/SC 29/WG 7, MPEG m58780 (2022)

57. J. Pang, M.A. Lodhi, D. Tian, A Software Framework for AI-based PCC. ISO/IEC JTC 1/SC 29/WG 7, MPEG m58961 (2022)
58. J. Pang, M.A. Lodhi, D. Tian, Geometric Residual Analysis and Synthesis for PCC. ISO/IEC JTC 1/SC 29/WG 7, MPEG m58962 (2022)
59. C.R. Qi, H. Su, K. Mo, L.J. Guibas, Pointnet: deep learning on point sets for 3d classification and segmentation, in *Proceedings of the IEEE Conference on Computer Vision and Pattern Recognition* (2017), pp. 652–660
60. M.A. Lodhi, J. Pang, D. Tian, Point cloud geometry compression using learned octree entropy coding. ISO/IEC JTC 1/SC 29/WG 7, MPEG m58965 (2022)
61. L. Huang, S. Wang, K. Wong, J. Liu, R. Urtasun, Octsqueeze: octree-structured entropy model for lidar compression, in *Proceedings of the IEEE/CVF Conference on Computer Vision and Pattern Recognition* (2020), pp. 1313–1323
62. C.R. Qi, L. Yi, H. Su, L.J. Guibas, Pointnet++: deep hierarchical feature learning on point sets in a metric space. Adv. Neural Inf. Proces. Syst. **30**, 5105–5114 (2017)
63. J. Wang, Z. Ma, H. Wei, Y. Yu, V. Zakharchenko, D. Wang, Point Cloud Geometry Compression using Sparse Tensor-based Multiscale Representation. ISO/IEC JTC 1/SC 29/WG 7, MPEG m59035 (2022)
64. J. Wang, Z. Ma, H. Wei, Y. Yu, V. Zakharchenko, D. Wang, Point Cloud Attribute Compression using Sparse Tensor-Representation. ISO/IEC JTC 1/SC 29/WG 7, MPEG m59037 (2022)
65. J. Wang, R. Xue, Z. Ma, H. Wei, Y. Yu, V. Zakharchenko, D. Wang, SparsePCGCv2: improved SparsePCGC with attention mechanism. ISO/IEC JTC 1/SC 29/WG 7, MPEG m59552 (2022)
66. A. Akhtar, Z. Li, G.V. der Auwera, A.K. Ramasubramonian, L.P. Van, M. Karczewicz, Dynamic Point Cloud Geometry Compression using Sparse Convolutions. ISO/IEC JTC 1/SC 29/WG 7, MPEG m59617 (2022)
67. MPEG-PCC-TMC13. https://github.com/MPEGGroup/mpeg-pcc-tmc13, accessed: 2021
68. J. Pang, M.A. Lodhi, D. Tian, Improved Geometric Residual Analysis and Synthesis for PCC. ISO/IEC JTC 1/SC 29/WG 7, MPEG m60342 (2022)
69. J. Ahn, J. Pang, M.A. Lodhi, D. Tian, Deep Distribution Aware (DDA) Point Feature Extractor for AI-based PCC. ISO/IEC JTC 1/SC 29/WG 7, MPEG m60349 (2022)
70. J. Wang, Z. Ma, H. Wei, Y. Yu, V. Zakharchenko, D. Wang, SparsePCGCv1 Update: Improvements on dense/sparse/LiDAR point clouds. ISO/IEC JTC 1/SC 29/WG 7, MPEG m60352 (2022)
71. R. Xue, J. Wang, Z. Ma, H. Wei, Y. Yu, V. Zakharchenko, D. Wang, SparsePCGCv2: Multihead Neighborhood Point Attention for Sparse Point Cloud. ISO/IEC JTC 1/SC 29/WG 7, MPEG m60353 (2022)
72. J. Wang, Z. Ma, H. Wei, Y. Yu, V. Zakharchenko, D. Wang, SparsePCGCv3: Dynamic SparsePCGC with Inter Frame Prediction. ISO/IEC JTC 1/SC 29/WG 7, MPEG m60354 (2022)
73. J. Wang, Z. Ma, H. Wei, Y. Yu, V. Zakharchenko, D. Wang, Dynamic SparsePCGC Update. ISO/IEC JTC 1/SC 29/WG 7, MPEG m61006 (2022)
74. R.B. Pinheiro, J.-E. Marvie, G. Valenzise, F. Dufaux, NF-PCAC—deep point cloud attribute compression with normalizing flow. ISO/IEC JTC 1/SC 29/WG 7, MPEG m61142 (2022)
75. M.A. Lodhi, J. Pang, D. Tian, Point cloud geometry compression with hierarchical feature propagation. ISO/IEC JTC 1/SC 29/WG 7, MPEG m61218 (2022)
76. J. Pang, D. Tian, Improved Geometric Residual Analysis and Synthesis for PCC. ISO/IEC JTC 1/SC 29/WG 7, MPEG m62099 (2023)
77. R. Xue, J. Wang, J. Li, Z. Ma, H. Wei, Y. Yu, V. Zakharchenko, D. Wang, Dynamic Point Cloud Geometry Compression for LiDAR Point Cloud with Ego-Motion Compensation. ISO/IEC JTC 1/SC 29/WG 7, MPEG m62177 (2023)
78. J. Behley, M. Garbade, A. Milioto, J. Quenzel, S. Behnke, C. Stachniss, J. Gall, Semantickitti: a dataset for semantic scene understanding of lidar sequences, in *Proceedings of the IEEE/CVF International Conference on Computer Vision* (2019), pp. 9297–9307

79. A. Akhtar, G.V. der Auwera, B. Kathariya, A.K. Ramasubramonian, M. Karczewicz, Update on baseline attribute compression for ML-based PCC. ISO/IEC JTC 1/SC 29/WG 7, MPEG m62180 (2023)
80. Y. Zhou, X. Ma, Y. Xu, K. Zhang, L. zhang, X. Zhang, Collaborative joint downsampling and upsampling for geometry compression. ISO/IEC JTC 1/SC 29/WG 7, MPEG m63059 (2023)
81. X. Ma, Y. Zhou, Y. Xu, K. Zhang, L. zhang, X. Zhang, Compression oriented geometry post-processing of point clouds. ISO/IEC JTC 1/SC 29/WG 7, MPEG m63061 (2023)
82. Y. Xu, S. Xia, T. Fan, V. Zakharchenko, H. Wei, Learning Dynamic Point Cloud Compression via Hierarchical Inter-frame Block Matching. ISO/IEC JTC 1/SC 29/WG 7, MPEG m64110 (2023)
83. M. Lee, J. Kim, K. Kim, H.-C. Moon, J. Jeong, S. Kim, Compressed AI-PCC Decoder Transmission with NNC. ISO/IEC JTC 1/SC 29/WG 7, MPEG m64315 (2023)
84. H. Yuan, X. Mao, M. Li, D. Zou, Harnessing Multi-scale Network for Enhanced 3D Point Cloud Attribute Compression with Geometry-Assisted Learning. ISO/IEC JTC 1/SC 29/WG 7, MPEG m66178 (2024)
85. H. Yuan, C. Sun, M. Li, D. Zou, Enhancing Context Models for Point Cloud Geometry Compression with Context Feature Residuals. ISO/IEC JTC 1/SC 29/WG 7, MPEG m66184 (2024)
86. D. Zuo, X. Cui, T. Dong, F. Liang, Efficient Dynamic Point Cloud Compression via Temporal Contextual Pyramid. ISO/IEC JTC 1/SC 29/WG 7, MPEG m67523 (2024)
87. A.F.R. Guarda1, N.M.M. Rodrigues, F. Pereira, IT/IST/IPLeiria Response to the Call for Evidence on JPEG Pleno Point Cloud Coding. ISO/IEC JTC 1/SC 29/WG 1, JPEG M90019 (2021)
88. A.F. Guarda, N.M. Rodrigues, F. Pereira, Adaptive deep learning-based point cloud geometry coding. IEEE J. Sel. Top. Sign. Proces. **15**(2), 415–430 (2020)
89. D. Lazzarotto, T. Ebrahimi, Performance evaluation of objective quality metrics on point clouds distorted with learning-based codecs. ISO/IEC JTC 1/SC 29/WG 1, JPEG M92040 (2021)
90. M. Quach, G. Valenzise, F. Dufaux, Improved deep point cloud geometry compression, in *2020 IEEE 22nd International Workshop on Multimedia Signal Processing (MMSP)* (IEEE, New York, 2020), pp. 1–6
91. M. Quach, G. Valenzise, F. Dufaux, Folding-based compression of point cloud attributes, in *2020 IEEE International Conference on Image Processing (ICIP)* (IEEE, New York, 2020), pp. 3309–3313
92. A.F.R. Guarda, N.M.M. Rodrigues, M. Ruivo, L. Coelho, A. Seleem, F. Pereira, IT/IST/IPLeiria Response to the Call for Proposals on JPEG Pleno Point Cloud Coding. ISO/IEC JTC 1/SC 29/WG 1, JPEG M96005 (2022)
93. D. Lazzarotto, T. Ebrahimi, EPFL Response to the Call for Proposals on JPEG Pleno Point Cloud Coding. ISO/IEC JTC 1/SC 29/WG 1, JPEG M96018 (2022)
94. D. Lazzarotto, T. Ebrahimi, EPFL Response to the Call for Proposals on JPEG Pleno Point Cloud Coding with extended description of color coding module. ISO/IEC JTC 1/SC 29/WG 1, JPEG M96076 (2022)
95. M. Ghafari, A. Guarda, N. Rodrigues, F. Pereiraa, Attention Models in the Geometry JPEG PCC VM: Performance and Core Experiment Proposal. ISO/IEC JTC 1/SC 29/WG 1, JPEG M99102 (2023)
96. W. Gao, G. Li, S. Liu, J. Wang, S. Ma, X. Zheng, L. Yu, L. Xie, End-to-End Point Cloud Compression Technology Based on Deep Learning Requirements, AVS M7820 (2023)
97. W. Gao, G. Li, S. Liu, J. Wang, S. Ma, X. Zheng, L. Yu, L. Xie, End-to-End Point Cloud Compression Technology Based on Deep Learning Requirements v2, AVS M7820 (2023)
98. W. Gao, L. Xie, X. Mou, Z. Yu, C. Zhang, K. Zheng, H. Liu, G. Li, X. Yang, R. Song, W. Zhang, Y. Yu, J. Sun, J. Tan, Z. Ma, R. Xue, J. Li, J. Wang, Y. Xu, S. Xia, J. Wang, Analysis of Requirements and Discussion of Use Cases for Point Cloud Encoding Based on Deep Learning, AVS M7879 (2023)
99. W. Gao, *AI-based Image and Video Coding: Methods, Standards, and Applications* (Springer, Berlin, 2025)

Chapter 10
Implementations, Streaming, and Rendering for 3D Point Cloud Coding

Abstract This chapter outlines the current landscape of point cloud implementation, streaming and rendering technologies, emphasizing the key challenges and recent progress of 3D point cloud coding and processing technologies. It discusses the lightweight neural network design principles and acceleration methods, which can benefit the hardware and software implementations of point cloud coding and processing methods. With the growing demand for high-quality 3D content in applications of virtual reality (VR), augmented reality (AR), and autonomous driving, the need for efficient point cloud delivery has become increasingly critical. This chapter presents key strategies aiming to optimize bandwidth usage, reduce transmission latency, and maintain high reconstruction quality. In addition, point cloud rendering methods are introduced, including traditional and learning-based methods, which are important for high-quality display of point clouds. This chapter introduces the latest research methods on implementation, streaming and rendering, demonstrating how these innovations are applied to overcome practical limitations and enhance real-world performance in diverse applications.

Keywords Point cloud streaming · Bandwidth optimization · Dynamic resolution adjustment · Semantic encoding · 3D data transmission · Point cloud coding · Point cloud rendering

10.1 Lightweight and Accelerated Point Cloud Computing

10.1.1 Lightweight Operators and Network Modules

Recent advancements in point cloud processing [1–11] have introduced lightweight operators and network modules optimized for sparse computations, significantly improving the efficiency of 3D vision tasks [12–22]. These innovations employ hardware-aware designs to address the computational challenges posed by the inherent sparsity and irregularity of point cloud data.

W. Gao, *AI-based 3D Point Cloud Coding*,
https://doi.org/10.1007/978-981-95-0660-6_10

Lightweight Computing Operators TorchSparse [23] is an efficient GPU-based inference engine tailored for point cloud processing, specifically designed to enhance the performance of sparse convolution operations. There are two primary challenges associated with sparse convolution: irregular computational patterns and inefficient data transfer. To mitigate these issues, TorchSparse introduces adaptive grouping techniques for matrix multiplication, improving computational regularity, and adopts localized memory access optimizations, including vectorization, quantization, and operator fusion, to streamline data movement. Experiments show that TorchSparse obtains significant speedups compared to SOTA sparse convolution libraries.

Furthermore, TorchSparse++ was developed on the basis of TorchSparse. Tang et al. [24] enabled high-performance sparse convolution, a critical operation in emerging workloads such as point cloud processing and graph understanding. It combines the implementation simplicity of the gather-GEMM-scatter dataflow with the high performance of overlapping computation and memory access dataflows, achieved through a sparse kernel generator and a sparse auto-tuner. This allows TorchSparse++ to significantly enhance the performance of sparse convolution libraries in both inference and mixed-precision training.

Although point cloud neural networks have achieved notable gains in accuracy, the growing volume of point cloud data continues to impose challenges on real-time processing. To address this, Liu et al. [25] proposed FusionArch, a fusion-oriented accelerator optimized for PCNN workloads. By applying three orthogonal algorithmic enhancements across key stages, including farthest point sampling (FPS), feature extraction, and aggregation, FusionArch significantly improves overall execution. The architecture also introduces optimized memory access mechanisms, enabling substantial speedup and energy savings across diverse PCNN models and applications. To enhance inference efficiency in point cloud-based deep neural networks, Park et al. [26] proposed an adaptive strategy that dynamically adjusts the number of input points based on frame-wise entropy. Their framework introduces a novel density-driven sampling technique, prioritizing points by density to optimize computational load while preserving performance.

Acceleration for Convolution Computing In pursuit of accelerating fundamental 3D operations including 3D submanifold sparse convolutions, 3D general sparse convolutions, and 2D sparse convolutions, Feng et al. [27] developed a unified 2D/3D sparse convolution accelerator. The design integrates several core technologies such as block-level sparse data control, high-throughput sparse convolution (SCONV) engines, and hybrid asynchronous-synchronous scheduling. Park et al. [28] proposed a convolutional strategy aimed at improving the efficiency of sparse pillar-based 3D object detection on embedded hardware. Their method, termed selectively dilated convolutions, dynamically modulates the receptive field to achieve a trade-off between computational cost and detection performance. This design allows the model to maintain high detection accuracy while significantly reducing processing overhead, making it highly applicable to real-time 3D perception tasks in constrained environments, such as autonomous vehicles.

In another line of work, Guo et al. [29] designed a lightweight scheme for road scene object segmentation task, such as vehicles, pedestrians, and cyclists, captured by autonomous navigation platforms. Their network builds upon the compact SqueezeNet architecture, enabling deployment on resource-constrained embedded systems. It processes 3D LiDAR point clouds transformed via a domain transform (DT), which sharpens object boundary alignment and results in high-resolution, point-wise semantic label maps. Li et al. [30] developed a robust point cloud-based approach for high-speed detection of solder joint shape defects in electronic manufacturing. Their method introduces a lightweight neural architecture named solder PointNet (SPNet), which incorporates local group attention to suppress the influence of outliers in scanned point cloud data and adaptively extract salient features.

Acceleration for Point Cloud Transformers In recent years, point cloud transformers have received widespread attention in industry and academia. By combining the conventional feature extraction schemes and the transformer, it can achieve significant performance. However, the existing point cloud neural network accelerators cannot fully utilize the properties of point cloud transformers. Therefore, researchers have proposed Sava [31], a collaborative design accelerator for point cloud transformers. Sava adopts a hybrid pruning strategy that is spatially and value-aware, which can effectively reduce redundant computation without significantly reducing accuracy. In addition, Sava also uses a reconfigurable mixed-precision systolic array and data reordering mechanism to handle the load imbalance problem of sparse computation workloads. Extensive experiments show that Sava is significantly better than existing point cloud neural network accelerators in terms of accuracy and performance.

In conclusion, these lightweight platforms address key challenges of irregular computations and inefficient data transfer. Additional software innovations include sparse convolution and density-driven techniques that optimize computational load while maintaining accuracy. Together, these software optimizations form a powerful toolkit for efficient point cloud processing, enabling practical deployment in real-time applications.

10.1.2 Hardware Accelerations

Conventional methods for point cloud processing often encounter limitations in computational speed and memory efficiency. To address these constraints, hardware acceleration has emerged as a compelling solution, enabling high-throughput processing and scalable management of large-scale 3D data. This paradigm shift significantly enhances point cloud operations, particularly in latency-sensitive applications.

GPU-Based Acceleration For massive LiDAR point cloud processing, especially in urban digital elevation model (DEM) extraction, Hu et al. [32] introduced a scan-line-based filtering algorithm. By leveraging the parallel processing capability of modern GPUs, each scan line is processed independently, leading to substantial reductions in runtime. This approach not only improves computational efficiency but also establishes the feasibility of hardware-accelerated point cloud processing. However, while GPUs excel at data-parallel tasks, their energy efficiency and flexibility for specialized neural network operations remain limited, motivating the exploration of alternative hardware platforms.

FPGA-Based Acceleration Building on the foundation of GPU acceleration, field-programmable gate arrays (FPGAs) have become a very competitive strategy for optimizing deep learning models on point clouds. Unlike GPUs, FPGAs offer customizable hardware architectures that can be tailored to specific neural network structures. For instance, Zheng et al. [33] proposed O-PointNet, a low-power accelerator designed specifically for the PointNet architecture. By reconfiguring hardware resources to match the computational patterns of PointNet's multilayer perceptrons and max-pooling operations, O-PointNet achieves significant improvements in both performance and energy efficiency. Similarly, Yoon et al. [34] introduced a Morton code-based representation that enables efficient sequential access to spatially adjacent points, reducing memory bandwidth requirements and computational overhead. These FPGA-based optimizations not only address the limitations of GPUs but also pave the way for deploying complex deep learning models in resource-constrained environments. While deep learning optimizations are critical, real-world applications often require acceleration for specific point cloud processing tasks. For example, in autonomous driving scenarios, real-time LiDAR data processing demands both high throughput and low power consumption. Latotzke et al. [35] addressed this challenge by developing an edge FPGA system that processes two 128-layer LiDAR streams with only 34.5W power consumption, significantly outperforming CPU-based solutions. Complementing this work, Chen et al. [36] introduced GDPCA, a geometry-aware accelerator that leverages spatial correlations between adjacent points to minimize redundant computations. By combining algorithmic insights with hardware design, GDPCA achieves a balance between computational efficiency and accuracy, demonstrating the potential of FPGAs for task-specific optimizations.

Edge Computing and Algorithm-Hardware Co-design As point cloud applications increasingly move to resource-constrained edge devices, the focus has shifted toward energy-efficient and algorithm-hardware co-designed solutions. Traditional CNN accelerators struggle to efficiently process the extreme sparsity of point cloud data, leading researchers to explore specialized architectures. Wang et al. [37] proposed an FPGA-based accelerator for submanifold sparse convolution networks (SSCNs) that incorporates a zero-removal mechanism to eliminate redundant operations, achieving 51× better power efficiency than GPUs. In a similar vein, Zhou et al. [38] introduced an accelerator for 3D point-based neural networks (PNNs) that uses filter pruning and block-wise MLP fusion to reduce memory access and improve parallelism. These co-design approaches not only optimize hardware utilization but also adapt algorithms to exploit the unique properties of point cloud data, marking a significant advancement in edge-based point cloud processing.

Optimizations for Sampling, Search, and Compression Beyond model acceleration, optimizing critical stages in point cloud analysis such as sampling, neighbor search, and compression has become increasingly important. Ying et al. [39] improved data locality using a Morton code-based structuring method, which accelerates key stages by up to 5.21× on edge devices. Meanwhile, Hong et al. [40] developed PCEngine to enhance sparse convolution performance through a coded-CSR memory format, reducing redundant access and improving GPU utilization. These techniques address bottlenecks in point cloud preprocessing and feature extraction, complementing the deep learning and task-specific optimizations discussed earlier. Additionally, solutions like QuickFPS [41] for farthest point sampling and Ying et al.'s [42] compression schemes further demonstrate the holistic approach to accelerating end-to-end point cloud pipelines. For real-time 3D registration, Sugiura et al. [43] introduced a FPGA-accelerated system based on PointNetLK, achieving up to 21.34× speedup over CPU-based methods with only 722 mW power consumption. Similarly, Chen et al. [44] designed ParallelNN for efficient k-nearest neighbor (KNN) search, leveraging high-bandwidth memory and parallel octree search to deliver 107.7× speedup over CPU/GPU implementations. These advancements collectively address the computational bottlenecks across various platforms of point cloud processing.

10.2 Point Cloud Streaming and Communication Systems

Point cloud streaming and communication technologies have garnered increasing attention due to their essential role in enabling real-time 3D data transmission [45–49]. These systems are especially critical for immersive applications such as virtual and augmented reality (VR/AR), remote sensing, and next-generation surveillance. Unlike conventional 2D media, point clouds encode rich 3D spatial information, capturing both the geometry and structural details of scenes or objects. This makes them ideal for applications requiring high interactivity and precision, including 3D reconstruction, autonomous navigation, and object recognition. Nevertheless, the transmission of point clouds poses considerable challenges due to their large data volume and the stringent latency requirements in real-time systems [50, 51]. A single frame may consist of millions of points, each embedded with multiple attributes (e.g., coordinates, color, intensity), leading to significant bandwidth and computation demands. To mitigate these issues, researchers have proposed various strategies, including adaptive resolution control, viewpoint-aware streaming, and semantic-driven encoding. Adaptive resolution dynamically adjusts point cloud fidelity based on scene content or object motion, optimizing resource use while preserving visual quality. Viewpoint-aware transmission selectively delivers spatial subsets relevant to the user's perspective, thereby minimizing unnecessary data flow and enhancing rendering efficiency in interactive environments. In addition, modern compression techniques, such as joint source-channel coding and learning-based super-resolution, have been developed to improve transmission quality under bandwidth-limited and high-latency conditions. These solutions not only reduce data redundancy but also ensure a smoother user experience by preserving perceptual quality, even in constrained network environments.

10.2.1 Point Cloud Streaming

Point cloud streaming is an emerging technology that enables the real-time transmission and rendering of 3D point cloud data over networks. Unlike traditional mesh-based 3D models, the point cloud data can represent objects or scenes as a collection of discrete points with attributes like color, intensity, and spatial coordinates. This format is widely used in diverse applications including augmented/virtual reality (AR/VR), autonomous driving, remote sensing, and telepresence. The key challenge in point cloud streaming lies in handling the massive data volume while ensuring low latency, high quality, and bandwidth efficiency. To address this, advanced compression techniques (*e.g.*, MPEG G-PCC or V-PCC), level-of-detail (LoD) adaptation, and progressive transmission are employed. Additionally, adaptive streaming protocols and edge/cloud processing help optimize performance for dynamic network conditions.

Point Cloud Video Streaming Delivering dynamic point cloud videos presents significant challenges for communication systems due to the dual demands of real-time performance and high-quality experiences across diverse users and application environments.

- **Adaptive streaming frameworks:** Liu et al. [52] investigated core challenges in point cloud video streaming, fundamental for delivering six degrees of freedom (6DoF) experiences in VR/AR/MR systems. Their work addresses key bottlenecks including massive data throughput and complex encoding-decoding workloads through an MPEG-DASH-based adaptive streaming framework. This system segments point cloud content for selective transmission according to user viewing direction and pose, integrates edge computing for real-time processing, and employs machine learning to forecast user movement for efficient resource allocation. Subramanyamet et al. [53] proposed a simplified tiling method for adaptive streaming that divides point cloud objects into independently encoded segments. Optimizing visual quality based on the user's current viewpoint, this approach leverages real-world navigation patterns from 26 participants in 6DoF environments. Performance evaluations demonstrate bitrate savings up to 57% compared to non-adaptive methods. Hosseini and Timmerer [54] developed DASH-PC, extending HTTP streaming protocols with view-dependent delivery mechanisms. The framework prioritizes visible portions of point clouds through spatial subsampling and introduces a point cloud-specific media presentation description (MPD) manifest for dynamic quality adaptation, significantly reducing bandwidth demands while maintaining visual quality.

- **Quality of experience (QoE) optimization:** Van et al. [55] explored quality of experience (QoE) for streaming 6DoF volumetric media. Through in-depth analysis of PCC-DASH, they investigated how bandwidth availability, rate adaptation algorithms, viewport prediction methods, and user movement influence perceived quality. The research identifies critical factors affecting user satisfaction and examines correlations between objective metrics and subjective feedback.
- **Codec comparative studies:** Yang et al. [56] conducted a comparative evaluation of five codecs, including three conventional (Draco, G-PCC, V-PCC) and two neural-based (PU-GCN+, MPU+). The study assesses efficiency and practicality across six volumetric video datasets, examining impacts of point cloud characteristics (i.e., quality, texture, scene complexity) and user viewing behaviors on QoE metrics, providing optimization insights for future systems.
- **Latency reduction techniques:** Rudolph et al. [57] introduced RABBIT, a novel technique reducing latency in dynamic point cloud streaming. While V-PCC compression suffers high encoding latency from computational demands of clustering and projection, RABBIT optimizes this process. The method maintains high compression efficiency while mitigating latency bottlenecks exacerbated by adaptive streaming techniques.
- **Viewport prediction advancements:** Li et al. [58] pioneered a DASH-compatible framework implementing adaptive bitrate strategies for volumetric video. Horizon enhances user experience through future viewing path prediction and deep reinforcement learning (DRL) for real-time streaming optimization, demonstrating high-quality 6DoF delivery on wireless networks. Li et al. [59] introduced Landscape, a high-precision viewport prediction scheme integrating video saliency and viewport trajectory. Featuring novel sampling methods and spatiotemporal saliency detection, this approach reduces computational load while improving prediction accuracy, validated through wireless network tests. Rudolph et al. [60] developed NoVA-PCC, compressing dynamic point clouds via surface-normal-based object segmentation. This enables independent encoding and adaptive streaming of view-specific segments, improving visual quality and bandwidth utilization when combined with user motion prediction.
- **Error resilience and compression:** Wu et al. [61] examined packet loss effects in MPEG V-PCC encoded streams, finding occupancy and geometry data losses cause the most severe quality degradation. They evaluate preliminary error concealment techniques for attribute/geometry data, highlighting needs for advanced resilience methods. Feng et al. [62] proposed a spatiotemporal compression system for real-time LiDAR point clouds. Leveraging spatial redundancies via plane fitting and temporal redundancies across frames, their range-image-based method achieves 90× compression rates while maintaining high application-level accuracy for autonomous systems.
- **Specialized streaming architectures:** Kang et al. [63] introduced a streaming framework utilizing PTD filters for point cloud filtering. By leveraging multi-core computing, the system improves processing efficiency and alleviates I/O

bottlenecks. Gamelin et al. [64] compared 2.5D streamed point-cloud versus 3D preconstructed avatars, demonstrating that higher kinematic fidelity—more critical than visual fidelity—enhances collaboration in spatial tasks within virtual environments.

In summary, these advancements collectively drive the development of efficient, low-latency, and user-centric point cloud streaming systems, though challenges in cross-device compatibility, real-world network variability, and neural codec scalability warrant further research.

Real-Time Point Cloud Streaming To tackle the challenge of streaming large-scale point cloud data over bandwidth-limited networks, Wang et al. [65] proposed a QoE-driven, tile-based adaptive streaming method. This approach minimizes transmission redundancy and enhances user experience by optimizing each 3D tile's quality based on its bitrate, user viewpoint, spatial position, occlusions, and device resolution. They frame the rate adaptation problem as a multiple-choice knapsack issue, aiming to allocate optimal bitrates to tiles within given bandwidth limits. By converting this into a submodular function maximization problem, they implement a greedy algorithm with theoretical performance guarantees. Hung et al. [66] developed a comprehensive error concealment framework for MPEG V-PCC to mitigate distortions caused by packet loss. This framework includes a suite of tools that can be combined into various algorithms to handle lost or distorted 3D point cloud frames effectively. Testing with seven diverse 3D point cloud sequences shows the methods outperform existing techniques. Operating in the 3D domain, the framework is codec-agnostic and compatible with future point cloud compression standards. Laniewski et al. [67] tackled real-time point cloud streaming from ongoing laser scans, essential for immersive 6DoF virtual environments. Traditional DASH methods are unsuitable as they require complete data before streaming. The solution enables real-time transmission directly from the laser scanner during the scan, adapting the data rate to network conditions using reinforcement learning. Nguyen et al. [68] proposed a novel method for real-time dynamic point cloud streaming. Experiments show that it can obtain visual quality improvement compared with existing methods while maintaining low computational overhead, particularly with the LM-based approach, which ensures stable real-time processing. This work advances efficient point cloud streaming for immersive applications under constrained resources. Han et al. [69] proposed streaming object detection in self-driving car perception systems. LiDAR, a crucial sensor in such systems, provides point cloud data, but traditional perception systems have latency issues due to waiting for a complete scan. They introduce a meta-architecture with modifications like stateful non-maximum suppression and recurrent architectures. Through experiments on the Waymo Open Dataset,[1] they demonstrate that streaming models can achieve competitive performance with reduced latency and computational demand and even exceed baseline performance with increased model

[1] https://waymo.com/open/download

size while maintaining favorable computational characteristics. Collectively, these methods advance real-time point cloud streaming toward efficient, resilient, and low-latency solutions for VR/AR, autonomous driving, and immersive technologies. Future research may focus on cross-scenario generalization, edge-computing integration, and hybrid neural-classical compression frameworks to further optimize performance across heterogeneous networks.

Real-Time Streaming System This part will be analyzed in the order of the technological evolution: from basic transmission to compression optimization, and then to intelligent decision-making.

- **Adaptive resolution and motion-based streaming:** Ishimaru et al. [70] segment point clouds into body parts and dynamically adjust resolution/frame rate based on motion and context. Chujo et al. [71] demonstrate a HoloLens-based prototype enabling uninterrupted live streaming. He et al. [72] implement view-dependent streaming that prioritizes user-focused content to reduce bandwidth while maintaining reconstruction quality.
- **Compression innovations:** Ainala et al. [73] employ kd-tree partitioning for scalable bitstreams adaptable to viewpoints. Rudolph et al. [74] introduce RABBIT, bypassing full V-PCC transcoding to achieve video-level latency. Zimmer et al. [75] present PointCompress3D for roadside LiDARs, achieving 50x compression at 10 FPS. Makiyah et al. [76] leverage HTTP/2 for efficient streaming, achieving 72.46 fps for 4M points.
- **Learning-driven adaptation:** Laniewski et al. [67] apply reinforcement learning for adaptive rate control during ongoing scans. Li et al. [58] predict user movement via rolling framework and DRL-based optimization. Gao et al. [77] employ RL for dynamic quality selection and federated learning for privacy-aware QoE maximization.
- **Progressive streaming and super-resolution techniques:** Moreno et al. [78] compare transmission schemes, proposing distributed octrees for progressive streaming. Deng et al. [79] implement super-resolution to reduce bandwidth by storing low-resolution tiles and upscaling via heuristic algorithms.
- **Semantic communication systems:** Liu et al. [80] design a semantic communication system (PCSC) with AI-based encoding and joint source-channel coding (JSCC). Akhtar et al. [81] implement JSCC with adaptive modulation, ensuring graceful degradation under varying channel conditions.
- **Application-specific implementations:** Liang et al. [82] develop Fumos for 6-DoF VR/AR, combining neural compression (N-PCC) with progressive refinement. Van der Hooft et al. [83] create PCC-DASH with viewport-aware rate adaptation for 6DoF content. Chandra et al. [84] enable real-time object detection/manipulation for Intel RealSense streams.

Collectively, these advancements drive the field toward intelligent, adaptive, and application-agnostic streaming solutions. Future research should focus on cross-modality generalization, energy-efficient edge learning, and hybrid semantic-classical compression to address diverse real-world network and device constraints.

Point Cloud Streaming Hardware To promote the application and development of point cloud technology in various advanced fields, this section reviews point cloud transmission hardware, hardware optimization techniques, and future directions.

- **Specialized hardware applications:** Fischer et al. [85] developed a VR telemedicine system based on Azure Kinect with Unreal Engine rendering to facilitate surgical collaboration. Egi et al. [86] combined 3D data with machine learning techniques to enable real-time spatial power loss prediction for wireless base station deployment. Lee et al. [87] implemented LiDAR-based object categorization (Object of Interest/Area of Interest) to enhance XR environments. Sultani et al. [88] created Kinect-based streaming systems with TLS authentication and octree compression for security. Yamazaki et al. [89] designed a ROS-compatible middleware for wireless streaming using IEEE 802.11ax in digital twin applications.
- **Hardware-optimized transmission:** Huang et al. [90] proposed AITransfer with bandwidth-aware model selection, achieving 30.72× compression. Zhang et al. [91] developed JCMPC, utilizing 3D convolution networks for end-to-end symbol encoding, which reduces decoding load by 80%. Additionally, Zhang et al. [92] combined Transformer-based prediction with RL-driven tile selection to maximize QoE.
- **Future hardware directions:** Point cloud hardware systems enable transformative applications across medical, industrial, and autonomous domains through (1) high-fidelity 3D transmission in VR/AR environments, (2) edge computing with AI-driven compression (G-PCC/V-PCC), and (3) emerging 6G/metaverse infrastructure. Continuous innovation overcomes latency/bandwidth constraints, enabling holographic telepresence and real-time digital twins.

In summary, point cloud streaming hardware is pivotal for bridging theoretical advancements with real-world applications. Future research should prioritize energy-efficient edge AI, standardized 6G protocols, and hybrid classical-neural compression architectures to unlock scalable, immersive, and latency-critical use cases.

10.2.2 Point Cloud Communication Systems

Point cloud communication systems represent a paradigm shift in 3D data transmission, with multiple innovations aimed at overcoming the limitations of traditional mesh-based approaches.

Historical Context and Foundational Work To understand the current advances, one must start from the foundational efforts in the field. At the early stage, 3D communication systems mainly transmit mesh data, which is time-consuming. Kajitani et al. [93] replaced polygonal models but transmit point cloud and render it at the client terminal exactly. Liu et al. [94] investigated point cloud video streaming within 5G infrastructures, providing simulation-based performance validation while documenting the complete processing pipeline. This work builds upon a substantial body of related research in volumetric media transmission [1–6, 95–98]. Taken together, these foundational efforts have laid the groundwork for modern volumetric transmission systems in both theory and application.

View-Dependent Transmission Frameworks A major breakthrough came with the shift toward user-centric delivery models. Li et al. [99] approached the optimization challenge from a resource allocation perspective, introducing a tile-based transmission scheme that selectively delivers 3D content within the user's field of view (FoV), achieving significant bandwidth efficiency through this view-dependent approach. The group of frames (GOF) is the minimum information unit and all information is stored in the MPD file style, similar to MPEG-DASH [100]. The server selectively transmits tiles based on the user's requests. The point cloud video is reconstructed after receiving and decoding all the tiles and sent into the buffer for playback. On the client side, the core mechanism is the tile selection module, which calculates the user's Fov and adaptively selects the tile residing inside the FoV. Each tile is encoded and transmitted with appropriate quality to enhance the user's QoE, where the bandwidth status, buffer status, and available computational resources are comprehensively considered during the selection procedure. Similarly, Liu et al. [101] connected the server and the user focus on the optimization of this connection wireless network. This paradigm enables bandwidth-efficient and user-tailored delivery, crucial for scalable and immersive 3D content experiences.

Semantic Communication and Lightweight Processing To further reduce complexity and boost efficiency, lightweight semantic strategies have been introduced. Huang et al. [102] proposed the ISCom, a region-of-interest (ROI) perceptual semantic communication system with lightweight point cloud video streaming. The system is equipped with the ROI selection module, lightweight encoder-decoder training module, and the learned scheduler to adaptively choose models according to different devices. The dual-stage ROI selection can dramatically reduce the number of transmitted data and achieve real-time point cloud video decoding and rendering at limited devices. As such, semantic awareness and model adaptivity present a practical solution for real-time performance under constrained computational budgets.

Protocol-Level Optimizations At the protocol level, further refinements have been made to enhance transmission efficiency. Leveraging the multiplexing capabilities of HTTP/2, Makiyah et al. [103] engineered a comprehensive web-based platform specifically optimized for the efficient delivery of high-density volumetric data. They compare the results under WiFi and 5G separate network scenarios. The results show that the inter-frame delay decreases by 16.8% with the HTTP/2 protocol compared with traditional methods. Moreno et al. [104] suggested adopting dynamic compression technology to adjust the compression ratio according to the network throughput. This method tackles the problem that a huge amount of changing data is transmitted with fixed bandwidths. They claim that dynamic compression is a promising strategy to be combined with frame skipping and progressive transmitting extra mechanisms to achieve the maximum quality of server (QoS) support. Previous streaming methods can hardly encode these data to small size in real time. These advancements at the protocol layer form a crucial component of a holistic point cloud streaming solution by mitigating network-related bottlenecks.

Specialized Compression Techniques Recent efforts have increasingly turned to specialized compression strategies tailored to the characteristics of 3D sensor data. Tu et al. [105] focused on the transmitting of 3D LiDAR sensor data. They propose compression method with a U-net. Specifically, they leverage the raw data packages from LiDAR sensors to save the 3D point cloud information as 2D matrices losslessly and transfer the streamed 3D point cloud data using the video-type format. They select some frames as a reference and interpolate other LiDAR frames via U-net, dramatically reducing temporal redundancy. They further present a filling algorithm to reduce the negative effect caused by the LiDAR noise. The proposed method outperforms the compression methods based on octree, MPEG standards, and SLAM. Overall, this approach exemplifies how deep learning-driven interpolation and representation strategies can significantly enhance compression performance in LiDAR-based systems.

QoE-Centric Optimization In parallel, maximizing user-perceived quality has become a central goal in streaming system design. Li et al. [106] proposed the DASH-based system for the task of streaming point cloud, which aims to increase the QoE performance. Wang et al. [107] customized an adaptive streaming method for point cloud to guarantee the user's QoE. Their research formalizes the complex interrelationships determining volumetric quality perception, establishing mathematical models that quantify how rendering device resolution, occlusion effects, spatial positioning, viewport geometry, and encoding parameters collectively influence perceived quality of individual 3D segments. This objective is formulated by a knapsack problem where coding bits are allocated between different 3D tiles. Together, these studies highlight the necessity of optimization strategies that account for both technical constraints and human perception in volumetric media delivery.

10.3 Point Cloud Rendering

10.3.1 Traditional Methods

As 3D data becomes increasingly central to applications ranging from robotics to digital content creation, the need for efficient and accurate rendering techniques has become paramount. Among various 3D representations, point clouds stand out for their directness and scalability. To harness their potential, a range of traditional rendering methods has been developed, forming the backbone of modern 3D visualization systems. Understanding these foundational techniques is essential to appreciate how current and emerging systems build upon them.

Foundation Framework Point cloud rendering has emerged as a fundamental technique in 3D computer vision and graphics, driven by the democratization of 3D sensing technologies, particularly the Microsoft Kinect [108]. The Point Cloud Library (PCL) established the foundational framework for modern 3D visualization systems, introducing a systematic three-stage approach, i.e., preprocessing for noise reduction and normal estimation, feature extraction for geometric understanding, and rendering for visualization. This modular pipeline has become the standard architecture for point cloud processing applications.

Rendering Techniques Traditional point cloud rendering primarily relies on direct point rasterization and view-dependent approaches adapted from image-based rendering [109]. These methods optimize rendering quality based on viewpoint position through projective texture mapping and hardware-accelerated rendering pipelines, enabling real-time visualization of complex scenes. Surface reconstruction techniques complement direct point rendering by generating more complete visual representations, often enhanced with spatially varying reflectance estimation through BRDF techniques [110]. This combination proves particularly valuable in applications requiring high-fidelity visualization, such as cultural heritage preservation and architectural documentation.

Data Structures and Optimization Efficient implementation of traditional rendering relies heavily on optimized data structures and acceleration methods. Modern frameworks like Open3D [111] demonstrate how careful algorithm design and data organization enable interactive performance with large-scale point cloud datasets [112–118]. These optimizations include spatial indexing structures, level-of-detail techniques, and memory-efficient processing pipelines that maintain visual quality while handling computational constraints.

Hybrid and Application-Specific Approaches The evolution of point cloud rendering has been shaped by diverse application requirements, leading to hybrid approaches that combine point-based and image-based methods. In photo tourism and cultural heritage documentation [119], these techniques successfully integrate photographic data with point cloud geometry, creating immersive visualization experiences while maintaining computational efficiency. Such domain-specific adaptations demonstrate the flexibility of traditional rendering frameworks in addressing specialized visualization needs.

Modern Integration and Evolution Contemporary developments have integrated traditional methods with modern computational approaches, exemplified by frameworks like PyTorch3D [120]. Rather than replacing established techniques, these advances build upon fundamental principles, leveraging the modular nature of traditional pipelines to incorporate new capabilities. This synthesis has expanded point cloud rendering applications to include autonomous vehicles, virtual and augmented reality, and 3D content creation, establishing it as an essential tool for 3D visualization across diverse domains [120].

10.3.2 Learning-Based Methods

With the rise of deep learning, learning-based point cloud rendering methods are becoming increasingly popular.

Neural Feature-Enhanced Rendering Early neural approaches focus on augmenting point clouds with learnable features to improve rendering quality. NPBG [121] pioneered this direction by preserving raw point geometry while augmenting each spatial element with trainable neural features that encapsulate localized appearance and structural information. This approach enables efficient scene representation without explicit mesh reconstruction and can handle complex scenes captured with handheld RGB-D sensors. Building upon this foundation, NPBG++ [122] significantly improved both fitting and rendering efficiency by better utilizing multi-view observations to predict neural descriptors for each point while maintaining high image quality [123–125]. Similarly, PAPR [126] addresses the vanishing gradient problem through a differentiable renderer that learns optimal point positions and associated features, enabling accurate scene geometry modeling even from poorly initialized point clouds.

Volumetric-Based Neural Rendering Several methods integrate point clouds with volumetric representations to leverage the advantages of both approaches. Dai et al. [127] proposed converting point clouds into layered camera cone volumes, where 3D CNN generates multiple planar images that are then blended through learned weights. This multiplane projection effectively handles visibility and occlusion issues. TriVol [128] takes a different approach by encoding point clouds into three slender volumetric layers and combining with NeRF technology, achieving efficient rendering through multi-scale feature fusion and volume reduction techniques. Point2Pix [129] further enhances this paradigm by introducing point-guided sampling techniques that focus on effective samples during the rendering process, particularly excelling in indoor scene rendering.

Surface-Aware and Ray-Based Methods Advanced techniques have emerged that treat point clouds more like surfaces while maintaining differentiable properties. Radiance Mapping [130] simplifies NeRF's complex representation into spatial mapping functions and corrects point coordinates to estimated ray-surface intersections, avoiding spatial frequency collapse and neighboring point interference. Pointersect [131] trains set transformers to directly infer ray-surface intersections, enabling surface normal estimation and global illumination effects without scene-specific optimization. For large-scale scenarios, READ [132] develops specialized neural rendering for autonomous driving scenes, learning descriptors from sparse point clouds through ω rendering networks to synthesize and edit realistic driving environments.

Acceleration and Optimization Techniques Recent work focuses on improving rendering efficiency through better data structures and sampling strategies. HashPoint [133] combines rasterization and ray tracing by organizing points into hash tables for optimized search while using adaptive sampling to accelerate the rendering process. These efficiency improvements are crucial for real-time applications and large-scale scenes.

3D Gaussian Splatting Integration With the emergence of 3D Gaussian Splatting, researchers have begun exploring its integration with point cloud rendering. PCRender [134] estimates 3D elliptical Gaussian distributions from arbitrary point clouds through neural networks, using differentiable Gaussian Splatting for real-time high-fidelity rendering without per-scene optimization. PFGS [135] pioneers a cascaded architecture that combines point-wise Gaussian property estimation with neural feature rasterization and progressive multi-scale decoding, achieving high-quality results from sparse inputs.

Joint Rendering with Compression Recognizing that point cloud compression introduces distortions, recent methods [136–138] explore the joint optimization of compression and rendering. These approaches combine differentiable rendering networks with point cloud encoding networks to achieve optimal tradeoff between compression efficiency and rendering quality.

10.4 Summary

This chapter explores advancements in lightweight operators and network modules designed to enhance efficiency in processing point cloud data. These innovations emphasize reduced computational complexity and optimized resource utilization, making them suitable for edge devices and large-scale deployments. Complementary to this, hardware acceleration techniques are examined, focusing on FPGA, GPU, and ASIC solutions to further expedite point cloud processing and support real-time applications. Additionally, this chapter delves into point cloud streaming and communication systems, proposing methods to improve transmission efficiency and maintain data integrity across various network conditions. This is critical for enabling seamless interaction with remote 3D environments. Lastly, this chapter investigates point cloud rendering techniques, offering novel solutions for high-quality visualization while balancing computational overhead. Together, these contributions aim to push the boundaries of point cloud applications in areas such as virtual reality, autonomous driving, and telepresence conference. For readers who are interested in the related technologies of AI-based image and video coding, please refer to [139].

Exercises

1. Please explain what the primary challenge is in point cloud streaming and communication systems.
2. Please describe how dynamic resolution adjustment improves point cloud streaming.
3. Please explain what view-dependent streaming is and how it benefits point cloud communication.
4. Please describe what role semantic encoding plays in point cloud transmission.
5. Please explain what the significance of AI-based encoding is in point cloud communication systems.
6. Please describe some methods for reducing spatial and temporal redundancies in point cloud streaming.
7. Please explain how bandwidth optimization contributes to the performance of point cloud communication systems.
8. Please describe the role of joint source-channel coding (JSCC) in point cloud communication systems.
9. Please explain why compression is important in point cloud streaming systems.
10. Please describe what impact real-time point cloud reconstruction has on immersive applications like VR and AR.

References

1. S. Fan, W. Gao, G. Li, Salient object detection for point clouds, in *European Conference on Computer Vision* (Springer, 2022), pp. 1–19
2. S. Luo, W. Gao, A general framework for rotation invariant point cloud analysis, in *ICASSP 2024-2024 IEEE International Conference on Acoustics, Speech and Signal Processing (ICASSP)* (IEEE, 2024), pp. 3665–3669
3. X. Lu, W. Gao, Attentivenet: Detecting small objects for lidar point clouds by attending to important points, in *2023 IEEE International Conference on Visual Communications and Image Processing (VCIP)* (IEEE, 2023), pp. 1–5
4. Z. Pan, N. Zhang, W. Gao, S. Liu, G. Li, Less is more: label recommendation for weakly supervised point cloud semantic segmentation, in *Proceedings of the AAAI Conference on Artificial Intelligence*, vol. 38(5), pp. 4397–4405 (2024)
5. Z. Pan, G. Liu, W. Gao, T.H. Li, Epcontrast: Effective point-level contrastive learning for large-scale point cloud understanding, in *2024 IEEE International Conference on Multimedia and Expo (ICME)* (IEEE, 2024), pp. 1–6
6. N. Zhang, Z. Pan, T.H. Li, W. Gao, G. Li, Improving graph representation for point cloud segmentation via attentive filtering, in *Proceedings of the IEEE/CVF Conference on Computer Vision and Pattern Recognition*, pp. 1244–1254 (2023)
7. W. Liu, W. Gao, X. Mu, Fast inter-frame motion prediction for compressed dynamic point cloud attribute enhancement, in *Proceedings of the AAAI Conference on Artificial Intelligence*, vol. 38(4), pp. 3720–3728 (2024)
8. Z. Yang, W. Gao, X. Lu, Danet: Density-adaptive network for geometry-based point cloud compression artifacts removal, in *2023 IEEE International Conference on Visual Communications and Image Processing (VCIP)* (IEEE, 2023), pp. 1–5

9. X. Fan, G. Li, D. Li, Y. Ren, W. Gao, T. H. Li, Deep geometry post-processing for decompressed point clouds, in *2022 IEEE International Conference on Multimedia and Expo (ICME)* (IEEE, 2022), pp. 1–6
10. X. Zhang, G. Liao, W. Gao, G. Li, Tdrnet: Transformer-based dual-branch restoration network for geometry based point cloud compression artifacts, in *2022 IEEE International Conference on Multimedia and Expo (ICME)* (IEEE, 2022), pp. 1–6
11. Z. Li, G. Li, T.H. Li, S. Liu, W. Gao, Semantic point cloud upsampling. IEEE Trans. Multimedia **25**, 3432–3442 (2023)
12. C. Fu, G. Li, R. Song, W. Gao, S. Liu, Octattention: Octree-based large-scale contexts model for point cloud compression, in *Proceedings of the AAAI Conference on Artificial Intelligence*, vol. 36(1), pp. 625–633 (2022)
13. C. Zhang, W. Gao, Adadpcc: Adaptive rate control and rate-distortion-complexity optimization for dynamic point cloud compression, in *Proceedings of the AAAI Conference on Artificial Intelligence* (2025)
14. K. Wang, W. Gao, Unipcgc: Towards practical point cloud geometry compression via an efficient unified approach, in *Proceedings of the AAAI Conference on Artificial Intelligence* (2025)
15. K. Zheng, W. Gao, H. Zheng, Octree-based learned point cloud geometry compression: A lossy perspective, in *2025 Data Compression Conference (DCC)* (IEEE, 2025)
16. Z. Qi, H. Liu, W. Gao, Variable-rate point cloud compression with channel-wise entropy modeling, in *2025 Data Compression Conference (DCC)* (IEEE, 2025)
17. H. Zheng, W. Gao, Z. Yu, T. Zhao, G. Li, Viewpcgc: View-guided learned point cloud geometry compression, in *Proceedings of the 32nd ACM International Conference on Multimedia*, pp. 7152–7161 (2024)
18. L. Xie, W. Gao, H. Zheng, G. Li, Roi-guided point cloud geometry compression towards human and machine vision, in *Proceedings of the 32nd ACM International Conference on Multimedia*, pp. 3741–3750 (2024)
19. W. Gao, H. Ye, G. Li, H. Zheng, Y. Wu, L. Xie, Openpointcloud: An open-source algorithm library of deep learning based point cloud compression, in *Proceedings of the 30th ACM International Conference on Multimedia*, pp. 7347–7350 (2022)
20. Y. Zhang, W. Gao, G. Li, Openpointcloud-v2: A deep learning based open-source algorithm library of point cloud processing, in *Proceedings of the 1st International Workshop on Advances in Point Cloud Compression, Processing and Analysis*, pp. 51–55 (2022)
21. L. Xie, W. Gao, Learningpcc: A pytorch library for learning-based point cloud compression, in *Proceedings of the 32nd ACM International Conference on Multimedia*, pp. 11234–11238 (2024)
22. L. Xie, W. Gao, Pchmvision: An open-source library of point cloud compression for human and machine vision, in *Proceedings of the 32nd ACM International Conference on Multimedia*, pp. 11239–11243 (2024)
23. H. Tang, Z. Liu, X. Li, Y. Lin, S. Han, Torchsparse: Efficient point cloud inference engine. Proc. Mach. Learn. Syst. **4**, 302–315 (2022)
24. H. Tang, S. Yang, Z. Liu, K. Hong, Z. Yu, X. Li, G. Dai, Y. Wang, S. Han, Torchsparse++: Efficient training and inference framework for sparse convolution on gpus, in *Proceedings of the 56th Annual IEEE/ACM International Symposium on Microarchitecture*, pp. 225–239 (2023)
25. X. Liu, Z. Song, G. Dai, G. Li, C. Xiao, Y. Xiang, D. Kong, K. Xu, X. Liang, Fusionarch: A fusion-based accelerator for point-based point cloud neural networks, in *2024 Design, Automation & Test in Europe Conference & Exhibition (DATE)* (IEEE, 2024), pp. 1–6
26. G. Park, S. Kang, W. Cheng, J.H. Ko, Dynamic inference acceleration of 3d point cloud deep neural networks using point density and entropy, in *IEEE/CVF Conference on Computer Vision and Pattern Recognition, CVPR 2023 - Workshops, Vancouver, BC, Canada, June 17–24, 2023* (IEEE, 2023), pp. 4725–4729
27. X. Feng, W. Sun, S. Fan, C. Tang, Y. Yang, J. Yue, Q. Liao, H. Yang, Y. Liu, A demonstration platform for large-scaled point cloud network based on 28nm 2d/3d unified sparse convolution

accelerator, in *2023 IEEE 5th International Conference on Artificial Intelligence Circuits and Systems (AICAS)* (IEEE, 2023), pp. 1–2
28. S. Park, M. Lee, J. Choi, J. Choi, Selectively dilated convolution for accuracy-preserving sparse pillar-based embedded 3d object detection, in *Proceedings of the IEEE/CVF Conference on Computer Vision and Pattern Recognition*, pp. 8104–8113 (2024)
29. G. Chen, B. Bai, Z. Mao, J. Dai, Real-time road object segmentation using improved lightweight convolutional neural network based on 3d lidar point cloud. Int. J. Ad Hoc Ubiquitous Comput. **39**(3), 113–121 (2022)
30. H. Li, K. Hao, B. Wei, X. Tang, Q. Hu, A reliable solder joint inspection method based on a light-weight point cloud network and modulated loss. Neurocomputing **488**, 315–327 (2022)
31. X. Liu, Z. Song, X. Liao, X. Li, T. Yang, F. Liu, X. Liang, Sava: A spatial-and value-aware accelerator for point cloud transformer, in *2024 Design, Automation & Test in Europe Conference & Exhibition (DATE)* (IEEE, 2024), pp. 1–6
32. X. Hu, X. Li, Y. Zhang, Fast filtering of lidar point cloud in urban areas based on scan line segmentation and GPU acceleration. IEEE Geosci. Remote. Sens. Lett. **10**(2), 308–312 (2013)
33. X. Zheng, M. Zhu, Y. Xu, Y. Li, An FPGA based parallel implementation for point cloud neural network, in *13th IEEE International Conference on ASIC, ASICON 2019, Chongqing, China, October 29–November 1, 2019* (IEEE, 2019), pp. 1–4
34. H. Yoon, J. Kim, Fused sampling and grouping with search space reduction for efficient point cloud acceleration, in *Proceedings of the 61st ACM/IEEE Design Automation Conference, DAC 2024, San Francisco, CA, USA, June 23–27, 2024*, V. De (Ed.) (ACM, 2024), pp. 194:1–194:6
35. C. Latotzke, A. Kloeker, S. Schoening, F. Kemper, M. Slimi, L. Eckstein, T. Gemmeke, Fpga-based acceleration of lidar point cloud processing and detection on the edge, in *IEEE Intelligent Vehicles Symposium, IV 2023, Anchorage, AK, USA, June 4–7, 2023* (IEEE, 2023), pp. 1–8
36. C. Chen, X. Zou, H. Shao, Y. Li, K. Li, Point cloud acceleration by exploiting geometric similarity, in *Proceedings of the 56th Annual IEEE/ACM International Symposium on Microarchitecture, MICRO 2023, Toronto, ON, Canada, 28 October 2023–1 November 2023* (ACM, 2023), pp. 1135–1147
37. Z. Wang, W. Mao, P. Yang, Z. Wang, J. Lin, An efficient fpga accelerator for point cloud, in *2022 IEEE 35th International System-on-Chip Conference (SOCC)* (IEEE, 2022), pp. 1–6
38. C. Zhou, Y. Fu, M. Liu, S. Qiu, G. Li, Y. He, H. Jiao, An energy-efficient 3d point cloud neural network accelerator with efficient filter pruning, mlp fusion, and dual-stream sampling, in *2023 IEEE/ACM International Conference on Computer Aided Design (ICCAD)* (IEEE, 2023), pp. 1–9
39. Z. Ying, S. Bhuyan, Y. Kang, Y. Zhang, M.T. Kandemir, C.R. Das, Edgepc: Efficient deep learning analytics for point clouds on edge devices, in *Proceedings of the 50th Annual International Symposium on Computer Architecture*, pp. 1–14 (2023)
40. K. Hong, Z. Yu, G. Dai, X. Yang, Y. Lian, N. Xu, Y. Wang, Exploiting hardware utilization and adaptive dataflow for efficient sparse convolution in 3d point clouds. Proc. Mach. Learn. Syst. **5**, 428–441 (2023)
41. M. Han, L. Wang, L. Xiao, H. Zhang, C. Zhang, X. Xu, J. Zhu, Quickfps: Architecture and algorithm co-design for farthest point sampling in large-scale point clouds. IEEE Trans. Comput. Aided Des. Integr. Circuits Syst. **42**(11), 4011–4024 (2023)
42. Z. Ying, S. Zhao, S. Bhuyan, C.S. Mishra, M.T. Kandemir, C.R. Das, Pushing point cloud compression to the edge, in *2022 55th IEEE/ACM International Symposium on Microarchitecture (MICRO)* (IEEE, 2022), pp. 282–299
43. K. Sugiura, H. Matsutani, An efficient accelerator for deep learning-based point cloud registration on fpgas, in *2023 31st Euromicro International Conference on Parallel, Distributed and Network-Based Processing (PDP)* (IEEE, 2023), pp. 68–75
44. F. Chen, R. Ying, J. Xue, F. Wen, P. Liu, Parallelnn: A parallel octree-based nearest neighbor search accelerator for 3d point clouds, in *2023 IEEE International Symposium on High-Performance Computer Architecture (HPCA)* (IEEE, 2023), pp. 403–414

45. W. Gao, G. Li, H. Yuan, R. Hamzaoui, Z. Li, S. Liu, Apccpa'22: 1st international workshop on advances in point cloud compression, processing and analysis, in *Proceedings of the 30th ACM International Conference on Multimedia*, pp. 7392–7393 (2022)
46. W. Gao, G. Li, Point cloud compression, enhancement and applications: From 3d perception to large models, in *Proceedings of the 32nd ACM International Conference on Multimedia*, pp. 11292–11293 (2024)
47. H. Sun, G. Li, S. Chen, L. Li, W. Gao, Special topic on 3d point cloud processing and applications. ZTE Commun. **21**(4), 1 (2023)
48. W. Gao, W. Gao, X. Mu, C. Peng, G. Li, Overview and comparison of avs point cloud compression standard. APSIPA Trans. Signal Inf. Process. **14**(2), 1–33 (2025)
49. W. Gao, S. Wang, X. Zhang, S. Kwong, Editorial for special issue on deep learning-based data compression. APSIPA Trans. Signal Inf. Process. **13**(6), 1–2 (2024)
50. G. Li, W. Gao, W. Gao, *Point Cloud Compression: Technologies and Standardization* (Springer, 2024)
51. W. Gao, G. Li, *Deep Learning for 3D Point Clouds* (Springer, 2024)
52. Z. Liu, Q. Li, X. Chen, C. Wu, S. Ishihara, J. Li, Y. Ji, Point cloud video streaming: Challenges and solutions. IEEE Network **35**(5), 202–209 (2021)
53. S. Subramanyam, I. Viola, A. Hanjalic, P. Cesar, User centered adaptive streaming of dynamic point clouds with low complexity tiling, in *Proceedings of the 28th ACM International Conference on Multimedia*, pp. 3669–3677 (2020)
54. M. Hosseini, C. Timmerer, Dynamic adaptive point cloud streaming, in *Proceedings of the 23rd Packet Video Workshop*, pp. 25–30 (2018)
55. J. van der Hooft, M.T. Vega, C. Timmerer, A.C. Begen, F. De Turck, R. Schatz, Objective and subjective qoe evaluation for adaptive point cloud streaming, in *2020 Twelfth International Conference on Quality of Multimedia Experience (QoMEX)* (IEEE, 2020), pp. 1–6
56. M. Yang, Z. Luo, M. Hu, M. Chen, D. Wu, A comparative measurement study of point cloud-based volumetric video codecs. IEEE Trans. Broadcast. **69**(3), 715–726 (2023)
57. M. Rudolph, S. Schneegass, A. Rizk, Transcoding v-pcc point cloud streams in real-time. ACM Trans. Multimedia Comput. Commun. Appl. **21**(9), 1–22 (2025)
58. J. Li, H. Wang, Q. Li, X. Liu, Z. Li, Z. Liu, Horizon: a real-time point cloud video streaming system over wireless networks, in *Proceedings of the 21st Annual International Conference on Mobile Systems, Applications and Services*, pp. 606–607 (2023)
59. J. Li, Z. Li, Q. Li, W. Sun, W. Li, H. Wang, Z. Liu, Landscape: Saliency and trajectory based viewport prediction in point cloud video streaming, in *Proceedings of the 21st Annual International Conference on Mobile Systems, Applications and Services*, pp. 604–605 (2023)
60. M. Rudolph, A. Rizk, View-adaptive streaming of point cloud scenes through combined decomposition and video-based coding, in *Proceedings of the 1st International Workshop on Advances in Point Cloud Compression, Processing and Analysis*, pp. 41–49 (2022)
61. C.-H. Wu, X. Li, R. Rajesh, W.T. Ooi, C.-H. Hsu, Dynamic 3d point cloud streaming: Distortion and concealment, in *Proceedings of the 31st ACM Workshop on Network and Operating Systems Support for Digital Audio and Video*, pp. 98–105 (2021)
62. Y. Feng, S. Liu, Y. Zhu, Real-time spatio-temporal lidar point cloud compression, in *2020 IEEE/RSJ International Conference on Intelligent Robots and Systems (IROS)* (IEEE, 2020), pp. 10766–10773
63. X. Kang, J. Liu, X. Lin, Streaming progressive tin densification filter for airborne lidar point clouds using multi-core architectures. Remote Sens. **6**(8), 7212–7232 (2014)
64. G. Gamelin, A. Chellali, S. Cheikh, A. Ricca, C. Dumas, S. Otmane, Point-cloud avatars to improve spatial communication in immersive collaborative virtual environments. Personal Ubiquitous Comput. **25**(3), 467–484 (2021)
65. L. Wang, C. Li, W. Dai, J. Zou, H. Xiong, Qoe-driven and tile-based adaptive streaming for point clouds, in *ICASSP 2021-2021 IEEE International Conference on Acoustics, Speech and Signal Processing (ICASSP)* (IEEE, 2021), pp. 1930–1934

66. T.-K. Hung, I.-C. Huang, S.R. Cox, W.T. Ooi, C.-H. Hsu, Error concealment of dynamic 3d point cloud streaming, in *Proceedings of the 30th ACM International Conference on Multimedia*, pp. 3134–3142 (2022)
67. D. Laniewski, N. Aschenbruck, Reinforcement learning-based rate adaptation for point cloud streaming, in *2023 IEEE 9th World Forum on Internet of Things (WF-IoT)* (IEEE, 2023), pp. 1–6
68. Q.L. Nguyen, D. Nguyen, H.T. Truong, Toward optimal real-time dynamic point cloud streaming over bandwidth-constrained networks, in *Proceedings of the 5th ACM International Conference on Multimedia in Asia*, pp. 1–7 (2023)
69. W. Han, Z. Zhang, B. Caine, B. Yang, C. Sprunk, O. Alsharif, J. Ngiam, V. Vasudevan, J. Shlens, Z. Chen, Streaming object detection for 3d point clouds, in *European Conference on Computer Vision* (Springer, 2020), pp. 423–441
70. H. Ishimaru, Y. Nakamura, M. Fujimoto, H. Suwa, K. Yasumoto, A qos-aware 3d point cloud streaming from real space for interaction in metaverse, in *2023 IEEE International Conference on Pervasive Computing and Communications Workshops and other Affiliated Events (PerCom Workshops)* (IEEE, 2023), pp. 68–73
71. Y. Chujo, K. Kanai, J. Katto, Implementation and demonstration of real-time point cloud streaming system using hololens, in *2022 IEEE International Conference on Consumer Electronics-Taiwan* (IEEE, 2022), pp. 221–222
72. L. He, W. Zhu, K. Zhang, Y. Xu, View-dependent streaming of dynamic point cloud over hybrid networks, in *Advances in Multimedia Information Processing–PCM 2018: 19th Pacific-Rim Conference on Multimedia, Hefei, China, September 21-22, 2018, Proceedings, Part I 19* (Springer, 2018), pp. 50–58
73. K. Ainala, *Point Cloud Compression and Low Latency Streaming* (University of Missouri-Kansas City, 2018)
74. M. Rudolph, S. Schneegass, A. Rizk, Rabbit: Live transcoding of v-pcc point cloud streams, in *Proceedings of the 14th Conference on ACM Multimedia Systems*, pp. 97–107 (2023)
75. W. Zimmer, R. Pranamulia, X. Zhou, M. Liu, A.C. Knoll, Pointcompress3d—a point cloud compression framework for roadside lidars in intelligent transportation systems (2024). arXiv preprint arXiv:2405.01750
76. E.H. Makiyah, N.N. Kliamees, Point cloud streaming over http/2, in *2023 6th International Conference on Advanced Communication Technologies and Networking (CommNet)* (IEEE, 2023), pp. 1–5
77. Y. Gao, P. Zhou, Z. Liu, B. Han, P. Hui, Fras: Federated reinforcement learning empowered adaptive point cloud video streaming (2022). arXiv preprint arXiv:2207.07394
78. C. Moreno, M. Li, A progressive transmission technique for the streaming of point cloud data using the kinect, in *2018 International Conference on Computing, Networking and Communications (ICNC)* (IEEE, 2018), pp. 593–598
79. J. Deng, F. Wen, Edge-based combined super-resolution point cloud video streaming, in *Fourth International Conference on Image Processing and Intelligent Control (IPIC 2024)*, vol. 13250 (SPIE, 2024), pp. 466–472
80. X. Liu, H. Liang, Z. Bao, C. Dong, X. Xu, Semantic communications system with model division multiple access and controllable coding rate for point cloud (2023). arXiv preprint arXiv:2307.06027
81. A. Akhtar, B. Kathariya, Z. Li, Low latency scalable point cloud communication, in *2019 IEEE International Conference on Image Processing (ICIP)* (IEEE, 2019), pp. 2369–2373
82. Z. Liang, J. Liu, M. Dasari, F. Wang, Fumos: Neural compression and progressive refinement for continuous point cloud video streaming. IEEE Trans. Visual. Comput. Graph. **30**(5), 2849–2859 (2024)
83. J. Van Der Hooft, T. Wauters, F. De Turck, C. Timmerer, H. Hellwagner, Towards 6dof http adaptive streaming through point cloud compression, in *Proceedings of the 27th ACM International Conference on Multimedia*, pp. 2405–2413 (2019)
84. G.R. Chandra, K. Ashritha, S. Jnaved, C.B. Teja, C. Poojitha, A framework for visualization of streaming 3d point cloud, in *2024 International Conference on Emerging Techniques in Computational Intelligence (ICETCI)* (IEEE, 2024), pp. 204–209

85. R. Fischer, A. Mühlenbrock, F. Kulapichitr, V.N. Uslar, D. Weyhe, G. Zachmann, Evaluation of point cloud streaming and rendering for vr-based telepresence in the or, in *International Conference on Virtual Reality and Mixed Reality* (Springer, 2022), pp. 89–110
86. Y. Egi, C.E. Otero, Machine-learning and 3d point-cloud based signal power path loss model for the deployment of wireless communication systems. IEEE Access **7**, 42507–42517 (2019)
87. Y. Lee, B. Yoo, S.-H. Lee, Sharing ambient objects using real-time point cloud streaming in web-based xr remote collaboration, in *Proceedings of the 26th International Conference on 3D Web Technology*, pp. 1–9 (2021)
88. Z. Sultani, R.F. Al-Tuma, S. Wefel, Color reduction in an authenticate live 3d point cloud video streaming system. Computers **5**(3), 17 (2016)
89. T. Yamazaki, N. Maeda, T. Miyoshi, T. Asaka, Wireless point cloud streaming experiment using IEEE 802.11 ax, in *2024 IEEE 21st Consumer Communications & Networking Conference (CCNC)* (IEEE, 2024), pp. 1058–1059
90. Y. Huang, Y. Zhu, X. Qiao, Z. Tan, B. Bai, Aitransfer: Progressive ai-powered transmission for real-time point cloud video streaming, in *Proceedings of the 29th ACM International Conference on Multimedia*, pp. 3989–3997 (2021)
91. W. Zhang, Z. Yu, H. Huang, X. Dong, K. Sun, K. Xu, Lightweight joint coding-modulation optical fiber communication system for point cloud. IEEE Trans. Commun. **73**(3), 1938–1949 (2025)
92. C. Zhang, Y. Cao, Z. Liu, R. Yin, Y. Zhu, X. Chen, Trans-rl: A prediction-control approach for qoe-aware point cloud video streaming, in *GLOBECOM 2022 IEEE Global Communications Conference* (IEEE, 2022), pp. 1899–1904
93. M. Kajitani, S. Takahashi, M. Okuda, Point cloud streaming for 3d avatar communication, in *Stereo Vision* (IntechOpen, 2008)
94. Z. Liu, Q. Li, X. Chen, C. Wu, J. Li, Y. Ji, et al., Point cloud video streaming in 5g systems and beyond: challenges and solutions. Authorea Preprints (2023)
95. K. Wen, N. Zhang, G. Li, W. Gao, Mpvnn: Multi-resolution point-voxel non-parametric network for 3d point cloud processing, in *2024 IEEE International Conference on Multimedia and Expo (ICME)* (IEEE, 2024), pp. 1–6
96. Z. Pan, N. Zhang, W. Gao, S. Liu, G. Li, Point cloud semantic segmentation with sparse and inhomogeneous annotations, in *Proceedings of the AAAI Conference on Artificial Intelligence* (2025)
97. R. Zhang, G. Li, W. Gao, S. Liu, A quantum-inspired framework in leader-servant mode for large-scale multi-modal place recognition. IEEE Trans. Intell. Transport. Syst. **26**(2), 2027–2039 (2025)
98. D. Yang, W. Gao, Pointchd: A point cloud benchmark for congenital heart disease classification and segmentation. IEEE J. Biomed. Health Inf. **29**(4), 2683–2694 (2025)
99. J. Li, C. Zhang, Z. Liu, W. Sun, Q. Li, Joint communication and computational resource allocation for qoe-driven point cloud video streaming (2020). arXiv preprint arXiv:2001.01403
100. I. Mpeg, Information technology-dynamic adaptive streaming over http (dash)-part 1: Media presentation description and segment formats. ISO/IEC MPEG, Tech. Rep. (2012)
101. Z. Liu, J. Li, X. Chen, C. Wu, S. Ishihara, Y. Ji, Fuzzy logic-based adaptive point cloud video streaming. IEEE Open J. Comput. Soc. **1**, 121–130 (2020)
102. Y. Huang, B. Bai, Y. Zhu, X. Qiao, X. Su, L. Yang, P. Zhang, Iscom: Interest-aware semantic communication scheme for point cloud video streaming on metaverse xr devices. IEEE J. Sel. Areas Commun. **42**(4), 1003–1021 (2024)
103. E.H. Makiyah, N.N. Khamees, Emulation of point cloud streaming over 5g network. Int. J. Inf. Technol., 1–15 (2024)
104. C. Moreno, Y. Chen, M. Li, A dynamic compression technique for streaming kinect-based point cloud data, in *2017 International Conference on Computing, Networking and Communications (ICNC)* (IEEE, 2017), pp. 550–555
105. C. Tu, E. Takeuchi, A. Carballo, K. Takeda, Real-time streaming point cloud compression for 3d lidar sensor using u-net. IEEE Access **7**, 113616–113625 (2019)

106. J. Li, C. Zhang, Z. Liu, W. Sun, W. Hu, Q. Li, Demo abstract: Narwhal: A dash-based point cloud video streaming system over wireless networks, in *IEEE INFOCOM 2020-IEEE Conference on Computer Communications Workshops (INFOCOM WKSHPS)* (IEEE, 2020), pp. 1326–1327
107. L. Wang, C. Li, W. Dai, S. Li, J. Zou, H. Xiong, Qoe-driven adaptive streaming for point clouds. IEEE Trans. Multimedia **25**, 2543–2558 (2022)
108. R.B. Rusu, S. Cousins, 3d is here: Point cloud library (pcl), in *2011 IEEE International Conference on Robotics and Automation* (IEEE, 2011), pp. 1–4
109. P. Debevec, Y. Yu, G. Borshukov, Efficient view-dependent image-based rendering with projective texture-mapping, in *Rendering Techniques' 98: Proceedings of the Eurographics Workshop in Vienna, Austria, June 29—July 1, 1998 9* (Springer, 1998), pp. 105–116
110. D.B. Goldman, B. Curless, A. Hertzmann, S.M. Seitz, Shape and spatially-varying brdfs from photometric stereo. IEEE Trans. Pattern Anal. Mach. Intell. **32**(6), 1060–1071 (2009)
111. Q.Y. Zhou, J. Park, V. Koltun, Open3d: A modern library for 3d data processing (2018). arXiv preprint arXiv:1801.09847
112. L. Xie, X. Mu, G. Li, W. Gao, et al., Pku-dpcc: A new dataset for dynamic point cloud compression. APSIPA Trans. Signal Inf. Process. **13**(6), 1–23 (2024)
113. H. Yuan, W. Gao, W. Gao, Opensep: An open source subjective experiment platform, in *Proceedings of the 32nd ACM International Conference on Multimedia*, pp. 11248–11251 (2024)
114. S. Fan, W. Gao, Screen-based 3d subjective experiment software, in *Proceedings of the 31st ACM International Conference on Multimedia*, pp. 9672–9675 (2023)
115. J. Wang, W. Gao, G. Li, Zoom to perceive better: No-reference point cloud quality assessment via exploring effective multiscale feature. IEEE Trans. Circuits Syst. Video Technol. **34**(7), 6334–6346 (2024)
116. J. Wang, W. Gao, G. Li, Applying collaborative adversarial learning to blind point cloud quality measurement. IEEE Trans. Instrum. Measur. **72**, 1–15 (2023)
117. H. Li, W. Gao, Information exploration of projected views for point cloud quality measurement. IEEE Trans. Instrum. Measur. **74**, 1–14 (2025)
118. S. Fan, W. Gao, Z. Chen, G. Li, G. Liu, Q. Wang, Stochasticity-aware no-reference point cloud quality assessment, in *International Joint Conference on Artificial Intelligence* (2025)
119. N. Snavely, S.M. Seitz, R. Szeliski, Photo tourism: exploring photo collections in 3d, in *ACM siggraph 2006 Papers*, pp. 835–846 (2006)
120. N. Ravi, J. Reizenstein, D. Novotny, T. Gordon, W.Y. Lo, J. Johnson, G. Gkioxari, Accelerating 3d deep learning with pytorch3d (2020). arXiv preprint arXiv:2007.08501
121. K.-A. Aliev, A. Sevastopolsky, M. Kolos, D. Ulyanov, V. Lempitsky, Neural point-based graphics, in *Computer Vision–ECCV 2020: 16th European Conference, Glasgow, UK, August 23–28, 2020, Proceedings, Part XXII 16* (Springer, 2020), pp. 696–712
122. R. Rakhimov, A.-T. Ardelean, V. Lempitsky, E. Burnaev, Npbg++: Accelerating neural point-based graphics, in *Proceedings of the IEEE/CVF Conference on Computer Vision and Pattern Recognition*, pp. 15969–15979 (2022)
123. B. Qu, X. Liang, S. Sun, W. Gao, Exploring aigc video quality: A focus on visual harmony, video-text consistency and domain distribution gap, in *Proceedings of the IEEE/CVF Conference on Computer Vision and Pattern Recognition Workshops* (2024)
124. B. Qu, H. Li, W. Gao, Bringing textual prompt to ai-generated image quality assessment, in *2024 IEEE International Conference on Multimedia and Expo (ICME)* (IEEE, 2024)
125. S. Sun, X. Liang, S. Fan, W. Gao, W. Gao, Ve-bench: Subjective-aligned benchmark suite for text-driven video editing quality assessment, in *Proceedings of the AAAI Conference on Artificial Intelligence* (2025)
126. Y. Zhang, S. Peng, A. Moazeni, K. Li, Papr: Proximity attention point rendering. Adv. Neural Inf. Process. Syst. **36**, 60307–60328 (2023)
127. P. Dai, Y. Zhang, Z. Li, S. Liu, B. Zeng, Neural point cloud rendering via multi-plane projection, in *Proceedings of the IEEE/CVF Conference on Computer Vision and Pattern Recognition*, pp. 7830–7839 (2020)

128. T. Hu, X. Xu, R. Chu, J. Jia, Trivol: Point cloud rendering via triple volumes, in *Proceedings of the IEEE/CVF Conference on Computer Vision and Pattern Recognition*, pp. 20732–20741 (2023)
129. T. Hu, X. Xu, S. Liu, J. Jia, Point2pix: Photo-realistic point cloud rendering via neural radiance fields, in *Proceedings of the IEEE/CVF Conference on Computer Vision and Pattern Recognition*, pp. 8349–8358 (2023)
130. X. Huang, Y. Zhang, B. Ni, T. Li, K. Chen, W. Zhang, Boosting point clouds rendering via radiance mapping, in *Proceedings of the AAAI Conference on Artificial Intelligence*, vol. 37(1), pp. 953–961 (2023)
131. J.-H.R. Chang, W.-Y. Chen, A. Ranjan, K. M. Yi, O. Tuzel, Pointersect: Neural rendering with cloud-ray intersection, in *Proceedings of the IEEE/CVF Conference on Computer Vision and Pattern Recognition*, pp. 8359–8369 (2023)
132. Z. Li, L. Li, J. Zhu, Read: Large-scale neural scene rendering for autonomous driving, in *Proceedings of the AAAI Conference on Artificial Intelligence*, vol. 37(2), pp. 1522–1529 (2023)
133. J. Ma, M. Liu, D. Ahmedt-Aristizabal, C. Nguyen, Hashpoint: Accelerated point searching and sampling for neural rendering, in *Proceedings of the IEEE/CVF Conference on Computer Vision and Pattern Recognition*, pp. 4462–4472 (2024)
134. Y. Hu, R. Gong, Q. Sun, Y. Wang, Low latency point cloud rendering with learned splatting, in *Proceedings of the IEEE/CVF Conference on Computer Vision and Pattern Recognition*, pp. 5752–5761 (2024)
135. J. Wang, Z. Zhang, J. He, R. Xu, Pfgs: High fidelity point cloud rendering via feature splatting, in *European Conference on Computer Vision* (Springer, 2025), pp. 193–209
136. Y. Hu, R. Gong, Y. Wang, Bits-to-photon: End-to-end learned scalable point cloud compression for direct rendering (2024). arXiv preprint arXiv:2406.05915
137. X. Huo, J. Ho, S. Wan, F. Yang, Rendering-oriented 3d point cloud attribute compression using sparse tensor-based transformer (2024). arXiv preprint arXiv:2411.07899
138. K. Wang, S. Li, Q. Yi, W. Gao, A novel benchmark and dataset for efficient 3d gaussian splatting with gaussian point cloud compression (2025). arXiv preprint arXiv:2505.18197
139. W. Gao, *AI-based Image and Video Coding: Methods, Standards, and Applications* (Springer, 2025)

Chapter 11
Open-Source Projects for 3D Point Cloud Coding

Abstract Open-source projects can benefit the development of AI research, as they facilitate the communicating of insights and the implementation of further improvements. This chapter introduces the open-source projects for AI-based point cloud coding. It is structured as follows. First, it provides a brief introduction of the open-source libraries for popular 3D point cloud coding algorithms, including Point Cloud Library and Draco. Second, it provides the introduction to the emerging open-source project, i.e., OpenPointCloud, which is an open-source algorithm library that focuses on deep learning-based point cloud coding and processing algorithms.

Keywords Open source · Deep learning · Point cloud coding · PyTorch · TensorFlow · Bit per point · Lossy compression · Lossless compression

11.1 Point Cloud Library

The Point Cloud Library (PCL) [1] is an open-source library designed for processing 2D/3D point clouds. It was initially developed by researchers at Willow Garage, a robotics research lab, to support their 3D vision projects. PCL has grown to be a comprehensive platform for various applications in fields like robotics, computer vision, augmented reality, and more [2–8]. Here, we explore the fundamentals of PCL, its capabilities, and its significance in the domain of point cloud processing. Point clouds are points of data in 3D space, representing the coordinates and sometimes additional attributes (like color or intensity) of a particular surface point. They are commonly obtained through techniques such as 3D scanning, Light Detection and Ranging (LiDAR), and stereo vision. Point clouds are crucial in modeling real-world environments for applications such as object recognition and industrial inspection [9–21].

The development of PCL began in 2010 at Willow Garage as a response to the need for a unified framework for 3D perception tasks. Over the years, it has been maintained and expanded by a vibrant community of developers and researchers

W. Gao, *AI-based 3D Point Cloud Coding*,
https://doi.org/10.1007/978-981-95-0660-6_11

worldwide. PCL is written in C + + and is compatible with Linux, Windows, macOS, and other platforms. The key features of PCL are as follows.

- **Point Cloud Processing**. The Point Cloud Library (PCL) offers a comprehensive suite of tools for manipulating 3D point cloud data, encompassing advanced techniques for filtering noise, segmenting structures, aligning datasets through registration, and extracting meaningful geometry features.
- **Visualization**. It offers tools for visualizing point clouds in both 2D and 3D environments, enabling developers to inspect and debug algorithms effectively.
- **Registration and Alignment**. PCL includes robust algorithms for aligning point clouds from different sources, which is essential for tasks such as mapping and localization.
- **Surface Reconstruction**. Surface reconstruction methods are available, allowing for the creation of 3D models from scanned data.
- **Machine Learning Integration**. Recent versions of PCL integrate machine learning techniques for tasks such as classification and object recognition within point clouds.

PCL offers a range of specialized libraries for different tasks. The pcl_filters library provides methods to eliminate outliers and noise from 3D point clouds. The pcl_features library helps estimate 3D features, while the pcl_keypoints library detects key points within point clouds. The pcl_registration library includes various algorithms for aligning organized and unorganized datasets. The pcl_kdtree library utilizes FLANN for efficient nearest neighbor searches, and the pcl_octree library constructs hierarchical structures from point clouds. The pcl_segmentation library divides point clouds into distinct clusters, and the pcl_sample consensus library features methods like RANSAC for model fitting. The pcl_surface library focuses on surface reconstruction from 3D scans, while the pcl_recognition module offers algorithms for object recognition. Finally, the pcl_io_library supports file operations and point cloud capture, and the pcl_visualization library enables rapid prototyping and visualization of results.

11.2 Draco Library

Draco is a specialized library developed for the efficient compression and decompression of 3D geometric meshes and point clouds [2, 3]. By significantly reducing the size of 3D assets—while preserving visual fidelity—Draco optimizes both storage and transmission, making it particularly valuable for applications in web-based 3D rendering, virtual reality (VR), and augmented reality (AR). It achieves high compression ratios across various data types, including vertex positions, mesh connectivity, texture coordinates, colors, and normals. As a result, it enables faster loading times, lower bandwidth usage, and smoother real-time rendering experiences. The library is provided as open-source C + + code for encoding and supports both C + + and JavaScript decoders, facilitating broad integration across platforms [22–26].

When you refer to the official website of Draco https://google.github.io/draco/, it provides a simple example on Codelab demonstrating how to compress and view 3D models using Draco, along with an exploration of various compression techniques and their impact on the models. You may also refer to the github page https://github.com/google/draco for the latest releases.

11.3 OpenPointCloud Library

Similar with the counterparts in image and video compression [27–41], enhancement [42–48], and analysis [49–56], OpenPointCloud is the first open-source algorithm library that focuses on point cloud deep learning algorithms, covering the main research areas of point cloud coding, processing, and analysis [57–66]. It brings together multiple categories of algorithms and provides code support for different deep learning programming frameworks. It also conducts baseline testing and comparative analysis of the performance of each algorithm.

The research on the open-source algorithm library for point clouds can reduce the research threshold for point cloud algorithms, encourage open source, facilitate academic research, and promote the development and progress of algorithms in the field of point clouds. You can refer to the official website for more information: https://openi.pcl.ac.cn/OpenPointCloud. Table 11.1 gives an overview of the OpenPointCloud open-source project.

11.4 Summary

This chapter introduces the open-source projects for AI-based point cloud coding. It first presents a brief introduction to popular open-source libraries for 3D compression algorithms, including Point Cloud Library and Draco. The main part of this chapter is the introduction of the newly developed open-source project for AI-based 3D point cloud coding and processing, i.e., OpenPointCloud. For readers who are interested in the related technologies of AI-based image and video coding, please refer to [77].

Exercises

1. Please briefly introduce the open-source library Point Cloud Library (PCL).
2. Please briefly introduce the open-source library Draco.
3. Please explain which aspects establishing an open-source project includes.

Table 11.1 Overview of OpenPointCloud (Source: Author)

Index	Category	Name & publication	Available frameworks	Brief introduction
1	Lossy	Pcc_geo_cnn_v1, ICIP 19 [67]	TensorFlow & PyTorch	This is the first effort to integrate arithmetic coding with convolutional neural networks (CNNs), making entropy coding applicable in point cloud coding (PCC)
2	Lossy	PCGCv1, TCSVT 21 [68]	TensorFlow & PyTorch & TensorLayer	PCGCv1 utilizes Voxception-ResNet blocks for both analysis and synthesis transformations, which not only increases the depth of the network but also mitigates the issue of gradient vanishing during training. Furthermore, it incorporates a hyper-prior network and a Laplacian function, enhancing the model's ability to capture and interpret complex probability distributions
3	Lossy	Pcc_geo_cnn_v2, MMSP 20 [69]	TensorFlow & PyTorch	Building on Pcc_geo_cnn_v1, Pcc_geo_cnn_v2 incorporates enhancements in five areas, with ablation tests conducted to evaluate the effectiveness of each improvement
4	Lossy	PCGCv2, DCC 21 [70]	PyTorch	PCGCv2 is an upgrade from PCGCv1. It introduces the Inception-Residual Network (IRN) unit, employs a multi-scale strategy, and utilizes a sparse convolution mechanism
5	Lossy	Pcc_attr_folding, ICIP 20 [71]	TensorFlow & TensorLayer	Pcc_attr_folding proposes a method for mapping 3D coordinates to 2D grids using overfitting deep learning, enabling the encoding of point cloud attributes with standard 2D image codecs
6	Lossy	NGS, ICIP 21 [72]	PyTorch	Efficient compression of point cloud geometry (PCG) is essential for optimizing networked applications, as PCG offers a compact and effective representation of intricate 3D objects and their corresponding physical environments. To fully exploit the inherent geometric correlations within the input PCG, a novel three-step neural graph sampling (NGS) method has been introduced
7	Lossless	VoxelDNN, ICASSP 21 [73]	TensorFlow & TensorLayer	VoxelDNN utilizes a deep generative model that incorporates masked convolutions to estimate occupancy probabilities for arithmetic coding
8	Lossless	MSVoxelDNN, ICMEW 21 [74]	PyTorch & TensorLayer	MSVoxelDNN employs multi-scale structures that encode subblocks in a coarse-to-fine manner, effectively mitigating the high time complexity associated with voxel-by-voxel decoding
9	Lossless	NNCTX, MMSP 21 [75]	PyTorch & TensorFlow	NNCTX develops a coding process that enables efficient decoding without the voxel-by-voxel approach used in VoxelDNN
10	Lossless	OctAttention, AAAI 22 [76]	PyTorch & TensorFlow	OctAttention integrates octree structures with transformers to predict distributions for entropy coding. Since the octree structure occupies less space than voxelization, OctAttention achieves superior performance in compression rates

4. Please describe which categories of algorithms OpenPointCloud contains.
5. Please discuss the point cloud coding algorithms included in OpenPointCloud.
6. Please describe what frameworks are provided.
7. Please discuss the future of AI-based 3D point cloud coding.
8. Please briefly summarize this chapter.
9. Please explain what the advantages of using OpenPointCloud as an open-source project for 3D point cloud coding and analysis are.
10. Please describe the role of deep learning in the evolution of point cloud coding, referencing specific algorithms.

References

1. R.B. Rusu, S. Cousins, 3D is here: point cloud library (PCL), in *2011 IEEE International Conference on Robotics and Automation* (IEEE, Piscataway, 2011), pp. 1–4
2. W. Gao, G. Li, *Deep Learning for 3D Point Clouds* (Springer, Berlin, 2024)
3. G. Li, G. Wei, W. Gao, *Point Cloud Compression: Technologies and Standardization* (Springer, Berlin, 2024)
4. W. Gao, G. Li, H. Yuan, R. Hamzaoui, Z. Li, S. Liu, Apccpa'22: 1st international workshop on advances in point cloud compression, processing and analysis, in *Proceedings of the 30th ACM International Conference on Multimedia* (2022), pp. 7392–7393
5. W. Gao, G. Li, Point cloud compression, enhancement and applications: from 3D perception to large models, in *Proceedings of the 32nd ACM International Conference on Multimedia* (2024), pp. 11 292–11 293
6. H. Sun, G. Li, S. Chen, L. Li, W. Gao, Special topic on 3D point cloud processing and applications. ZTE Commun. **21**(4), 1 (2023)
7. W. Gao, W. Gao, X. Mu, C. Peng, G. Li, Overview and comparison of AVS point cloud compression standard. APSIPA Trans. Signal Inf. Proces. **14**(2), 1–33 (2025)
8. W. Gao, S. Wang, X. Zhang, S. Kwong, Editorial for special issue on deep learning-based data compression. APSIPA Trans. Signal Inf. Proces. **13**(6), 1–2 (2024)
9. W. Liu, W. Gao, X. Mu, Fast inter-frame motion prediction for compressed dynamic point cloud attribute enhancement. Proc. AAAI Conf. Artif. Intell. **38**(4), 3720–3728 (2024)
10. Z. Yang, W. Gao, X. Lu, DANet: density-adaptive network for geometry-based point cloud compression artifacts removal, in *2023 IEEE International Conference on Visual Communications and Image Processing (VCIP)* (IEEE, Piscataway, 2023), pp. 1–5
11. X. Fan, G. Li, D. Li, Y. Ren, W. Gao, T.H. Li, Deep geometry post-processing for decompressed point clouds, in *2022 IEEE International Conference on Multimedia and Expo (ICME)* (IEEE, Piscataway, 2022), pp. 1–6
12. X. Zhang, G. Liao, W. Gao, G. Li, TDRNet: transformer-based dual-branch restoration network for geometry based point cloud compression artifacts, in *2022 IEEE International Conference on Multimedia and Expo (ICME)* (IEEE, Piscataway, 2022), pp. 1–6
13. S. Fan, W. Gao, G. Li, Salient object detection for point clouds, in *European Conference on Computer Vision* (Springer, Berlin, 2022), pp. 1–19
14. S. Luo, W. Gao, A general framework for rotation invariant point cloud analysis, in *ICASSP 2024-2024 IEEE International Conference on Acoustics, Speech and Signal Processing (ICASSP)* (IEEE, Piscataway, 2024), pp. 3665–3669
15. X. Lu, W. Gao, AttentiveNet: detecting small objects for lidar point clouds by attending to important points, in *2023 IEEE International Conference on Visual Communications and Image Processing (VCIP)* (IEEE, Piscataway, 2023), pp. 1–5

16. Z. Pan, N. Zhang, W. Gao, S. Liu, G. Li, Less is more: label recommendation for weakly supervised point cloud semantic segmentation. Proc. AAAI Conf. Artif. Intell. **38**(5), 4397–4405 (2024)
17. Z. Pan, G. Liu, W. Gao, T.H. Li, EPContrast: effective point-level contrastive learning for large-scale point cloud understanding, in *2024 IEEE International Conference on Multimedia and Expo (ICME)* (IEEE, Piscataway, 2024), pp. 1–6
18. S. Fan, W. Gao, Screen-based 3D subjective experiment software, in *Proceedings of the 31st ACM International Conference on Multimedia* (2023), pp. 9672–9675
19. J. Wang, W. Gao, G. Li, Zoom to perceive better: no-reference point cloud quality assessment via exploring effective multiscale feature. IEEE Trans. Circuits Syst. Video Technol. **34**(7), 6334–6346 (2024)
20. J. Wang, W. Gao, G. Li, Applying collaborative adversarial learning to blind point cloud quality measurement. IEEE Trans. Instrum. Measure. **72**, 1–15 (2023)
21. H. Li, W. Gao, Information exploration of projected views for point cloud quality measurement. IEEE Trans. Instrum. Measure. **74**, 1–14 (2025)
22. L. Xie, W. Gao, H. Zheng, G. Li, ROI-guided point cloud geometry compression towards human and machine vision. arXiv preprint arXiv:2504.14240 (2025)
23. W. Gao, H. Ye, G. Li, H. Zheng, Y. Wu, L. Xie, OpenPointCloud: an open-source algorithm library of deep learning based point cloud compression, in *Proceedings of the 30th ACM International Conference on Multimedia* (2022), pp. 7347–7350
24. Y. Zhang, W. Gao, G. Li, OpenPointCloud-V2: a deep learning based open-source algorithm library of point cloud processing, in *Proceedings of the 1st International Workshop on Advances in Point Cloud Compression, Processing and Analysis* (2022), pp. 51–55
25. L. Xie, W. Gao, LearningPCC: a pytorch library for learning-based point cloud compression, in *Proceedings of the 32nd ACM International Conference on Multimedia* (2024), pp. 11 234–11 238
26. L. Xie, W. Gao, PCHMVision: an open-source library of point cloud compression for human and machine vision, in *Proceedings of the 32nd ACM International Conference on Multimedia* (2024), pp. 11 239–11 243
27. Y. Wu, L. Xie, S. Sun, W. Gao, Y. Yan, Adaptive intra period size for deep learning-based screen content video coding, in *2024 IEEE International Conference on Multimedia and Expo Workshops (ICMEW)* (IEEE, Piscataway, 2024), pp. 1–6
28. H. Zheng, W. Gao, End-to-end RGB-D image compression via exploiting channel-modality redundancy. Proc. AAAI Conf. Artif. Intell. **38**(7), 7562–7570 (2024)
29. L. Tao, W. Gao, G. Li, C. Zhang, AdaNIC: towards practical neural image compression via dynamic transform routing, in *Proceedings of the IEEE/CVF International Conference on Computer Vision* (2023), pp. 16 879–16 888
30. Y. Wu, W. Gao, End-to-end lossless compression of high precision depth maps guided by pseudo-residual, in *2022 Data Compression Conference (DCC)* (IEEE, Piscataway, 2022), pp. 489–489
31. Y. Wu, Z. Qi, H. Zheng, L. Tao, W. Gao, Deep image compression with latent optimization and piece-wise quantization approximation, in *Proceedings of the IEEE/CVF Conference on Computer Vision and Pattern Recognition* (2021), pp. 1926–1930
32. W. Gao, L. Tao, L. Zhou, D. Yang, X. Zhang, Z. Guo, Low-rate image compression with super-resolution learning, in *Proceedings of the IEEE/CVF Conference on Computer Vision and Pattern Recognition Workshops* (2020), pp. 154–155
33. W. Gao, S. Sun, H. Zheng, Y. Wu, H. Ye, Y. Zhang, OpenDMC: an open-source library and performance evaluation for deep-learning-based multi-frame compression, in *Proceedings of the 31st ACM International Conference on Multimedia* (2023), pp. 9685–9688
34. W. Gao, H. Zheng, C. Zhang, K. Zheng, Z. Yu, Y. Li, H. Ye, Y. Zhang, OpenDIC: an open-source library and performance evaluation for deep-learning-based image compression, in *Proceedings of the 32nd ACM International Conference on Multimedia* (2024), pp. 11 202–11 205

35. Y. Li, W. Gao, G. Li, S. Ma, Saliency segmentation oriented deep image compression with novel bit allocation. IEEE Trans. Image Proces. **34**, 16–29 (2025)
36. C. Zhang, W. Gao, Learned rate control for frame-level adaptive neural video compression via dynamic neural network, in *European Conference on Computer Vision* (Springer, Berlin, 2024)
37. Z. Yang, W. Gao, G. Li, Y. Yan, SUR-driven video coding rate control for jointly optimizing perceptual quality and buffer control. IEEE Trans. Image Proces. (2023)
38. F. Shen, Z. Cai, W. Gao, An efficient rate control algorithm for intra frame coding in AVS3, in *2021 IEEE International Conference on Systems, Man, and Cybernetics (SMC)* (IEEE, Piscataway, 2021), pp. 3164–3169
39. H. Yuan, W. Gao, J. Wang, Dynamic computational resource allocation for fast inter frame coding in video conferencing applications, in *2021 IEEE International Conference on Multimedia and Expo (ICME)* (IEEE, Piscataway, 2021), pp. 1–6
40. W. Gao, Q. Jiang, R. Wang, S. Ma, G. Li, S. Kwong, Consistent quality oriented rate control in HEVC via balancing intra and inter frame coding. IEEE Trans. Ind. Inf. **18**(3), 1594–1604 (2021)
41. H. Yuan, W. Gao, A new coding unit partitioning mode for screen content video coding, in *Proceedings of the 2021 5th International Conference on Digital Signal Processing* (2021), pp. 66–72
42. Z. Li, G. Li, T. Li, S. Liu, W. Gao, Information-growth attention network for image super-resolution, in *Proceedings of the 29th ACM International Conference on Multimedia* (2021), pp. 544–552
43. L. Zhou, W. Gao, G. Li, H. Yuan, T. Zhao, G. Yue, Disentangled feature distillation for light field super-resolution with degradations, in *2023 IEEE International Conference on Multimedia and Expo Workshops (ICMEW)* (IEEE, Piscataway, 2023), pp. 116–121
44. L. Zhou, W. Gao, G. Li, End-to-end spatial-angular light field super-resolution using parallax structure preservation strategy, in *2022 IEEE International Conference on Image Processing (ICIP)* (IEEE, Piscataway, 2022), pp. 3396–3400
45. W. Gao, L. Zhou, L. Tao, A fast view synthesis implementation method for light field applications. ACM Trans. Multimedia Comput. Commun. Appl. (TOMM) **17**(4), 1–20 (2021)
46. X. Zhang, W. Gao, G. Li, Q. Jiang, R. Cong, Image quality assessment–driven reinforcement learning for mixed distorted image restoration. ACM Trans. Multimedia Comput. Commun. Appl. **19**(1s), 1–23 (2023)
47. X. Zhang, W. Gao, H. Yuan, G. Li, Je 2 net: joint exploitation and exploration in reinforcement learning based image restoration, in *ICASSP 2022-2022 IEEE International Conference on Acoustics, Speech and Signal Processing (ICASSP)* (IEEE, Piscataway, 2022), pp. 2090–2094
48. X. Zhang, W. Gao, HIRL: hybrid image restoration based on hierarchical deep reinforcement learning via two-step analysis, in *ICASSP 2022-2022 IEEE International Conference on Acoustics, Speech and Signal Processing (ICASSP)* (IEEE, Piscataway, 2022), pp. 2445–2449
49. X. Zang, W. Gao, G. Li, H. Fang, C. Ban, Z. He, H. Sun, A baseline investigation: transformer-based cross-view baseline for text-based person search, in *Proceedings of the 31st ACM International Conference on Multimedia* (2023), pp. 7737–7746
50. G. Liao, W. Gao, G. Li, J. Wang, S. Kwong, Cross-collaborative fusion-encoder network for robust RGB-thermal salient object detection. IEEE Trans. Circuits Syst. Video Technol. **32**(11), 7646–7661 (2022)
51. W. Gao, G. Liao, S. Ma, G. Li, Y. Liang, W. Lin, Unified information fusion network for multi-modal RGB-D and RGB-T salient object detection. IEEE Trans. Circuits Syst. Video Technol. **32**(4), 2091–2106 (2021)
52. Y. Chen, S. Sun, G. Li, W. Gao, T.H. Li, Closing the gap between theory and practice during alternating optimization for gans. IEEE Trans. Neural Networks Learn. Syst. **35**(10), 14005–14017 (2024)
53. Y. Chen, C. Jin, G. Li, T.H. Li, W. Gao, Mitigating label noise in gans via enhanced spectral normalization. IEEE Trans. Circuits Syst. Video Technol. **33**(8), 3924–3934 (2023)
54. X. Zang, G. Li, W. Gao, Multidirection and multiscale pyramid in transformer for video-based pedestrian retrieval. IEEE Trans. Ind. Inf. **18**(12), 8776–8785 (2022)

55. X. Zang, G. Li, W. Gao, X. Shu, Learning to disentangle scenes for person re-identification. Image Vis. Comput. **116**, 104330 (2021)
56. X. Zang, G. Li, W. Gao, X. Shu, Exploiting robust unsupervised video person re-identification. IET Image Proces. **16**(3), 729–741 (2022)
57. T. Qin, G. Li, W. Gao, S. Liu, Multi-grained point cloud geometry compression via dual-model prediction with extended octree. ACM Trans. Multimedia Comput. Commun. Appl. **20**(9), 1–30 (2024)
58. Y. Shao, W. Gao, S. Liu, G. Li, Advanced patch-based affine motion estimation for dynamic point cloud geometry compression. Sensors **24**(10), 3142 (2024)
59. Y. Shao, F. Song, W. Gao, S. Liu, G. Li, Texture-guided graph transform optimization for point cloud attribute compression. Appl. Sci. **14**(10), 4094 (2024)
60. Y. Shao, X. Yang, W. Gao, S. Liu, G. Li, 3D point cloud attribute compression using diffusion-based texture-aware intra prediction. IEEE Trans. Circuits Syst. Video Technol. **34**(10), 9633–9646 (2024)
61. J. Zhang, Y. Chen, G. Liu, W. Gao, G. Li, Efficient point cloud attribute compression framework using attribute-guided graph fourier transform, in *ICASSP 2024-2024 IEEE International Conference on Acoustics, Speech and Signal Processing (ICASSP)* (IEEE, Piscataway, 2024), pp. 8426–8430
62. W. Gao, H. Yuan, G. Li, Z. Li, H. Yuan, Low complexity coding unit decision for video-based point cloud compression. IEEE Trans. Image Proces. **33**, 149–162 (2023)
63. Y. Shao, G. Li, Q. Zhang, W. Gao, S. Liu, Nonrigid registration-based progressive motion compensation for point cloud geometry compression. IEEE Trans. Geosci. Remote Sens. **61**, 1–14 (2023)
64. F. Song, G. Li, X. Yang, W. Gao, S. Liu, Block-adaptive point cloud attribute coding with region-aware optimized transform. IEEE Trans. Circuits Syst. Video Technol. **33**(8), 4294–4308 (2023)
65. Y. An, Y. Shao, G. Li, W. Gao, S. Liu, A fast motion estimation method with hamming distance for lidar point cloud compression, in *2022 IEEE International Conference on Visual Communications and Image Processing (VCIP)* (IEEE, Piscataway, 2022), pp. 1–5
66. H. Yuan, W. Gao, G. Li, Z. Li, Rate-distortion-guided learning approach with cross-projection information for V-PCC fast CU decision, in *Proceedings of the 30th ACM International Conference on Multimedia* (2022), pp. 3085–3093
67. M. Quach, G. Valenzise, F. Dufaux, Learning convolutional transforms for lossy point cloud geometry compression, in *2019 IEEE International Conference on Image Processing (ICIP)* (IEEE, Piscataway, 2019), pp. 4320–4324
68. J. Wang, H. Zhu, H. Liu, Z. Ma, Lossy point cloud geometry compression via end-to-end learning. IEEE Trans. Circuits Syst. Video Technol. **31**(12), 4909–4923 (2021)
69. M. Quach, G. Valenzise, F. Dufaux, Improved deep point cloud geometry compression, in *2020 IEEE 22nd International Workshop on Multimedia Signal Processing (MMSP)* (IEEE, Piscataway, 2020), pp. 1–6
70. J. Wang, D. Ding, Z. Li, Z. Ma, Multiscale point cloud geometry compression, in *2021 Data Compression Conference (DCC)* (IEEE, Piscataway, 2021), pp. 73–82
71. M. Quach, G. Valenzise, F. Dufaux, Folding-based compression of point cloud attributes, in *2020 IEEE International Conference on Image Processing (ICIP)* (IEEE, Piscataway, 2020), pp. 3309–3313
72. L. Gao, T. Fan, J. Wan, Y. Xu, J. Sun, Z. Ma, Point cloud geometry compression via neural graph sampling, in *2021 IEEE International Conference on Image Processing (ICIP)* (IEEE, Piscataway, 2021), pp. 3373–3377
73. D.T. Nguyen, M. Quach, G. Valenzise, P. Duhamel, Lossless coding of point cloud geometry using a deep generative model. IEEE Trans. Circuits Syst. Video Technol. **31**(12), 4617–4629 (2021)
74. D.T. Nguyen, M. Quach, G. Valenzise, P. Duhamel, Multiscale deep context modeling for lossless point cloud geometry compression, in *2021 IEEE International Conference on Multimedia & Expo Workshops (ICMEW)* (IEEE, Piscatawa, 2021), pp. 1–6

75. E.C. Kaya, I. Tabus, Neural network modeling of probabilities for coding the octree representation of point clouds, in *2021 IEEE 23rd International Workshop on Multimedia Signal Processing (MMSP)* (IEEE, Piscataway, 2021), pp. 1–6
76. C. Fu, G. Li, R. Song, W. Gao, S. Liu, Octattention: octree-based large-scale contexts model for point cloud compression. Proc. AAAI Conf. Artif. Intell. **36**(1), 625–633 (2022)
77. W. Gao, *AI-based Image and Video Coding: Methods, Standards, and Applications* (Springer, Berlin, 2025)

Chapter 12
Future Works for AI-Based 3D Point Cloud Coding

Abstract The future of AI-based 3D point cloud coding has numerous research opportunities and challenges. Key areas include advancing deep learning-based compression techniques to optimize geometry and attribute coding, with a focus on lightweight neural networks to reduce computational overhead and enable large-scale applications. Robust point cloud quality assessment methods are needed, integrating both subjective and objective evaluations to address geometry and attribute quality. Dynamic point cloud coding requires improved temporal context acquisition and computational efficiency for real-time processing. Human and machine perception oriented coding methods demand adaptive compression frameworks to balance bit rates, signal fidelity, and perception performance. Compression artifact removal, particularly for sparse LiDAR point clouds and dynamic scenarios, remains a critical challenge. Standardization efforts must evolve to address dynamic point clouds and integrate low-level and high-level tasks. Implementation systems should leverage hardware acceleration and edge computing for efficient streaming and rendering. Open-source projects and large language models (LLMs) offer promising avenues for innovations, though LLMs require enhanced spatial understanding for effective point cloud coding. Collectively, these advancements aim to enhance point cloud coding efficiency, perceptual quality, low latency, flexibility, and scalability across diverse applications like autonomous driving and virtual reality.

Keywords Point cloud coding · Point cloud quality assessment · Point cloud geometry coding · Point cloud attribute coding · Dynamic point cloud coding

12.1 Future Work on Fundamentals for Deep Learning-Based Point Cloud Coding

With the rapid development of deep learning technologies [1–10], point cloud coding has seen substantial advances, particularly through the use of deep learning models such as convolutional neural networks, sparse convolutional networks, and transformer-based architectures. These models are increasingly capable of handling

W. Gao, *AI-based 3D Point Cloud Coding*,
https://doi.org/10.1007/978-981-95-0660-6_12

the irregular and sparse nature of point cloud data, a key advantage over traditional methods like G-PCC and V-PCC [11, 12]. However, despite these advancements, several critical challenges remain, demanding focused research and innovation.

One of the key challenges in deep learning-based point cloud coding is the variability in point cloud geometry. The nature of point clouds can differ significantly across different datasets and applications, requiring models to generalize well across diverse data types. Sparse convolution techniques, while offering state-of-the-art performance, still face limitations in dealing with the diverse geometry structures present in point clouds. Therefore, future work must explore more robust and uniform operators that can effectively preserve the geometry features of point clouds across various types, ensuring consistent performance across applications ranging from autonomous driving to virtual reality.

The encoder-decoder architecture used in deep learning-based point cloud coding is highly effective in mapping point cloud data into compact latent representations. However, the large number of parameters in these models poses a significant challenge, particularly when it comes to large-scale applications. The practical deployment of deep learning-based codecs requires the development of more lightweight models that can operate efficiently without sacrificing compression performance. This is where research in lightweight neural networks becomes crucial. By designing neural networks with fewer parameters, yet retaining their ability to perform robust compression, we can achieve more scalable and practical solutions for real-time point cloud processing.

Another avenue for future research involves optimizing the coding process for point cloud streaming. While deep learning-based approaches have shown promise in enhancing compression efficiency, the dynamic allocation of bitstreams based on the user's needs remains a topic of active exploration. In video and image compression, adaptive streaming technologies have been developed to ensure quality and stability in real-time media transmission. Similarly, point cloud streaming needs to be optimized for dynamic and efficient bitstream allocation, especially in bandwidth-constrained environments. Further research is needed to develop smart algorithms that can dynamically adjust bit rates depending on the context and user requirements.

Additionally, point cloud quality assessment remains a major challenge. Current methods rely on subjective evaluation, but robust objective evaluation techniques are still under development. Future work should focus on creating more reliable quality assessment metrics that address both the geometry and attributes of point clouds [13–25], along with their structural integrity. This will help improve the efficiency of deep learning-based point cloud coding by ensuring that only relevant and high-quality data is encoded and transmitted.

These challenges collectively outline a roadmap for advancing the fundamentals of deep learning-based point cloud coding. Solutions in these areas will lay the groundwork for robust, efficient, and intelligent 3D data coding frameworks capable of supporting next-generation applications such as autonomous navigation, telepresence, and immersive content delivery.

12.2 Future Work on Quality Assessment and Perception Models for 3D Point Cloud

As 3D point clouds are increasingly applied in immersive experiences and intelligent systems [26–31] and the performance of machine-related tasks [32–48], the need for effective quality assessment and perceptual modeling becomes ever more urgent. However, research in this area is still at an early stage, and several critical challenges remain unresolved.

In subjective quality assessment, one key limitation stems from current rendering techniques. Due to hardware constraints, most subjective tests still present 3D content using 2D display devices, which undermines perceptual accuracy and reduces immersion. To better simulate realistic consumption scenarios, future work should leverage advancements in virtual reality and head-mounted displays to design truly 3D-aware subjective experiments. This includes refining rendering schemes, viewing protocols, and scoring strategies, which together affect the outcome and consistency of opinion scores.

From the perspective of objective quality assessment, current approaches are dominated by full-reference (FR) metrics such as point-to-point and point-to-plane distances. While these methods provide valuable geometry measurements, they often fail to reflect perceptual distortions, particularly in color and texture. Future research should focus on designing no-reference (NR) and reduced-reference (RR) models that can function without access to pristine reference data, thereby improving applicability in real-world streaming or lossy compression scenarios. Additionally, there is a need for more accurate perceptual quality metrics that take human visual system (HVS) characteristics into account, integrating both geometry and attribute fidelity.

The integration of just-noticeable-distortion (JND) models into point cloud quality assessment presents another important direction. JND reflects the minimum perceptual threshold at which visual distortion becomes noticeable. While this concept has been well-explored in 2D images and video, its adaptation to 3D point clouds is limited by the lack of suitable datasets and subjective testing protocols. Developing large-scale, annotated JND datasets specifically for point clouds, and modeling perceptual redundancy in spatially irregular 3D data, will play a vital role in advancing perceptual coding and efficient compression algorithms.

Visual attention modeling also holds promise for perceptually guided processing. Most existing work in point cloud attention modeling focuses on saliency detection using hand-crafted features, which limits robustness and generalization. Future efforts should explore deep learning-based saliency detection models that automatically extract attention cues from raw data. Given the limited amount of annotated saliency data, weakly supervised or unsupervised learning paradigms offer viable solutions, especially when paired with synthetic datasets or domain adaptation from 2D saliency tasks.

Furthermore, research on salient object detection (SOD) for point clouds is still in its infancy. The recently proposed PCSOD dataset and PointSal baseline network represent first steps toward solving this problem. However, SOD models tailored for images do not transfer well to the irregular structure of point clouds. Future work should investigate geometry-aware transformer architectures or multi-view aggregation mechanisms to better localize salient objects from arbitrary perspectives. Enhancing the resolution of segmentation maps, reducing background interference, and integrating multi-scale semantics will also be essential for practical deployment in perception-driven applications.

Finally, it is important to bridge the gap between quality assessment and downstream tasks such as compression, segmentation, and recognition. Quality-driven optimization strategies could be embedded into learning-based point cloud coding frameworks, using perceptual cues like saliency maps and JND regions to prioritize high-value data. This synergy between perception and compression will be crucial in enabling efficient, human-centered 3D content delivery.

12.3 Future Work on Deep Learning-Based Static Point Cloud Geometry Coding

Although deep learning-based static 3D point cloud geometry coding has made significant progress in recent years, there remain multiple research directions requiring breakthroughs. Addressing current technical limitations and practical application requirements, future studies need to resolve several critical issues.

At the model architecture level, effectively integrating advantages of different data representations remains crucial. Current voxel-based and octree-based methods show scenario-dependent bottlenecks: Voxel methods perform well on dense point clouds but incur high computational costs, while octree methods enable fast coding for sparse clouds but struggle with geometry details. Developing a unified architecture accommodating both dense and sparse characteristics may require redefining 3D spatial representation paradigms. More promising directions involve exploring intrinsic geometry-topological features through graph neural networks or geometric deep learning frameworks that directly process raw point cloud structures, thereby avoiding quantization-induced precision loss.

Emerging generative models present notable application potential. Traditional approaches rely on manually designed probability prediction mechanisms, whereas diffusion models can enhance compression efficiency through data distribution learning for context modeling. Particularly for complex 3D geometries, their fine-grained modeling of local point distributions might overcome current entropy coding limitations. Concurrently, 3D Gaussian distribution models demonstrate unique advantages in surface representation, suggesting new paradigms combining geometry continuity with compression efficiency when integrated with traditional frameworks.

Practical deployment constraints drive exploration of efficient architectures. Existing autoregressive models face real-time application limitations due to sequential decoding dependencies, necessitating noncausal yet high-fidelity alternatives. Lightweight network design for edge computing must address parameter-heavy 3D convolutions, where dynamic sparse convolution and structured pruning could enable mobile-compatible encoders.

Robustness improvement for noisy environments and low-density point clouds requires multidimensional innovations: (1) Physics-based data augmentation simulating real acquisition conditions could create comprehensive training datasets; (2) attention mechanisms combined with graph reasoning may suppress outliers; and (3) self-supervised pretraining could enhance feature generalization from imperfect data.

Perception-driven coding mechanisms could expand application boundaries. Traditional rate-distortion optimization emphasizes geometry fidelity while neglecting human/machine visual perception characteristics. Developing task-adaptive coding strategies for specific scenarios might involve multimodal joint optimization, such as fusing LiDAR-camera data complementarity or transferring high-precision model reasoning through knowledge distillation.

Green computing principles demand algorithm-hardware co-optimization. Sustainable coding solutions should include energy-aware training strategies with dynamic precision control and customized 3D processing units for hardware acceleration. Intelligent bitrate allocation algorithms balancing critical-region fidelity and noncritical compression through semantic coordination could optimize resource utilization.

Standardization and practical deployment require addressing generalization challenges. Establishing multi-device, multi-density validation benchmarks and cross-domain adaptation techniques will help models confront real-world complexity. Compatibility studies with traditional codecs (G-PCC/V-PCC) and open industry-academia frameworks could accelerate technological transition.

In summary, future deep point cloud coding research must balance algorithmic innovation with practical implementation considerations. New model exploration should pursue theoretical breakthroughs while accounting for deployment conditions. Systematic solutions should leverage inherent 3D data characteristics across architecture design, efficiency optimization, and application adaptation. With theoretical advancements and computational paradigm innovations, deep point cloud coding technology will continue evolving toward smarter, more efficient, and more universal solutions.

12.4 Future Work on Deep Learning-Based Static Point Cloud Attribute Coding

As deep learning-based methods continue to evolve, point cloud attribute compression presents a wide range of opportunities for further research and practical deployment. Although significant progress has been achieved in both lossless and lossy compression paradigms, several open challenges remain that merit future investigation.

One of the primary research directions lies in developing flexible and adaptive compression frameworks that can operate effectively across diverse point cloud densities. Existing models often show limited robustness when dealing with varying levels of sparsity and density, which are commonly encountered in real-world scenarios such as autonomous driving and 3D reconstruction. Future approaches should consider designing data-adaptive mechanisms that can dynamically adjust compression strategies based on the local or global density of the input point clouds, thus ensuring consistent performance across heterogeneous data sources.

Another crucial avenue involves enhancing the computational efficiency of attribute compression models. While transformer-based architectures and sparse convolutional networks have shown impressive compression capability, they also introduce significant computational overhead. This constraint limits their usability in resource-constrained environments such as edge devices or embedded systems. Future work could explore lightweight model design, pruning strategies, quantization techniques, or knowledge distillation to reduce the model complexity without compromising performance, thereby enabling efficient real-time compression.

Moreover, task-oriented or perception-aware attribute compression methods offer promising potential. Unlike conventional approaches that prioritize minimizing reconstruction error alone, future models could incorporate human or machine perception as an optimization objective. For instance, compression techniques that emphasize preserving visually or semantically important features, such as color gradients, texture consistency, or object related regions, could better support downstream tasks like visualization, recognition, or classification. Such perceptual optimization can bridge the gap between raw data representation and application-oriented utility.

Additionally, integrating cross-modal compression strategies represents a compelling future direction. Current methods typically process geometry and attribute information separately, but jointly modeling them could lead to improved compression ratios and better contextual understanding. Leveraging unified neural architectures to simultaneously encode geometry structure and associated attributes can exploit intermodal correlations and reduce redundancy, ultimately improving compression efficiency and semantic fidelity.

Collectively, advancing static point cloud attribute compression will require addressing challenges in adaptability, resource constraints, perceptual fidelity, and multimodal integration. Tackling these challenges will lay a solid foundation for deploying deep learning-based compression solutions in real-world, large-scale 3D applications across domains such as robotics, virtual reality, digital twin systems, and intelligent transportation.

12.5 Future Work on Deep Learning-Based Dynamic Point Cloud Coding

Dynamic point cloud coding, akin to traditional image and video coding, has witnessed rapid progress [49–55], especially with the incorporation of deep learning techniques. By leveraging the capability of neural networks to model complex spatial and temporal correlations in 3D data, these approaches have significantly improved both compression efficiency and reconstruction quality. Nevertheless, several open challenges must be addressed before such methods can be reliably deployed in real-world dynamic applications [1, 2].

One of the foremost challenges lies in computational efficiency. Existing deep learning models for dynamic point cloud coding are often resource-intensive, requiring powerful GPUs for both training and inference. This high computational cost restricts their usability in time-sensitive or resource-constrained environments, such as autonomous vehicles or embedded systems. Future work should prioritize the design of lightweight and efficient architectures, potentially through model compression techniques such as pruning, quantization, and neural architecture search, to achieve a balance between performance and deployability.

A second critical issue is the temporal modeling capability of current compression frameworks. Although recent efforts have incorporated temporal context to reduce frame to frame redundancy, the methods for precisely capturing and utilizing temporal dependencies are still in early stages. Developing architectures that can more effectively encode inter-frame motion, deformation, and temporal continuity will be essential. Attention mechanisms, recurrent models, or temporal transformers may serve as promising tools to enhance temporal feature extraction and improve long-term coherence in the reconstructed point clouds.

Another important future direction involves improving the interpretability and transparency of deep learning-based compression models. Unlike traditional codecs with well-defined and controllable encoding pipelines, neural compression models often function as “black boxes," making it difficult to trace how specific input characteristics affect the output. Enhancing interpretability, such as via attention visualization, feature attribution, or layer wise analysis, would provide valuable insights into model behavior, facilitate debugging and optimization, and improve user trust in the compression system.

Beyond these technical challenges, there is also a need to explore task-driven dynamic compression, where the compression process is optimized not solely for reconstruction fidelity but also for downstream applications like scene segmentation, object tracking, or motion prediction. Embedding semantic awareness into the compression pipeline could lead to more efficient and intelligent coding frameworks tailored to specific tasks or perceptual requirements.

Driven by rapid advancements in deep learning and hardware acceleration, dynamic point cloud coding is poised for continued growth. Future research that addresses these key challenges like efficiency, temporal modeling, interpretability, and task-awareness will contribute to the development of robust, scalable, and intelligent compression systems, enabling widespread deployment in applications such as autonomous driving, virtual and augmented reality, and remote collaboration.

12.6 Future Work on Human and Machine Perception Oriented Point Cloud Coding

As point cloud applications continue to expand across human-centric visualization and machine-centric perception tasks, achieving collaborative coding frameworks that satisfy both modalities has become a significant research frontier. Current methods have laid a foundation for joint optimization, but several critical directions require further exploration to fully realize the potential of perception-oriented point cloud coding.

One pressing challenge is the design of flexible and scalable compression frameworks that can dynamically balance visual fidelity for human observers and semantic integrity for machine tasks. Approaches like SPC-Net and SM-PCC have demonstrated early successes by utilizing scalable bitstream designs or task-specific latent space separation. However, their adaptability across diverse application scenarios remains limited. Future work should focus on hierarchical architectures that can intelligently adjust compression granularity based on task priority, device capability, or network condition.

A second promising direction lies in enhancing semantic awareness within the compression pipeline. Methods such as HM-PCGC and SAVD-PCGC have shown that integrating semantic priors or attention-guided modules can help allocate more bitrate to task-relevant regions, improving classification and detection outcomes without excessive overhead. Future research should further explore multitask feature decoupling, enabling shared representations that preserve both signal and semantic fidelity for downstream tasks.

Another area of interest is adaptive compression guided by real-time task requirements. Most existing methods operate under fixed compression configurations, which limit their responsiveness to changing system contexts. By integrating real-time feedback from downstream modules, such as perception confidence scores or environment complexity levels, compression algorithms could be adjusted on the fly, leading to smarter resource allocation and improved efficiency in mission-critical scenarios like autonomous driving or robotics.

To expand the universality of perception-oriented coding, future systems must also support generalization to unseen tasks and categories. Current approaches are often trained with limited task-specific supervision. Incorporating techniques such as zero-shot learning, large-scale pretraining, and knowledge distillation from multimodal sources may enhance the generalization and scalability of point cloud codecs, especially for open-world applications.

From a deployment perspective, the development of low-power, edge-friendly coding architectures is critical. Deep neural networks used in dual-branch or feature-based coding schemes often involve significant computational costs. Research into lightweight designs and hardware-aware neural compression models will be essential for enabling real-time inference on embedded systems or mobile devices.

Lastly, a growing need exists for joint optimization frameworks that unify rate-distortion and task-loss objectives. Inspired by the formalization of collaborative objectives, future codecs can incorporate multi-objective learning strategies that directly optimize human-perceived distortion and machine task accuracy under a unified loss. Such frameworks would promote holistic performance and enable shared deployment across human-machine interaction platforms.

By addressing these emerging challenges, future research in human or machine collaborative point cloud coding can significantly enhance the synergy between perception, efficiency, and generalization ultimately enabling intelligent, adaptive, and perceptually consistent 3D content delivery in real-world applications.

12.7 Future Work on Compression Artifacts Removal for 3D Point Cloud Coding

As point cloud coding technologies are increasingly deployed in applications such as autonomous driving, virtual/augmented reality, and smart city modeling, the presence of compression-induced artifacts has become a critical obstacle to high-fidelity reconstruction and downstream perception tasks. While current methods have demonstrated promising results in geometry and attribute artifact removal [56–63], several open problems remain that point to key directions for future research.

A foremost challenge is the development of joint geometry-attribute artifact removal frameworks. Real-world compression scenarios often involve hybrid distortions, and treating geometry and attribute restoration as isolated processes may lead to suboptimal outcomes. Future systems should incorporate multibranch network architectures that allow for collaborative feature extraction and enhancement between geometry and attributes. Leveraging generative sparse convolution and spatial attention mechanisms, as in GPCC + +, offers a solid foundation for such integrated designs.

Another essential direction involves the incorporation of multi-scale and multi-task learning. Since point cloud geometry and attribute information are distributed across various spatial scales, fusing multi-resolution features can provide richer contextual cues for artifact removal. Additionally, coupling related tasks, such as occupancy prediction, coordinate refinement, and color restoration into a multitask training framework can promote feature reuse and improve overall restoration quality. Models like MS-GAT and DAE already hint at this potential by introducing multi-scale graph reasoning and motion-guided attribute enhancement.

With the growing use of dynamic point clouds, addressing temporal consistency and motion-aware artifact removal has become increasingly important. Dynamic scenarios introduce challenges such as inconsistent point correspondences and inter-frame motion blur. Future methods should consider spatiotemporal architectures, incorporating temporal attention, recurrent networks, or motion-guided residual learning to better align features across frames. Fast inter-frame motion estimation frameworks like DAE provide a strong starting point, but further optimization is needed for high speed and high accuracy scenarios.

Given the high computational cost of many existing approaches, especially in real-time or mobile contexts, the design of lightweight and efficient networks is vital. Techniques such as sparse convolution, network pruning, quantization, and knowledge distillation should be applied to reduce complexity while retaining performance. Furthermore, the use of self-supervised or unsupervised learning paradigms can eliminate the dependence on large annotated datasets. By designing geometry- or contrast-based pretext tasks, models can learn artifact patterns directly from unlabeled compressed data, improving generalization to unseen compression types or sensor formats.

To further enhance model adaptability and application scope, future research should explore cross modal and cross domain collaborative learning. Information from additional modalities can assist in restoring missing details and correcting ambiguous regions. Additionally, adapting visual priors and techniques from image super-resolution, texture synthesis, or optical flow estimation could provide novel perspectives for point cloud artifact correction.

Another practical concern is the lack of diverse benchmarks and evaluation metrics. Current datasets and metrics may not reflect the full spectrum of compression artifacts encountered in varying density levels, motion patterns, and sensor types. It is imperative to develop comprehensive datasets encompassing both static and dynamic scenes with controlled distortions and realistic annotations. At the same time, perceptual quality metrics that capture geometry accuracy, color consistency, temporal smoothness, and downstream task performance should be incorporated into evaluation pipelines.

Finally, the emergence of edge computing and real-time applications requires attention to hardware acceleration and flexible deployment. Compression artifact removal methods must be compatible with real-time constraints and embedded system environments. Future work can explore GPU/TPU optimization, edge-friendly architectures, and parallel inference strategies, enabling widespread adoption in latency-sensitive domains.

By addressing these challenges in joint modeling, scalability, adaptability, and deployment, artifact removal technologies will continue to play a crucial role in ensuring high-quality point cloud reconstruction and analysis under compression constraints.

12.8 Future Work on AI-Based 3D Point Cloud Coding Standards

For the issue of point cloud coding based on deep learning, many related proposals have been put forth by both MPEG, JPEG, and AVS. These proposals cover datasets, metrics, specific frameworks, and more. The frameworks include various network structures for geometry coding, attribute coding, joint compression of geometry and attributes, static point cloud coding, and dynamic point cloud coding. These standards play a significant role in the reuse of the subsequent research on point clouds. These proposals still have a lot of room for future work that can be further improved as follows:

In the real world, especially with the ongoing development of autonomous driving and general artificial intelligence, dynamic point cloud coding represents a very tangible and highly applicable challenge. However, JPEG has almost no related proposals, while MPEG, despite having a number of proposals for dynamic point clouds, still has many areas that could be improved, for instance, joint compression of both geometry and attributes in dynamic point clouds, among others.

As mentioned above, the effectiveness of metrics for subsequent point cloud processing tasks such as classification, detection, and recognition is an issue. On one hand, there's the impact of metrics, and on the other, the encoding itself, as part of the low-level tasks, is closely related to high-level tasks. For instance, in processing the low-level task of encoding, they can draw on the results of high-level tasks to allocate bits across different channels during encoding. This issue is not yet addressed in current proposals, but it is indeed a problem that needs to be solved in practical applications.

Overall, there are still many directions worth optimizing and exploring on the standard of point cloud coding based on deep learning.

12.9 Future Work on Implementations, Streaming, and Rendering for 3D Point Cloud Coding

The rapid growth of 3D scanning technologies, computer vision, and immersive environments has driven significant progress in point cloud processing. However, several challenges remain, particularly in the areas of lightweight computation, streaming and communication systems, and rendering. As these fields continue to evolve, the following outlines the future technological advancements that can shape the next generation of point cloud applications.

Point clouds inherently possess a large volume of data, and processing these datasets can be computationally intensive. Future advancements in lightweight and accelerated computing for point cloud processing will focus on two primary objectives: reducing computational overhead while maintaining high-quality results and enabling real-time processing on edge devices with limited resources. To achieve these objectives, hardware acceleration through specialized hardware such as graphics processing units (GPUs), field-programmable gate arrays (FPGAs), and application-specific integrated circuits (ASICs) will play a central role. These devices, paired with optimized deep learning models and sparse representations, will allow for faster and more efficient point cloud processing. Researchers are likely to focus on developing lightweight neural network architectures capable of operating with lower memory requirements and faster inference times, without compromising on accuracy. Furthermore, quantization techniques and model pruning will continue to advance, enabling point cloud models to be deployed in real-time applications on devices such as mobile phones, drones, and autonomous vehicles. Additionally, distributed and parallel computing frameworks will continue to gain prominence, allowing for the efficient handling of large-scale point cloud datasets by distributing the workload across multiple nodes or processors. The combination of efficient hardware and innovative software architectures will make it feasible to process massive point cloud datasets quickly and affordably, even in constrained environments.

As point clouds become an integral part of applications in areas such as augmented reality (AR), virtual reality (VR), and remote sensing, there is a growing need for efficient streaming and communication systems that can deliver high-quality and real-time point cloud data with minimal latency. The large size of point cloud datasets presents a challenge for efficient data transmission, particularly in bandwidth-limited environments like mobile networks or remote sensor networks. In the near future, compression techniques specifically tailored for streaming will continue to evolve. The use of deep learning-based compression methods for point clouds will allow for real-time, lossless or lossy compression, significantly reducing the bandwidth required for transmitting point clouds. Further advancements in adaptive streaming protocols, which adjust the quality of the point cloud based on available bandwidth and device capabilities, will enable smoother and more flexible experiences for end users. Another exciting development is the integration of edge computing with point cloud streaming. By processing point cloud data at the edge, closer to the data source (such as sensors or cameras), it will be possible to reduce the amount of raw data that needs to be sent over the network. This will not only improve latency but also reduce the burden on network infrastructure, making real-time streaming of point clouds more feasible in applications like autonomous driving or remote surgical procedures. Moreover, 5G and future communication technologies will provide the bandwidth and low-latency capabilities necessary to support high-resolution point cloud streaming, making real-time interaction with 3D environments more immersive and accessible, even in mobile or distributed contexts.

Rendering point clouds in real time with high visual quality remains a challenging task due to the large data size and complex structures. However, significant advancements are expected in point cloud rendering, especially with the integration of machine learning and graphics processing innovations. One of the most promising directions is the use of neural rendering techniques to generate high-quality point cloud visualizations. Deep neural networks (DNNs) can be trained to enhance point cloud rendering by predicting missing data, improving texture mapping, and generating high-resolution images from sparse point cloud data. Techniques such as point cloud upsampling, where missing or low-density points are inferred, will become more accurate, allowing for smoother and more detailed renders in real time. Moreover, real-time ray tracing technologies, enhanced by specialized hardware, will enable photorealistic rendering of point clouds, even in complex lighting and environmental conditions. This will be critical for applications in virtual and augmented reality, where realistic and immersive experiences rely heavily on high-quality point cloud rendering. The integration of point cloud and mesh-based representations will also be a focus, as hybrid methods that combine the benefits of both approaches (the flexibility of point clouds and the efficiency of meshes) can help achieve higher rendering performance. Additionally, level-of-detail (LOD) techniques will be further refined to enable the real-time rendering of large-scale point clouds by dynamically adjusting the complexity of the rendered data based on the viewer's perspective and distance from the scene. Lastly, the development of interactive point cloud rendering systems will allow for intuitive exploration and manipulation of point clouds in virtual spaces. These systems will incorporate advanced user interfaces, enabling users to seamlessly zoom in, rotate, and interact with point clouds in immersive AR/VR environments [64].

Looking ahead, the convergence of lightweight implementation, real-time communication, and high-fidelity rendering will be central to the next generation of point cloud systems. By addressing these interrelated challenges through coordinated algorithmic and system-level innovations, it will become possible to deploy scalable, responsive, and immersive point cloud applications across a wide range of domains from autonomous systems to immersive media and beyond.

12.10 Future Work on Open-Source Projects for AI-Based Point Cloud Coding

Open-source projects are expected to play a vital role in the future development of AI-driven 3D point cloud coding. As 3D data becomes increasingly essential across diverse fields, including virtual reality, autonomous driving, gaming, and medical imaging, the demand for efficient, scalable, and intelligent compression methods continues to grow. Open-source initiatives provide a collaborative foundation for accelerating innovation in this area.

AI-based compression offers significant advantages over traditional approaches by learning complex geometry and attribute patterns from data. Machine learning models can adaptively capture structural redundancies and semantic features, enabling compact representations without sacrificing reconstruction quality. Open-source platforms serve as fertile ground for developing and validating such models, fostering community-wide contributions and promoting the rapid evolution of state-of-the-art techniques.

A major benefit of open-source collaboration lies in the acceleration of algorithm development and benchmarking. Contributions from a global research and developer community allow for faster prototyping, reproducibility, and refinement of new methods. This shared environment also facilitates the creation of standardized toolkits and datasets, promoting consistency and comparability across implementations and experiments.

Moreover, open-source projects significantly improve transparency and accessibility. By making codebases and model architectures publicly available, they allow for broader scrutiny and adaptation, reducing reliance on proprietary technologies. This openness encourages community-driven optimization while also helping to identify potential limitations or biases in AI-based codecs.

Looking forward, the convergence of AI techniques and open-source collaboration will likely drive key advancements in 3D point cloud coding. Future research should focus on building modular, extensible, and hardware-friendly open source frameworks, along with standard evaluation pipelines for compression quality and perceptual fidelity. These efforts will accelerate the transition of research prototypes into practical tools for industry adoption, supporting scalable 3D data management across diverse application domains.

12.11 Future Work on Large Language Model-Based Point Cloud Coding

The key to effective point cloud coding lies in obtaining a robust context model that aligns with the intricate and complex structures of point cloud data. Recent advancements in large language models (LLMs) have demonstrated their dual capabilities as both powerful generators for in-context learning and generation and as highly effective compressors. These unique attributes position LLMs as promising candidates for addressing the challenges of point cloud coding. However, directly applying LLMs to this task presents significant hurdles that must be overcome to fully leverage their potential.

One of the primary challenges is that LLMs, in their current form, lack an inherent understanding of the structural and spatial characteristics of point clouds. Point clouds, as representations of 3D objects or environments, consist of vast amounts of unstructured data points, each carrying spatial and geometric information. Bridging the gap between the textual domain, where LLMs excel, and the spatial domain of point clouds is a nontrivial task. While text descriptions can provide high-level semantic information about the scene or object represented by a point cloud, they often fail to capture the fine-grained details and geometric intricacies, especially for large, complex, or small, shapeless point clouds. This limitation hinders the ability of LLMs to fully comprehend and compress such data effectively.

Future work in this area should focus on developing innovative methods to enhance LLMs' understanding of point cloud structures. One potential direction is to explore multimodal approaches that integrate visual, spatial, and textual information, enabling LLMs to better interpret and process 3D data. Techniques such as embedding point clouds into a latent space that aligns with LLM representations or leveraging pretrained vision-language models could be investigated. Additionally, parameter-efficient fine-tuning methods, such as low-rank adaptation (LoRA), could be employed to adapt LLMs specifically for point cloud coding tasks, allowing them to learn the unique characteristics of 3D data without extensive retraining.

Another critical area for future research is the development of efficient context modeling strategies tailored to point clouds. The in-context learning capabilities of LLMs can be harnessed to capture the spatial dependencies and geometric relationships within point clouds, enabling more accurate and efficient compression. Furthermore, exploring hierarchical or multi-scale approaches to represent point clouds could help LLMs handle the varying levels of detail and complexity inherent in 3D data.

Finally, the scalability and computational efficiency of LLM-based point cloud coding methods must be addressed. Given the large size of point cloud datasets and the computational demands of LLMs, future work should investigate optimization techniques, such as quantization, pruning, or distillation, to reduce memory consumption and inference time while maintaining high compression performance.

By addressing these challenges and exploring these directions, future research can unlock the full potential of LLMs for point cloud coding, paving the way for innovative and efficient solutions in the field of 3D data processing and storage.

12.12 Summary

The rapid evolution of AI-based 3D point cloud coding presents a wealth of research opportunities and technical challenges that span multiple critical domains. In deep learning-based point cloud coding, future work must focus on developing more robust and generalizable models capable of handling diverse geometry structures while maintaining computational efficiency through lightweight neural architectures. The field urgently requires advanced dynamic bitstream allocation techniques and reliable quality assessment metrics that holistically evaluate both geometry and attribute fidelity. Quality assessment and perception modeling represent another crucial frontier, where innovations in 3D-aware subjective testing protocols, no-reference quality metrics, and just-noticeable-distortion (JND) models will be essential. The integration of deep learning-based visual attention mechanisms and saliency detection could revolutionize perceptually optimized coding strategies. For static point cloud coding, researchers should pursue the unified architectures that handle both dense and sparse representations, potentially leveraging emerging generative approaches like diffusion models for enhanced entropy coding while simultaneously addressing the pressing need for edge-compatible lightweight solutions.

Attribute coding demands special attention to adaptive compression frameworks that maintain performance across varying point densities and incorporate perception-aware optimization. The dynamic point cloud coding domain faces significant challenges in computational efficiency, temporal modeling, and interpretability—areas where transformer architectures and attention mechanisms may offer transformative solutions. A particularly promising direction lies in human-machine collaborative coding frameworks that dynamically balance visual quality and semantic preservation based on application requirements. Compression artifact removal remains a critical challenge, especially for real-world applications. Future solutions should emphasize joint geometry-attribute restoration, multi-scale feature learning, and temporal consistency preservation in dynamic scenarios. The standardization landscape must evolve to address dynamic point clouds and better integrate compression with high-level vision tasks, while implementation efforts should focus on hardware acceleration, edge computing, and advanced neural rendering techniques for real-time performance. Open-source initiatives will play a pivotal role in accelerating progress through community-driven development and benchmarking. Perhaps most intriguing is the potential of large language models (LLMs) for point cloud coding, though significant work remains to adapt these text-optimized architectures to spatial 3D data understanding through multimodal learning and efficient fine-tuning strategies.

Across all these domains, the convergence of algorithmic innovation, hardware optimization, and standardization efforts will be crucial for advancing AI-based point cloud coding toward its full potential in applications ranging from autonomous vehicles to immersive reality systems. The field stands at an exciting inflection point where interdisciplinary collaboration and open innovation can overcome current limitations and unlock new possibilities in 3D data representation and processing. For readers who are interested in the related technologies of AI-based image and video coding, please refer to [65].

Exercises

1. Please provide several key points to discuss the future research of deep learning-based point cloud coding.
2. Please provide several key points to discuss the future research of point cloud quality assessment and perception models.
3. Please provide several key points to discuss the future research of static point cloud geometry and attribute coding.
4. Please provide several key points to discuss the future research of dynamic point cloud coding.
5. Please provide several key points to discuss the future research of human and machine vision oriented point cloud coding.
6. Please provide several key points to discuss the future research of point cloud compression artifacts removal.
7. Please provide several key points to discuss the future research of AI-based point cloud coding standards.
8. Please provide several key points to discuss the future research of point cloud coding implementation systems.
9. Please provide several key points to discuss the future research of point cloud open source projects.
10. Please provide several key points to discuss the future research of large model-based point cloud coding.

References

1. G. Li, G. Wei, W. Gao, *Point Cloud Compression: Technologies and Standardization* (Springer, Berlin, 2024)
2. W. Gao, G. Li, *Deep Learning for 3D Point Clouds* (Springer, Berlin, 2024)
3. W. Gao, G. Li, Point cloud compression, enhancement and applications: from 3D perception to large models, in *Proceedings of the 32nd ACM International Conference on Multimedia* (2024), pp. 11 292–11 293
4. H. Sun, G. Li, S. Chen, L. Li, W. Gao, Special topic on 3D point cloud processing and applications. ZTE Commun. **21**(4), 1 (2023)
5. W. Gao, W. Gao, X. Mu, C. Peng, G. Li, Overview and comparison of AVS point cloud compression standard. APSIPA Trans. Signal Inf. Proces. **14**(2), 1–33 (2025)
6. W. Gao, S. Wang, X. Zhang, S. Kwong, Editorial for special issue on deep learning-based data compression. APSIPA Trans. Signal Inf. Proces. **13**(6), 1–2 (2024)
7. W. Gao, H. Ye, G. Li, H. Zheng, Y. Wu, L. Xie, OpenPointCloud: an open-source algorithm library of deep learning based point cloud compression, in *Proceedings of the 30th ACM International Conference on Multimedia* (2022), pp. 7347–7350
8. Y. Zhang, W. Gao, G. Li, OpenPointCloud-V2: a deep learning based open-source algorithm library of point cloud processing, in *Proceedings of the 1st International Workshop on Advances in Point Cloud Compression, Processing and Analysis* (2022), pp. 51–55
9. L. Xie, W. Gao, LearningPCC: a pytorch library for learning-based point cloud compression, in *Proceedings of the 32nd ACM International Conference on Multimedia* (2024), pp. 11 234–11 238
10. L. Xie, W. Gao, PCHMVision: an open-source library of point cloud compression for human and machine vision, in *Proceedings of the 32nd ACM International Conference on Multimedia* (2024), pp. 11 239–11 243
11. W. Gao, G. Li, Introduction to 3D point clouds: datasets and perception, in *Deep Learning for 3D Point Clouds* (Springer, Berlin, 2024), pp. 1–27
12. W. Gao, G. Li, Learning basics for 3D point clouds, in *Deep Learning for 3D Point Clouds* (Springer, Berlin, 2024), pp. 29–70
13. T. Qin, G. Li, W. Gao, S. Liu, Multi-grained point cloud geometry compression via dual-model prediction with extended octree. ACM Trans. Multimedia Comput. Commun. Appl. **20**(9), 1–30 (2024)
14. Y. Shao, W. Gao, S. Liu, G. Li, Advanced patch-based affine motion estimation for dynamic point cloud geometry compression. Sensors **24**(10), 3142 (2024)
15. Y. Shao, F. Song, W. Gao, S. Liu, G. Li, Texture-guided graph transform optimization for point cloud attribute compression. Appl. Sci. **14**(10), 4094 (2024)
16. Y. Shao, X. Yang, W. Gao, S. Liu, G. Li, 3D point cloud attribute compression using diffusion-based texture-aware intra prediction. IEEE Trans. Circuits Syst. Video Technol. **34**(10), 9633–9646 (2024)
17. J. Zhang, Y. Chen, G. Liu, W. Gao, G. Li, Efficient point cloud attribute compression framework using attribute-guided graph Fourier transform, in *ICASSP 2024-2024 IEEE International Conference on Acoustics, Speech and Signal Processing (ICASSP)* (IEEE, Piscataway, 2024), pp. 8426–8430
18. W. Gao, H. Yuan, G. Li, Z. Li, H. Yuan, Low complexity coding unit decision for video-based point cloud compression. IEEE Trans. Image Proces. **33**, 149–162 (2023)
19. Y. Shao, G. Li, Q. Zhang, W. Gao, S. Liu, Nonrigid registration-based progressive motion compensation for point cloud geometry compression. IEEE Trans. Geosci. Remote Sens. **61**, 1–14 (2023)
20. F. Song, G. Li, X. Yang, W. Gao, S. Liu, Block-adaptive point cloud attribute coding with region-aware optimized transform. IEEE Trans. Circuits Syst. Video Technol. **33**(8), 4294–4308 (2023)

21. Y. An, Y. Shao, G. Li, W. Gao, S. Liu, A fast motion estimation method with hamming distance for lidar point cloud compression, in *2022 IEEE International Conference on Visual Communications and Image Processing (VCIP)* (IEEE, Piscataway, 2022), pp. 1–5
22. H. Yuan, W. Gao, G. Li, Z. Li, Rate-distortion-guided learning approach with cross-projection information for V-PCC fast CU decision, in *Proceedings of the 30th ACM International Conference on Multimedia* (2022), pp. 3085–3093
23. F. Song, G. Li, W. Gao, T.H. Li, Rate-distortion optimized graph for point cloud attribute coding. IEEE Signal Proces. Lett. **29**, 922–926 (2022)
24. F. Song, G. Li, X. Yang, W. Gao, T.H. Li, Fine-grained correlation representation for graph-based point cloud attribute compression, in *2022 IEEE International Conference on Multimedia and Expo (ICME)* (IEEE, Piscataway, 2022), pp. 1–6
25. F. Shen, W. Gao, A rate control algorithm for video-based point cloud compression, in *2021 International Conference on Visual Communications and Image Processing (VCIP)* (IEEE, Piscataway, 2021), pp. 1–5
26. L. Xie, X. Mu, G. Li, W. Gao et al., PKU-DPCC: a new dataset for dynamic point cloud compression. APSIPA Trans. Signal Inf. Proces. **13**(6), 1–23 (2024)
27. H. Yuan, W. Gao, W. Gao, OpenSEP: an open source subjective experiment platform, in *Proceedings of the 32nd ACM International Conference on Multimedia* (2024), pp. 11 248–11 251
28. S. Fan, W. Gao, Screen-based 3D subjective experiment software, in *Proceedings of the 31st ACM International Conference on Multimedia* (2023), pp. 9672–9675
29. J. Wang, W. Gao, G. Li, Zoom to perceive better: no-reference point cloud quality assessment via exploring effective multiscale feature. IEEE Trans. Circuits Syst. Video Technol. **34**(7), 6334–6346 (2024)
30. J. Wang, W. Gao, G. Li, Applying collaborative adversarial learning to blind point cloud quality measurement. IEEE Trans. Instrum. Measure. **72**, 1–15 (2023)
31. H. Li, W. Gao, Information exploration of projected views for point cloud quality measurement. IEEE Trans. Instrum. Measure. **74**, 1–14 (2025)
32. S. Fan, W. Gao, G. Li, Salient object detection for point clouds, in *European Conference on Computer Vision* (Springer, Berlin, 2022), pp. 1–19
33. S. Luo, W. Gao, A general framework for rotation invariant point cloud analysis, in *ICASSP 2024-2024 IEEE International Conference on Acoustics, Speech and Signal Processing (ICASSP)* (IEEE, Piscataway, 2024), pp. 3665–3669
34. X. Lu, W. Gao, AttentiveNet: detecting small objects for lidar point clouds by attending to important points, in *2023 IEEE International Conference on Visual Communications and Image Processing (VCIP)* (IEEE, Piscataway, 2023), pp. 1–5
35. Z. Pan, N. Zhang, W. Gao, S. Liu, G. Li, Less is more: label recommendation for weakly supervised point cloud semantic segmentation. Proc. AAAI Conf. Artif. Intell. **38**(5), 4397–4405 (2024)
36. Z. Pan, G. Liu, W. Gao, T.H. Li, EPContrast: effective point-level contrastive learning for large-scale point cloud understanding, in *2024 IEEE International Conference on Multimedia and Expo (ICME)* (IEEE, Piscataway, 2024), pp. 1–6
37. N. Zhang, Z. Pan, T.H. Li, W. Gao, G. Li, Improving graph representation for point cloud segmentation via attentive filtering, in *Proceedings of the IEEE/CVF Conference on Computer Vision and Pattern Recognition* (2023), pp. 1244–1254
38. K. Wen, N. Zhang, G. Li, W. Gao, MPVNN: multi-resolution point-voxel non-parametric network for 3D point cloud processing, in *2024 IEEE International Conference on Multimedia and Expo (ICME)* (IEEE, Piscataway, 2024), pp. 1–6
39. Z. Pan, N. Zhang, W. Gao, S. Liu, G. Li, Point cloud semantic segmentation with sparse and inhomogeneous annotations, in *Proceedings of the AAAI Conference on Artificial Intelligence* (2025)
40. R. Zhang, G. Li, W. Gao, S. Liu, A quantum-inspired framework in leader-servant mode for large-scale multi-modal place recognition. IEEE Trans. Intell. Transport. Syst. **26**(2), 2027–2039 (2025)

41. D. Yang, W. Gao, PointCHD: a point cloud benchmark for congenital heart disease classification and segmentation. IEEE J. Biomed. Health Inf. **29**(4), 2683–2694 (2025)
42. S. Fan, W. Gao, G. Li, Point-MPP: point cloud self-supervised learning from masked position prediction. IEEE Trans. Neural Networks Learn. Syst. **36**(7), 12964–12976 (2025)
43. Z. Pan, W. Gao, G. Li, Distribution guidance network for weakly supervised point cloud semantic segmentation. Adv. Neural Inf. Proces. Syst. (2024)
44. R. Zhang, G. Li, W. Gao, T.H. Li, ComPoint: can complex-valued representation benefit point cloud place recognition? IEEE Trans. Intell. Transport. Syst. **25**(7), 7494–7507 (2024)
45. X. Zang, W. Gao, G. Li, H. Fang, C. Ban, Z. He, H. Sun, A baseline investigation: transformer-based cross-view baseline for text-based person search, in *Proceedings of the 31st ACM International Conference on Multimedia* (2023), pp. 7737–7746
46. G. Liao, W. Gao, G. Li, J. Wang, S. Kwong, Cross-collaborative fusion-encoder network for robust RGB-thermal salient object detection. IEEE Trans. Circuits Syst. Video Technol. **32**(11), 7646–7661 (2022)
47. W. Gao, G. Liao, S. Ma, G. Li, Y. Liang, W. Lin, Unified information fusion network for multi-modal RGB-D and RGB-T salient object detection. IEEE Trans. Circuits Syst. Video Technol. **32**(4), 2091–2106 (2021)
48. Y. Chen, S. Sun, G. Li, W. Gao, T.H. Li, Closing the gap between theory and practice during alternating optimization for gans. IEEE Trans. Neural Networks Learn. Syst. **35**(10), 14005–14017 (2024)
49. H. Yuan, W. Gao, S. Ma, Y. Yan, Divide-and-conquer-based RDO-free CU partitioning for 8k video compression. ACM Trans. Multimedia Comput. Commun. Appl. **20**(4), 1–20 (2024)
50. L. Tao, W. Gao, A hardware implementation of entropy encoder for 8k video coding, in *2022 IEEE International Conference on Multimedia and Expo (ICME)* (IEEE, Piscataway, 2022), pp. 1–6
51. Y. Guo, W. Gao, S. Ma, G. Li, Accelerating transform algorithm implementation for efficient intra coding of 8k UHD videos. ACM Trans. Multimedia Comput. Commun. Appl. (TOMM) **18**(4), 1–20 (2022)
52. Z. Cai, W. Gao, Efficient fast algorithm and parallel hardware architecture for intra prediction of AVS3, in *2021 IEEE International Symposium on Circuits and Systems (ISCAS)* (IEEE, Piscataway, 2021), pp. 1–5
53. W. Liu, W. Gao, G. Li, S. Ma, T. Zhao, H. Yuan, Enlarged motion-aware and frequency-aware network for compressed video artifact reduction. IEEE Trans. Circuits Syst. Video Technol. (2024)
54. W. Gao, H. Yuan, Y. Guo, L. Tao, Z. Cai, G. Li, OpenHardwareVC: an open source library for 8k UHD video coding hardware implementation, in *Proceedings of the 30th ACM International Conference on Multimedia* (2022), pp. 7339–7342
55. W. Gao, S. Kwong, H. Sang, Low-cost memory data scheduling method for reconfigurable FFT bit-reversal circuits. Electron. Lett. **51**(3), 217–219 (2015)
56. W. Liu, W. Gao, X. Mu, Fast inter-frame motion prediction for compressed dynamic point cloud attribute enhancement. Proc. AAAI Conf. Artif. Intell. **38**(4), 3720–3728 (2024)
57. Z. Yang, W. Gao, X. Lu, DANet: density-adaptive network for geometry-based point cloud compression artifacts removal, in *2023 IEEE International Conference on Visual Communications and Image Processing (VCIP)* (IEEE, Piscataway, 2023), pp. 1–5
58. X. Fan, G. Li, D. Li, Y. Ren, W. Gao, T.H. Li, Deep geometry post-processing for decompressed point clouds, in *2022 IEEE International Conference on Multimedia and Expo (ICME)* (IEEE, Piscataway, 2022), pp. 1–6
59. X. Zhang, G. Liao, W. Gao, G. Li, TDRNet: transformer-based dual-branch restoration network for geometry based point cloud compression artifacts, in *2022 IEEE International Conference on Multimedia and Expo (ICME)* (IEEE, Piscataway, 2022), pp. 1–6
60. Z. Li, G. Li, T.H. Li, S. Liu, W. Gao, Semantic point cloud upsampling. IEEE Trans. Multimedia **25**, 3432–3442 (2023)
61. Z. Li, S. Liu, W. Gao, G. Li, G. Li, S4r: rethinking point cloud sampling via guiding upsampling-aware perception. IEEE Trans. Multimedia **27**, 6677–6689 (2025)

62. R. Zhang, W. Gao, G. Li, T.H. Li, QINet: decision surface learning and adversarial enhancement for quasi-immune completion of diverse corrupted point clouds. IEEE Trans. Geosci. Remote Sens. **60**, 1–14 (2022)
63. R. Bao, Y. Ren, G. Li, W. Gao, S. Liu, Flow-based point cloud completion network with adversarial refinement, in *ICASSP 2022-2022 IEEE International Conference on Acoustics, Speech and Signal Processing (ICASSP)* (IEEE, Piscataway, 2022), pp. 2559–2563
64. L. Xie, W. Gao, H. Zheng, G. Li, ROI-guided point cloud geometry compression towards human and machine vision. arXiv preprint arXiv:2504.14240 (2025)
65. W. Gao, *AI-based Image and Video Coding: Methods, Standards, and Applications* (Springer, Berlin, 2025)

Index

W. Gao, *AI-based 3D Point Cloud Coding*,
https://doi.org/10.1007/978-981-95-0660-6

The manufacturer's authorised representative in the EU is Springer Nature Customer Service Centre GmbH, Europaplatz 3, 69115 Heidelberg, Germany. If you have any concerns regarding our products, please contact ProductSafety@springernature.com

Printed and bound by CPI Group (UK) Ltd, Croydon, CR0 4YY
07/10/2026
02229349-0006